Financial Risk Management

Domestic and International Dimensions

Philippe Jorion

Sarkis Joseph Khoury

To: Our Alexes
Our Natalies

Financial Risk Management

Domestic and International Dimensions

Philippe Jorion

University of California, Irvine

Sarkis Joseph Khoury

University of California, Riverside

Blackwell Publishers Inc.
238 Main Street
Cambridge, Massachusetts 02142
USA

Blackwell Publishers Ltd
108 Cowley Road
Oxford OX4 1JF
UK

Library of Congress Cataloging-in-Publication Data

Jorion, Philippe, 1955–
    Financial risk management: domestic and international dimensions / Philippe Jorion,
Sarkis J. Khoury.
        p. cm.
    Includes bibliographical references and index.
    ISBN 1-55786-591-4:
    1. Financial futures. 2. Risk management. 3. Interest rate risk. 4. Foreign exchange
rates.
    5. Portfolio management. I. Khoury, Sarkis J. II. Title.
    HG6024.3J68   1996
    332.64'5—dc20   94-46751
                                                                                        CIP

British Library Cataloguing in Publication Data

A CIP catalogue record for this book is available from the British Library.

Typeset by AM Marketing

Printed in the USA

This book is printed on acid-free paper

Contents

Preface

This book represents years of planning, research, and writing. The project was started in 1991 by Sarkis Joseph Khoury but had to be put on hold during 1992 due to a political engagement. The project was resurrected jointly by Sarkis Joseph Khoury and Philippe Jorion in 1993. Jorion joined in as a full research partner and a minority stakeholder.

The objective of the book is to offer the most rigorous analysis of domestic and international risk management issues. We believe that no text currently available in the marketplace approaches the risk management strategy and techniques in the same fashion. Current texts lack our emphasis on the international dimension of portfolio management and its full integration in the development of an effective, geocentric portfolio strategy.

Practically all the chapters represent in-depth reviews of the latest research on the topics under discussion. Several of the chapters could have been written as review articles destined for a variety of journals. Throughout the book we were motivated to keep the concept intact to ensure comprehensive discussions, which we hope to be thorough and easy to read.

The book is targeted to graduate students and money managers who appreciate and use quantitative techniques for portfolio management. The book may also be used for an introductory course in investment for students with reasonable quantitative skills.

The book has benefitted enormously from the excellent research and word processing assistance provided by Peter Holthe, Joyce Khoury, and Siew-Huey Pang. We are deeply grateful to them but are solely responsible for any errors that may remain.

We are most grateful to our families for their tolerance and support and their willingness to make, occasionally, major sacrifices to see this project through.

We trust that the reader will enjoy this book as much as we enjoyed writing it. It has been a happy partnership.

Philippe Jorion
Sarkis Joseph Khoury

Introduction: The Nature of Financial Risks

Theory without practice is pointless
Practice without theory is mindless
Lenin

This book is about the global management of financial risks. Unlike other texts, it takes an integrated approach to the topic and provides an in-depth coverage of interest rate risk, stock portfolio risk, and exchange rate risk. Most textbooks, reflecting the domestic orientation of authors, view the international dimension as worthy of an appendix or, perhaps, a "special item" to which little space is devoted. This may explain the astonishing lack of international diversification by U.S. investors. In contrast, this book argues that the size of global financial markets is such that it is irresponsible to give secondary consideration to foreign investments. Given the increasing integration of financial markets, equal importance should be given to the international and domestic financial environments.

Because we believe in a global approach to risk management, we have written the first textbook that, to our knowledge, provides detailed coverage of international investment methods, including security and currency selection, and of the effect of barriers to capital movements. We show that domestic investment is a subset of the global asset allocation decision and that it is impossible to evaluate the risk of domestic securities without reference to international factors. The purpose of this first chapter is to motivate the reader to think globally.

In this chapter, we explain why financial risk management is important. This concept applies to any corporation or investor dealing with financial assets or liabilities, which probably involves just about everybody. Banks, for instance, have to deal with the fact that their deposits and liabilities may be differentially exposed to interest rates. Corporations involved in international trade must assess the impact of movements in exchange rates on their profitability. Investors are now turning increasingly to international markets and must be aware of factors driving stock prices and the interaction between movements in stock prices and exchange rates. Understanding financial risks is a prerequisite for venturing into new financial markets. Speculative positions can be taken only after a firm understanding of financial risk management exists.

Risk Management

Financial risk management has become a tool essential to the survival of all business activity. This affects all firms: industrial corporations, banking institutions, and investment management firms. Nowhere is this more evident than for commercial banks. Walter Wriston, former chairman of Citicorp, has argued that "The fact is that bankers are in the business of managing risk. Pure and simple, that is the business of banking." Banks now realize that they must precisely measure sources of risk as a prelude to controlling and properly pricing risks.

Understanding risk means that financial managers can consciously plan for the consequences of adverse outcomes and, by so doing, be better prepared for the inevitable uncertainty and offer better prices for managing risks than the competition.

But what exactly is risk? *Risk* can be defined as the volatility of unexpected outcomes, usually the value of assets or liabilities of interest. In general, managers face two types of risks: business risk and financial risk. Business, or operating risk pertains to the product market in which a firm operates and includes innovations, technology changes, and marketing. Financial risk relates to movement in financial variables.

Enterprises are in the business of seeking exposure to business risk. This is how they create a competitive advantage and add value for shareholders. Financial risk, in contrast, can be carefully hedged if so desired, so that firms can concentrate on what they do best – exposure to business risks. In contrast to industrial corporations, the function of financial institutions is primarily to manage financial risks.

In the absence of views on financial markets, there are many arguments why financial risk should be hedged by corporations. Hedging may allow firms to better plan ahead, by projecting cash flows that will not be affected by the whims of financial markets. In some situations, hedging can also lessen the probability of costly bankruptcy. Hedging may lower the average tax burden if it leads to more stable profits over time. For instance, wildly gyrating prices could cause large profits in some years, taxed at high rates, and in other years losses that cannot be credited against future profits; the net effect is to pay higher taxes when earnings are not hedged against financial risks. In general, hedging is useful if there are "frictions" (costs or taxes) in capital markets.

Corporations and financial managers are too often ignorant of the effect of financial variables. Broadly, there are four different types of financial risks: interest rate risk, foreign exchange risk, equity risk, and commodity risk. This book provides a thorough and integrated coverage of the first three types of risks.

Taking a global approach to financial risk management usefully shows that a number of important concepts are pervasive to all markets. Risk is measured by the standard deviation of unexpected outcomes, or "sigma" (σ). Measurements of linear exposure to movements in underlying risk variables appear everywhere under different guises. For instance, in the fixed income market, exposure to movements in interest rates is called *duration*. In the stock market, this exposure is called *systematic risk,* or beta (β); according to the capital asset pricing model (CAPM), if investors efficiently diversify across stocks, this should be the only component of priced risk. In the foreign exchange market, this exposure is called *exchange rate exposure.* In derivatives markets, the exposure to movements in the value of the underlying asset is called *delta* (δ). Second derivatives are called *convexity* and *gamma* in the fixed income and derivatives markets, respectively.

Risk management is the tightest in the derivatives market, because almost all the movements in the value of derivatives contracts are explained by price movements in the underlying asset. This is why this market has become quite quantitative: one talks of delta (the first-order partial derivative of the option premium with respect to the underlying stock price), gamma (the second-order derivative of the option premium with respect to the stock price), theta (a sensitivity measure of a call option to the time of expiration), vega (the first-order partial derivative of the option premium with respect to volatility), and rho (the first-order partial derivative of the option premium with respect to the risk-free interest rate). Next comes the fixed income market, where perhaps three-fourths of the volatility of bond prices is explained by a common interest rate factor. Finally, in the equity market, general market movements explain perhaps one-third of the typical stock movements. Individual stocks are differentially affected by many other factors, such as interest rates, commodity prices, exchange rates, and most important, idiosyncratic business risk. The attempt to explain systematic movements in terms of marketwide pervasive factors has led to the "arbitrage pricing theory," which states that expected returns should be linearly related to their exposure to these pervasive factors. But multifactor models have also appeared in the fixed income markets and are now being extended to the international environment.

Financial Risk

The single most important reason for the growth of the risk management industry is the dramatic increase in the volatility of interest rates, exchange rates, and commodity prices in the 1970s. Exhibit 1.1 compares movements in exchange rates, long-term government bond yields, stock market values, and the price of oil since 1962.

Over the last decades, financial markets have become far more volatile. Consider the following fundamental changes:

- The breakdown of the fixed exchange rate system in 1971;
- The oil price shocks, accompanied by high inflation and wild swings in interest rates, starting in 1973;
- The recycling of petro-dollars to less developed countries (LDCs), followed by widespread defaults in the early 1980s due to the LDCs' inability to service high interest payments;
- The drive toward economic and monetary unification in Europe, accelerated by the 1989 Maastricht treaty;
- The wide-scale conversion of communist countries to free-market policies, best symbolized by the fall of the Berlin Wall in 1989.

What is dramatic about these developments is their unpredictability, their speed, their impact, and most interesting, their dominolike

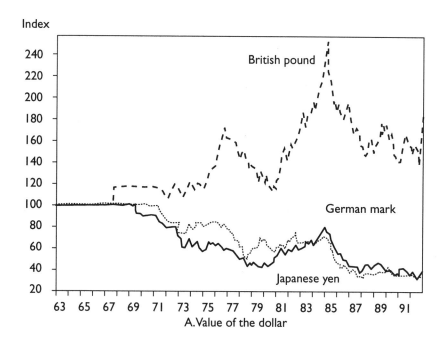

A. Value of the dollar

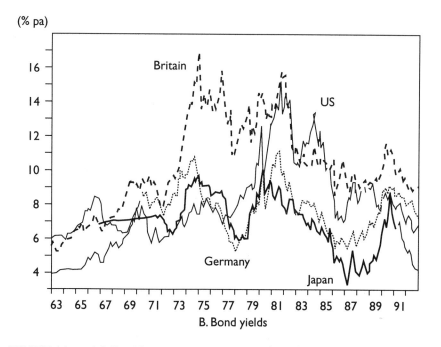

B. Bond yields

EXHIBIT 1.1a and 1.1b   Movements in Financial Prices

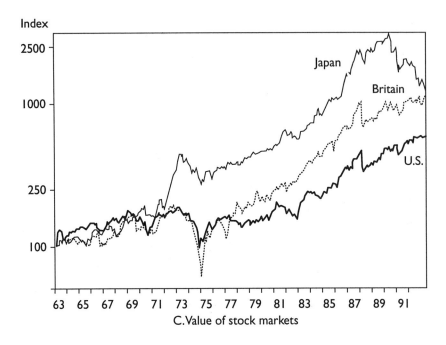

C. Value of stock markets

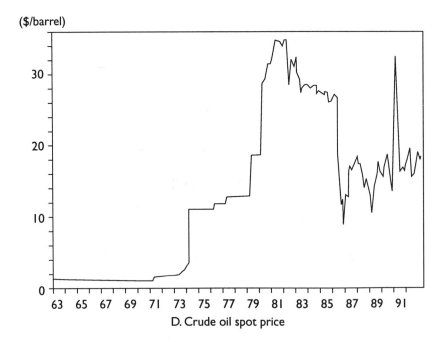

D. Crude oil spot price

EXHIBIT 1.1c and 1.1d   Movements in Financial Prices Continued

nature. We know of no single person, not even the head of the CIA or the KGB, who, even in early 1989, predicted that the Berlin Wall would soon become a relic in the Reagan library or that all Eastern European countries would discard communism and openly embrace free markets. Again, unpredictability is the only constant for all these events.

No country in the world has been spared the impact of these events. Even corporations with no foreign operations have been affected by these tumultuous changes. Worldwide events do affect domestic interest rates and domestic economic activity; movements in exchange rates can suddenly change the competitive position of corporations, as demonstrated by the recent resurgence of U.S. domestic automobile manufacturers.

Investment and corporate managers operate in this sea of change and unpredictability. These events represent tremendous challenges and opportunities, and they emphasize the need for tightly controlled risk management. To illustrate the forces of changes in the last 30 years, Exhibit 1.1 displays movements in exchange rates, long-term bond yields, stock market values, and the spot price of oil. Four countries are analyzed: the United States, Japan, Germany, and Great Britain.

Exhibit 1.1a graphs movements in the U.S. dollar against the deutsche mark (DM), the Japanese yen (JY), and the British pound (BP). In 30 years, the dollar has lost about two-thirds of its value against the yen and mark: the yen/$ rate has slid from 361 to about 100, and the DM/$ rate has fallen from 4.2 to 1.6. The pound, however, has fallen against the dollar, from 2.8 to 1.6 $/BP over the same period. In between, the dollar has reached dizzying heights, just to fall to unprecedented lows, thereby creating wild swings in the competitive advantage of nations – and nightmares for unhedged firms.

Exhibit 1.1b also shows that bond yields have widely fluctuated in the 1980s, reflecting creeping inflationary pressures spreading throughout national economies. These were created in the 1960s by the United States, trying to simultaneously finance the Vietnam War and a domestic government assistance program, and they spread to other countries through the rigid mechanism of fixed exchange rates. Eventually, the persistently high U.S. inflation led to the breakdown of the fixed exchange rate system and a sharp fall in the value of the dollar. In October 1979, the Federal Reserve Bank changed its operating policies in an attempt to squash inflation. As a result, interest rates immediately increased, became more volatile, and led to a sustained appreciation of the dollar. In the United States, bond yields increased from 4 percent in the early 1960s to 15 percent at the height of the monetarist squeeze on the money supply, thereby creating havoc in savings and loans that had made long-term loans, primarily for housing, using short-term funding.

In addition, Exhibit 1.1d shows that the sharp increases in the price of oil in the 1970s are correlated with increases in bond yields all over the world. These also had an impact on the value of national stock markets, displayed in Exhibit 1.1c; the great bear market of 1973–1975 occurred all over the world and happened after the three-fold increase in the price of crude oil in 1973. This episode clearly shows that it is difficult to understand the mechanics of the fixed income markets without a good grasp of the links between interest rates, exchange rates, and commodity prices.

The risk imparted by these movements can be measured by short-term volatility. Exhibit 1.2 presents the standard deviation of trailing 12-month relative price changes, expressed in percent per annum. Exhibit 1.2a shows that the volatility of the DM/$ rate has increased sharply after 1973. The demise of the system of fixed exchange rates has added to financial risks. Note that this volatility, on the order of 10–15 percent per annum, is large enough to wipe out typical profit margins for firms with substantial exposure to foreign currencies.

The volatility in U.S. bond prices is presented in Exhibit 1.2b. Here, the typical volatility was about 5 percent per annum, except in the early 1980s, where it reached 20 percent per annum, and has subsided since. Exhibit 1.2C measures risk in the U.S. stock market. Volatility here appears to be more stable, on the order of 10–20 percent per annum. Risk is more consistent in this market, reflecting residual claims on corporations subject to business risks in a mature stock market. Notable peaks in volatility occurred in October 1974, when U.S. stocks went up by 17 percent, after three large consecutive drops, and during the October 1987 crash, when U.S. equities lost 20 percent of their value. Volatility therefore occurs because of large unexpected price changes, whether positive or negative. This symmetric treatment is logical since players in these markets can be long or short, domestic or foreign, consumers or producers. In the energy market, the once stable price of oil has become subject to the brutal pressures of supply and demand. Overall, the greater volatility of financial markets creates risks and opportunities, which must be measured and controlled.

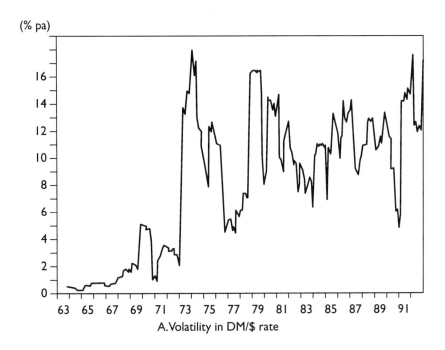

A. Volatility in DM/$ rate

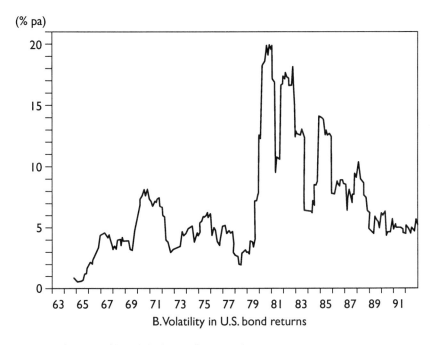

B. Volatility in U.S. bond returns

EXHIBIT 1.2a and 1.2b   Volatility in Financial Prices

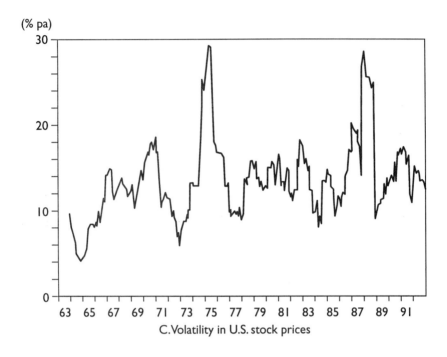

C. Volatility in U.S. stock prices

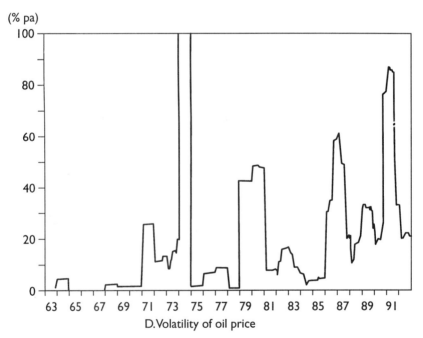

D. Volatility of oil price

EXHIBIT 1.2c and 1.2d   Volatility in Financial Prices Continued.

The World Financial Markets

To convey a better sense of the evolution of world financial markets, we now describe the global stock and bond markets. First, as a benchmark measure, Exhibit 1.3 compares the size of major national economies using the gross domestic product (GDP) over 1971, 1981, and 1991, translated into a common currency, the U.S. dollar. Although the United States is still the most important single economic power,

EXHIBIT 1.3 World Gross Domestic Product: 1971–1991 (billions of U.S. dollars)

	1971	1981	1991	Growth 1971–91
Europe:				
Austria	17	71	164	12.1
Belgium	29	99	201	10.2
Denmark	18	57	130	10.5
France	159	582	1,200	10.6
Germany	215	679	1,566	10.4
Italy	118	408	1,150	12.1
Netherlands	39	141	287	10.5
Norway	13	57	106	11.2
Spain	42	184	527	13.5
Sweden	36	114	237	9.8
Switzerland	25	94	229	11.7
United Kingdom	141	519	1,017	10.4
All Europe	835	2,936	6,650	10.9
Australia	42	172	293	10.1
Asia:				
China	93	280	371	7.2
India	62	185	268	7.6
Japan	231	1,167	3,356	14.3
Korea	10	70	283	18.4
Singapore	2	14	40	15.5
No. America:				
Canada	96	297	593	9.5
United States	1,097	3,031	5,673	8.6
World	2,485	8,223	17,691	10.3

Source: International Monetary Fund, various issues.

it is dominated by the European Union (EU) as an economic entity. In 1991, the total U.S. GDP amounted to $5.7 trillion, versus $6.7 trillion for Europe as a whole. Further, over the past two decades, the rate of growth in the United States has been lower than that in most other countries.

Exhibit 1.4 now presents the size of major stock markets as of the end of 1971, 1981, and 1991. Clearly, no market is dominant. Even the United States, which accounted for more than 55 percent of total stock market capitalization in 1971, now accounts for less than 38 percent of the total. At some point, it was eclipsed by the Japanese

EXHIBIT 1.4   The World Stock Markets: 1971–1991 (billions of U.S. dollars)

	1971	1981	1991	Growth 1971–91
Austria	1	2	27	17.9
Belgium	7	8	73	12.4
Denmark	1	4	45	21.0
France	24	37	347	14.3
Germany	36	63	369	12.3
Italy	12	24	154	13.6
Netherlands	12	20	129	12.6
Norway	1	2	23	17.0
Spain	14	17	120	11.3
Sweden	6	17	104	15.3
Switzerland	14	41	199	14.2
United Kingdom	111	177	954	11.4
Europe	239	412	2,544	12.6
Australia	22	58	137	9.6
Hong Kong	4	42	119	18.5
Japan	67	403	2,996	20.9
Singapore	3	35	82	18.0
"EAFE"	335	950	5,878	15.4
Canada	45	104	232	8.5
USA	762	1,145	3,702	8.2
World	1,142	2,199	9,812	11.4

Source: Morgan Stanley Capital International, various issues. "EAFE" represents Europe, Australia, and Far Eastern countries.

market. Japan has been growing at the astounding annual rate of 21 percent over the last 20 years, thereby increasing its share of the global stock market from 6 percent to 31 percent. Even after the recent slide in Japanese equity prices, investing in Japan in the last decade would have produced huge excess returns. Global investors are now actively scanning emerging markets in the hope of uncovering another Japanese-style growth market.

In general, foreign markets have been growing much more rapidly, especially during the last decade, than the U.S. stock market. European markets as a whole have increased at a rate of about 13 percent per annum, versus only 8 percent for the United States. Admittedly, some of this growth reflects the privatization of state-owned firms, but more fundamentally, it represents a dramatic shift toward entrepreneurship in Europe.

Next, Exhibit 1.5 presents a breakdown of the global bond markets by currency and issuer type. The U.S. dollar accounts for 44 percent of the total market, which is higher than the stock market share. This is hardly a virtue, however, because the large size of the U.S. bond market primarily reflects large accumulated government deficits, and it is not clear whether spendthrift governments should be rewarded by a large portfolio allocation. From the viewpoint of U.S. investors, foreign bond markets are now large, quite liquid, and easily accessible; in addition, foreign bond markets allow investors to efficiently diversify away the risk of one's own monetary and political risk.

Exhibit 1.5 also shows that the international bond markets, composed of the so-called foreign and Eurobond markets, are quite large, accounting for more than 10 percent of the total bond market. For some sectors, international bonds exceed the domestic corporate bond market. For debt-issuing corporations and investment managers alike, international bonds should be given as much attention as domestic bonds.

We now turn to a description of global capital flows. Exhibit 1.4 clearly illustrates that world stock markets have been growing very rapidly in the last decade. This unprecedented growth has occurred at the same time as capital started to chase investment opportunities all over the world, spurred by the liberalization of financial markets.

Volatility has also increased because of the surging flows of capital across borders. Exhibit 1.6 displays recent movements in international equity flows. These are becoming huge. It is reckoned that 1 in 5 equity transactions now includes a foreign investor. In 1981, before

EXHIBIT 1.5   The World Bond Markets: 1991 Public Issues (billions of U.S. dollars)

Market	Total	Central Gov't	Gov't Agencies	State, Local	Corp.	Bank Debt	Foreign Bonds	Euro-bonds
U.S. Dollar	6,238	1,881	1,563	894	1,168	117	87	527
Japanese Yen	2,503	1,287	160	59	236	588	49	123
Deutsche Mark	1,257	326	50	32	2	686	162	
Italian Lira	868	686	28	–	4	126	3	22
French Franc	654	256	242	5	103	–	6	42
U.K. Pound	376	225	–	–	26	–	8	117
Canadian Dollar	361	136	–	110	54	1	1	59
Belgian Franc	301	151	80	–	6	47	17	1
Swedish Krone	270	116	–	1	12	138	–	4
Danish Krone	219	70	–	–	–	144	–	5
Dutch Guilder	201	134	–	3	43	–	7	13
Swiss Franc	191	9	–	12	30	54	87	–
ECU	160	52	–	–	–	–	–	109
Spanish Peseta	119	71	4	–	24	12	8	–
Australian Dollar	88	28	22	–	14	–	–	24
Austrian Schilling	78	25	2	1	3	46	2	–
Norwegian Krone	44	12	3	6	3	20	–	2
Finnish Markka	36	9	–	1	6	19	–	–
Port. Escudo	30	21	–	1	4	3	1	–
Irish Pound	25	24	1	–	–	–	–	–
New Zealand Dollar	11	7	2	–	–	–	–	3
Total	14,028	5,525	2,155	1,123	1,738	2,001	1,487	

Source: Salomon Brothers, "How Big is the World Bond Market?," 1991.

countries lifted capital controls, the ratio was 1 in 16. Emerging markets attracted about $14 billion a year in new money over 1989–1991, and their share is expected to sharply increase, because these markets offer substantial diversification benefits due to a low correlation with "developed" markets.

The internalization of capital markets is reflected in the large flows of capital across borders and in the cross-listing of equities. Today the New York Stock Exchange (NYSE) lists more than 100 foreign securities, and foreign securities account for the lion's share of the total capitalization of the London Stock Exchange; SEAQ international lists more than 600 foreign firms, with an annual trading volume of more than $500 billion.

EXHIBIT 1.6   International Equity Flows: 1986–1991 (billions of U.S. dollars)

	1986	1987	1988	1989	1990	1991
Global Gross Equity Flows:						
Cross-Border Trading	801	1,344	1,213	1,598	1,441	1,320
Cross-Exchange Trading	101	509	343	583	874	764
Of which,						
Foreign Firm Trading on						
NYSE	NA	75	53	67	81	88
(Number of firms listed)	(63)	(67)	(76)	(86)	(95)	(105)
SEAQ International	NA	90	72	136	284	530
(Number of firms listed)	(584)	(597)	(585)	(599)	(608)	(625)

Source: Howell and Cozzini, "International Equity Flows, 1992 Edition." Cross-border trading refers to trading by foreigners in domestic securities; cross-exchange trading refers to trading in foreign securities on a domestic exchange.

Another measure of international financial activity is the volume of transactions in the foreign exchange (Forex) markets. Recent surveys estimate the amount of *daily* trading to be about $800 billion in 1992. In comparison, the average daily trading volume on the New York Stock Exchange, the largest stock exchange in the world, is only $5 billion. The only market to come close to the Forex market is the U.S. Treasury market, with average trading volume of $170 billion daily. The volume of foreign exchange activity dwarfs that of any other market: the Forex market is truly the most active of all financial markets.

The Forex market has become a reflection of the activity in international capital markets and is the final arbitrator of currency values. The power of central banks to set exchange rates has slowly disappeared in the 1980s, following the removal of barriers to capital movements. Given that the total stock of central bank reserves is barely higher than one day's trading, about $1,000 billion, attempts to fix unrealistic exchange rates have become futile. Ten years ago, no one would have thought that a single speculator, George Soros, could have made profits of $2 billion from staring into the eyes of that venerable lady, the Bank of England, and speculating that the British pound would have to devalue. Speculators correctly anticipated that the British government would not have the courage to raise interest rates at the time the country was suffering from one of its worst recessions this century. Suffice to say, investors who were not paying attention to the exchange rate exposure of their portfolio were badly hurt by the currency turmoil of September 1992.

The increasing globalization of capital markets is also reflected in the way corporations raise funds. Exhibit 1.7 breaks down sources of funds into equities, domestic bonds, and international bonds for U.S., Japanese, German, and British corporations. In 1991, the total volume of issues in the Eurobond market, $248 billion, was larger than the total debt raised by U.S. industrial corporations, $170 billion. British corporations appear to raise more bonds off-shore than domestically. Today, corporations in need of funds can issue debt in any currency and then swap payments back into another preferred currency to minimize total funding costs. Corporations that do not play this game are now saddled with a competitive disadvantage vis-à-vis more globally oriented firms.

The purpose of this book is to help the portfolio and bank managers to cope with the dynamics of international financial markets and the unique risk they represent. The book is structured to provide a strong analytical basis for analyzing risks and returns in the fixed income, foreign exchange, and stock markets. At the same time, we reflected our own biases in presenting materials that we thought would be of practical relevance for readers. We focus on interest rate risk, foreign

EXHIBIT 1.7   New Security Issues: 1991 (billions of U.S. dollars)

	U.S.	Japan	Germany	Britain	Total Int'l
Equities:	84	10	8	19	
Bonds:	1,223	831	266	26	
Central Gov't	492	287	76	23	
Local Gov't	154	19	5	0	
Financial Institutions	189	141	176	1	
Nonfinancial Corp.	170	379	8	2	
Foreign Bonds	13	3	20	0	
Memorandum:					
Eurobonds by Residents	17	61	3	25	248
Foreign Bonds by Residents	2	10	0	2	49

Source: Organization for Economic Cooperation and Development, various issues. Average exchange rates are 135 Yen/$, 1.66DM/$, 1.77$/BP.

currency risk, and portfolio risk, attaching equal importance to each and attempting to integrate the various facets of risk. Derivatives are covered in the context of controlling exchange rate risk but could be presented as easily for other types of contracts; one virtue of the methods of risk management is that they can easily be transferred to other sources of financial risk.

Chapter Review

The book is organized by source of financial risk. Chapters 2, 4, and 6 focus on interest rate risk, exchange rate risk, and stock market risk, respectively. Chapters 3 and 5 deal with the management of interest and exchange rate risk. The last chapters are more integrative in nature.

Chapter 2 presents the nature and dynamics of fixed income markets. We summarize the major bond markets and analyze the various aspects of yield curves, the determinants of interest rates, and theories of the term structure of interest rates.

Chapter 3 focuses on the management of interest rate risk. We first introduce duration as a characteristic of fixed income assets or liabilities. Duration also measures the sensitivity of prices to movements in interest rates. Therefore, duration is an essential tool for the management of interest rate risk. The chapter illustrates how duration can be used to manage the assets and liabilities of a banking institution. We also introduce off-balance-sheet instruments such as forwards, futures, and swap contracts and show how these can be used to hedge interest rate risk. Because duration involves a first-order, linear, approximation to interest rate exposure, we discuss other measures of exposure, such as convexity and M^2.

Chapter 4 looks at the nature and dynamics of the foreign exchange markets. It covers the various international financial systems; the spot, forward, and Eurocurrency markets; the major theories explaining movements in exchange rates; the efficiency of the Forex markets; and the various methods for forecasting spot exchange rates and their effectiveness. We show that exchange rates should be analyzed in the same fashion as other asset markets such as bond or equity markets.

Chapter 5 takes a comprehensive look at risk management in the foreign exchange market using derivatives markets. We show how to use and price futures and options and cover advanced strategies for speculation and hedging. These methods can be easily converted to futures and options on other sources of financial risk.

Chapter 6 looks at the domestic dimensions of portfolio diversification. The development of the efficiency frontier, some methods for outperforming it, the capital asset pricing model, the arbitrage pricing model, and various methods for evaluating the performance of portfolio managers are presented in a rigorous and comprehensive fashion.

Chapter 7 looks at the international dimensions of portfolio theory. After reviewing the globalization of financial markets, it concludes with an assertion that no portfolio manager can afford to ignore the other markets of the world and still claim to have a truly optimal portfolio. The chapter integrates domestic portfolio diversification and exchange rates and shows how to optimally structure portfolios with exchange rate risk. Using an equilibrium argument, that is, assuming that all investors behave optimally, we derive and discuss the international capital asset pricing model. The chapter also looks at the impact of government restrictions on capital flows, which create "segmentations" in capital markets. Understanding these segmentations is important, since they create additional opportunities for global portfolio managers.

Chapter 8 looks at the anomalies (inefficiencies) in the financial markets and the risks and opportunities they present. We strongly believe that, before taking speculative positions, managers must be fully aware of financial market risks. Managers should first fully master hedging techniques and only then speculate on the basis of strong opinions on a market. The chapter presents anomalies in major financial markets, which can be used for the active management of portfolios. By judiciously deviating from their benchmark, portfolio managers can use these anomalies to create value.

Conclusion

This chapter sets the scene for all the chapters to follow by giving the reader an idea about the need to have portfolios reflect the realities of the world. We have come ever closer to fully integrated financial markets. Perfect integration may remain a dream, however.

The rest of the chapters will show the reader how to cope and how to capitalize on the multiplying opportunities in the international marketplace.

The Fixed Income Markets: Nature and Dynamics

A fixed income security usually is a government, corporate, or municipal bond that pays a fixed rate of interest until the bond matures. The value of fixed income securities fluctuates as market yields change over time, creating a potential for loss but also profit opportunities for portfolio managers. It is therefore essential to understand the sources of risk in the fixed income markets and how they affect fixed income instruments.

This chapter discusses the nature and dynamics of the fixed income market. We first review elements of bond valuation as well as the yield concept. The major sectors of the bond market are explored in the next section. This section covers in great detail government securities, agency securities, and municipal and corporate debt. Convertible bonds are also covered. Given the increasing importance of nondollar bond markets, we cover foreign government bond markets, as well as international bonds. Knowledge of institutional aspects of these markets is essential to the management of bond portfolios.

As the first two sections show, bond prices are differentially affected by changes in yields. It is therefore important to understand how yields vary across maturities and are expected to change over time. The third section then provides an overview of the supply and demand factors that are thought to affect short-term interest rates. The term *structure of interest rates* is also developed in the third section, and theories of the term structure are presented in the fourth. We present classical theories: the expectations theory, the liquidity theory, and the market segmentation theory. We also discuss the more recent general-equilibrium approach to the term structure.

Finally, we show how these theories can be applied to the management of bond portfolios. We also show how to use information about the term structure to select an optimal maturity, as well as to identify mispriced securities.

This chapter serves as a necessary introduction to the next chapter, which is devoted to the management of interest rate risk. We will then study in more detail duration hedging and asset/liability management.

Bond Valuation

Bond Prices and Yields

The market value of a bond P can be written as the present value of future cash flows expected from the bond:

$$P = \sum_{t=1}^{T} \frac{C_t}{(1 + y)^t},\qquad(2.1)$$

where

C_t = the coupon or principal payment in period t,

t = the number of periods (annual, semiannual, or other) of coupon or principal payments,

T = the number of periods to final maturity,

y = the yield to maturity for this particular bond.

For a bond with a constant coupon and final repayment of the face value F at maturity (a "balloon" payment), we can write

$$P = \sum_{t=1}^{T} \frac{C}{(1 + y)^t} + \frac{F}{(1 + y)^T}.\qquad(2.2)$$

In this definition, the discount rate y is the internal rate of return that equates the present value of the cash flows to the market value of the bond. It is also the reinvestment rate, or the rate of return on the bond if all coupons are reinvested at the same rate.

Equation (2.1) assumes that coupon payments are made annually. If coupon payments were paid semiannually or m times a year, the annual yield or coupon must be divided by m and the number of periods is multiplied by the same factor, m.

If a bond has an infinite life and a fixed coupon, it is called a *consol.* Its market price can be found from an infinite series expansion,

$$P = \sum_{t=1}^{\infty} \frac{C}{(1 + y)^t} = \frac{C}{y}. \qquad (2.3)$$

Equation (2.3) clearly shows the inverse relationship between the price P and y, the yield to maturity.

The yield to maturity represents the rate of return on the face value of the bond adjusted for the amortization of the premiums (paid) or the discount (saved) on the bond at the time of purchase. It can be calculated precisely using Equation (2.1) or it can be approximated. Equation (2.1) requires an iterative process where various rates are plugged into the equation for y, given the observable market price. The process should begin with the "current yield," defined as C/P, an approximation of the yield to maturity, which is then adjusted upward or downward–upward when the bond is selling at a discount and downward when it is selling at a premium.

An approximation of the yield to maturity is provided by the following equation:

$$y = \frac{[(F - P)/T] + C}{(F + P)/2}, \qquad (2.4)$$

where the $(F - P)/T$ term represents the periodic amortization of the premium (if $P > F$) or discount (if $F > P$) on the bond, and the denominator is the average value of the investment in the bond.

As an example, we find the yield to maturity on a 10 percent coupon bond selling at a market price of $850 with a remaining life of five years. The coupon is paid once a year, and annual compounding is used for the yield.

$$y = \frac{[(1{,}000 - 850)/5] + 0.10 \times 1{,}000}{(1{,}000 + 850)/2}$$

$$= \frac{[150/5] + 100}{925} = 130/925 = 14.05 \text{ percent.}$$

In fact, the exact yield is 14.4126 percent. This example shows that the yield to maturity (14.05 percent) is always higher than the coupon rate (10 percent) and the current yield, 11.76 percent (100/850), when the bond is selling at a discount. If the bond were sold at a premium, its yield to maturity would be lower than its coupon rate. Bonds selling at par would, therefore, have a current yield equal to the yield to maturity equal to the coupon rate.

Yields for callable bonds are different than for "straight" bonds, because the exact maturity date is uncertain. The general convention is to compute the yield to final maturity if the current clean price is less than par; it is then assumed that the bond will not be called. When the bond sells at a premium, yield is generally calculated to the first call date.

It should be noted that the yield-to-maturity on a bond does not necessarily represent a promised rate of return. It is only with a zero coupon bond that locking in the initial yield guarantees a nominal rate of return. When a bond pays coupons, these payments have to be reinvested at a future unknown rate. Even when yields do not change over time, coupons will be reinvested at different rates if the yield curve is not flat. For coupon-paying bonds, therefore, the yield represents a rate of return only under the strict condition of a constant flat yield curve.

Yields are convenient measures of the value of a bond. They can be used to compare bonds differing in maturity, coupon, and market prices. Because yields are used to discount fixed future cash flows, an increase in yield lowers the present value of the cash flow or the market price of the bond. Conversely, lower yields increase the price of the bond.

Bond prices are inversely related to bond yields. This relationship follows directly from Equations (2.1) and (2.3), where y appears in the denominator. For a consol, for example, $P = C/y$, which leads to

$$\frac{dP}{dy} = \frac{-C}{y^2},$$

hence the inverse relationship. The inverse relationship holds for most types of bonds and is displayed in Exhibit 2.1.

Bond Quotations and Accrued Interest

The previous bond pricing formula assumes that the next coupon will be paid in exactly one period. If this is not the case, the market value of the bond will include *accrued interest*, which is the part of the future coupon due to the seller of the bond.

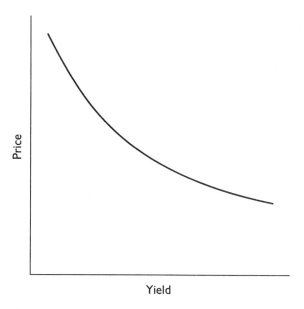

Yield

EXHIBIT 2.1   Price–Yield Relationship

The total sale price, also known as *gross price*, includes the *clean price* plus the *accrued:*

$$P_{\text{gross}} = P_{\text{clean}} + \text{accrued}. \tag{2.5}$$

Different markets have different conventions for the computation of the accrued interest. In the U.S. Treasury bond market, for instance, accrued is computed as

$$\text{accrued} = \text{coupon} \tag{2.6}$$
$$\times \frac{\text{actual number of days since last coupon}}{\text{actual number of days between last coupon and next}}$$

For most markets, bonds are generally quoted on a "clean" basis and as a percentage of the face value. If the bond sells at a (clean) price higher than its face value, it is said to be at a *premium*. If its price is equal to its face value, the bond is selling at *par*. If the bond sells at a (clean) price lower than its face value, it is said to be selling at a *discount*.

For example, on March 31, 1993, the U.S. Treasury bond of 7¹/₈ of February 23 was quoted at a price of 102-17. Because Treasuries are quoted in thirty-seconds, the clean price is 102.53125 percent of face value. The buyer must pay the seller for accrued interest, which corresponds to the next coupon payment of 3.5635 percent of face value, since Treasuries pay coupons semiannually. The last coupon payment occurred on February 15, and the next would be on August 15. There are therefore 181 days between the two coupon dates. If settlement (actual payment) occurs on April 1, a total of 44 days will have elapsed since the last coupon.

The price the buyer will have to pay will therefore be, as a percentage of the face value,

$$P_g = (102 + 17/32) + (1/2)(7 + 1/8) \times (44/181) = 103.39727.$$

This particular bond is trading at a premium, since its yield of 6.92 percent is lower than its coupon rate. Note that, because the gross price determines the invoice payment, the computation has to be carried out with great precision. Both the buyer and seller must agree on the exact valuation of the accrued interest.

Bond Price Theorems

At this point, we present bond price theorems that are useful in explaining bond price movements.

> *Theorem 1:* Bond prices are inversely related to bond yields.
> *Theorem 2:* Bond price changes are an increasing function of maturity, all else (coupon and yield) equal.
> *Theorem 3:* The percentage change in the price of a bond increases at a diminishing rate as maturity increases.
> *Theorem 4:* For a given maturity, capital gains resulting from a decrease in yields are always higher than capital losses resulting from an increase in yields.
> *Theorem 5:* The higher is the coupon rate, the smaller is the percentage change resulting from a change in yields.

Fixed Income Securities

This section examines the operation of fixed income financial markets. The fixed income market includes the so-called money market, which consists of short-term instruments, with maturities less than a year, and the bond market, which consists of longer instruments that generally pay regular coupons.

As seen in the introduction, U.S.-dollar-denominated bonds account for about 45 percent of the world bond market. This is why we focus on the U.S. bond market, which is the largest and most liquid bond market in the world. Bond markets can be classified into three borrower categories: government and agency bonds, state and local government (municipal) bonds, and corporate debt.

Government Securities

We first examine government and agency securities with substantial investor participation. These markets generally have their counterparts in other countries, each with its own institutional arrangements. In the United States, government securities do not trade on a centralized exchange but rather "over the counter" (OTC). That is, orders to buy or sell go through a "market maker," who will quote a price at which he or she is willing to buy or sell. The U.S. Treasury market is by far the most active and liquid bond market in the world.

Treasury Bills.   Treasury bills (T-bills) are short-term obligations of the federal government. They do not carry a coupon and are sold at a discount from par value. As a result, income on T-bills is calculated as the difference between the purchase price and the sale price.

T-bills are quoted in terms of their *discount rate*, expressed on a 360-day period. Using the following definition, the investor can convert the discount rate to a price, and vice versa:

$$\text{discount rate} = \frac{\text{face value} - \text{actual issue price}}{\text{face value}} \times \frac{360}{\text{days to maturity}}.$$
$$(2.7)$$

The *investment yield* allows the investor to compare the yield on a T-bill with that on a coupon-bearing financial instrument. Because it is calculated using the initial purchase price of the bill and 365 days to maturity, it is, therefore, higher than the discount rate.

$$\text{yield} = \frac{\text{face value} - \text{actual issue price}}{\text{actual issue price}} \times \frac{365}{\text{days to maturity}} \cdot (2.8)$$

For example, a T-bill selling at 97 and maturing in 90 days has a discount rate of

$$DR = \frac{100 - 97}{100} \times \frac{360}{90} = 12 \text{ percent.}$$

Its investment yield is

$$Y = \frac{100 - 97}{97} \times \frac{365}{90} = 12.54 \text{ percent.}$$

In the primary market, U.S. T-bills are issued with maturities of 13 weeks, 26 weeks, and 52 weeks, and they are sold in minimum amounts of $10,000 and in multiples of $5,000 over this minimum. Investors in T-bills do not receive certificates from the Treasury; instead, their ownership is recorded as a book entry at the Treasury. This reduces the issuance costs to the Treasury as well as the probability of theft, loss, or counterfeit.

T-bills are issued by the Federal Reserve System through a bidding process. Bids can take two forms. Competitive bids are submitted to the Treasury on the basis of a price (e.g., 98.753) using a tender (a special form used for submitting a bid). Noncompetitive bidders do not specify the price in their bid. They simply agree to purchase a certain number of T-bills at the weighted average price of accepted competitive bids. An investor may submit only one noncompetitive bid for a maximum of $500,000. All competitive tenders for a T-bill issue must be made before 1:30 P.M. of the deadline day.

The offering schedule for T-bills depends on the maturity period; 13-week and 26-week maturities are offered every week. The offering is announced on Tuesday, the bills are auctioned the following Monday, and the bills are issued (recorded) on the Thursday after the auction. The 52-week maturity is offered every 4 weeks. The offering is announced every fourth Thursday, the auction takes place the following Wednesday, and the bills are recorded (issued) the following Tuesday.

The secondary market for T-bills is quite deep. It is characterized by very high liquidity at very low transaction costs. Bid–ask spreads are probably the tightest of any money market instrument. The T-bill in the preceding example might be quoted 12.02 percent bid, 12.00 percent ask. This translates into a bid price of 96.995 and an ask price of 97.000; in other words, the bid–ask spread is only 0.005 percent of the value of the bond, which is extremely small.

Treasury Notes and Bonds.   Treasury notes and bonds are, respectively, medium- and long-term obligations of the U.S. government. They are coupon-bearing instruments issued with 2-year to 10-year maturities for notes and a longer maturity, up to 30 years, for bonds. Some long-term bonds have been issued with a call feature.

U.S. Treasury notes and bonds pay interest semiannually. Accrued interest is computed using the "actual over actual" rule. This involves computing the actual number of days since the last coupon payment, divided by the actual number of days between the last and next coupons. Treasury bonds are quoted as a percentage of par value (100) with changes expressed in 32nds of a percentage point.

Notes may be issued in $1,000, $5,000, $10,000, $100,000, and $1 million denominations. The minimum denomination is at the discretion of the Treasury. Bonds and notes generally are available in registered or bearer forms. Registered notes or bonds bear the owner's name and are recorded on the Treasury's books. Transfer of ownership requires the owner's written assignment (certified by a commercial bank or a trust company) on the back of the certificate. Bearer notes or bonds, on the other hand, do not bear the name of their owner. They are, therefore, easier to transfer but more susceptible to theft because of the presumption that the holder is the owner. Bearer bonds and notes have coupons attached to them. When the coupons become due, the owner submits them to a savings or commercial bank or to a Federal Reserve bank and collects the semiannual interest payment.

In the primary market, the Treasury sells its notes and bonds through the Federal Reserve System using an auction system similar to that used to sell T-bills. The auction may be on a price basis or a yield basis. Investors, as in the T-bill case, may submit a competitive or a noncompetitive bid. A noncompetitive bid does not require the specification of a percentage yield. The noncompetitive bidder agrees, however, to accept the average yield or equivalent price determined by the accepted competitive bids. A commercial bank or a primary security dealer may submit, for a fee, a bid on behalf of the investor.

Treasury notes and bond offerings are not as regular as those of T-bills. The *Wall Street Journal* and other financial publications report on current Treasury offerings and the results of the auction.

Notes and bonds are not redeemable by the Treasury prior to maturity. They can, however, be sold in the secondary markets. The market for Treasury notes and bonds is an extremely active over-the-counter market. It is characterized by depth (size of issues), breadth (various maturities), and low transaction costs.

The riskiness of these securities emanates from changes in market yields. Interest income from T-notes and T-bonds is taxable as ordinary income; profits (losses) from their sale are taxed at capital gains (losses) rates if the securities are held for more than a year. However, interest on T-notes and T-bonds is exempt from state and local income taxes.

Federal Agency Securities

Agency securities involve securities issued by institutions that are either part of the government or quasi-government institutions, some privately owned, involving federal sponsorship or guarantees. Because the market perceives that the government would not allow these agencies to default, agency securities are considered the closest to government debt in terms of credit risk.

The volume of agency securities has expanded at a substantial rate. In July 1981, the outstanding debt of federal and federally sponsored agencies totaled $214 billion. By 1992, the total had grown to $490 billion.

There are five federally sponsored credit agencies. The *Farm Credit System* provides credit to the agricultural sector. The *Student Loan Marketing Association* provides funds to support higher education. Three agencies, *Federal Home Loan Bank, Federal Home Loan Corporation*, and *Federal National Mortgage Association,* provide credit to the housing sector. In addition, the *Government National Mortgage Association* is a government-owned corporation that provides guarantees for mortgages. We shall concentrate our discussion on the last two organizations.

Federal National Mortgage Association.   The Federal National Mortgage Association (FNMA or "Fannie Mae") is a profit-making corporation wholly owned by its stockholders. FNMA is supervised by a 15-member board of directors, 5 of whom are appointed by the president of the United States; the remaining 10 are elected by the stockholders.

FNMA was formed in 1954 under the FNMA Act. Its function is to provide liquidity in the secondary market for mortgages and special assistance in the mortgage area as may be requested by the president or Congress. FNMA's 56 million outstanding shares are actively traded on the New York Stock Exchange. Institutions servicing mortgages on behalf of FNMA must own FNMA stock.

Although classified as federal agency securities, debt instruments issued by the FNMA are *neither* federal government obligations *nor* federally guaranteed. However, FNMA has authority to borrow directly from the U.S. Treasury. Interest on these securities is taxable at the federal, state, and local levels.

The primary function of FNMA is to supplement the secondary market for residential mortgages. It does so by injecting funds into the mortgage market when conditions are not very accommodating to home buyers, home builders, and mortgage lenders. FNMA issues various types of securities, among them FNMA discount notes (30- to 360-day maturity, tailored – as to maturity date – to the specific needs of investors) and secondary-market notes and debentures with maturities ranging from 1.5 to 25 years. As of December 1992, total FNMA debt outstanding equaled $170 billion. More recently, FNMA has issued bonds secured by mortgages, which will be described further.

Government National Mortgage Association. The Government National Mortgage Association (GNMA or "Ginnie Mae") was created in 1968 to assume programs that were originally part of FNMA: (1) special assistance functions like the extension of financial aid to certain types of housing programs of the federal government and (2) management functions relating to existing FNMA mortgage portfolios. GNMA made possible the origination of federally insured and guaranteed mortgages at below-market rates; that is, it allowed for the subsidization of home ownership. Securities issued by GNMA are taxed on the federal, state, and local levels.

Beginning in 1970, GNMA began to guarantee the timely payment of interest and principal on securities issued by private institutions and backed by pools of government-insured mortgages. These securities, called *passthrough mortgages*, are created when a mortgage originator, often a mortgage banker or a savings and loan association, assembles a pool ($500,000 minimum) of mortgages insured by the Federal Housing Administration (FHA) or the Veterans Administration (VA), with identical maturities and interest rates and consisting of mortgages on homes in one geographical area, and deposits them at a custodial bank. Upon approval by GNMA, the originator issues securities against the mortgage pool and assumes the responsibility for making monthly payments of interest and principal to holders of GNMAs, less a servicing fee.

If the payments date coincides with that of the underlying mortgages, the securities are referred to as straight GNMA *passthroughs*. If, on the other hand, the payments date does not coincide with that of the underlying mortgages – that is, the originator makes payments on GNMA securities prior to or after the receipt of payments form the underlying mortgages – the securities are referred to as GNMA *modi-fied passthroughs*. What GNMA guarantees, therefore, is the payment of interest and principal on a given date. Unlike passthroughs issued by FNMA, GNMA passthroughs are guaranteed by the U.S. government.

They offer opportunities for investors interested in the mortgage market while providing liquidity. Since their introduction in 1970, GNMA passthroughs have been most popular with thrift institutions, which currently hold about 30 percent of outstanding securities. Since their introduction in 1975, mortgage passthroughs have grown to more than $1 trillion, and now cover a third of the U.S. residential mortgage market.

Foreign Government Bonds

Foreign government bond markets consist of sovereign bonds issued within the domestic market. In the past ten years, foreign markets have become increasingly liquid and more attractive to global investors.

Trading methods vary across markets. The U.S. market is mainly an OTC (dealer) market, where market makers quote bid and ask prices. In Europe, most of the trading occurs on exchange floors through brokers, who charge a commission. Trading in Japan occurs both OTC and on the stock exchange. In the continental European markets, transactions are cleared through one of two major clearing systems, Euroclear or Cedel, which are also linked to the domestic clearing systems. The clearing systems create transactions as book entries, without any physical movement of the underlying securities.

Bonds also differ in the frequency of the coupon payments, as well as in the computation of the accrued interest. Exhibit 2.2 compares the characteristics of major bond markets. Most countries pay semiannual interest, except France and Germany, which pay annual coupons. The pricing of foreign government bonds is similar to that of U.S. Treasuries, allowing for different frequencies in interest payments.

Many countries impose a withholding tax on interest paid to foreign nationals. The United States eliminated its tax in 1984, but some countries still levy a tax, which, however, may be reduced by bilateral tax treaties. The net tax for U.S. investors, listed in Exhibit 2.2, is not necessarily a cost for a taxable investor because it can generally be credited against domestic taxes. Withholding taxes, however, make foreign bonds less attractive than otherwise for tax-exempt investors such as pension funds.

EXHIBIT 2.2   Characteristics of Government Bond Markets (1991)

Country	Coupon Frequency	Day Count	Withholding Tax for U.S. Investors	Settlement	Clearing for U.S. Investors
United States	Semiannual	Act/Act	–	1 day	Book entry
Canada	Semiannual	Act/365	0	5 days	Physical
Japan ("JGBs")	Semiannual	Act/365	10	5 days	Book entry
Britain ("gilts")	Semiannual	Act/365	0	1 day	Physical
Germany ("bunds")	Annual	30/360	0	5 days	Cedel/Euroclear
France	Annual	Act/Act	0	5 days	Cedel/Euroclear
Italy	Semiannual	30/360	12.5	5 days	Cedel/Euroclear
Australia	Semiannual	Act/365	10	5 days	Physical

Because government bonds are denominated in different currencies, yields are affected by currency risk. Investors would hold currencies expected to depreciate only if they are compensated by higher
yields. The relationship between interest rates and currency movements is further detailed in the foreign exchange chapter.

Another factor entering yields is credit risk. As governments accumulate more debt, their ability to repay long-term debt holders becomes
increasingly questionable. The total government debt of Italy, for
instance, exceeds the annual Italian GNP. This credit risk is reflected
in higher yields than otherwise and a low credit rating for some foreign
governments.

Municipal Bonds

The increasing size of state and local governments, the increased need
for synchronization of receipts and payments, and the political realities
requiring the distribution of the cost of major capital projects over
many tax years have led to substantial increases in the outstanding
debt of these political entities. During 1992, total borrowing by U.S.
state and local governments amounted to $215 billion, of which $120
billion was new capital and the remainder used for refunding old
bond issues.

In the United States, municipal bonds are debt obligations issued
by a state, territory, or possession of the United States; by any municipality or political subdivision of the United States (city, county, school
district, etc.); or even by a university. They can take the following
forms:

- *General obligation bonds.* General obligation bonds are bonds guaranteed (interest and principal) by the full faith, credit, and taxing power of the issuing authority. If the general tax is subject to a ceiling or if the obligation is to be discharged using a specific tax (e.g., gasoline tax) or a fixed portion of a certain type of tax, then the general obligation bond is referred to as a *limited-tax bond.*
- *Revenue bonds.* Revenue bonds are payable from the revenue generated by the facilities they financed or by other facilities owned by the issuer. Water, sewer, electric, and gas systems as well as port authorities, toll bridges, and the like are primary issuers of this type of bond. The yield on this type of bond is generally higher than that on a general obligation bond.

Municipal bonds generally enjoy an excellent safety record, because they are backed by the taxation power of local government. Under adverse economic conditions, however, the full taxing power of a municipality may not help, because taxes have a maximum level of tolerance. Creditworthiness is assessed by municipal ratings services, who assign credit ratings to municipal bonds. Nevertheless, municipal bonds are still considered second only to U.S. government bonds in terms of safety.

The main distinguishing feature of municipal bonds is their tax exemption. Interest on municipal bonds is exempt from federal income taxes, from the taxes of the issuing state, and usually from the taxes of the political entity in which the bondholder resides. The exemption from federal income taxes derives from the constitutional doctrine of reciprocal immunity. State and local governments do not tax federal property, and the federal government reciprocates in kind. However, appreciation in the value of municipal bonds is subject to capital gains taxes.

Because it was perceived that many municipalities were abusing their tax privileges, for instance, by issuing bonds for funds used for private investments, the Tax Reform Act of 1986 restricted the tax-exempt status of municipal bonds to "public purpose" bonds, where the funds are invested in projects deemed essential to the government function, such as roads or schools.

The yield on a municipal bond y_M will be equivalent to that on a fully taxable bond y if the following relationship holds true:

$$y(1 - \tau) = y_M,$$

where τ is the investor's marginal income tax rate. If $y_M > y(1 - \tau)$, investors will prefer to buy municipal bonds because they provide a higher after-tax return, even if nominal yields are less than those on fully taxable bonds.

The over-the-counter market dealing in municipal bonds is extensive, allowing the investor to buy and sell at low spreads. In contrast with Treasuries, quoted on a price basis, municipal bonds are usually quoted on a *yield basis*. More than a thousand municipal bond dealers operate throughout the United States. The diversity of the issues allows investors to best tailor the bonds to their own needs and diversify the risk of their bond portfolios.

Corporate Debt

Corporations issue debt instruments to finance investment projects. Because of the tax deductibility of interest expenses, issuing debt reduces the cost of financing and improves the rate of return on equity capital when leverage is operating in the intended direction. Corporate debt securities can be classified into money market securities, generally with maturities of less than a year, and bond issues. These are very active markets. In 1992, for instance, U.S. corporations raised $449 billion in bond issues, as opposed to $83 billion in stock issues. We first examine short-term securities issued by corporations.

Commercial Paper.   A commercial paper is an unsecured short-term note issued by a business to dealers or investors in return for funds. The commercial paper market is very large. By the end of 1992, $570 billion in commercial paper was outstanding. It has become a very potent substitute to bank lending.

Commercial paper is sold at a discount and typically has maturities from 30 to 270 days. Because of these short maturities, commercial paper is exempt from registration with the Securities and Exchange Commission (SEC). The market for commercial paper is generally limited to creditworthy corporations and has a relatively low default rate. Rates on commercial paper parallel T-bill rates and are generally below the prime rate, making them more desirable than bank credit.

The majority of commercial paper is "directly placed"; that is, the issuer sells the commercial paper directly to the lender. Directly placed paper has a secondary market, since the lender may resell the paper to a bank or dealer to receive funds. The remainder of the commercial paper market consists of "dealer paper," which is sold by the issuer to a dealer who, in turn, resells it in the market. There is no secondary market for this type of paper.

Banker's Acceptances. To understand banker's acceptances requires some knowledge of the financing of international trade. Banker's acceptances typically arise from international trade. Start with a U.S. importing firm that wishes to assure the exporter of the quality of its credit. The importer asks its bank to issue a letter of credit as evidence of availability of funds to pay for the imports. The letter of credit represents a payment guarantee by the bank if certain specific conditions are met. It effectively substitutes the bank's credit for that of the importer. The exporting firm receives payment from its local bank by drawing a draft against the letter of credit and discounting it at its local bank. To receive payment, the exporter must present appropriate documents as indicated in the letter of credit (e.g., bill of lading, invoice, insurance form). The exporter's bank forwards the discounted draft to its correspondent bank in the United States, which, in turn, presents it to the bank that issued the letter of credit. The "acceptance" of the draft by the latter is what is referred to as a *banker's acceptance.*

The accepting bank may purchase the acceptance. In this case, its position is equivalent to that of extending an outright loan to the importer. The practice of accepting banks is not to purchase their own acceptances, but rather to buy the acceptances of other banks. These have much higher liquidity because they bear three signatures – that of the exporter, that of the bank that discounted the draft, and that of the accepting bank. Accepting banks ordinarily trade their own acceptances for those of other banks to improve the marketability of their portfolios.

Banker's acceptances range in maturity from 30 to 180 days, with 90 days maturity being the most common. The market for banker's acceptances is made up primarily of foreign banks and financial institutions (the most active being the Federal Reserve banks, particularly in New York; large banks and nonbank dealers; and other private investors). Nonbank dealers, mainly in New York City, have created an active secondary market. At the end of 1992, $38 billion in banker's dollar acceptances was outstanding. Foreign financial institutions are attracted by the quality, liquidity, breadth, and depth of the market for banker's acceptances.

Certificates of Deposit. A certificate of deposit (CD) is a time deposit evidenced by a negotiable or nonnegotiable receipt. CDs grew from investors' reluctance to commit funds in bank deposits, where early redemption is subject to substantial penalties. Since 1961, security dealers have provided a secondary market for negotiable CDs. This increased their liquidity and hence their popularity with investors. Negotiable CDs are issued by banks to corporations, pension funds, and other large investors and are issued in bearer form. CDs command yields generally higher than those on T-bills.

Federal Funds.   The market for federal funds arises directly from the reserve requirements imposed on deposits in financial institutions. These funds are on deposit with Federal Reserve banks and do not earn interest. Commercial banks with insufficient reserves must borrow from those with surplus reserves and other sources to meet their reserve requirements. Federal funds include one-day federal funds, repurchase agreements, term federal funds, and other forms of borrowing nonreservable, immediately available funds. The interbank federal funds lending takes place because banks with excess reserves wish to transform idle funds into income-generating assets.

The manner in which the transaction is effected depends on many factors. If the banks belong to the same Federal Reserve district, the lending bank instructs the Federal Reserve bank to transfer funds from its account to that of the borrowing bank. The following day the process is reversed. The decision to borrow federal funds depends on the cost of alternative sources of funds. Banks with reserve deficiencies can alternatively raise funds by selling securities, calling a loan with a government securities dealer, raising dealer loan rates to discourage borrowing, or if they are members of the Federal Reserve System, using the discount window (borrowing from the Federal Reserve bank).

Federal funds rates, which are highly correlated with T-bill rates, are good indicators of the level and direction of interest rates for the short run. Their level represents the pressures in the market for bank reserves, which ultimately determine the extent to which banking institutions can accommodate the financial needs of business institutions.

Considering the high levels of substitution and sometimes complementarity between federal funds and repurchase agreements, a brief discussion of repurchase agreements is warranted.

Repurchase agreements (or simply RPs) are contractual arrangements whereby a holder of securities sells them to a lender who, in turn, agrees to sell the securities back to the same party at the same price. For this the lender charges a fee – interest. This arrangement is similar to a bank loan, with the securities used as collateral. The maturity is usually a day, although it can be as long as 30 days or even indefinitely.

The Federal Reserve System ("the Fed") enters into repurchase agreements with nonbank dealers in U.S. government securities. By buying the securities, the Fed is adding to the reserves of the banking system, for it credits the accounts of the sellers' banks and thus increases their reserves. This addition is temporary, for the agreements have a typical life of a single day with maximum maturity of 15 days. When a reduction in the level of bank reserves is desired, the Fed enters into a reverse repurchase agreement (the Fed is the original seller of securities), also known as a *matched sale-purchase transaction*, with a bank or with nonbank securities dealers.

Similarly, banks enter into RPs or reverse RPs with their clients or securities dealers to utilize idle cash or generate reserves. In this case, the increase (decrease) in reserves is a decision for the bank to make. Total bank reserves for the banking system as a whole do not increase as a result of the initiative of the bank. New York banks typically use RPs to adjust actual reserves to desired reserve levels. RP transactions entered into by the Fed, however, increase or decrease the reserves of the banking system as a whole.

Domestic Corporate Bonds.   As the name implies, corporate bonds are issued by corporations. Generally, these are of the following types:

- *Debenture bonds.* Debenture bonds are securities backed by the creditworthiness of the issuing corporation and by any asset not otherwise pledged by the issuing corporation. In the event of liquidation, the holders of debenture bonds are placed ahead of holders of common and preferred stocks.
- *Subordinated debentures.* Subordinated debentures are unsecured debt instruments that rank behind bank loans and regular debentures but ahead of common and preferred stocks.
- *Mortgage bonds.* Mortgage bonds are debt instruments secured by real property (land and buildings).
- *Income bonds.* An income bond is an unsecured debt instrument that pays interest only if it is earned. These bonds typically arise from corporate reorganization.
- *Collateral trust bonds.* A collateral trust bond is a debt instrument generally backed by securities pledged to the trustee, who is empowered to liquidate them in the event of default.

- *Convertible bonds.* Convertible bonds are debt instruments that
  are convertible into common stock under specified terms.

All the important facts dealing with the rights of the holder and
the obligations of the bond issuer are contained in the "indenture"
agreement. The agreement details the face value of the bond, the
coupon, and the frequency of payment, as well as provisions for
repayment.

Some indenture agreements require that the issuer maintain a sink-
ing fund to facilitate the retirement of the bond issue. Under this
provision the firm may buy and retire a certain percentage of its
outstanding bonds on an annual basis. Other bonds are callable by
the issuing corporation, and details of the call feature are contained
in the indenture agreement. Typically, the bond can be recalled at a
fixed price, above the face value, at specified intervals. Companies
may recall bonds if market yields have fallen below coupon payments,
so that the debt could be reissued at a lower cost.

Unlike Treasuries, corporate debt is exposed to credit risk. Credit
risk refers to the probability that the firm will default on its obligation.
This risk is measured by the credit rating provided by commercial
ratings agencies. Exhibit 2.3 shows the different ratings currently available for corporate bonds. Using the Standard & Poor's (S&P) classification, securities rated BBB or above are considered *investment grade*;
lower rated bonds are more speculative and are sometimes given the
derogatory, and somewhat unjustified, name of *junk* bonds.

Corporate debt securities are sold through a public distribution in
the primary market or through direct placement. In a public distribution, the underwriter typically buys the bond issue for resale to institutions or individual investors. Direct or private placement, on the other
hand, avoids the details of public offerings and allows for greater
flexibility in structuring the terms of the issue and for earlier access
to the funds. The issuer in this case sells the bonds to institutions,
mostly life insurance companies. Investment bankers, if they play any
role, would act as brokers for the transaction. Direct placement is the
domain of industrial bonds, because railroad and utility bonds must
be sold under competitive bidding. Out of $390 billion issued in 1991,
74 percent were public offerings, 19 percent were directly placed,
and 7 percent were placed abroad. Of $318.6 billion in new bond
issues in 1989, 36 percent were sold through direct placement.

EXHIBIT 2.3   Credit Rating for Corporate Debt

	Explanation
Moody's	
Aaa	Best quality
Aa	High quality
A	Upper medium grade
Baa	Medium grade
Ba	Possess speculative elements
B	Generally lack characteristics of desirable investment
Caa	Poor standing; may be in default
Ca	Speculative in a high degree; often in default
C	Lowest grade; very poor prospects
Standard & Poor's	
AAA	Highest grade
AA	High grade
A	Upper medium grade
BBB	Medium grade
BB	Lower medium grade
B	Speculative
CCC-CC	Outright speculation
C	Reserved for income bonds
DDD-D	In default, with rating indicating relative salvage value

Corporate bonds are traded on the floor of organized exchanges or over the counter. Most of the exchange trading is on the New York Stock Exchange. Trading on the American Stock Exchange is much less active. The bulk of the bond transactions takes place in the over-the-counter market. This market consists of bond dealers connected by a sophisticated electronic network, allowing for quick price discovery and consummation of transactions.

Convertible Bonds

Convertible bonds are debt instruments that can be converted into equity securities at the option of the holder during a specified period of time. They are usually debenture bonds with no collateral pledged by the issuing corporation.

Elements of Convertible Bonds.   A convertible bond represents a combination of a straight bond and a warrant, a long-term option to purchase common stock from the issuing corporation under specified terms. A convertible bond involves the following elements:

- The *Investment Value* (*IV*) is the price at which a convertible bond would have to sell to provide a yield equivalent to that of a nonconvertible bond of equal maturity and risk. If the bond were to sell for this price, the value of the conversion privilege would be zero. Investment value represents a support level, a cushion in the event of excessive decline in the price of the common stock, assuming no accompanying changes in the bond risk.
- The *Conversion Ratio* (*N*) is the number of shares to which a bond can be converted. This number is stated in the indenture agreement.
- The *Conversion Price* (*CP*) is the reciprocal of the conversion ratio multiplied by face value (*FV*). It is equal to $1,000/*N*.
- The *Conversion Value* (*CV*) is the market value of the bond if conversion takes place. It equals the conversion ratio multiplied by the market value of the common stock: $CV = N \times P^S$, where P^S = market price per common stock.
- The *Premium over Conversion Value* (*PC*) is the percentage difference between the conversion value and the market price of the convertible bond, P: $PC = (P - CV)/CV$.
- The *Premium over Investment value* (*PI*) is the percentage difference between the investment value and the market price of the convertible bond: $PI = (P - IV)/IV$. *PI* measures the worth of the conversion privilege and concurrently the proportion of the market value of the convertible bond subject to risk resulting from the fluctuation in the price of the common stock.
- The *Price of Latent Warrant* (*W*) represents the value of the conversion privilege per warrant – that is, per each share to which the bond can be converted: W = price per warrant = $(P - IV)/N$ (or number of latent warrants).

For example, a corporation issues an 8 percent coupon bond at par convertible into 20 shares of common stock. The stock is currently trading at $40. We calculate the values of the relevant variables just listed, assuming the values shown in the first two rows of Exhibit 2.4.

For the yield on this convertible bond to equal to the market yield 10.00 percent on a straight bond, the price must be

EXHIBIT 2.4   Analysis of a Convertible Bond

Variable Name	Symbol	Values at Time of Purchase	Values if Stock Price Appreciates by 25%	Values if Stock Price Appreciates by 87.5%	Values if Stock Price Drops by 50%
Market price of bond	MP^n	$1,000	$1,200 (an assumed value)	$1,500 (an assumed value)	$878
Current yield	C/MP^n	$\dfrac{8\% \times 1,000}{1,000} = 8$	$\dfrac{8\% \times 1,000}{1,200} = 6.66$	$\dfrac{8\% \times 1,000}{1,500} = 5.33$	$\dfrac{8\% \times 1,000}{878} = 9.11$
Conversion ratio	N	20	20	20	20
Conversion price	CP	$\dfrac{1,000}{20} = 50$	$\dfrac{1,000}{20} = 50$	$\dfrac{1,000}{20} = 50$	$\dfrac{1,000}{20} = 50$
Market price of stock	P	$40	$50	$75	$20
Conversion value	CV	$40 \times 20 = \$800$	$50 \times 20 = \$1,000$	$75 \times 20 = \$1,500$	$20 \times 20 = \$400$
Premium over conversion value	PC	$\dfrac{1,000 - 800}{800} = 25$	$\dfrac{1,200 - 1,000}{1,000} = 20$	$\dfrac{1,500 - 1,500}{1,500} = 0$	$\dfrac{878 - 400}{400} = 94.5$
Investment value	IV	878	878	878	878
Premium over investment value	PI	$\dfrac{1,000 - 878}{878} = 13.9$	$\dfrac{1,200 - 878}{878} = 36.7$	$\dfrac{1,500 - 878}{878} = 70.8$	$\dfrac{878 - 878}{878} = 0$
Price per warrant	W	$\dfrac{1,000 - 878}{20} = \$6.1$	$\dfrac{1,200 - 878}{20} = \$16.1$	$\dfrac{1,500 - 878}{20} = \$31.1$	0 (The price never actually drops this low unless the bond is approaching maturity.)

$$P = \sum_{t=1}^{10} \frac{80}{(1 + 0.10)^t} + \frac{1,000}{(1 + 0.10)^{10}} = 878.$$

We observe from Exhibit 2.4 that the premium over conversion value moves in the direction opposite from the premium over investment value. As the premium over conversion value (*PC*) shrinks toward zero, the convertible bond would behave (at zero) exactly like a common stock. Conversely, as *PC* rises, the convertible bond would approach its investment value, and its behavior would correspond exactly, when *PI* = 0 percent, to that of a straight bond.

A conservative investor would, therefore, choose a convertible bond with a higher *PC* and a lower *PI*, because the behavior of the bond under these conditions is less dependent on the behavior of the stock. An aggressive investor would choose a convertible bond with a lower *PC* and a higher *PI* because its price more closely follows that of the common stock. The following observations are also worth making:

1. The percentage increase in the market price of the bond lags behind that of the stock. The reasons for this and the extent of the lag will be explained later. For a 25 percent increase in the price of the stock, the premium over conversion value would drop by only 5 percent. For an additional 62.5 percent increase in the price of the stock, (87.5 percent − 25 percent), *PC* would drop by 20 percent, or a ratio of 20/62.5 = 0.32, as compared with an earlier ratio of 5/25 = 0.2. This simply indicates that the faster the price of the stock rises, the more quickly the behavior of the bond corresponds to that of the stock until a one-to-one correspondence is achieved. Again, aggressive investors would be most interested in convertible bonds with a low *PC* because they offer higher appreciation potential.
2. The lower is the premium over conversion value, the lower is the yield.
3. The investment value represents a cushion of considerable importance in a bear market. When the market price of the bond is equal to its investment value, the convertible bond behaves exactly like a straight bond and its price is then determined by market rates of interest, supply and demand, and the financial position of the issuing company.

Our discussion can be summarized diagrammatically as shown in Exhibit 2.5. The heavy line from *IV* through *S* to *CV'* represents the

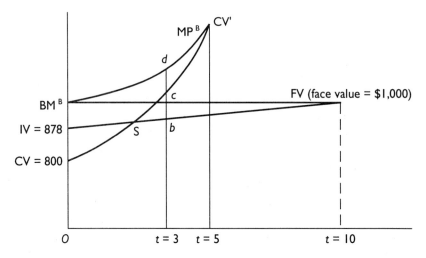

EXHIBIT 2.5   Relationships among Various Values of a Convertible Bond

minimum price of the bond. The bond cannot sell below its conversion value; otherwise investors would buy bonds, convert them immediately, and sell the stocks in the market. The conversion value curve CV to CV' is sloped as such because of the assumed constant geometric growth rate in the price of the underlying stock, $P_t = P_0(1 + g)^t$. This obviously excludes the 50 percent decline in the price of the stock discussed in Exhibit 2.4.

The curve from MP^B to $MP^{B'}$ represents the bond market value curve over a portion of the bond's life. This value is higher than the conversion value curve, initially because of the protection convertible bonds provide (in a bear market) through their investment value. The difference between P and CV represents the value of the "safety net" that convertible bonds provide. This protection diminishes in significance as the price of the stock rises in value.

At $t = 5$, in this particular case, the market value of the bond is equal to its conversion value (premium over conversion value is equal to zero), and the bond is equivalent to holding 20 shares of the underlying security. The investment value of the bond is shown in Exhibit 2.5 to converge linearly to the face value of the bond as the maturity date of the bond approaches.

Determinants of the Market Price of a Convertible Bond.   The pricing of a convertible bond is considerably more involved than that of a straight bond. The complications result from the unpredictability of future stock prices (and consequently the conversion value) and from the relationship between the conversion value and the investment value. If the convertible bond is callable, the pricing mechanism is complicated further.

The problem in pricing convertible bonds results primarily from the asymmetric effects on the convertible bond price when different conditions hold. This asymmetry can best be understood through a reexamination of Exhibit 2.4. The market price of the bond equals or exceeds the investment value because of the equity aspect of the convertible bond – that is, because of the price appreciation potential the convertible bond offers. This is observed at $t = 0$, where $MP^B > IV > CV$. The difference $MP^B - IV = P - IV$ represents the value of the conversion privilege. Beyond point S, the market price P of the convertible bond would exceed the conversion value. At $t = 3$, the difference $P - CV$ is equal to the distance cd in the graph and represents the value of the safety net provided by the investment value. This safety factor is nonexistent if the convertible bond is replaced by an equivalent number of common stocks; it becomes meaningless when the conversion premium equals zero. A stock position could theoretically fall to zero, but an equivalent convertible bond position would fall to the investment value. It is important to note, however, that the investment value is not constant. It is affected by changes in market yields and in the riskiness of the firm. A falling stock price is generally reflective of a deteriorating position within the firm. This increases the risk of default and of bankruptcy. As this risk increases, the investment value falls. The safety net is not as strong as it may appear to be.

Ingersoll (1977) and Brennan and Schwartz (1977) employed the option pricing methodology to value convertible bonds. They derive a differential equation and boundary conditions governing the value of the bond. This is followed by an algorithm to solve the differential equation. Because numerical methods are employed to solve the differential equation, the valuation procedure is quite flexible.

Raymond King (1986) conducted an empirical test on an equilibrium model for valuing convertible securities derived by Brennan and Schwartz. An algorithm was used to calculate theoretical values for a sample of 103 convertible bond issues. When actual market prices were compared to the calculated values, the means were not significantly different. Additionally, 90 percent of model predictions were within 10 percent of market values. King divided the sample on the basis of whether the calculated values were greater or less than market prices. Returns on these two subsamples were then compared over the subsequent three years. The results indicate that without risk adjustment, the returns for the undervalued (model prices > market prices) bonds are significantly greater than the returns for the overvalued (model prices < market prices). This valuation model provides unbiased estimates of market values, and model values were found to be better predictors of future market prices than current market prices. The model valuation is economically useful in practical valuation applications.

International Bonds

Although there is no unified international bond market, we can distinguish three broad market groups:

- *Domestic bonds* are issued locally by a domestic borrower, either by a federal, state, or local government or a corporation. Domestic bonds are subject to the regulatory authority of the country in which they are issued.
- *Foreign bonds* are issued in a local market by a foreign borrower and are also subject to the supervision of local market authorities. Foreign bonds have existed for a long time and have colorful names such as Yankee (in the United States), Samurai (in Japan), Bulldog (in Britain), and Rembrandt (in the Netherlands).
- *Eurobonds* are underwritten by a multinational syndicate of banks and are generally placed in a country other than the one in whose currency bonds are denominated. For instance, a dollar Eurobond might be placed anywhere outside the United States.

The Eurobond market initially developed in the 1960s as a way for corporations and investors to avoid capital controls in the United States. At that time, the United States experienced balance of payments deficits, which led the government to impose taxes on capital outflows. These taxes forced non-U.S. corporations to pay higher interest to U.S. investors, and at the same time withholding taxes decreased the attractiveness of the U.S. bond market for foreign investors. As a result, corporations and investors decided to create a market for dollar-denominated debt outside the United States. Thus the Eurobond market was born.

Even after the restrictions on capital movements were lifted, the Eurobond market continued to grow because it offers an efficient, innovative, and less costly market in which to issue debt. In the absence of government regulations, Eurobonds offer the following advantages:

- *No withholding taxes.* Because payments in Eurobonds are not taxed, investors are willing to accept a lower yield than on a taxable bond. For instance, up to 1984, U.S. corporations could raise funds at a cheaper rate in the Eurobond market than in the U.S. domestic bond market, because Eurobond investors did not have to pay the 10 percent U.S. withholding tax levied on coupon payments from U.S. bonds to foreign investors. This advantage has been slowly reduced, because withholding taxes are being eliminated by governments eager to finance their public deficits with foreign capital.
- *No registration requirements.* Because Eurobonds need not go through a tedious and slow SEC registration process, the Eurobond market is a fast and efficient market in which to raise funds. Its appeal, however, has again been blunted by the creation of Rule 415 in the United States, which allows "shelf-registration" in preparation for future debt issuance. Note that Eurobonds cannot be directly sold to U.S. investors in the primary market; they can be offered in the United States only after a 90-day "seasoning" period.
- *Investor anonymity.* Because Eurobonds are all bearer bonds, the confidentiality of the owner is protected. Investors may be induced to accept a lower yield in exchange for this feature.

Credit risk with Eurobonds is generally low. Because there is no registration requirement, investors have less information about issuing firms and tend to prefer companies with well-known names. Consequently, Eurobonds have experienced a much lower default rate than the U.S. corporate bonds.

Eurobonds are principally traded over the counter. Some bonds are listed on the London or Luxembourg exchanges, principally to allow some investors, restricted to buy exchange-listed securities, to hold the bonds, but the volume of trading is minimal.

Because investors are spread all over the world, coupon payments are made only once a year, which lowers the payment costs. Accrued interest is, by convention, calculated on a 30/360 basis. Note that yields in the Eurobond market are compounded annually and therefore are generally higher than if computed with semiannual compounding.

Because of the international nature of this market, Eurobonds can be denominated in many different currencies and often contain currency-related features. Some Eurobonds, for instance, contain long-term currency options; others offer payments of coupon and principal in different currencies (dual-currency bonds); still others offer denomination in a currency basket, such as the ECU. The Eurobond market has thrived because it constantly offers innovative products, without the supervision of government regulators.

The Term Structure of Interest Rates

The term structure of interest rates is summarized by the yield curve, which represents the relationship, at a given point in time, between time to maturity and yield to maturity on fixed income securities within a given risk class.

The yield curve is a snapshot of the term structure at a point in time. Its level can change over time, as well as its shape, which can be upward sloping, flat, downward sloping, or even humped. Exhibit 2.6 presents the different possible shapes. The accurate forecasting of changes in the yield curve can pay handsome dividends, as we shall demonstrate later in this chapter. We first present methods to construct the term structure of interest rates from observed bond prices.

Fitting a Yield Curve

The construction of yield curves is an art to some and a science to others. Originally, yield curves were typically constructed using the methodology of the U.S. Treasury. The method requires, as a first step, a collection of homogeneous securities – that is, securities that have the same characteristics in terms of riskiness and type (e.g., all noncallable) and differ only in the length of time to maturity. The second step is to plot, on a given day or hour, the yield to maturity as a dependent variable, against the time to maturity as an independent variable. The scatter of points usually exhibits a pattern through which a curve is fitted. The procedure used by the Treasury locates "the

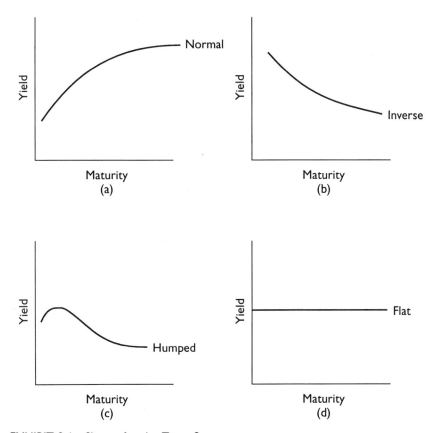

EXHIBIT 2.6   Shapes for the Term Structure

yield curve in the middle of the data scatter for Treasury bonds, bill, and notes."

This method has been subject to two criticisms. The first is that the freehand approach may not give consistent results and may be less reliable than fitting the econometric model to the data. The second is that the Treasury method ignores the impact of coupon rate differentials on the shape of the yield curve.

Echols and Elliott (1976), for instance, postulated the following function for yields:

$$\ln(1 + y_t) = a_0 + a_1(1/t) + a_2(t) + a_3(c) + \epsilon, \qquad (2.9)$$

where t measures time-to-maturity, the a_i is the coefficient to be estimated, and c is added to account for the fact that bonds with different coupon rates are not homogeneous.

Equation (2.9) is flexible enough to explain the various shapes of the yield curves by different values for a_1 and a_2:

Condition   **Curve Shape**
(1) $a_1 < 0$, $a_2 < 0$ Humped
(2) $a_1 < 0$, $a_2 > 0$ Rising
(3) $a_1 > 0$, $a_2 < 0$ Falling
(4) $a_1 > 0$, $a_2 > 0$ Flat.

The Zero Coupon Curve

Fitting a yield curve using bonds with different coupons, however, is unsatisfactory. The fact that the coupon variable in Equation (2.9) is significant suggests a model misspecification. Furthermore, observed yields are not realizable returns unless measured from zero coupon bonds.

Consider a pure discount bond, which has only one cash flow equal to the face value of the bond:

$$P = \frac{F}{(1 + y_N)^N}. \tag{2.10}$$

In this case, the yield to maturity is well-defined since it corresponds to the n-period compounded return on the bond $y_N = R_N$.

A coupon bond, on the other hand, has one or many cash flows prior to the payment of face value. Its market price is equal to

$$P = \frac{C_1}{(1 + R_1)} + \frac{C_2}{(1 + R_2)^2} + \ldots + \frac{C_N}{(1 + R_N)^N} + \frac{F}{(1 + R_N)^N}, \tag{2.11}$$

where R_N are the current (spot) market rates making up the term structure at time t.

Equation (2.11) can be viewed as the present value of a series of pure discount bonds. The first coupon payment represents the maturity value of a one-period pure discount bond. The second coupon represents the maturity value of a two-period discount bond, and so on up to the last payment, consisting of principal and coupon.

Using the yield to maturity (a unique rate) as a discount factor in Equation (2.11) distorts the effective rate of return on the bond. Only if all the values of R_n were equal to each other and to y_N would the yield to maturity equal the effective rate of return on the bond. If the yield curve were rising, the expected return on a debt security would be higher than the yield to maturity, and the opposite would material-ize if a descending yield curve were observed. This is so because of higher reinvestment rates in the first case and lower reinvestment rates in the second. These problems, it must be noted again, would not occur if the bonds did not carry coupons that may have to be reinvested at a rate different from the yield to maturity.

Clearly, it is preferable to estimate a zero coupon curve to the usual yield curve. A zero coupon curve, however, is not directly observable and must be estimated from outstanding coupon bonds. Consider, for instance, a situation where we have two bonds, one with six months to expiration and the other with exactly one year to expiration; coupons are paid semiannually. The question is how to estimate the 6- and 12-month spot rates, defined as R_1 and R_2, respectively.

Since the first bond expires in six months, there is no intervening coupon payment, and it is effectively a zero coupon bond. Its price is

$$P_1 = \frac{(F_1 + C_1)}{(1 + R_1/2)},$$

from which we can solve for R_1. Since the second bond pays a coupon in six months and a final payment later, its price is

$$P_2 = \frac{C_2}{(1 + R_1/2)} + \frac{(F_2 + C_2)}{(1 + R_2/2)^2}.$$

Substituting the value found for R_1, we can then solve for R_2. Thus coupon bonds, viewed as a package of zeroes, can be used to recover spot rates by forward substitution.

Fitting a Discount Function

The approach just presented cannot be applied directly to the bond market because bond maturities may not be regularly spaced and also because there may be many more bonds than chosen maturities.

The objective in empirical estimation of the term structure is to construct a spot rate curve that fits the data reasonably well and is sufficiently smooth. To do this, first define the *discount function* as the present value of a dollar paid in the future:

$$D(t) = (1 + R_t)^{-t},$$

for which a functional form is chosen.

For instance, it is computationally convenient to choose a cubic spline:

$$D(t) = a_{i0} + a_{i1}t + a_{i2}t^2 + a_{i3}t^3, \quad t_i < t < t_{i+1}, \qquad (2.12)$$

where the values of the parameters a_{ij} are allowed to differ across knot points t_i, $i = 1, \ldots, K$. This functional form consists of cubic functions "splined" at a number of knot points and is sufficiently flexible to fit most curves. To ensure continuity and smoothness of the spline curve, the function value and its first and second derivatives are restricted to be the same at the knot points. In addition, the discount function is set equal to one at time zero. For K knot points, this yields $3 + K$ parameters to estimate.

Second, the theoretical prices of the sample of selected bonds are computed from this discount function. For instance, if a bond pays the cash flows c_n, $n = 1, \ldots, N$ at respective times t_n, the model price is set at the present value of the future cash flows,

$$\hat{P} = \sum_n c_n D(t_n),$$

which can be written as a linear function of the spline parameters,

$$\hat{P} = a_0 f_0(c_n) + a_1 f_1(c_n) + a_2 f_2(c_n) + \ldots$$

The parameters $\{a\}$ can be estimated by comparing the theoretical prices $\hat{P}$ with the market prices P for the selected bonds. For instance, one could choose to minimize the square of discrepancies between observed market prices and model prices. Because we chose a cubic spline as a functional form, the parameters can be computed by simply running a linear regression of the market prices on the model prices expressed as a linear function of the parameters of interest.

Cubic splines can be estimated easily using conventional regression packages and have been so used by McCulloch (1971) with satisfactory results. Vasicek and Fong (1982), however, argue that cubic splines are inherently less well-suited to fitting exponential curves like term structures and propose replacing Equation (2.12) with exponential splines. Although theoretically more appropriate, the latter are more difficult to estimate because they involve a nonlinear optimization.

Implied Forward Rates

Once the discount rate function is estimated, implied *forward rates* can be measured from the spot rate curve. These give a dynamic picture of future movements in interest rates and can be used for speculation on interest rates.

The N-period spot rate can be written as a geometric average of the spot and forward rates, defined as follows:

$$(1 + {}_tR_N) = [(1 + {}_tR_1)(1 + {}_{t+1}F_1) \ldots (1 + {}_{t+N-1}F_1)]^{1/N}, \quad (2.13)$$

where ${}_{t+N}F_N$ is the forward rate of interest to prevail at time $t + N$ over period N.

To illustrate how the forward rate is calculated, assume we observe the spot rate for one and two years. From Equation (2.13), the two-period rate is equal to

$$(1 + {}_tR_2) = [(1 + {}_tR_1)(1 + {}_{t+1}F_1)]^{1/2}; \quad (2.14)$$

therefore

$$_{t+1}F_1 = \frac{(1 + {}_tR_2)^2}{1 + {}_tR_1} - 1 \quad (2.15)$$

and in general

$$_{t+N-1}F_1 = \frac{(1 + {}_tR_N)^N}{(1 + {}_tR_{N-1})^{N-1}} - 1. \quad (2.16)$$

For example, in the two-period case, assume we observe that ${}_tR_2 =$ 8 percent and ${}_tR_1 = 7$ percent. Thus we have a rising yield curve. The forward rate equals 9 percent, which is obtained as follows:

$$_2F_1 = \frac{(1 + 0.08)^2}{(1 + 0.07)} - 1 = 9 \text{ percent.}$$

For intervals different from one year, the appropriate spot rates must be used. If the three-month forward rate to prevail three months from now is to be calculated, we need the six-month rate and the three-month rate. If, on the other hand, the three-month rate to prevail one year from now is to be calculated, then the investor must use the one-year and three-month rates as well as the one-year rate. In general,

$$_{t+(Nm-1)}F_1 = \frac{(1 + R_N/m)^{Nm}}{(1 + R_{N-1}/m)^{Nm-1}} - 1, \qquad (2.17)$$

where the subscript after F indicates the subperiod (a quarter, a month, etc.) and m is the number of subperiods in a year (four in the case of quarters).

For example, if R_N (the five-quarter rate) = 10.5 percent and R_{N-1} (the four-quarter or one-year rate) = 10 percent, the one-quarter rate to prevail one year from now is equal to

$$_4F_{1qtr} = \frac{(1 + 0.105/4)^5}{(1 + 0.10/4)^4} - 1 = \frac{1.13832}{1.1038} - 1 = 3.13 \text{ percent/quarter.}$$

Theories of Term Structure

There are various theories to explain the term structure of interest rates. Some overlap and the others have little in common. We shall focus our attention on three major theories: the expectations theory, the liquidity preference theory, and the market segmentation theory.

The Expectations Theory

The expectations theory is a demand-based theory. The expectations of investors about the future course of interest rates determine their demand for certain maturities. The theory asserts that no supplier of securities, not even the federal government, is large enough to exert influence over the structure of interest rates.

The assumptions of the expectations theory are as follows:

1. Perfect capital markets, that is, zero transactions costs and no taxes;
2. Universality of markets – no segmentation, investors are indifferent as to maturity;
3. Rational investors operating to maximize the expected return over the investment horizon;
4. Initially, assumption of complete certainty about future rates, which can be relaxed to an uncertain environment, but then investors must be risk neutral.

Based on these assumptions, the expectations theory states that the long rate is the geometric average of expected future short rates:

$$(1 + {}_tR_N) = \{(1 + {}_tR_1)(1 + E[{}_{t+1}r_1]) \ldots (1 + E[{}_{t+N-1}r_1])\}^{1/N}, \quad (2.18)$$

where $E[{}_{t+1}r_1]$ is the one-period spot rate expected to prevail at the beginning of period $t + 1$.

From Equation (2.13), this implies that the forward rate is an unbiased forecast of the expected future spot rate:

$$_{t+N-1}F_1 = E[{}_{t+N-1}r_1]. \quad (2.19)$$

The expectations theory explains every type of yield curve. If rates are expected to rise in the future, the yield curve would be rising; if rates are expected to fall, yield curves would be descending; if rates are expected to remain at their current level, the curves would be flat; and if rates were expected to rise in the near future and fall later on, the yield curve would be humped.

In practical terms, the expectations theory asserts that investors should be indifferent between investing in long-term securities or in a series of short-term securities. This indifference relies heavily on the absence of transactions costs and a preference function for certain maturities. Any changes in the supply of bonds of a given maturity would not affect the term structure unless it somehow affected expectations.

If interest rates deviate from expectations, arbitrageurs would enter the market on the demand side or the supply side to ensure equality between the expected and the forward rate. If, for instance,

$$E[{}_{t+n-1}r_1] < {}_{t+n-1}F_1 = \frac{(1 + {}_tR_N)^N}{(1 + {}_tR_{N-1})^{N-1}} - 1,$$

arbitrageurs (or speculators) would borrow for $N - 1$ periods and lend for N periods. An opposite strategy would be employed if

$$E[{}_{t+N-1}r_1] > {}_{t+N-1}F_1.$$

Assume that the one-year and two-year spot rates are 7 and 8 percent, respectively, which implies a one-year forward rate of 9 percent. If investors instead expect the future one-year spot rate to be 7.5 percent, they will speculate by locking in 9 percent and (they hope) borrow at the expected 7.5 percent. This can be achieved as follows:

1. Take $1 million and invest for two years at 8 percent. This will yield $1(1 + 0.08)^2 = $1.166 million in two years.
2. These funds are obtained by borrowing $1 million for one year, at the end of which $1.070 million will need to be repaid.
3. The following year, the loan is rolled over at the expected 7.5 percent interest cost, which grows to $1.070(1 + 0.075) = $1.150 million.
4. The proceeds from the investment are used to repay the loan and leave an excess profit of $1.166 − $1.150, which is about $16,000.

The most serious of the early attempts at testing the validity of the expectations hypothesis was made by Meiselman (1962). The model proposed by Meiselman is the "error-learning" model. As investors observe that the actual rate of interest differs from the forward rate, they should revise their forecast of the next one-period rate by a fraction of the previous error.

The test conducted by Meiselman purports to show that forward rates do, in fact, conform to the error-learning model. The equation tested is

$$_{t+N}F_{1,t} - {}_{t+N}F_{1,t-1} = a_N + b_N(R_{1,t} - {}_tF_{1,t-1}) + \epsilon, \qquad (2.20)$$

where

$_{t+N}F_{1,t}$ = forecast one-year rate to prevail at time $t + N$ (the forecast is made at time t),

$_{t+N}F_{1,t-1}$ = forecast one-year rate to prevail at time $t + N$ (the forecast is made at time $t - 1$),

$(R_{1,t} - {}_tF_{1,t-1})$ = difference between the actual one-year rate and the forecast rate.

The error-learning model would be vindicated if $a \approx 0$ and if $0 < b_i < b_{i-1} < 1$ for $i = 2, \ldots, n$. Using data covering 1901–54 and the ordinary least squares technique, Meiselman found supportive results, confirming the validity of the expectations theory.

The Achilles' heel of Meiselman's test was the data used. Meiselman used the "basic yield" curves of Durand, which by Durand's own admission do not lend themselves to "refined analysis or precise computation."

Grant (1967) tried to duplicate Meiselman's results with British data and found that the error-learning model is not supported using unsmoothed data (as opposed to Durand's smoothed data). Buse (1967), using smoothed yield curves for British and U.S. government securities, found the constant term to be positive and significant, which contradicts the error-learning model.

Santomero (1975), using Eurodollar spot rate observations – which bypass the problems of yield to maturity and the differential in coupon rates – found substantial support for the error-learning model. Kugler (1988) analyzed the short end of the term structure using Swiss, German, and U.S. data from 1974 to 1986. He found that the predictive power of the expectations hypothesis was statistically highly significant in the Swiss and German cases but not for the U.S. case. The expectations theory fails to explain the short end of the term structure both before and after the change in operating procedures in the monetary policy that occurred in October 1979. This can be explained by the interest rate smoothing procedure used by Kugler and by the Federal Reserve's renewed emphasis on targeting interest rates after October 1982.

Campbell (1986) defended the expectations theory against the contention of Cox, Ingersoll, and Ross (1981) that the theory is internally inconsistent and has no value in empirical work unless a strict arbitrage pricing model is first specified. In Shiller, Campbell, and Schoenholtz, the authors state that "The simple expectations theory, . . . , has been rejected many times in careful econometric studies. But the theory seems to reappear perennially in policy discussions as if nothing had happened to it. It is uncanny how resistant superficially appealing theories in economics are to contrary evidence." Campbell argued that the criticisms of Cox, Ingersoll, and Ross are second-order effects that disappear in linear approximations of term structures. Hence the expectations theory may indeed be false, but it is useful as a starting point for empirical research outside of the confines of a tightly specified arbitrage pricing model.

Shiller, Campbell, and Schoenholtz (1983) and Campbell and Shiller (1984), however, reported that the expectations theory is strongly rejected in postwar U.S. data. Hsieh and Leiderman (1986) went one step further and explored the portfolio implications of empirical rejections of the expectations hypothesis. In summary, there has been a growing consensus on the lack of empirical validity of the expectations hypothesis. Expectations alone do not determine the shape of the yield curve.

The Liquidity Preference Theory

The fundamental assertion of the liquidity preference theory is that Equations (2.13) and (2.18) are not perfect substitutes. Restating Equation (2.13),

$$(1 + {}_tR_N) = [(1 + {}_tR_1)(1 + {}_{t+1}F_1) \ldots (1 + {}_{t+N-1}F_1)]^{1/N}, \qquad (2.21)$$

we can define the forward rate as the expected future spot rate plus a "liquidity premium," LP:

$$_{t+N-1}F_1 = E[_{t+N-1}r_1] + {}_{t+N-1}LP_1,$$

where the liquidity premium is an increasing function of maturity

$$_{t+N-1}LP_1 > {}_{t+N-2}LP_1 > {}_{t+N-3}LP_1 > \ldots > {}_{t+1}LP_1.$$

The liquidity premium, Hicks (1946) argued, is necessary to compensate risk-averse speculators in the financial markets. Borrowers have a propensity to borrow long term to lock in the interest rate costs and ensure the availability of funds. Lenders are more interested in lending short term; they require compensation for assuming longer-term maturities because of the risk involved in investing in long-term securities. Risk-averse investors tend to view distant dates with greater uncertainty (about interest and principal payments) and hence require compensation for the additional risk. The size of the premium, its value over time, its sign, and even its very existence are subject to much controversy.

In equilibrium, the expectations hypothesis asserts that the liquidity premium is equal to zero, while the liquidity preference theory asserts that the value is positive. The size, sign, and behavior of the term premiums distinguishes one theory from another. The immediate implication of the liquidity theory, some may superficially argue, is that it can explain only rising yield curves. This is not true, however, because the shape of the yield curves may well be determined by factors that offset the rising liquidity premium. If the expected-rate component of the forward rate is expected to fall by a value larger than the rise in the liquidity premium, the forward rate would be falling and consequently also the yield curve. These and other factors explaining a downward-sloping yield curve were documented by Kessel (1965), Scott (1963), and Gray (1973). Kessel offered evidence that accounting for the liquidity premium substantially contributes to the explanatory power of the yield curve.

DeGennaro (1988) found that if payment delays due to entities such as check-clearing or brokerage accounts are priced, but not explicitly incorporated into pricing equations, they cause the true time to maturity and that reported in the financial press to diverge. This spurious premium causes yield curves constructed from observed rates to slope up even if all forward rates are equal and if the pure expectations hypothesis is true. These apparent premiums vary in a manner consistent with important empirical results, which calls into question the evidence concerning liquidity premiums.

The Market Segmentation Theory

The fundamental argument of the market segmentation theory is that both supply and demand – which are determined by many factors, including expectations – determine the yield to maturity. The elasticity of substitution (or the extent to which bonds of differing maturities are substitutes) is assumed to equal zero for bonds with substantially different maturities. The elasticity of substitution between close maturities (three months with six-month bills) may be nonzero, however. This stems from the fact that institutions, because of the nature of their business and their attempts to match the maturity structure of their liabilities with that of their assets to reduce if not eliminate exposure to interest rate fluctuations, would have a natural affinity for securities with certain maturities. Insurance companies would, for instance, demand longer-term bonds to match their long-term obligations, and commercial banks may have a preference for short-term securities to invest time or demand deposits and ensure a certain level of liquidity.

This implies, therefore, that the bond market is "segmented" by maturity. For each maturity, identifiable demand and supply curves determine the yield and, consequently, the liquidity premium, which can be positive, zero, or negative. Changes in the yield structure are, therefore, determined by changes in the supply or demand for a given maturity.

Exhibit 2.7 shows how the yield to maturity is determined by the intersection of supply and demand. The supply of funds and its compo-

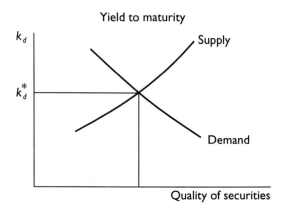

EXHIBIT 2.7   Equilibrium Determination of Yields

nents are identifiable and allow for the determination of the equilibrium yield for a given term to maturity.

This theory has considerable currency among practitioners in the field of managing fixed income securities portfolios. Academicians, however, have not emphasized this theory as much as the expectations theory. Nonetheless, practitioners persist in their belief. The board of governors of the Federal Reserve System, for example, publishes on a regular basis, in the *Federal Reserve Bulletin*, a flow-of-funds statement showing in detail the sources and uses of funds for the entire U.S. economy. Statements of sources and uses of funds per term to maturity are also made, allowing for the prediction of the corresponding interest rates. The effects of changes in the supply and demand for funds depends on the elasticity of the supply and demand curves. For a given change in supply, the resultant change in yield will be greater the less elastic is the demand curve.

The supply of funds basically comes from three sources: savings, changes in the money supply, and changes in the money balances held for speculative purposes (hoarding, dishoarding). The demand for loans comes from government (federal, state, and local), businesses, and consumers. The correct anticipation of the size and direction of the supply and demand components translates itself into a forecast of interest rates, as we shall discuss later.

The empirical evidence gives some support to the segmentation hypothesis. Kane and Malkiel (1967) examined the issue by surveying banks, insurance companies, and nonfinancial corporations. They concluded: "Our various findings each support a single conclusion:

that the demands for various maturities of debt are not infinitely elastic at going rates, and, therefore, that changes in the relative supplies of different maturities . . . can alter the term structure." Trudgian and Scott (1971) also found evidence of market segmentation in their survey of government securities dealers. Supply and demand factors were closely monitored by the dealers in the formulation of investment strategies.

Modigliani and Sutch (1966) attempted to reconcile the three theories by suggesting an alternative theory that relies on all three. They dubbed it the *preferred habitat theory*. Their hypothesis states that investors, who are not as risk averse as their counterparts under the segmentation hypothesis, can be induced out of their preferred maturity, the one that minimizes their risk, by paying them a positive or a negative premium, depending on the relationship between their time horizon and the time to maturity of the bond. An investor with a two-year liability would be interested in two-year investments because shorter maturities price risk reinvestment risk and longer maturities increase exposure to price risk. To get this investor interested in securities with a one-year maturity, a negative risk premium must be paid.

The reason for the negative risk premium can be explained by restating Equation (2.18):

$$(1 + {}_1R_2) = \{(1 + {}_1R_1)(1 + E[{}_2r_1])\}^{1/2}.$$

The concern of the investor is with the probability that his or her expectations (summarized by $E[{}_2r_1]$) would not materialize. In particular, the concern is that the actual one-period rate prevailing at the beginning of the record period, ${}_2R_1$, would fall short of $E[{}_2r_1]$. Because of risk aversion, the investor would demand a risk premium L_1. Therefore, for the investor with a two-year horizon to be interested in a one-year bond, the following must be true:

$$(1 + {}_1R_2) < \{(1 + {}_1R_1)(1 + E[{}_2r_1])\}^{1/2}.$$

Since

$$(1 + {}_1R_2) = [(1 + {}_1R_1)(1 + {}_2F_1)]^{1/2},$$

this implies that

$${}_2F_1 = E[{}_1r_1] + LP_1 < E[{}_2r_1],$$

or that the risk premium LP_1 must be negative. Using logic opposite that of the preceding, a positive risk premium would be required for a bond with a maturity exceeding two years.

Therefore, provided risk is adequately compensated for, there can be a cross elasticity in maturities. Risk-averse investors do not necessarily have a preference for short maturities but do hedge by staying in their preferred maturity habitat unless other maturities (longer or shorter) offer a sufficient inducement through a risk premium. Thus, the "liquidity premium" can assume positive, zero, or negative values, depending on the nature of the supply and demand factors for a given maturity and across maturities. The empirical tests conducted by Modigliani and Sutch did not confirm that changes in the supply of government securities affect the term structure of interest rates.

It can be said, in conclusion, that to understand the behavior of interest rates one must pay attention to expectations, liquidity premiums, and supply and demand factors.

The Cox, Ingersoll, and Ross Theory

The expectations hypothesis, the liquidity preference hypothesis, and the market segmentation hypothesis are theories of the term structure that predict only if the implied forward rate is equal or not equal to the expectation of future spot rates.

The Cox, Ingersoll, and Ross (CIR) (1985) theory models the term structure in a competitive equilibrium environment. In CIR, anticipations, risk aversion, investment alternatives, and preferences about the timing of consumption interact to determine bond prices. Thus many of the factors present in the more traditional theories of the term structure are incorporated in a manner that is wholly consistent with maximizing behavior and rational expectations. The model can thus be used to endogenously derive the current prices and stochastic properties of all contingent claims, including bonds and options on fixed income securities.

A different approach to modeling the term structure is the "arbitrage" approach. This starts from assumptions about the stochastic movements in one or more interest rates and derives the price of all contingent claims by imposing the condition that there are no arbitrage opportunities. Brennan and Schwartz (1979), for instance, derived a two-factor model based on short and long interest rates. The equilibrium approach, however, is generally considered superior because the term structure, its dynamics, and the functional form of the market prices of risk are endogenously determined as part of the equilibrium, which is not the case for the arbitrage approach.

The single-factor CIR model was intuitively derived by Brown and Dybvig (1986), whereby the dynamics of the interest rate process are given by

$$dr = k(\theta - r)dt + \sigma\sqrt{r}dz, \tag{2.22}$$

where $k(\theta - r)$ is the instantaneous rate drift and dz is a standard Gauss-Wiener process.

This process is important because it provides a simple description of the stochastic nature of interest rates that is consistent with empirical observations. If $k < 1$, there is mean-reversion toward the long-run value θ; situations where interest rates are high, such as $r > \theta$, would have a negative drift and therefore a tendency to revert to θ. Also note that the variance of this process is proportional to the level of interest rates; as the interest rate moves toward zero, the variance decreases, so that r can never fall below zero.

Let $P[r,t,T]$ represent the price of a riskless pure discount bond maturing at period T. Using Ito's Lemma, the instantaneous rate of return on the bond is

$$dP/P = \left[P_r dr + \frac{1}{2}P_{rr}(dr)^2 + P_t dt \right] P. \tag{2.23}$$

Substituting dr from Equation (2.22), we have

$$dP/P = [k(\theta - r)P_r/P + P_t/P + \frac{1}{2}\sigma^2 rP_{rr}/P]dt + [\sigma\sqrt{r}P_r/P]dz. \tag{2.24}$$

The instantaneous interest rate on the zero coupon bond can also be written as

$$dP/P = \mu(r,t,T)dt + v(r,t,T)dz. \tag{2.25}$$

In perfect markets, the instantaneous expected rate of return for any asset can be written as the instantaneous risk-free return, r, plus a risk premium. Cox, Ingersoll, and Ross (1985) show that, in this economy,

$$\mu(r,t,T) = r + \lambda\dot{}(r,t)v(r,t,T). \tag{2.26}$$

Assuming the risk premium factor, λ^*, to be of the form $\lambda\sqrt{r}/\sigma$, substituting the expression for the expected return (Equation (2.26)) into Equation (2.24) yields

$$rP + \lambda rP_r = P_r k(\theta - r) + P_t + \frac{1}{2}P_{rr}\,\sigma^2 r. \tag{2.27}$$

Equation (2.27) describes the price of any asset having a value that depends solely on the instantaneous rate, r, and the time to maturity, $T - t$.

Adding the boundary condition that $P(r,T,T) = 1.0$ and setting $\tau = T - t$, the solution of Equation (2.27) takes the form

$$P[r,t,T] = A[t,T]e^{-B[t,T]r}, \tag{2.28}$$

$$A[t,T] \equiv \left\{ \frac{\phi_1 exp(\phi_2\tau)}{\phi_2[exp(\phi_1\tau) - 1] + \phi_1} \right\}^{\phi_3}, \quad B[t,T] \equiv \left\{ \frac{exp(\phi_2\tau) - 1}{\phi_2[exp(\phi_1\tau) - 1] + \phi_1} \right\} \tag{2.29}$$

with

$$\phi_1 \equiv [(k + \lambda)^2 + 2\sigma^2]^{1/2}, \quad \sigma_2 \equiv (k + \lambda + \phi_1)/2, \quad \phi_3 \equiv 2k\theta/\sigma^2. \tag{2.30}$$

Brown and Dybvig performed tests of the one-factor CIR model on the prices of U.S. Treasury notes, bills, and bonds traded from 1952 to 1983. Under CIR, they estimated from a cross-section of bonds both the instantaneous default-free interest rate and the variance of changes in that rate. These estimates were compared with those derived from the time series of short-term rates. Brown and Dybvig reported that the model systematically overestimates short interest rates and, in addition, misprices premium and discount bonds. Thus the one-factor CIR model does not appear to be flexible enough to explain the term structure of interest rates. Results in Stambaugh (1988) suggest that the fit will be improved by going to two or three variable CIR models.

Another drawback of the one-factor model is that it implies that all bond prices are perfectly correlated, since there is only one source of risk, which is inconsistent with the data. Longstaff and Schwartz (1992) analyzed a two-factor model, where the factors are the short-term rate and its variance. They found that the two-factor model provides an acceptable description of the cross-section of bond prices, whereas the single-factor model is rejected by the data. In addition to providing endogenous consistency, these models have the advantage of providing closed-form solutions for bond options.

Bond Portfolio Management

Active bond management involves views on interest rates, on the shape of the yield curve, and on the pricing of individual bonds. We now examine methods to guide portfolio managers in these three decisions.

By far, the most important decision is the forecasting of interest rates. Rises in the yield curve lead to capital losses for long-maturity bonds. A falling yield curve creates capital gains for long-term bonds. In contrast, very short-term investments such as Fed funds are essentially unaffected by changes in interest rates. Therefore an investor expecting rates to increase should shorten the maturity of the bond portfolio and, conversely, lengthen the maturity of the portfolio if rates are expected to fall. Given the impact of yields on bond prices, substantial profits can be realized by appropriately changing the maturity of the portfolio in anticipation of yield changes. Of course, forecasting interest rates is also the riskiest proposition, since erroneous forecasts can lead to large losses.

For global fixed income portfolios, investment managers must forecast not only movements in interest rates in each bond market but also in exchange rates. Given the high correlations among bond markets, as well as comovements between exchange rates and interest rates, constructing a portfolio requires processing an enormous amount of information. This is best achieved by (i) forecasting interest rates in each bond market using the techniques presented in this chapter, (ii) forecasting exchange rates using techniques developed in the foreign exchange chapter, (iii) measuring risk and correlations using techniques developed in the domestic portfolio diversification chapter, and (iv) integrating all this information in a mean–variance optimizer as explained in the international portfolio diversification chapter.

Forecasting Interest Rates

The correct anticipation of the direction of interest rates is most valuable in the management of fixed income portfolios. The ideal state, however, is to forecast not only the direction but also the exact level of interest rates to prevail in the future. Unfortunately, to accurately forecast the level of interest rates has been all but impossible for economists. Judging the economists' dismal record, one observer has stated that "Anybody who can go out and say what interest rates will be at the end of the year has rocks in his head."[1] As a result, most portfolio managers have learned over time to settle for just forecasting the direction of change in interest rates.

The payoffs from using forecasting techniques depend on the efficiency of the market. If the financial markets were strongly efficient, no amount of forecasting skill would produce risk-adjusted returns higher than those obtained by buying a bond and holding it to maturity. That is, successive trades based on forecasts of interest rates would not outperform the naive buy-and-hold strategy in an efficient market.

A semistrong form efficient market is one in which all publicly available information is impounded in the observed yield curve. The best predictor of the future course of interest rates is the yield curve, which represents all the investors' expectations – that is, the collective wisdom of the market.

The evidence presented earlier in this chapter showed the deficiencies in the expectations hypothesis. Investors do not have homogeneous expectations, and bonds of differing maturities are not perfect substitutes for each other. Thus, forward rates are at best an approximation of yields that will prevail in the future.

We now discuss a few of the forecasting techniques used by money managers and academicians. They range from the simple to the very complex.

Simple Forecasting Techniques. Some of the simple models are of the following form:

$$y_t^l = a + \sum_{i=0}^{t} b_i y_{t-i}^S + \epsilon_t, \tag{2.31}$$

$$y_t^S = a + b_1 y_{t-1}^S + b_2 (\Delta P/P)_t + \epsilon_t, \tag{2.32}$$

where

y_t^l = long-term yield to maturity,

y_t^S = short-term yield to maturity,

$(\Delta P/P)_t$ = current rate of inflation.

The coefficients a and b_i are estimated using regression techniques. A technique that is gaining popularity involves the usage of *expected*

---

[1]These are the words of George W. McKinley, Jr., chairman of the economic advisory committee of Irving Trust Co., as quoted in the *Wall Street Journal* of Jan. 5, 1981.

inflation and *expected* short rates (ordinarily estimated using rational expectations theory) to predict long rates of interest.

Another frequently used method is that of developing a table showing the source and use of funds for each maturity and for the economy as a whole. Having arrived at the expected level of supply and demand for the period under consideration, the next step would involve the determination of that level of the interest rate that would equate supply to demand, given some assumptions about the elasticities of the supply and demand.

Forecasting with the Wharton Model.   Wharton Econometric Forecasting Associates, Inc. (WEFA), makes available to subscribers forecasts of various interest rates. The model follows these steps:

1. Forecast excess reserves. These are computed from a regression model using lagged values of free reserves, changes in commercial loan demand, in reserve requirements and in nonborrowed reserves, T-bill rates, and seasonal dummy variables.
2. Calculate the monetary base H (high-powered money), as $H = RR + FR +$ currency held by nonbank public, where RR is required reserves, FR is free reserves.
3. Using the money multiplier m, estimate the money supply as $M = Hm$.
4. Using the money supply figures, estimate the three-month T-bill rate.
5. On the basis of the T-bill rate, estimate the other short-term rates, using single-equation models. This is possible because of the high correlation among short-term rates.
6. Estimate long-rates using distributed lag models.

These large structural models have recently come under increasing criticism, because they assume that the relationships will remain stable in the future. However, if these models can indeed predict interest rates, investors will take positions that will affect future prices and in the process invalidate the econometric relationship underlying the models. As a result, econometric models such as those require frequent revisions.

Riding the Yield Curve

Riding the yield curve is a strategy intended to capitalize on certain shapes of the yield curve that are expected to hold over a period of time. Given the shape of the yield curve, the question for an investor with a certain time horizon t is whether to purchase a security maturing at time t or to purchase a longer-term security and sell it at time t.

Consider the zero coupon spot curve shown in Exhibit 2.8. Assume that this curve is expected to hold for a period of time. An investor with a five-year horizon can invest (i) in a five-year security, (ii) in a security with a maturity longer than five years and sell it after five years, or (iii) in shorter-term securities (say one year) and reinvest the proceeds every year for five years.

We first consider investing in a five-year zero coupon bond. The initial price is $1/(1 + 8 \text{ percent})^5 = \$68.06$, which locks in a sure return of 8 percent. Next, we assume that the ten-year zero is initially selling with a 9 percent annual yield to maturity; its price is $1/(1 + 9 \text{ percent})^{10} = \$42.24$. As the bond moves closer to maturity ($t \rightarrow 0$, that is, moving from right to left down the yield curve), its price will increase as the yield on similar issues decreases. At $t = 5$, the price of the ten-year zero with five years' remaining maturity equals \$68.06, producing a total return of $(68.06 - 42.24)/42.24 = 0.6112$, or an annually compounded return of $\$1.6112^{1/5} - 1 = 10$ percent. The 10 percent return is higher than the 8 percent return from the five-year zero. Buying the long-term bond benefits from sliding down the yield curve, which generates capital gains in addition to the normal yield to maturity. This strategy can be generalized to coupon-paying bonds, by reinvesting each of the cash flows at the appropriate discount rate.

Of course, this strategy hinges on the fact that the shape and the position of the yield curve remain intact or do not move unfavorably.

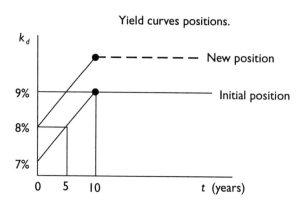

EXHIBIT 2.8   Riding the Yield Curve

It assumes that the expectation theory does not hold or that forward rates do not provide the best forecasts of future spot rates. If the yield curve shifts upward and its slope remains the same as in Exhibit 2.8, the investor would have been better off investing in a series of shorter-term maturities.

Security Selection

Finally, we turn to the selection of individual securities. The most systematic method is to use the theoretical spot curve to create a theoretical price for all outstanding bonds; from Equation (2.11), we can derive a theoretical price $\hat{P}$, which can be compared to the market price P. The difference, $P - \hat{P}$, indicates to what extent the bond is mispriced. Undervalued bonds should be purchased, and overvalued bonds should be sold from the portfolio.

Of course, the mispricing may reflect only a model misspecification. On-the-run bonds, for example, will generally be more expensive than other bonds because they trade at tighter bid–ask spreads and therefore provide a liquidity service. Tax effects may also affect the relative pricing of high-coupon and low-coupon bonds. If capital gains are taxed at a lower rate than income, low-coupon bonds are attractive to taxable investors, because part of the bond return is taxed at a low rate. This may increase low-coupon bond prices relative to other bonds. Although some of these factors can be explicitly modeled in the derivation of the discount function, there is no substitute for knowledge of the institutional factors that affect individual bond prices.

In general, the selection of bonds can be implemented through "bond swaps," which involve the exchange of bonds and take the following forms:

- *Swapping Equivalent Bonds Selling at Different Prices.* Two bonds of exactly the same characteristics (same coupon, rating, maturity, and liquidity) must sell at the same price whether issued by the same party or by different issuers of a similar profile. If not, the lower priced bond can be swapped for the higher priced bond.
- *Swapping Bonds with Differing Coupon, Maturity, or Quality.* Two bonds can be swapped if the yield spread between the bonds is very different from the historical norm to which it is

expected to converge. The yield spread normally falls in a range known to hold over long periods of time. If the yield spread between A-rated bonds and AAA-rated bonds has historically equaled 75 basis points, and the investor observes that it is currently at 40 because of an undue appreciation in the price of the A-rated bond, he or she would sell the A-rated bond and buy the AAA-rated bond and reverse the transactions when the yield spread moved back to the normal range. Spreads of this type require considerable knowledge of the behavior of yields over time.

■ *Tax Swaps.* Tax swapping is a technique used ordinarily to establish a capital loss at the end of the tax year. For tax losses to be allowed on a swap, the acquired bonds must differ from those sold in two of the following three characteristics: coupon, maturity, and issuer. If the two bonds are not sufficiently distinct, the IRS would not permit the tax deduction on the basis that the swap constitutes a wash sale. Capital losses realized from bond swaps can be used to offset capital gains, if any, or to reduce taxable income up to the maximum allowed.

Conclusion

This chapter has provided a thorough introduction to fixed income markets. We first presented the mechanics of bond pricing and the inverse relationship between bond prices and yields. The chapter then surveyed the major money and bond markets.

The term structure of interest rates was explored next. We showed that the usual yield curve is an ill-defined concept and should be replaced by a zero coupon spot rate curve, from which implied forward rates can be easily derived. The expectation theory states that these forward rates are the best predictors of future spot rates; in contrast, the liquidity theory emphasizes that risk premiums may exist in forward rates. The more recent CIR theory provides a more comprehensive general-equilibrium approach to the term structure that accounts for different sources of risk in the economy and can explain risk premiums.

References

Balback, R. B., 1977. "The effects of changes in inflationary expectations," *Federal Reserve Bank of St. Louis Review*: 10–15.

Brennan, M., and E. Schwartz. 1977. "Convertible bonds: Valuation and optimal strategies for call and conversion," *Journal of Finance*: 1699–1715.
——. 1979. "A continuous-time approach to the pricing of bonds," *Journal of Banking and Finance*: 133–55.

Brown, S. J., and P. H. Dybvig. 1986. "The empirical implications of the Cox, Ingersoll, Ross theory of the term structure of interest rates," *Journal of Finance*: 617–32.

Buse, A. B. 1967. "Interest rates, the Meiselman model and random numbers," *Journal of Political Economy*.

Campbell, J. Y. 1986. "A defense of traditional hypotheses about the term structure of interest rates," *Journal of Finance*, 183–93.

—— and R. J. Shiller. 1984. "A simple account of the behavior of long-term interest rates," *American Economic Review*: 44–48.

Carlson, K. M., and S. E. Hein. 1980. "Monetary aggregates as monetary indicators," *Review*, Federal Reserve Bank of St. Louis.

Cohen, K. J., R. L. Kramer, and W. H. Waugh. 1966. "Regression curves for U.S. government securities," *Management Science*: 168–175.

Cox, J., J. Ingersoll, and S. A. Ross. 1981. "A re-examination of traditional hypotheses about the term structure of interest rates," *Journal of Finance*: 769–99.

——. 1985. "A theory of the term structure of interest rates," *Econometrica*: 385–407.

DeGennaro, R. P. 1988. "Payment delays: Bias in the yield curve," *Journal of Money, Credit, and Banking*: 684–90.

Echols, M. E., and J. W. Elliot. 1976. "A quantitative yield curve model of estimating the term structure of interest rates," *Journal of Financial and Quantitative Analysis*.

Fama, E. F. 1975. "Short-term interest rates as predictors of inflation," *American Economic Review*: 269–82.

——. 1984. "The information in the term structure," *Journal of Financial Economics*: 509–28.

—— and R. Bliss. 1988. "The information in long-maturity forward rates," *American Economic Review*: 680–92.

Grant, J. A. 1967. "Meiselman on the structure of interest rates: A British test," *Economica*.

Gray, J. M. 1973. "New evidence on the term structure of interest rates, 1884–1900," *Journal of Finance*: 635–46.

Hardouvelis, G. 1988. "The predictive power of the term structure during recent monetary regimes," *Journal of Finance* 43: 339–56.

Hicks, J. R. H. 1946. *Value and Capital*, Clarendon Press, Oxford.

Hsieh, D. A., and L. Leiderman. 1986. "Portfolio implications of the expectations hypothesis," *Review of Economics and Statistics*: 680–84.

Huizinga, J., and Mishkin, F. S. 1984. "Inflation and real interest rates on assets with different risk characteristics," *Journal of Finance* 39: 699–712.

Ingersoll, J. 1977. "A convertible-claims valuation of convertible securities," *Journal of Financial Economics*: 289–322.

Jordan, J. 1984. "Tax effect in term structure estimation," *Journal of Finance* 39: 393–406.

Kane, E. J., and B. G. Malkiel. 1967. "The term structure of interest rates: An analysis of a survey of interest rate expectations," *Review of Economics and Statistics*. 354–364.

Kessel, A. R. K. 1965. *The Cyclical Behavior of the Term Structure of Interest Rates*, Occasional Paper 91, National Bureau of Economic Research, New York.

King, R. 1986. "Convertible bond valuation: An empirical test," *Journal of Financial Research*: 53–69.

Kugler, P. K. 1988. "An empirical note on the term structure and interest rate stabilization policies," *Quarterly Journal of Economics*, 789–792.

Longstaff, F., and E. Schwartz. 1992. "Interest rate volatility and the term structure: A two-factor general equilibrium model," *Journal of Finance*: 1259–83.

Malkiel, B. G. M. 1970. *The Term Structure of Interest Rates: Theory, Empirical Evidence, and Applications*, McCabb-Seiler, New York.

Mankiw, N. G., and Summers, L. H. 1984. "Do long-term interest rates over-react to short-term interest rates?" *Brookings Papers on Economic Activity* 1: 223–42.

McCulloch, H. 1987. "The monotonicity of the term premium: A closer look," *Journal of Financial Economics* 18: 185–192.

McCulloch, J. H. 1975. "An estimate of the liquidity premium," *Journal of Political Economy*: 95–119.

McCulloch, J. H. 1971. "Measuring the term structure of interest rates," *Journal of Business*: 19–31.

Meiselman, D. M. 1962. *The Term Structure of Interest Rates*, Prentice-Hall, Englewood Cliffs, N.J.

Nelson, C. R., and G. W. Schwert. 1977. "Short-term interest rates as predictors of inflation, on testing the hypothesis that the real rate of interest is con-stant," *American Economic Review* 67: 478–86.

Modigliani, F. M., and R. Sutch. 1966. "Innovations in interest rate policy," *American Economic Review*.

Santomero, A. M. S., 1975. "The error-learning hypothesis and the term structure of interest rates in Eurodollars," *Journal of Finance*.

Schap, K. S. 1990a. "Swaps II: Trading for a convertible currency," *Futures*: 42–44.

———. 1990b. "Swaps III: Reducing risks with synthetic swaps," *Futures*: 42–44.

Scott, R. H. S. 1963. "A 'liquidity' factor contributing to those downward sloping yield curves, 1900–1916," *Review of Economics and Statistics*: 328–29.

Shiller, R. J., J. Y. Campbell, and K. L. Schoenholtz. 1983. "Forward rates and future policy: Interpreting the term structure of interest rates," *Brookings Papers on Economic Activity* 1: 173–217.

Shiller, R. and H. McCulloch. 1987. "The term structure of interest rates," Working paper (National Bureau of Economic Research, Boston, MA).

Stambaugh, R. 1988. "The information in forward rates: Implications for models of the term structure," *Journal of Financial Economics* 21: 41–70.

Smith, C. W. S., Jr., C. Smithson, and L. M. Wakeman. 1986. "The evolving market for swaps," *Midland Corporate Finance Journal*: 20–32.

Trudgian, W. T., and R. H. Scott. 1971. "A survey of maturity pattern of yields," *University of Washington Business Review*: 65–76.

Vasicek, O., and G. Fong. 1982. "Term structure modeling using exponential splines," *Journal of Finance*: 339–48.

3

Interest Rate Management: Hedging Assets and Liabilities

Interest rates are one of the major sources of financial risk facing financial managers. Unfortunately, forecasting of interest rates is an unnatural science if not an art form. The overwhelming evidence is that interest rates cannot be predicted with sufficient precision and consistency to generate superior performance. In the absence of special forecasting skills, risk-averse managers should try to control the impact of unanticipated movements in the term structure on the value of their assets or liabilities. New techniques, however, have emerged to do just that.

Because duration measures the exposure of an asset to interest rate risk, understanding duration is essential for managing interest risk. Bond portfolio managers, for example, can "immunize" their bond portfolios from interest rate changes by setting the portfolio duration to zero. *Immunization* refers to the need to guarantee a minimum rate of return over a planning horizon. Duration can also be used to manage the assets and liabilities of banking institutions. Thus, asset/liability management has become an essential part of bank risk management.

Institutions that operate without knowledge of the net duration of their assets are essentially going blind in the maelstrom of changing financial markets. As witnessed by the savings and loans debacle of the 1980s, the duration gap can lead to huge losses if interest rates change in unexpected ways. At the very least, financial institutions should be aware of their net duration and then take informed action to immunize their portfolios or to take speculative positions. But even if speculative positions are undertaken, duration is useful because it helps to gauge the extent of gains or losses from movements in interest rates.

This chapter develops the use of duration and other measures of interest rate exposure for fixed income assets and asset/liability management. The first section defines *duration* as the exposure of a bond's rate of return to changes in yields and details important properties of duration. When a portfolio must be assured a minimum return over a given planning horizon, duration can be used to immunize a portfolio against interest rate moves. The second section illustrates how duration analysis can be used for managing the financial risk of banking institutions. This discussion is concentrated on banks; however, the concept of duration gap analysis is equally valid for pension funds with a defined benefits plan. The next section shows how derivative products can be used to manage the interest rate risk of an institution. These instruments are called *off-balance sheet* products because they do not directly appear on the balance sheet of financial institutions, thus allowing banks to bypass some regulatory requirements. Derivative instruments include forwards, futures, swaps, and options. This chapter introduces future, forward, and swap contracts. We show how to use these contracts to hedge against interest rate risk. The chapter on the management of foreign currency risk will show how forward, futures, and options contracts are priced and can be used to manage currency risk. The fourth section develops alternative measures of duration under more general processes. Since duration can be viewed as a first-order measure of exposure, convexity is introduced as a second-order term. Because of the risk of nonparallel moves in the term structure, a measure of reinvestment risk, M^2, is presented. The next section briefly covers the measurement of duration for bonds with imbedded options. Finally, a factor model approach is presented, which is shown to be a generalization of the duration and convexity concepts.

Duration

Definition

Duration is a characteristic of an asset or portfolio. In simple terms, duration is the weighted maturity of the bonds, where the weights are given by the present value of the cash flows. Duration also measures the sensitivity of an asset price to movements in yields. This is why it is such a valuable tool.

To see the link between duration and bond price changes, recall that the market price P of a bond can be written in terms of the present value of future cash flows as

$$P = \sum_{t=1}^{T} C_t/(1 + y)^t, \tag{3.1}$$

where

C_t = the interest or principal payment in period t,
$\quad t$ = the number of periods (annual, semiannual, or other) of coupon or principal payments,
T = the number of periods to final maturity,
y = the yield to maturity for this particular bond.

The sensitivity of the bond price to instantaneous changes in yield is

$$dP/dy = \sum_{t=1}^{T} \frac{(-t)C_t}{(1 + y)^{t+1}} = -\frac{1}{(1 + y)} \sum_{t=1}^{T} \frac{(t)C_t}{(1 + y)^t}. \tag{3.2}$$

Macauley's duration is formally defined as the weighted-average maturity of an investment, where the weights are proportional to the present value of the future cash flows:

$$D = (1/P) \sum_{t=1}^{T} tC_t/(1 + y)^t. \tag{3.3}$$

Equation 3.3 shows duration to be time (t) weighted by $\frac{C}{1 + y}$ relative to the initial investment P. Consequently, the sensitivity of the bond price to changes in yields can be written as

$$(1/P)\frac{dP}{dy} = -\frac{D}{(1 + y)}. \tag{3.4}$$

If yields are small, the denominator $(1 + y)$ can be approximated by unity, and duration measures the linear relationship between a bond return and changes in yields. Otherwise, for a better approximation, *modified duration* should be used:

$$D^* = -(1/P)\frac{dP}{dy} = D/(1 + y). \tag{3.5}$$

When yields are measured using m compounding periods in a year, the resulting duration measure is expressed in number of subperiods. To convert duration to an annual measure, it should be divided by m. For example, a duration of 20 semiannual periods in the U.S. Treasury market is converted to ten years. Duration is always measured in units of time. Exhibit 3.1 shows how duration is computed for a five-year bond with a 12 percent coupon payable semiannually.

Duration also expresses the time dimension of an investment, taking into account intervening payments and can be interpreted as a measure of the "effective" maturity of a bond. Focusing on maturity gives an inaccurate picture of the layout of cash flows because it ignores coupon payments. Indeed only in the case of zero coupon instruments is the maturity equal to the duration measure. If F is the face value of the "zero," setting $C_t = 0$ and $C_T = F$ in (3.1) and in (3.3) yields $P = F/(1 + y)^T$ and $D = (1/P)TF/(1 + y)^T$. Replacing P in the duration measure, we see that duration simplifies to maturity $D = T$ for a zero coupon bond.

Therefore, duration approximates changes in the prices of coupon-paying bonds by changes in the price of zero coupon bonds and can be used to compare bonds with differing maturities, payment schedules, and interest rates. It is a mechanism for homogenizing different bonds in terms of price sensitivity to yield changes.

However, duration is strictly valid only as a measure of exposure for (i) instantaneous, (ii) small, and (iii) "parallel" movements in yields; that is, where the whole yield curve is shifted up or down by the same increment. Yield movements need to be instantaneous because the change in the bond price keeps time-to-maturity constant; yield movements need to be small for the linear approximation to be valid; yield movements need to be parallel, because the same yield change is applied to all intervening coupon payments whatever their maturity. If more precision is needed, additional factors can be added to more precisely capture movements in bond prices, as will be explained in the rest of this chapter.

Dollar duration measures the impact of a given change in yield on the bond price, measured in dollars. It is defined as

$$\text{Dollar duration} = D^*P, \tag{3.6}$$

EXHIBIT 3.1   Computation of Duration (five-year, $1,000 face value, 12% semiannual coupon bond)

Time (t) (1)	Payment (2)	$(1 + y)^{-t}$ (3)	(3)*(2) (4)	(4)/P (5)	(5)*(1) (6)
			Par Bond		
0.5	60	0.9434	56.60	0.0566	0.0283
1.0	60	0.8900	53.40	0.0534	0.0534
1.5	60	0.8396	50.38	0.0504	0.0756
2.0	60	0.7921	47.53	0.0475	0.0951
2.5	60	0.7473	44.84	0.0448	0.1121
3.0	60	0.7050	42.30	0.0423	0.1269
3.5	60	0.6651	39.90	0.0399	0.1397
4.0	60	0.6274	37.64	0.0376	0.1506
4.5	60	0.5919	35.51	0.0355	0.1598
5.0	1,060	0.5584	591.9	0.5919	2.9595
			$P = 1,000.00$		$D = 3.9008$
		Premium Bond – spot rates = 8%			
0.5	60	0.9615	57.69	0.0496	0.0248
1.0	60	0.9246	55.47	0.0477	0.0477
1.5	60	0.8890	53.43	0.0459	0.0688
2.0	60	0.8548	51.29	0.0441	0.0883
2.5	60	0.8219	49.32	0.0424	0.1061
3.0	60	0.7903	47.42	0.0408	0.1224
3.5	60	0.7599	45.60	0.0392	0.1373
4.0	60	0.7307	43.84	0.0377	0.1509
4.5	60	0.7026	42.16	0.0363	0.1632
5.0	60	0.6756	716.10	0.6161	3.0807
			$P = 1,162.22$		$D = 3.9903$
		Discount Bond – spot rates = 14%			
0.5	60	0.9320	55.92	0.0615	0.0307
1.0	60	0.8686	52.11	0.0573	0.0573
1.5	60	0.8095	48.57	0.0534	0.0801
2.0	60	0.7544	45.26	0.0497	0.0995
2.5	60	0.7031	42.18	0.0464	0.1159
3.0	60	0.6552	39.31	0.0432	0.1296
3.5	60	0.6107	36.64	0.0403	0.1409
4.0	60	0.5691	34.15	0.0375	0.1501
4.5	60	0.5304	31.82	0.0350	0.1574
5.0	60	0.4943	523.97	0.5758	2.8791
			$P = 909.95$		$D = 3.8406$

and can be used to approximate the *dollar value of a basis point,* which is the amount by which the bond price changes if yields change by one basis point.

For a portfolio of fixed income instruments, an approximation to the overall portfolio duration is a simple weighted average of the components of the portfolio durations. If x_i represents the proportions invested in n different bonds, the portfolio duration can be approximated by

$$\text{Portfolio duration} = \sum_i^n x_i D_i, \tag{3.7}$$

where D_i is the duration of bond i. For more precision, however, one must first identify the cash flows from the portfolio and find the discount rate at which the present value of the portfolio equals its market price. Once this discount rate is identified, Macauley's duration can be computed by weighing the maturity of each payment by the fraction of the portfolio's total value represented by the present value of the payment.

Factors Affecting Duration

In the case where interest payments are constant throughout the life of the bond, a closed-form solution can be found for duration. Defining c as the constant coupon rate, or C/F, we have

$$D = \frac{c(1 + y)[(1 + y)^T - 1] + yT(y - c)}{cy[(1 + y)^T - 1] + y^2}. \tag{3.8}$$

This expression is useful to derive expressions for duration in special cases. For instance, when the coupon rate is zero, the duration expression simplifies to $y^2 T/y^2$, which is also T, the maturity of the zero coupon bond. Also, for a consol, which is a coupon-paying bond for which maturity tends to infinity, the $(1 + y)^T$ term dominates, and since it appears in both the numerator and denominator, duration tends to $c(1 + y)/cy$, or $(1 + y)/y$.

Duration and Maturity. For a zero coupon bond, duration equals maturity. At the other end of the spectrum, a perpetuity has a duration that is unrelated to maturity since its maturity is infinite. As already shown, a perpetuity's duration is approximated by $(1 + y)/y$.

For coupon-paying bonds, duration is always less than maturity. But the relationship between a coupon bond's duration and its maturity is not uniform. As shown in Exhibit 3.2, the duration of par and premium bonds increases as maturity increases, holding coupon and yield fixed; the duration of these securities approaches but will always be less than the perpetuity duration. In contrast, the duration of some discount bonds can exceed that of perpetuities. Asymptotically, the duration of all bonds tend to that of perpetuities.

Applying Equation (3.8) to par bonds, when $y = c$, duration simplifies to

$$D = \frac{y(1 + y)}{y^2 + y^2[(1 + y)^T - 1]^{-1}}.$$ (3.9)

Because the second term in the denominator is positive, duration will be less than $(1 + y)/y$, which is the duration of a consol. For premium $(c > y)$ or discount $(c < y)$ bonds, duration is composed of two terms: the first corresponds to that of an equivalent par bond, and the second is proportional to $yT(y - c)$. This shows that the duration of premium (discount) bonds must be less (higher) than that of par bonds.

Duration and Coupon.   The duration of a security decreases as the coupon rate increases, holding maturity and yield constant. This is

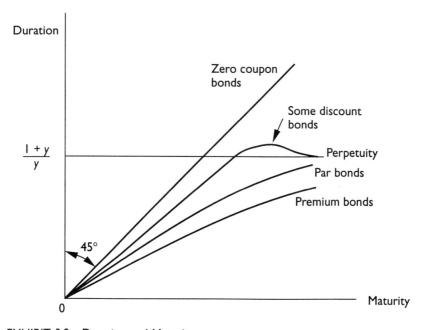

EXHIBIT 3.2   Duration and Maturity

because the cash flows occur relatively earlier for higher coupons. Exhibit 3.3 displays the negative relationship between duration and coupon rate.

Duration and Yield.   The duration of a security decreases as the yield increases, holding maturity and coupon constant. The reason for this is that, with higher yields, early cash flows and their time measure are given a higher weight in the computation of duration. Exhibit 3.4 displays the negative relationship between duration and yield.

Duration-Based Immunization

We now examine the risk of a portfolio that needs to be held until a certain horizon date. As yields increase, the market price of a bond will fall, but the income received from reinvestment of interim cash flows will be in general higher than expected. Conversely, a decrease in market rates will result in a higher than expected realized price and a lower than expected income from cash flow reinvestment. Stated another way, consider the two components of total yield – capital gains and reinvestment income. If we assume zero transaction costs and zero taxes, as interest rates rise the capital gains effects are negative and the reinvestment income effects are positive. The reverse is true if interest rates fall.

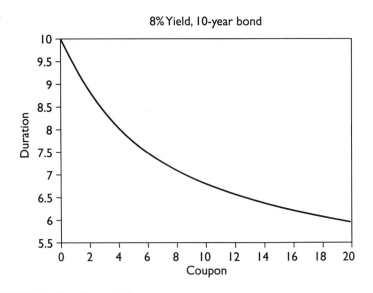

EXHIBIT 3.3   Duration and Coupon

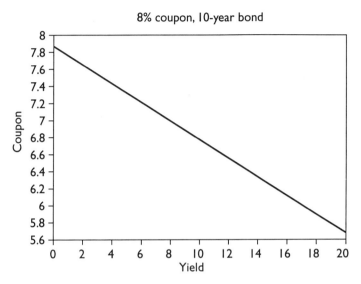

8% coupon, 10-year bond

EXHIBIT 3.4   Duration and Yield

Clearly, a portfolio manager would like to eliminate the net impact of yield movements on the final value of the portfolio. Fisher and Weil (1971) found that duration can be used to "immunize" a portfolio against both risks. A portfolio is said to be immunized from interest rate risk when the duration of a portfolio equals the desired investment horizon.

Consider, for instance, a pension fund manager with $1 million to invest on September 15, 1990, over a time horizon of 3.2913 years. The rate should be sufficiently high to guarantee the receipt of $1,467,500 when pension payments come due on January 1, 1994. The required rate is 12 percent compounded semiannually, as

$$\$1,000,000 \ (1 + 0.12/2)^{2\times3.2913} = \$1,467,500.$$

This can be achieved by investing in a four-year 12 percent bond, selling at par and with a duration of 3.2913.

As shown in Exhibit 3.5, if the reinvestment rate falls permanently to 11 percent on December 1, 1990, the bond price appreciates, so that it can be resold on January 1, 1994, at slightly higher than par, $1,006.64, with accrued interest of $35 ($60 times 3.5 months/6 months). Further, the first coupon payment on March 15, 1991, will grow to $60(1 + 0.11/2)^{2\times2.791} = \$80.90$. Cumulating all the interim payments yields a total of $426.36. Therefore the final payoff on

EXHIBIT 3.5   Impact of Changes in the Reinvestment Rate

Time Period	11% Interest Total Wealth	Yield if Sold	13% Interest Total Wealth	Yield	12% Interest Total Wealth	Yield
.0	1,031.67	–	969.56	–	1,000.00	12
.5	1,088.41	17.68	1,032.58	6.52	1,060.00	12
1.0	1,148.28	14.32	1,099.69	9.73	1,123.60	12
1.5	1,211.43	13.20	1,171.17	10.82	1,191.02	12
2.0	1,278.06	12.65	1,247.30	11.36	1,267.48	12
2.5	1,348.35	12.32	1,328.38	11.69	1,338.23	12
3.0	1,422.51	12.10	1,414.73	11.91	1,418.52	12
3.291	1,468.00	12.01	1,468.07	12.01	1,467.95	12
3.5	1,500.75	11.94	1,506.69	12.06	1,503.63	12
4.0	1,583.29	11.82	1,604.62	12.18	1,593.85	12

January 1, 1994, is ($1,006.64 + 35 + 426.36)1,000 = $1,468,000, which is a realized yield of 12.01 percent relative to the initial investment. Because the realized yield is quite close to the initial yield to maturity, the final payoff is not affected by the intervening fall in yield: the bond is said to be immunized against interest rate moves.

Exhibit 3.6 shows the final wealth as a function of time for different reinvestment rates. The numbers are graphed in Exhibit 3.6. At the point on the graph where time = duration = 3.2913 years, the return from the bond is nearly identical regardless of the reinvestment rate. For shorter horizons, the capital gain effect dominates; the reinvestment income effect dominates for longer horizons. Duration, consequently, balances the capital gains effects with the income (reinvestment) effects.

If duration does not equal the investment horizon, the realized yield will be higher or lower than the initial yield y depending on the relationship between duration and the holding period. McEnally (1980) noted that the realized yield is a weighted average of the yield to maturity and the reinvestment rate:

$$RY = (D/H)y + [1 - (D/H)]RR, \qquad (3.10)$$

where

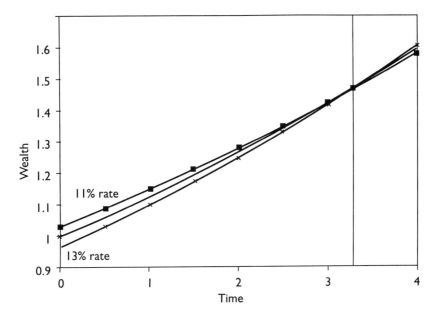

EXHIBIT 3.6   Total Wealth vs. Time for Selected Rates

RY = realized yield,
D = portfolio duration,
H = holding period,
RR = average reinvestment rate.

The realized yield equals the yield to maturity if the duration of the bond is equal to the time horizon of the investor $RY = y$. This demonstrates that setting duration equal to the planning horizon achieves a situation where the price risk and the reinvestment risk of a bond cancel each other. Duration can therefore be used to immunize a portfolio against interest rate shifts.

In practice, because market yields and time to maturity change, duration will change over the planned horizon. Only for zero coupon bonds will duration always match the planned horizon at any point in time. As a result the portfolio will have to be rebalanced if duration moves significantly far from the remaining horizon. Duration-based immunization requires a dynamic strategy. This often translates into monthly reimmunizations.

It is important to note, however, that immunization is effective only for parallel shifts in interest rates. Alternative models of interest rate behavior lead to different definitions of duration, as will be shown. Unfortunately, immunity is achieved against only the assumed type of rate change.

Limitations of Duration

Duration is clearly preferable to other methods of timing cash flows, such as term to maturity and weighted average term to maturity. As such, duration has emerged as an essential tool to measure interest rate exposure and to manage interest rate risk.

Using duration as a measure of exposure to interest rate risk, however, relies on a number of assumptions. It is essential to understand the implications of these assumptions, as well as the resulting limitations of duration. Failure to properly apply duration may result in unpleasant surprises and suboptimal results.

Cash Flows.   Since duration is concerned with the timing of cash flows, they must be known with certainty. In the presence of uncertainty, duration would simply become a probabilistic number reflecting a likely rather than actual effective maturity; cash flows must still be assumed to be independent of each other.

Duration must also be modified if there is default risk, early retirement, or early withdrawal. A paper by Chance (1990) addressed the issue of default risk. He found that the duration of a default-prone bond is a value-weighted combination of the duration of a default-free bond and the duration of a short put on the underlying asset.

Using Chance's example, let a holder of a risky zero coupon bond purchase a European put option on the assets of the firm. The exercise price is set to the face value of the bond F, the bond price is P_B, the put price is Put, and the firm's assets value is A. If $A < F$, the firm will default on the bond, but the bondholder will exercise the put. The holder will receive A from the bond and $F - A$ from the put for a net payoff of F. If $A > F$, the bond will be paid off and the put will expire worthless for a total payoff of F. Since the portfolio of the risky bond and the put yields a total payoff of F independent of A, it is a riskless portfolio. Its value must equal the sum of the bond price and the put price (i.e., $P = P_B +$ Put). Rearranging to isolate the bond price yields $P_B = P -$ Put, which shows that the risky bond is equivalent to a risk-free bond and a short put on the firm's assets.

Term Structure Process.   Duration is limited to a specific stochastic process for the term structure. Macauley's duration assumes a flat term

structure and parallel or equal movements in the entire term structure
that maintain the flatness. Other types of movements in the term structure such as multiplicative, additive, or log movements would make
Macauley's duration inaccurate.

Macauley's duration assumes a flat yield curve, because each cash
flow is discounted at the same rate. And for coupon bonds, the yield
to maturity is equal to only the simple average of the one-period rates
with a flat term structure. The term structure is rarely flat, so changes
in discount rates are usually not equal to changes in the yield to
maturity. However, alternative measures of duration consistent with
different stochastic processes have been developed and are detailed
later in this chapter.

In practice, although long-duration bonds are more price sensitive
to a given change in yield to maturity than short-duration bonds,
short-duration yields are more volatile than long-duration yields. As
a result, duration measures perhaps only half the risk associated with
a bond investment. Both duration and yield volatility must be considered in evaluating the riskiness of a bond.

Exhibit 3.7, taken from Yawitz and Marshall (1981), compares measures of duration, yield volatility, and total return volatility. Because

EXHIBIT 3.7   The Joint Effects of Duration and Yield Volatility on Bond Price
Volatility

(1)	(2)	(3)	(4)	(5)
Years to Maturity	Relative Duration*	Mean Absolute Change in Yield (%)	Relative Yield Volatility	Relative Price Volatility (2) × (4)
1	1	0.212	1	1
2	1.94	0.210	0.99	1.92
3	2.83	0.193	0.91	2.58
4	3.67	0.181	0.85	3.12
5	4.46	0.170	0.80	3.57
10	7.78	0.128	0.60	4.67
20	12.12	0.101	0.48	5.82
30	14.47	0.089	0.42	6.08

*Relative duration is computed as the ratio of each bond's duration to the duration of the
one-year bond. Relative yield volatility is computed similarly.

Source: Yawitz, J. B. and W. J. Marshall, "The shortcomings of duration as a risk measure for
bonds," *Journal of Financial Research*, (1981) 91–101.

yield volatility decreases with maturity, total return volatility is not proportional to duration. For instance, going from 1-year bonds to 30-year bonds, duration is multiplied by a factor of 14.47, while return volatility increases by only a factor of 6.08. This shows that the total risk of individual securities is not proportional to the magnitude of its duration index. Because movements in the term structure are not parallel, duration can be considered only an approximation to the risk index of a bond.

Infinitesimal Yield Changes. A third limitation of duration is that it is only a linear approximation of interest rate exposure. It is valid only with infinitesimal changes in yields, even when the term structure is flat and undergoes parallel shifts. When there are large shocks to the term structure, higher-order terms in the price derivative must be incorporated into the valuation. This is why convexity is sometimes also considered a second-order measure of exposure. Convexity will be analyzed in more detail later in this chapter.

Asset/Liability Management

Approaches

Duration is an essential tool to help banking institutions manage their assets and liabilities (A/L). Ideally, an institution would seek to finance long-term assets with long-term liabilities and finance short-term assets with short-term liabilities. Hedging in this fashion should ensure that the firm will have sufficient cash to prevent liquidity problems. However, it is unlikely that funds with the preferred maturity will always be available. In addition, adjusting the loan portfolio to match the maturity of available funds may result in the acquisition of unacceptably risky assets. Thus, although there is some flexibility in the composition of the portfolio of assets and liabilities, there are limits to the degree hedging can serve as an absolute guide to A/L management.

Instead, banks and thrifts have turned to A/L management (ALM) through maturity gap analysis or duration gap analysis. Maturity gap analysis classifies assets and liabilities into time periods ("buckets") by maturity. For instance, the first bucket might be 0–90 days, the second 90–180 days, and so on. Maturity gap management then consists of managing each bucket separately to control interest rate exposure. Although the maturity gap model is conceptually easy to understand, it presents several limitations.

First, there is no single number index of the interest rate risk of the bank, which obscures the total exposure to interest rates. Second, maturity gap management unnecessarily constrains the bank's choice of assets and liabilities to hedge the risk, because the maturity gap buckets must usually be managed with securities in the same maturity category. Also, maturity gap management constrains the bank's ability to accommodate consumer demands for services. In the rapidly changing financial services market, the need to maintain a certain balance in a particular maturity bucket may put the bank at a competitive disadvantage. For example, if a new hybrid security is devised and becomes popular rapidly, a bank may not be able to adjust its maturity bucket structure so as to make it available to its customers. Finally, as we have seen in the first section, maturity is an imperfect measure of interest rate exposure.

Given the inherent flaws in the maturity gap model, another model has been developed that, although not perfect, corrects many of the defects of the maturity gap approach. This more accurate approach is known as *duration gap analysis.*

Duration Gap Analysis

Many of the problems of maturity gap analysis can be overcome with duration gap analysis (DGA). Duration gap analysis summarizes the interest rate risk facing an institution in a single number. With that single number, a manager can chart a course through the sea of volatility underlying today's interest rate environment.

DGA starts with the identification of the target account. A target account whose value is to be controlled must first be selected, usually by senior management. Four accounts commonly chosen for management are the nominal value of capital, capital/asset ratio, net income, and the net income/asset ratio. These ratios are of importance to the bank's shareholders and for regulatory purposes.

Next, the gathering of the relevant data is required. This is the primary hurdle to DGA, since a tremendous volume of data is required. Complete data on each account or homogeneous group of accounts is needed, involving account balances, estimated mean maturity, and market yield or cost. Once the relevant data are acquired, the duration for each account must be calculated, taking into account repricing information and prepayment provisions. For instance, if a five-year floating-rate bond reprices in six months, its price behavior is comparable to a six-month bond rather than a five-year bond. Thus, variable rate securities and securities with imbedded options have effective maturities less than their contractual maturities.

In the following example, a simple bank balance sheet has been created. We will show the effects of both interest rate increases and decreases on the balance sheet and in the process demonstrate the usefulness of duration. Only a few asset and liability classes will be utilized, but the example will illustrate the principles of duration gap analysis. The same principles can be applied to more complex balance sheets. All of the assets, except cash, generate monthly cash flows. To simplify the example, assume the yield curve is flat, all payments are made on time, and there are no defaults, prepayments, or early withdrawals.

Initially, as shown in Exhibit 3.8, the hypothetical institution has $2,500 in assets with an asset duration of 3.77 years, $2,100 in liabilities with a deposit duration of 2.71 years, and capital of $400 with a duration of 6.67 years. The duration of the combined liabilities and equity is 3.35 years, which yields a positive institutional duration gap of $3.77 - 3.35 = 0.42$ years.

If we now increase interest rates by 50 basis points for all accounts, the market value of all interest-bearing accounts is decreased, as shown in Exhibit 3.9. The effect is not uniform as it can be seen that longer-term accounts are more severely affected by the interest rate change. As a result of this rate rise, capital (K) has decreased by 5.22 percent, the capital-to-asset ratio has decreased by 0.55 percent, the net income (NI) has decreased by 2.38 percent, and the net-income-to-assets (NI/A) ratio has decreased by 0.02 percent. Thus, as is usually the case, the institution has been hurt by the rate rise. This is a direct result of the positive duration gap. The combination of a positive duration gap and rising rates results in asset returns falling faster than liability costs. The result of this disparity is decreased profitability for the institution.

If we take the same initial balance sheet and subject it to a 50 basis point interest rate decrease, the effect is just the converse, as shown in Exhibit 3.10. The institution benefits from the rate increase. Capital has increased by 5.54 percent, the capital-to-asset ratio has increased by 0.56 percent, the net income (NI) has increased by 2.56 percent, and the net-income-to assets (NI/A) ratio has increased by 0.03 percent.

The value of duration can be seen in its applicability to analyzing a financial institution's situation under the influence of interest rate

EXHIBIT 3.8   Initial Balance Sheet

Account	Balance	Rate	Term	Duration
Assets (A)				
Cash	200	0.00%	0	0.00
Short-term treasuries	500	7.00%	0.25	0.17
Commercial loans	800	10.00%	5	2.52
Consumer loans	1,000	14.00%	15	7.32
Total	2,500			3.77
Liabilities and Equity				
Demand deposits	400	0.00%	0	0.00
1-year CDs	700	8.00%	1	1.00
5-year CDs	1,000	9.50%	5	5.00
Capital (K)	400	15.00%		6.67
Total	2,500			3.35

Deposit duration (D_p) (700*1 + 1,000*5)/2,100 = 2.71

PROJECTED INITIAL INCOME STATEMENT

	Interest Yield	Market Value/ Total Assets	Annual Income	Interest/Total Assets (%)
Revenues				
Cash	0.00%	8.00%	$0.00	0.00%
Short-term treasuries	7.00%	20.00%	$35.00	1.40%
Commercial loans	10.00%	32.00%	$80.00	3.20%
Consumer loans	14.00%	40.00%	$140.00	5.60%
	Sum	100.00%	$255.00	10.20%
Expenses				
Demand deposits	0.00%	16.00%	$0.00	0.00%
1-year CDs	8.00%	28.00%	$56.00	2.24%
5-year CDs	9.50%	40.00%	$95.00	3.80%
Capital	15.00%	16.00%	$0.00	0.00%
	Sum	100.00%	$151.00	6.04%
Net Income (NI)			$104.00	4.16%

Summary Accounts
K = $400.00   K/A = 16.00%
NI = $104.00   NI/A = 4.16%

EXHIBIT 3.9   Effect of a 50 Basis Point Rise

Account	Balance	Rate	Term	Duration
Assets				
Cash	200.00	0.50%	0	0.00
Short-term treasuries	499.38	7.00%	0.25	0.17
Commercial loans	784.49	10.00%	5	2.52
Consumer loans	969.51	14.00%	15	7.32
Total	2,453.38			3.73
Liabilities and Equity				
Demand deposits	400.00	0.00%	0	0.00
1-year CDs	696.77	8.00%	1	1.00
5-year CDs	977.48	9.50%	5	5.00
Capital	379.13	15.00%		6.67
Total	2,453.38			3.29

Deposit duration (D_p) $(700*1 + 1,000*5)/2,100 = 2.71$

PROJECTED INCOME STATEMENT WITH 50 BASIS POINT INCREASE

	Interest Yield	Market Value/ Total Assets	Annual Income	Interest/Total Assets (%)
Revenues				
Cash	0.50%	8.15%	$1.00	0.04%
Short-term treasuries	7.00%	20.35%	$34.96	1.42%
Commercial loans	10.00%	31.98%	$78.45	3.20%
Consumer loans	14.00%	39.52%	$135.73	5.53%
	Sum	100.00%	$250.14	10.20%
Expenses				
Demand deposits	0.00%	16.30%	$0.00	0.00%
1-year CDs	8.00%	28.40%	$55.74	2.27%
5-year CDs	9.50%	39.84%	$92.86	3.79%
Capital	0.00%	14.72%	$0.00	0.00%
	Sum	100.00%	$148.60	6.06%
Net Income			$101.53	4.14%

Summary Accounts
K = $379.13   K/A = 15.45%
NI = $101.53   NI/A = 4.14%

EXHIBIT 3.10   Effect of a 50 Basis Point Fall

Account	Balance	Rate	Term	Duration
Assets				
Cash	200.00	−0.50%	0	0.00
Short-term treasuries	500.62	7.00%	0.25	0.17
Commercial loans	815.86	10.00%	5	2.52
Consumer loans	1,032.09	14.00%	15	7.32
Total	2,548.57			3.80
Liabilities and Equity				
Demand deposits	400.00	0.00%	0	0.00
1-year CDs	703.26	8.00%	1	1.00
5-year CDs	1,023.15	9.50%	5	5.00
Capital	422.16	15.00%		6.67
Total	2,548.57			3.40

Deposit duration (D_p) $(700*1 + 1,000*5)/2,100 = 2.71$

PROJECTED INCOME STATEMENT WITH 50 BASIS POINT DECREASE

	Interest Yield	Market Value/ Total Assets	Annual Income	Interest/Total Assets (%)
Revenues				
Cash	−0.50%	7.85%	($0.00)	−0.04%
Short-term treasuries	7.00%	19.64%	$35.04	1.38%
Commercial loans	10.00%	32.01%	$81.59	3.20%
Consumer loans	14.00%	40.50%	$144.49	5.67%
	Sum	100.00%	$260.12	10.21%
Expenses				
Demand deposits	0.00%	15.70%	$0.00	0.00%
1-year CDs	8.00%	27.59%	$56.26	2.21%
5-year CDs	9.50%	40.15%	$97.20	3.81%
Capital	0.00%	17.29%	$0.00	0.00%
	Sum	100.00%	$153.46	6.02%
Net Income			$106.66	4.19%

Summary Accounts
K = $422.16   K/A = 16.56%
NI = $106.66   NI/A = 4.19%

changes. Duration can be used to relate changes in interest rates to changes in securities prices. This equation was presented previously (Equation (3.4)) and follows:

$$\Delta P/P = -D[\Delta y/(1 + y)], \tag{3.11}$$

where

P = price of a security,
y = yield to maturity,
Δ = change from previous value,
D = duration.

To estimate the effect of interest rates on specific accounts, one needs only calculate the duration for the account and multiply that duration by the rate change. We have done this for a number of accounts and presented both the predicted and actual balances under our interest rate changes in Exhibit 3.11. Most of the predicted values are reasonably close to the actual values. Thus, to the extent that price changes reflect the degree of interest rate risk assumed, duration represents a good first approximation risk measure, as it is proportional to the price change.

As stated before, an institution must choose a target account for duration gap analysis. We elaborate on each duration gap measure in the following paragraphs.

Portfolio Equity (Capital).   An institution's net portfolio (i.e., equity) can have a duration of nearly any value including a negative one. The duration of equity reflects the interest rate sensitivity of the claim on the bank by equity holders. Thus a small value for equity duration simply indicates that the current equity position has little exposure to changes in interest rates. The duration gap of portfolio equity $DGAP_E$ is defined as

$$DGAP_E = D_E. \tag{3.12}$$

The effect of the equity duration gap on the market value of equity under a dynamic interest rate environment can be calculated as follows:

$$\Delta V_E \approx V_E[-D_E/(1 + y)]\Delta y = [V_L D_L/(1 + y) - V_A D_A/(1 + y)]\Delta y, \tag{3.13}$$

where

EXHIBIT 3.11   Changes in Market Value

| | 50 BASIS POINT INCREASE | | | | | |
	D	MV	% Change in MV	Actual Balance	Predicted Balance	%
Short-term treasuries	0.17	500	-0.0835	499.38	499.58	0.04%
Consumer loans	7.32	800	-3.66	969.51	963.40	-0.63%
Commercial loans	2.52	1,000	-1.26	784.49	789.92	0.69%
1-year CDs	1.0	700	-0.5	696.77	696.5	-0.04%
5-year CDs	5	1,000	-2.5	977.48	975.00	-0.25%
Capital	6.67	400	-3.335	379.13	386.66	1.99%*
Total Assets	3.77	2,500	-1.885	2,453.38	2,452.87	-0.02%
Total Liabilities	3.35	2,500	-1.675	2,453.38	2,458.13	0.19%

| | 50 BASIS POINT DECREASE | | | | | |
	D	MV	% Change in MV	Actual Balance	Predicted Balance	%
Short-term treasuries	0.17	500	0.0835	500.62	500.42	-0.04%
Consumer loans	7.32	800	3.66	1,032.09	1,036.60	0.44%
Commercial loans	2.52	1,000	1.26	815.86	810.08	-0.71%
1-year CDs	1.00	700	0.5	703.26	703.5	0.03%
5-year CDs	5	1,000	2.5	1,023.15	1,025	0.18%
Capital	6.67	400	3.335	422.16	413.34	-2.09%*
Total Assets	3.77	2,500	1.885	2,548.57	2,447.125	-0.06%
Total Liabilities	3.35	2,500	1.675	2,548.57	2,541.875	-0.26%

*Price effect only. The total liabilities account includes both the price and income effect.

$DGAP_E$ = duration gap of equity,
  D_E = duration of equity,
  ΔV_E = change in market value of equity,
  V_L = market value of liabilities,
  D_L = duration of liabilities,
  V_A = market value of assets,
  D_A = duration of assets,
  Δy = change in interest rates.

Equation (3.13) is useful since it redefines the duration gap of equity as a difference between the value-weighted durations of assets and liabilities. This enables a manager to know how much either asset or liability durations must be altered to effect a desired change in the value of the duration gap of equity. This also helps the manager to hedge incrementally. For example, suppose that current equity duration is 3.45 years, and we calculate that to make the duration gap of equity equal to zero, D_A should be 3.11 years. The manager now knows that any transaction that shifts D_A toward a value of 3.11 years will reduce the interest rate exposure of equity.

  Asset to Equity (Leverage).   Capital adequacy is a major concern in today's financial environment. Regulators are focusing on capital adequacy as a means to assess the health of financial institutions. Toevs and Haney (1986) approached the problem by considering the issue of capital adequacy in terms of economic leverage, which is the ratio of the market value of assets to the market value of portfolio equity. The duration gap for economic leverage is

$$DGAP_L = D_E - D_A, \qquad (3.14)$$

where $DGAP_L$ is the duration gap of economic leverage. The effect of $DGAP_L$ on the change in value of economic leverage under a dynamic interest rate environment can be calculated as follows:

$$\Delta(A/E) \approx (A/E)[(D_E - D_A)/(1 + y)]\Delta y. \qquad (3.15)$$

With these equations, a manager can quickly determine the effect of interest rate changes on the value of economic leverage and take steps to capitalize on change or mitigate the effects of the change in interest rates. To determine the degree of restructuring necessary to alter current risk exposures to desired levels, Equation (3.15) can be restated in terms of asset and liability durations:

$$\Delta(A/E) = [(AL)/E^2][(D_A - D_L)/(1 + y)]\Delta y. \qquad (3.16)$$

At this point it is instructive to note that simultaneous hedging of two specific target accounts is often impossible. Comparing the $DGAP_E(= D_E)$ with the $DGAP_L(= D_E - D_A)$, it is obvious that the achievement of complete hedges for both target accounts are mutually exclusive events. The exception here is in the unlikely event of $D_A = D_L = D_E = 0$. This points out a weakness in all ALM models in which interest rate risk must be endured in one target account for it to be hedged in another target account. The art of ALM is to establish a primary target account, hedge it, and then work to minimize, if possible, interest rate risk in target accounts of lesser importance.

Total Return on Equity.   As discussed earlier, the total return on a bond over an investment period can be immunized against changes in interest rates if the duration of the bond is equal to the holding period and if duration drift is corrected periodically. The same principle can be extended to portfolio equity, which is actually a net bond. The duration gap for immunizing total returns on the market value of equity is the following:

$$DGAP_{TR} = D_E - H, \qquad (3.17)$$

where H is the holding period over which the manager wishes to assure the currently available return. This duration gap is straightforward in its application. When $D_E = H$, the total market-valued return on equity over the investment period is immunized.

Book Value of Net Interest Income.   The final duration gap to be considered is the book value of net interest income. This account is the one most frequently followed by stock analysts, investors, and not the least, by risk managers. The duration gap for this target account was defined by Toevs and Haney (1986) as the amount earned from currently booked assets plus reinvestment of those earnings to the end of the accounting period, minus the interest expense-booked and refinanced to the end of the accounting period. The duration gap for the book value of net interest income is

$$DGAP_{NII} = V_{RSA}(1 - D_{RSA}) - V_{RSL}(1 - D_{RSL}), \qquad (3.18)$$

where

$DGAP_{NII}$ = duration gap of the book value of net interest income,
V_{RSA} = market value of rate-sensitive assets,
D_{RSA} = duration of rate-sensitive assets,
V_{RSL} = market value of rate-sensitive liabilities,
D_{RSL} = duration of rate-sensitive liabilities.

Choice of Passive or Active Strategy

A *passive strategy* consisting of setting the duration gap to zero is referred to as *immunization*. For whatever reasons, an institution may wish to maintain a constant nominal value of its target account regardless of changes in interest rates. This is where immunization is useful as a complete hedging strategy. A key point to remember is that profits can be earned by assuming some degree of interest rate risk and managing it effectively. Immunization may reduce or eliminate this income altogether. Thus, a completely immunized portfolio may not be desirable, especially when management has strong views on the direction of interest rates. On the positive side, immunization protects an institution against losses if the risk is mismanaged.

To achieve full immunization, the appropriate duration gap must be set to zero. However, it is very important to remember that duration is a function of time and therefore, to remain immunized, a bank must continually restructure its balance sheet to offset this duration "drift." Even in the absence of interest rate changes, periodic restructuring will be necessary. This is a result of the differential decay rates of duration and time. Duration generally decreases more slowly than time, although at times duration will increase as time passes. Because it is improbable that the two sides of the balance sheet will change equally over time, periodic restructuring is inevitable. For optimal results, an institution would want to restructure its balance sheet every day. However, this may not be profitable or practical.

Active management of interest rate risk involves assuming a certain amount of interest rate risk and profitably exploiting it. Clearly, if interest rates move opposite to the expected direction, the bank would be subject to losses. If rates are predicted to increase, the gap should be negative. This effectively makes the bank behave as a net liability whose value grows as rates rise. Conversely, if rates are predicted to be decreasing, a net asset position resulting from a positive gap would be profitable. The precise value of the gap depends upon the institution's risk/return preference, as determined by senior management and the asset/liability committee.

On- or Off-Balance Sheet Hedging

There are two types of immunization, natural percent (on-balance sheet) and artificial (off-balance sheet). Immunization through on-balance sheet methods involves matching the durations of assets and liabilities. While it may seem logical to assume that a manager could use on-balance sheet methods to immunize the entire institution, in practice, it is quite difficult, given that the few securities have a duration greater than ten years. The desired securities may also be expensive or trade at wide bid–ask spreads.

Given that on-balance sheet methods are often inadequate, other approaches have been developed to manage interest rate risk. In this section, we show how to use *derivative* instruments to control interest rate risk. Derivative instruments are products that are priced in relation to the underlying asset price; they include forwards, futures, swaps, and options. This chapter introduces futures, forwards, and swap contracts. We show how to use these contracts to hedge against interest rate risk. The chapter on the management of foreign currency risk will show how forwards, futures, and options contracts are priced and can be used to manage currency risk.

As seen from the method used for pricing them, derivatives are generally redundant instruments, in the sense that they can be replicated by positions in underlying assets. A long position in a forward contract, for example, is exactly replicated by a long position in the cash market plus some borrowing and lending. Derivatives, however, offer important advantages in terms of liquidity, transaction costs, and tax or regulatory benefits. The liquidity provided by derivatives often makes them preferable over cash market operations. With futures, one can generally move more quickly and more efficiently on narrower bid–offer spreads than is possible in the cash market.

Forwards

Forwards are contracts to buy or sell a given commodity at a given price at a given point in time. There are no cash flows between the origination and termination of the contract. The exercise price of the contract is initially set so that the current market price of the contract is zero. As expectations about future events change, the value of the contract may become either positive or negative. If you buy a forward contract, you are obligated to buy the commodity at the mandated time and price. If you are on the buy side of the transaction, you must buy the commodity at the mandated time and price.

Futures

Futures are exactly the same as forwards except that there are cash flows between the origination and termination of the contract. Futures contracts are revalued daily so as to maintain a zero market value for the contract. As an example, assume you enter into a futures contract to sell a commodity for $1,000 in 60 days. The next day the identical contract is priced at $950 for delivery in 59 days. Since the price fell while you were short, the contract accrues a net gain of $50, and your margin account would be credited for the product of $50 times the number of contracts that you own. The same forward contract would simply assume a positive value.

Duration Hedging with Futures

Futures enable a portfolio manager to alter the duration of a fixed income portfolio to conform to his or her rate expectations and yet not change the actual composition of his or her portfolio. A high-duration (i.e., longer term) investment is vulnerable to rising interest rates. By selling futures, the effective duration of this instrument can be reduced and thereby lessen its exposure to the rising rates. Conversely, futures could be purchased to extend the effective duration of the instrument in the face of falling interest rates.

For example, suppose a bank has a positive $DGAP_E$ and anticipates an interest rate increase. The combination of the positive duration and an interest rate increase will lead to a decrease in capital levels. The bank wishes to avoid this but is unable to restructure the balance sheet quickly enough to achieve the goal of reducing its $DGAP_E$ to desired levels. The bank could sell futures contracts, such as T-bill futures, and achieve the desired decrease in duration. Similar manipulations could be accomplished with forwards.

To accomplish the hedge, the manager who has a current long position in securities must sell a given number of futures contracts. The task is to determine the number of futures contracts necessary to hedge the portfolio. Let $V(r)$ be the value of the cash portfolio, where r is the yield to maturity of the securities held. Similarly, let $F(r)$ be the futures price for future delivery of a unit of some security. For both contracts, the price V or F will move inversely with interest rates. Also let h be the number of units of contracts bought or sold for future delivery. Note that $h > 0$ represents a long position (securities bought) and $h < 0$ represents a short position (securities sold). Let r_0 be the initial interest rate. After entering the futures market, r_0 changes to r, which changes the futures price from $F(r_0)$ to $F(r)$. Thus the margin account will change by $h[F(r) - F(r_0)]$. If $h > 0$ and $r > r_0$, futures prices will fall so $F(r) - F(r_0) < 0$, which means $h[F(r) - F(r_0)] < 0$. Hence, there is a decrease in the margin account. If $h < 0$, an increase to the margin account would have resulted.

The total value of the investor's portfolio is

$$P(r) = V(r) + h[F(r) - F(r_0)]. \qquad (3.19)$$

The hedge operates as follows. As r increases, $V(r)$ will decrease but be offset by $h[F(r) - F(r_0)]$ (given $h < 0$). If r decreases, $V(r)$ will increase while $h[F(r) - F(r_0)]$ will decrease (given $h < 0$). Provided that h is correctly determined, interest rate changes will occur but $P(r)$ will never fall below $V(r_0)$. Thus the original value of the portfolio will be retained. However, there will also be limited upside gain.

Duration can be used as follows in setting up the hedge. Taking the derivative of Equation (3.19) with respect to r and evaluating at r_0, we obtain

$$P'(r_0) = V'(r_0) + hF'(r_0). \qquad (3.20)$$

As we know, the durations of the securities are

$$V'(r_0) = -DV(r_0)/(1 + r_0), \qquad (3.21)$$
$$F'(r_0) = -D_F F(r_0)/(1 + r_0),$$

where D is the duration of the cash portfolio, D_F is the duration on the delivery date of the security sold in the futures market. Substituting these definitions into Equation (3.20) yields

$$P'(r_0) = -DV(r_0)/(1 + r_0) + h[-D_F F(r_0)/(1 + r_0)]. \qquad (3.22)$$

If D_P is the duration of the total portfolio, then

$$P'(r_0) = -D_P P(r_0)/(1 + r_0), \qquad (3.23)$$

which when substituted into Equation (3.22) gives

$$-D_P P(r_0)/(1 + r_0) = -DV(r_0)/(1 + r_0) + h[-D_F F(r_0)/(1 + r_0)].$$
(3.24)

Since $P(r_0) = V(r_0)$, Equation (3.24) simplifies to

$$D_P = D + hD_F[F(r_0)/V(r_0)].$$
(3.25)

For D_P to equal 0, h must assume the following value:

$$h = -(D/D_F)[V(r_0)/F(r_0)].$$
(3.26)

Thus the hedge ratio is the negative of the price ratio multiplied by the ratio of durations. An example is now presented.

An investor holds a one-year T-bill having a face value of $1 million with an interest rate of 11 percent. Since the T-bill is a zero coupon instrument, its duration is exactly one year. The investor wants to hedge the one-year bill by selling three-month T-bills futures contracts, with a face value of $1 million and a duration of 0.25 years. If the investor wants to use the three-month futures, the hedge ratio is

$$h = -(1/0.25)[(\$1,000,000(1 + 0.11/4)^{-4})/(\$1,000,000(1 + 0.11/4)^{-1})]$$
$$= -4(1 + 0.11/4)^{-3}$$
$$= 3.687351.$$

The investor would have to buy four futures contracts and would therefore be somewhat imperfectly hedged, because only integer amounts can be purchased.

Unfortunately, this example and the preceding derivations are predicated on two major assumptions. The first assumption was that the yields to maturity on the securities in the portfolio and the security underlying the futures contract were identical. The second assumption was that both yields changed by the same amount. However, neither assumption is generally valid. Bierwag (1987) provided a more detailed hedging procedure.

Let r_0^c and r_0^f be the current yields to maturity on a cash asset and a futures security respectively. Let $V(r_0^c)$ and $F(r_0^f)$ be the corresponding values of the cash asset and the futures security. The total value of the portfolio can now be written as

$$P = P(r^c, r^f) = V(r^c) + h[F(r^f) - F(r_0^f)],$$
(3.27)

where r^c is the yield on the cash asset and r^f is the yield on the futures security. Taking the total derivative of Equation (3.27) with respect to r^c, where dr^f/dr^c represents the change in r^f relative to a change in r^c, we obtain

$$\frac{dP}{dr^c} = V'(r^c) + hF'(r^f)\left[\frac{dr^f}{dr^c}\right]. \tag{3.28}$$

We now need to determine h so that

$$V'(r^c) + hF'(r^f)\delta = 0, \tag{3.29}$$

where δ is the derivative dr^f/dr^c evaluated at the initial point (r_0^c, r_0^f). Proceeding as before with the definitions of duration, Equation (3.29) can be rewritten as

$$-\frac{DV(r_0^c)}{1 + r_0^c} - \frac{\delta hD_F F(r_0^f)}{1 + r_0^f} = 0, \tag{3.30}$$

where annual compounding and the calculation of durations at the initial yields are assumed. Modified duration is generally represented as $D/(1 + r_0^c) = D^*$ and $D_F/(1 + r_0^f) = D^*_F$. This gives us

$$-D^*V(r_0^c) - hD^*_F F(r_0^f)\delta = 0, \tag{3.31}$$

which yields the new hedge ratio

$$h = -(D^*/D^*_F)[V(r_0^c)/F(r_0^f)](1/\delta). \tag{3.32}$$

This modified hedge ratio differs from the previously derived ratio in two respects. The first is that prices and durations are determined at security-specific yields; the second is that relative motion of yields is introduced through the variable δ. If the maturities of the cash asset and the security underlying the futures contract are approximately equal, δ will be close to unity. Otherwise, δ can be estimated by the slope of the regression of r^f on r^c.

Swaps

Swaps are agreements by two parties to exchange cash flows in the future according to a prearranged formula. The first swap contracts were arranged in 1981. At that time, August 1981, the World Bank raised $290 million in fixed-rate loans and swapped it for IBM floating-rate liabilities in Swiss francs and deutsche marks. Since then, the market for swaps has grown very rapidly and in 1992 reached $4 trillion in terms of outstanding face value (notional), of which perhaps 80 percent are interest rate swaps.

Currency swaps involve the exchange of currencies. An *interest rate swap* is a mechanism for transforming a cash flow stream from fixed to floating or vice versa or from floating against a certain index to floating against another. This transformation allows the participants to improve the performance of their assets or reduce the cost of their liabilities or both.

Swaps can also be used as an effective tool for interest or currency exposure management. A gap – the difference between rate-sensitive assets and rate-sensitive liabilities – can be reduced or eliminated through swap transactions.

As an example of an interest rate swap, consider two companies, A and B, that can each borrow either fixed or floating. We assume that B ultimately wants to borrow at a fixed rate, and that A wants to borrow at a floating rate. Floating-rate debt is typically based on the London interbank offer rate (LIBOR), which is the benchmark cost of funds in international markets. The terms are as follows.

	Fixed	Floating
Company A	10.00%	6-month LIBOR + 0.20%
Company B	11.00%	6-month LIBOR + 0.80%

Even though Company A has an absolute advantage in raising funds because it has a higher credit rating, Company B has a comparative advantage in issuing floating debt. This is because it is paying 1 percent more than A for fixed debt but only 0.60 percent more for floating debt. Thus the benefit to be shared is 40 basis points.

The two companies can benefit from issuing in the sector in which each has the greatest *comparative* advantage, then swapping the debt payments. For instance, A could raise fixed debt at 10 percent, receive 9.95 percent from B to which it would pay LIBOR. In exchange, B would raise floating-rate debt at LIBOR + 0.80 percent, and then swap floating-rate payments for fixed-rate payments. Overall, A would be paying LIBOR + 0.05 percent, and B would be paying 10.75 percent. Company A gains 15 basis points, and B gains 25 basis points, which sums to the total benefit of 40 basis points.

Interest swaps involve swapping only the interest payments on the respective loans. No principal changes hands. The "exchange" of cash flows can be done on a net basis (that is, the party expected to receive the lower cash flow could simply pay the counterparty expecting the higher cash flows the net difference), but this is not the normal practice. Should the swap also involve different currencies (e.g., paying floating dollars, receiving fixed DM) the counterparties would exchange principals at a specified exchange rate.

Reasons for Interest Rate Swaps.   Swaps generally represent an arbitrage between seemingly different quality borrowers or an arbitrage between different tax and regulatory environments. In the first instance, the World Bank was able to borrow cheaper in dollars than IBM because lenders of dollars are more familiar with the World Bank and consider it of lower risk. And in the second, debt is issued in a country with the lower tax rate and preferred regulatory environment and swapped for debt in a country with higher taxes and stricter regulatory environment. Swaps are also convenient to use because of their complete anonymity, without SEC registration and reporting requirements and with no negative impact on the credit rating of the participating parties.

Valuation of Swaps.   If we assume no default can occur, a swap can be valued simply as a long position and a short position in two bonds. Consider, for instance, the swap described previously. Company A makes floating-rate payments in exchange for receiving fixed-rate payments. If P_1 is the value of the fixed-rate bond and P_2 is the value of the floating-rate bond, the value of the swap is $V = P_1 - P_2$. At the beginning of its life, the value of the swap is zero and $P_1 = P_2$.

If interest rates fall, A's swap will be more valuable, because it receives higher coupons than prevailing market yields. P_1 will then increase to the present value of fixed cash flows, using the appropriate discount rates, while P_2 will barely change, because interest payments are reset at regular intervals. The swap value can be recomputed at any time during its life.

Whereas interest rate risk is straightforward to measure, swaps are also exposed to default risk. If company B defaults because it cannot keep up with the high fixed-rate payments, company A will suffer a financial loss. The loss, however, is not in the face value of the principal involved, but rather the change in the value of the swap. In recent years, swaps have involved lower quality credit ratings, and default rates have sharply increased.

Market. The function of banks and investment banks in the swap market is either that of an intermediary ("pure broker") or a principal ("market maker"). When acting as an intermediary, the bank could charge three different fees: a *finder's fee, guarantee fee,* and *processing fee.* The "guarantee fee," rarely used, is the fee charged for replacing the credit of the bank for that of the counterparty in a swap, whenever the credit worthiness of the counterparty is questionable. Here the role of the bank is similar to that provided by the Clearing Corporation for futures contracts, where every buyer or seller looks to the Clearing Corporation for performances against the contract and is not concerned about the identity or the creditworthiness of the party on the opposite side of the transaction. Similarly the bank must honor the contract in the event of default by one of the counterparties.

When acting as a principal the bank "warehouses" the swap, that is, it takes a position in the swap by assuming the other side of the transaction. The fee structure in a principal transaction is imbedded in the bid and ask spread quoted by the bank.

The bank's net swap position determines its risk exposure at any point in time. Competition in the swap markets is increasing rapidly. The margins have shrunk steadily, allowing little room for market makers to charge rates that sufficiently discriminate among counterparties with differing risk profiles. This phenomenon has led to a much reduced participation by several banks in the swap market.

Swaps lack a strong secondary market because of their heterogeneity. This considerable drawback is being addressed partially by requiring a collateral for the party with a weaker credit, by marking the weaker credit to market, and by the purchase of implicit or explicit insurance. None of these methods represents a permanent solution, and the market, in this regard, remains in the evolutionary state.

Other Duration Measures

Duration measures have been derived for more general stochastic processes of the term structure than the flat term structure assumed by Macauley's duration. Each of these durations is specific to its underlying stochastic process and therefore should be more appropriate if the assumed process is closer to the actual behavior of interest rates. We consider three alternative duration measures.

But, first, the discount function can be modified to account for the fact that it may not be necessarily flat:

$$(1 + y)^t = [1 + h(0, t)]^t, \tag{3.33}$$

where $h(0, t)$ is now interpreted as the rate of return appropriate for discounting the cash flow C_t and where $h(0, t)$ may take on different values for different terms of t.

Additive Stochastic Process Duration

The additive stochastic process is one where a constant is added to the existing term structure to arrive at the new instantaneous term structure. This process, often referred to as a *parallel shift,* can be represented as

$$h^*(0, t) = h(0, t) + \lambda, \tag{3.34}$$

where λ is a constant. The slopes are the same for parallel shift yield curves at any time point. Exhibits 3.12 and 3.13 illustrate the additive stochastic process under upward- and downward-sloping yield curves.

The duration for the additive stochastic process is derived by Bierwag (1987) as

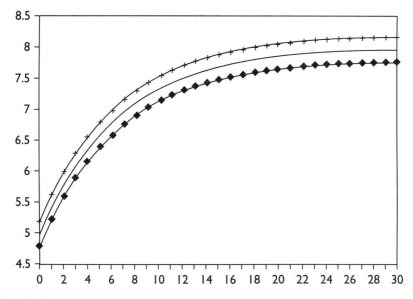

EXHIBIT 3.12   Additive Stochastic Process (upward-sloping yield curve)

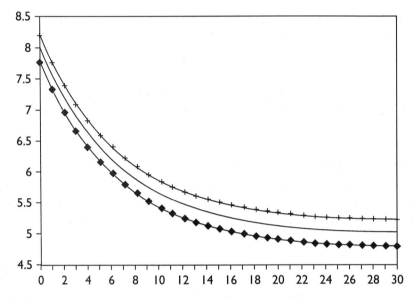

EXHIBIT 3.13   Additive Stochastic Process (downward-sloping yield curve)

$$\frac{D_A}{1 + b(0, D_A)} = (1/P)\sum_{t=1}^{n} C_t \frac{t}{1 + b(0, t)}[1 + b(0, t)]^{-t}, \qquad (3.35)$$

with the percentage price change approximated by

$$dP/P = -\frac{D_A}{1 + b(0, D_A)}d\lambda. \qquad (3.36)$$

This is very similar to Macauley's duration measure, except that all occurrences of the yield y are replaced by a time-specific measure $b(0, t)$.

Multiplicative Stochastic Process Duration

The multiplicative stochastic process is one where the existing term structure is multiplied by a constant to arrive at the new instantaneous term structure. This process can be represented as

$$1 + b^*(0, t) = [1 + b(0, t)]\lambda. \qquad (3.37)$$

Thus, there may be differential shifts in the term structure. If $\lambda > 1$, the term structure shifts upward, and if $\lambda < 1$, the shift is downward. This phenomenon is illustrated in Exhibit 3.14.

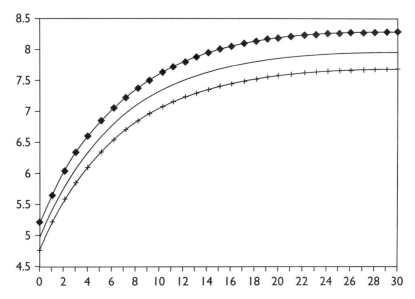

EXHIBIT 3.14   Multiplicative Stochastic Process (upward-sloping yield curve)

The duration for the multiplicative stochastic process is with the percentage price change approximated by

$$D_M = (1/P)\sum_{t=1}^{n} tC_t\,[1 + h(0, t)]^{-t} \tag{3.38}$$

$$dP/P = -D_M d\lambda. \tag{3.39}$$

Log-Stochastic Process Duration

Finally, two log-stochastic processes allow short-term rates to fluctuate instantaneously more than long-term rates for both upward- and downward-sloping term structures. The log-additive process, which adds a log function to the term structure, was derived by Khang (1979) as follows:

$$h^*(0, t) = h(0, t) + \frac{\lambda \ln(1 + \beta t)}{\beta t}, \tag{3.40}$$

where λ is a random variable and β is a positive parameter. Bierwag (1987) noted that the logarithmic function $\ln(1 + \beta t)$ increases with t

at a slower rate than βt so that the ratio $\ln(1 + \beta t)/\beta t$ decreases as t increases. This causes short-term rates to be instantaneously shocked by larger increments than long-term rates. The value of β thus regulates the degree to which short-term rates fluctuate more than long-term rates.

The duration for the log-additive process $D_{LA}(\beta)$ is implicitly defined in

$$\frac{\ln[1 + \beta D_{LA}(\beta)]}{1 + b(0, D_{LA})} = (1/P)\sum_{t=1}^{n} C_t \frac{\ln(1 + \beta t)}{1 + b(0, t)}[1 + b(0, t)]^{-t}, \quad (3.41)$$

with the percentage price change approximated by

$$dP/P = -\frac{\ln(1 + \beta D_{LA})}{\beta[1 + b(0, D_{LA})]}d\lambda. \quad (3.42)$$

The log-multiplicative process can be specified as

$$b^*(0, t) = b(0, t)\left[1 + \frac{\lambda \ln(1 + \beta t)}{\beta t}\right] + \frac{\lambda \ln(1 + \beta t)}{\beta t}. \quad (3.43)$$

The duration for the log-multiplicative process is implicitly defined as

$$\ln[1 + \beta D_{LM}(\beta)] = (1/P)\sum_{t=1}^{n} C_t \ln(1 + \beta t)[1 + b(0, t)]^{-t}, \quad (3.44)$$

and the price change approximating equation is

$$dP/P = -\frac{\ln(1 + \beta D_{LM})}{\beta}d\lambda. \quad (3.45)$$

Bierwag, Kaufman, and Toevs (1983) examined the effectiveness of duration hedging over a given planning period. They compared the performance of immunized portfolios with a simple strategy of holding a portfolio with maturity equal to the planning horizon. Simulating ten-year horizons over 1925 to 1978, they found that, in 86 percent of cases, a simple Macauley duration achieves returns closer to promised returns than the maturity strategy. Duration is therefore much more effective than maturity for immunization.

The Macauley duration was also compared to additive, multiplicative, and log-multiplicative process duration. Somewhat unexpectedly, they reported little difference among duration strategies and concluded that the simplest Macauley duration provides the most cost-effective immunization method. This result, however, is probably due to the averaging of various shapes in term structure over long horizons. There are some environments, such as sharply (upward or downward) sloping yield curves, where the log-multiplicative process duration should perform better because these are environments where short rates are generally more volatile than long rates.

Convexity

Although duration is useful for predicting the effect of interest rate changes on the value of fixed income accounts, it should be regarded as a first-order approximation valid only for small changes in yield. Further precision can be obtained by considering convexity. If duration is set to immunize a portfolio, minimizing convexity will keep the portfolio duration from moving too quickly from its target value.

Definition. Convexity is a second-order effect that describes the way in which duration changes as yield changes. The convexity measure can be obtained by differentiating Equation (3.3) twice with respect to yield and dividing by price:

$$C = \frac{dD^*}{dy} = -\frac{1}{P}\frac{d^2P}{dy^2} = \frac{1}{P}\frac{1}{(1+y)^2}\sum_{t=1}^{T}\frac{t(t+1)C_t}{(1+y)^t}. \tag{3.46}$$

Convexity is measured in periods squared. As before with duration, an annual measure is obtained by dividing convexity by the square of the number of compounding periods m in a year.

To see why convexity may be important, we can approximate a bond rate of return, or relative change in bond price, by a Taylor expansion with two terms:

$$(1/P)dP = (1/P)\frac{dP}{dy}dy + (1/2)P\frac{d^2P}{dy^2}(dy)^2 = -D^*dy + (1/2)C(dy)^2. \tag{3.47}$$

When the changes in yield are small, the convexity term can be ignored. Otherwise, we can rewrite the preceding as $-[D^* - (1/2)Cdy]dy$. This shows that convexity causes duration to increase in response to a decrease in rates and to decrease in response to an increase in rates.

For noncallable bonds, convexity is a positive number, implying that the true price–yield curve lies above the duration line. This effect is considered advantageous because it implies that bond prices rise more than by the linear approximation and decrease less than by the linear approximation.

Exhibit 3.15 presents the actual bond price changes resulting from changes in spot rates. Also displayed are the estimates of those price changes using duration alone and using a combination of duration and convexity. The estimates are graphed in Exhibit 3.16. Duration provides a reasonable estimate of bond price changes when the interest rate changes are small. However, the accuracy of duration in predicting bond price changes is poor for large rate changes. These deviations occur because duration is a linear estimate of a curvilinear relationship. When both duration and convexity are used together, the prediction is far better over a broader spectrum of rate changes.

As for duration, the convexity of a portfolio of fixed income instruments can be derived from a simple weighted average of the compo-

EXHIBIT 3.15   Comparison of Duration and Convexity Approximation

Settlement Date:	October 1, 1990
Maturity Date:	October 1, 2005
Yield:	9.00%
Price:	$1,000
Duration:	10.32564
Convexity:	170.3485

Yield	Change in Yield (bp)	Actual Price ($)	Duration Projected Price ($)	Duration Difference ($)	Duration + Convexity Projected Price ($)	Duration + Convexity Difference ($)
4.00%	−500	1,785.590	1,516.2820	269.3080	1,729.2170	56.3724
5.00%	−400	1,567.246	1,413.0256	154.2204	1,549.3040	17.9416
6.00%	−300	1,385.946	1,309.7692	76.1768	1,386.4260	−0.4800
7.00%	−200	1,234.556	1,206.5128	28.0432	1,240.5820	−6.0265
8.00%	−100	1,107.411	1,103.2564	4.1546	1,111.7730	−4.3628
9.00%	0	1,000.000	1,000.0000	0.0000	1,000.0	0.0000
10.00%	100	908.720	896.7436	11.9764	905.2610	3.4590
11.00%	200	830.685	793.4872	37.1978	827.5569	3.1281
12.00%	300	763.572	690.2308	73.3412	766.8876	−3.3156
13.00%	400	705.572	586.9744	118.5356	723.2532	−17.7430
14.00%	500	654.981	483.7180	171.2630	696.6536	−41.6726
15.00%	600	610.756	380.4616	230.2944	687.0889	−76.3329

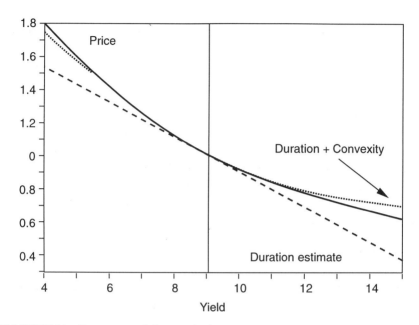

EXHIBIT 3.16 Duration and Convexity Approximations

nents of the portfolio convexity. If x_i is the proportion invested in bond i with convexity C_i, portfolio convexity can be approximated by

$$\text{Portfolio convexity} = \sum_{i=1}^{n} x_i C_i. \qquad (3.48)$$

Factors Affecting Convexity.   In the case of constant coupon payments, a closed-form solution for convexity was derived by Nawalka, Lacey, and Schneeweis (1990) as

$$C = \frac{2c\{(1 + y)^2[(1 + y)^T - 1] - Ty(1 + y)\} + y^2T(T + 1)(y - c)}{[y(1 + y)]^2\{c[(1 + y)^T - 1] + y\}}, \qquad (3.49)$$

where c is the coupon payment as a proportion of the face value, y is the yield to maturity, and T is the maturity. This expression can be simplified in some cases. For instance, the convexity of zero coupon bonds is $T(T + 1)/(1 + y)^2$.

Convexity is increased by a lower coupon, a lower yield level, and longer term. Because convexity is based on measures of squared time, it increases sharply with duration. Even when duration is matched, different portfolios can have very different convexities. "Barbell" port-folios, for instance, composed of bonds with short and long maturities, typically have higher convexity than "bullet" bonds with intermediate maturities.

Consider a bullet portfolio composed of one zero coupon bond with maturity of ten years and a yield of 8 percent. Its duration is 10 years and convexity is 94.31 years-squared. The same duration can be achieved by a portfolio consisting of 50 percent cash, with zero duration, and 50 percent invested in a 20-year bond, with a duration of 20 years and convexity of 360.08 years-squared. The convexity of the barbell portfolio is $0.5 \times 0 + 0.5 \times 360.08 = 180.04$, which is twice that of the 10-year bond.

Is "Benter" Better?   Positive convexity implies that prices increase at a faster rate as yields drop than prices decrease as rates rise. Thus convexity is more desirable when the market perceives interest rate volatility to be high. In theory, bonds with a high convexity should outperform bonds with a low convexity, assuming equal duration and yield. A high-convexity bond duration will increase more in price as rates drop than a bond with low convexity. The same is true when rates rise. As duration drops more for the high-convexity bond, it becomes more defensive, outperforming a low-convexity bond. This is why higher convexity was hailed as "the benter, the better" by Grantier (1988).

It should be recognized, however, that these results hold only under the assumption of parallel shifts in the term structure. To examine the benefits of convexity, Kahn and Lochoff (1990) analyzed returns in the U.S. Treasury market between January 1980 and October 1986. They found that a portfolio of bonds with duration and yield equal to that of the market, but with convexity one standard deviation above that of the market, outperforms only in down markets. According to the theory, the high convexity portfolio should also outperform the market in up markets, but this was not the case. Hence their results call into question the absolute superiority of convexity. When the term structure twists, that is, changes shape instead of simply moving up or down, it may not be optimal to maximize convexity, which is why another measure, called M^2, has been developed.

M²

In the traditional theory of immunization, interest rate risk is eliminated by setting the portfolio duration D equal to the investment horizon

H. When yields can move only in parallel shifts, the portfolio value cannot fall below the target value. With twists in the yield curve, however, immunization can fail. To measure this "immunization risk," Fong and Vasicek (1983b and 1984) developed a model of risk control that accounts for nonparallel shifts in the term structure.

Definition.   Fong and Vasicek demonstrated that the change in the end-of-horizon value of an immunized portfolio $\Delta P(H)$ resulting from an arbitrary change in interest rates is approximated by

$$\Delta P(H)/P(H) = -M^2\Delta_s, \tag{3.50}$$

where Δ_s is the change in the slope of the term structure and

$$M^2 = (1/P)\sum_{t=1}^{T}(t - H)^2C_t/(1 + y)^t. \tag{3.51}$$

M^2 is therefore a weighted average variance around the horizon date of the cash flows generated by the portfolio. Although Δ_s is clearly beyond the control of the investor, M^2 can be controlled. The value of Δ_s can be characterized as the twist in the term structure with M^2 representing the investor's exposure to such twists. M^2 is therefore a measure of risk for the immunized portfolio because it measures the remaining exposure of the portfolio to rate changes.

In the case of constant coupon payments, a closed-form solution for M^2 was derived by Nawalka, Lacey, and Schneeweis (1990) as

$$M^2 = \frac{c[(1 + y)^T - 1]\{(1 + y)[2(1 - Hy) + y] + H^2y^2\}}{cy^2[(1 + y)^T - 1] + y^3},$$

$$+ \frac{Ty[y(y - c)(T - 2H) - 2c(1 + y)] + H^2y^3}{cy^2[(1 + y)^T - 1] + y^3}, \tag{3.52}$$

where c is the coupon payment as a proportion of the face value, y is the yield to maturity, and T is the maturity. When $c = 0$, $M^2 = (T - H)^2$.

M^2 and Convexity. M^2 is always nonnegative and attains its lowest value, zero, for a zero coupon bond with a maturity equal to the length of the horizon. Therefore other portfolios are, to varying degrees, vulnerable to term structure shifts.

It is not difficult to see that a barbell portfolio, for instance, should be more risky than a bullet portfolio. For a 10-year zero coupon bond, for instance, no change in yield can affect the final value because there is no reinvestment risk: the bond is perfectly immunized against any movement in the term structure. In contrast, the barbell portfolio, consisting, for instance, of cash and of a 20-year zero, will sharply decrease in value if short rates decline and long rates increase: the cash will be reinvested at lower rates, and the 20-year zero will be valued at a lower price after 10 years. Therefore, M^2 actually measures how much the portfolio differs from the ideally immunized portfolio composed of a single zero coupon bond.

The relationship between M^2 and convexity now becomes clear. Schnabel (1990), for instance, expanded Equation (3.50) in terms of duration and convexity and found that it can be written as a general form

$$M^2 \approx \text{convexity} - \text{duration}. \qquad (3.53)$$

The danger in maximizing convexity is clear from this equation. For immunized portfolios, maximizing convexity is the same as maximizing M^2. Thus, by maximizing convexity, the investor is also maximizing the exposure to twists in the term structure. Therefore, investors should seek to either maximize convexity or minimize M^2, depending on whether they expect parallel moves or term structure twists, respectively.

Immunization Using Risk and Return. Fong and Vasicek (1983a) extended the traditional immunization strategy as follows. First, they maintained the duration of the portfolio equal to the time horizon H of the investor, thereby immunizing the portfolio against parallel shifts in the term structure. Second, they aimed at an optimal tradeoff between risk and return instead of seeking to minimize the portfolio's vulnerability to arbitrary term structure shifts.

The objective function is

$$\text{Minimize } M^2 - \lambda E(R),$$
$$\text{subject to } D = H, \qquad (3.54)$$

where $E(R)$ is the portfolio expected rate of return and λ is a parameter representing the tradeoff between risk and return. When λ is zero, by (3.53), this is equivalent to minimizing convexity.

This method is quite flexible because it combines risk and return in the same fashion as mean–variance optimization. By varying the parameter λ, it is possible to obtain an efficient frontier for immunized portfolios. This expanded immunization technique incorporates elements of active investment strategies to enhance the target return, yet offers tight control of portfolio risk.

Bonds with Options

Duration and convexity cannot be directly measured for callable bonds and mortgages with prepayment options. In the case of the noncallable bond, the price/yield relationship measures return when the cash flow stream is, by definition, known and certain. Neither maturity or cash flow is certain for callable bonds. Thus duration and convexity cannot be reliably computed.

According to Dunetz and Mahoney (1988), the most effective method of analysis for callable bonds is to use option valuation techniques to characterize the bond duration. The assumption here is that the callable bond can be thought of as consisting of two instruments, a noncallable bond and a short option (held by the issuer) to call the bond according to contractual specifics: $P_C = P_{NC} - \text{call}$. Taking the derivative with respect to the noncallable bond price, we have

$$\frac{dP_C}{dP_{NC}} = 1 - \frac{d\,\text{call}}{dP_{NC}}. \tag{3.55}$$

Since $dP/dy = -P \times D$, where D is the modified duration, the first term is also $(dP_C/dy)/(dP_{NC}/dy) = P_C D_C/P_{NC} D_{NC}$, and the analysis yields the following formulas for duration and convexity:

$$D_C = (P_{NC}/P_C) \times D_{NC}(1 - \delta), \tag{3.56}$$

where

D_C = duration of callable bond,
P_{NC} = price of noncallable bond,
P_C = price of callable bond,
D_{NC} = duration of noncallable bond,
δ = change in the option value for a given change in the price of the underlying, noncallable security.

Convexity is then

$$C_C = (P_{NC}/P_C)[C_{NC}(1 - \delta) - (P_{NC}\gamma)D_{NC}^2], \tag{3.57}$$

where

C_C = convexity of callable bond,
C_{NC} = convexity of noncallable bond,
γ = change in δ for a given change in the
price of the underlying, noncallable security.

When the callable bond carries a coupon much lower than the market yield, it sells at a deep discount because it has a low probability of being called; the option δ is close to zero. As a result, its price, duration, and convexity are very close to those of a noncallable bond. In contrast, a callable bond with a very high coupon sells at a premium, in which case the option δ is close to one and duration is very short.

On the other hand, Winkelmann (1989) believed that duration and convexity provide little insight into the interest rate risk of a callable bond. Here the bondholder is less concerned with small movements in the term structure than with large downward movements that would cause the bond to be called. Exhibit 3.17 displays the price–yield relationship of a typical callable bond. Starting at point A, the bond shows positive convexity for increases in yield (point B), as for regular bonds. As yields fall to point C, bond prices first increase, then may decrease because of the higher probability the bond will be called at par (point D). Thus the relationship between bond prices and yields is initially convex, as for noncallable bonds, then becomes concave as yields fall. Negative convexity plagues callable bonds.

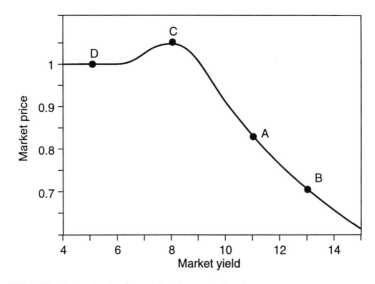

EXHIBIT 3.17   Price–Yield Curve for Callable Bonds

Duration and convexity therefore should be considered local measures of interest rate exposure. Because they may not be valid estimates of exposure for large rate moves, their severe limitations for bonds containing options should not be overlooked.

Factor Models for Bond Returns

The discussion of duration, convexity, and M^2 showed that duration can be considered a good first approximation to the exposure of bonds to movements in yields but that it is harder to control exposure to a second factor. Proper positioning, using either maximum convexity or M^2, requires anticipating the type of movement in the term structure, either parallel or twisted. Given that the main objective of risk management is to control portfolio risk without necessarily forecasting changes in risk factors, this requirement appears unsatisfactory. Instead, another approach, called the *arbitrage pricing theory* (APT), based on factor models, can be applied to bond returns.

The idea is to try to explain bond returns by a small number of pervasive factors. Assuming a linear K-factor model, returns on bond i can be written as

$$\tilde{r}_i = E_i + \beta_{i1}\tilde{\delta}_1 + \beta_{i2}\tilde{\delta}_2 + \ldots + \beta_{iK}\tilde{\delta}_K + \tilde{\epsilon}_i, \qquad (3.58)$$

where $\tilde{\delta}_K$ is the unexpected component on factor K, E_i is the expected return on bond i, β_{iK} is the beta – or loading – on factor K, and $\tilde{\epsilon}_i$ is an error term. Note that this approach is similar in philosophy to the "arbitrage pricing theory," developed primarily for pricing stocks, that also postulates a factor model then derives the implications for expected returns.

Although this example assumed that the factors are observable, one could also derive unobservable factors, given a sufficiently large sample of assets, through a statistical technique called *factor analysis*. The factors can then be given an economic interpretation after proper transformation. Litterman and Scheinkman (1988) examined a three-factor model for the U.S. Treasury bond market and found that the model fits the data quite well: it explains a minimum of 96 percent of the variability of excess returns. Exhibit 3.18 displays the impact of each of these factors on the yield curve, measured as a function of maturity.

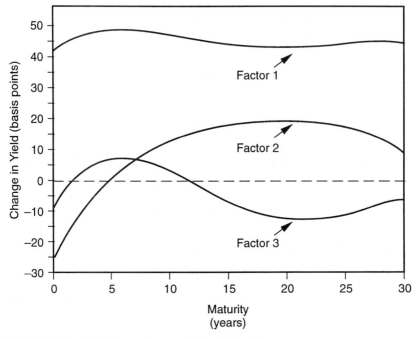

EXHIBIT 3.18   Yield Curve Impact of Bond Factors

EXHIBIT 3.19   Relative Importance of Factors

Maturity	Total Variance Explained	Proportion of Variance Explained by		
		Factor 1	Factor 2	Factor 3
6 months	99.5	79.5	17.2	3.3
1 year	99.4	89.7	10.1	0.2
2 years	98.2	93.4	2.4	4.2
5 years	98.8	98.2	1.1	0.7
8 years	98.7	95.4	4.6	0.0
10 years	98.8	92.9	6.9	0.2
14 years	98.4	86.2	11.5	2.2
18 years	95.3	80.5	14.3	5.2
Average	98.4	89.5	8.5	2.0

Because the first factor affects all maturities about equally, it is called a *level* factor. Factor 2 shows that a shock lowers the yields up to five years and increases yields for longer maturities; hence, it is termed a *steepness* factor. The third factor, called *curvature,* increases the curvature of the yield curve in the range of maturities below 20 years.

Exhibit 3.19 uses a variance decomposition of Equation (3.58) to show the relative importance of the three factors. The level factor is by far the most important and explains about 89.5 percent of total variance. The exposure to this factor can be interpreted as duration. Thus duration hedging provides a good, first-order, hedging tool. Factor 2, steepness, explains about 8.5 percent of the total variance, which is 81 percent of the remaining variance; this represents the twists in the yield curve.

Suppose a bond portfolio has the following sensitivities. Realized factor returns, scaled by their standard deviation, are described for a given week.

Factor	Sensitivity	Factor Movement	Gain/Loss
I (Level)	−$84,010	−1.482	+$124,503
2 (Steepness)	$6,510	−2.487	−$ 16,191
3 (Curvature)	−$444,950	+1.453	−$646,512
Net			−$538,200

Over this week, rates came down sharply, the yield curve became flatter (less steep), and the curvature increased. Because the portfolio had a negative exposure to the first factor, equivalent to a slightly positive duration, it gained from the down move in rates. However, this gain was more than offset by the additional curvature, which led to a net loss of $538,200. The example given here is a particularly severe case, where duration was ineffective in controlling risk, but it still illustrates a real-life situation where movements in the yield curve would have created serious losses for a manager focusing on duration hedging.

Knowledge of the driving factors, as well as of the factor loadings for candidate bonds, can be used for tight control of portfolio risk. For instance, the portfolio can be structured so that the net exposure to the three factors is very small. This will considerably improve upon duration hedging and yet require no forecast of future twists in the yield curve.

Conclusions

Duration is an essential tool in the management of fixed income assets or liabilities because it provides a convenient, closed-form measure of the exposure of bonds to changes in interest rates. In particular, duration can be used to immunize a portfolio against interest rate risk. Immunization refers to the need to guarantee a minimum rate of return over a planning horizon. This happens, for instance, when pension funds need to make nominal payments from a defined benefits plan or when insurance companies sell guaranteed investment contracts, where a fixed payout is promised at some future date. For banking institutions, duration gap analysis is a valuable technique for managing assets and liabilities.

Although duration is a useful first-order measure of exposure, it is exact only under the restrictive assumptions of small, parallel, and instantaneous movements in the term structure. This is why additional measures, called *convexity*, M^2, are also widely used.

A more general approach to controlling risk in bond portfolios is to create a factor model, which includes duration hedging as a special case. Such methods are particularly successful at explaining bond returns and are currently used by leading investment banks to control the total risk of their aggregate bond portfolios.

References

Bierwag, G. O. 1987. *Duration Analysis: Managing Interest Rate Risk*, Ballinger Publishing Company, Cambridge, Mass.

——, and G. G. Kaufman. 1985. "Duration gap for financial institutions," *Financial Analysts Journal:* 68–71.

——, G. G. Kaufman, R. Schweitzer, and A. Toevs. 1981. "The art of risk management in bond portfolios," *Journal of Portfolio Management:* 27–36.

——, G. G. Kaufman, and A. Toevs. 1983. "Duration: Its development and use in bond portfolio management," *Financial Analysts Journal:* 15–35.

Chance, D. M. 1990. "Default risk and the duration of zero coupon bonds," *Journal of Finance:* 265–74.

Cox, J., J. Ingersoll, and S. Ross. 1979. "Duration and measurement of basis risk," *Journal of Business*.

Dunetz, M. L., and J. M. Mahoney. 1988. "Using duration and convexity in the analysis of callable bonds," *Financial Analysts Journal:* 53–72.

Fisher, L., and R. Weil. 1971. "Coping with risk of interest rate fluctuations: Returns to bondholders from naive and optimal strategies," *Journal of Business:* 408–431.

Fong, H. G., and O. A. Vasicek. 1983a. "The tradeoff between return and risk in immunized portfolios," *Financial Analysts Journal:* 73–78.

———. 1983b. "Return maximization for immunized portfolios," in *Innovations in Bond Portfolio Management*, ed. G. Kaufman, G. Bierwag, and A. Toevs, JAI Press, Greenwich, Conn.

———. 1984. "A risk minimizing strategy for portfolio immunization," *Journal of Finance:* 1541–46.

Gardner, M. J., and D. L. Mills. 1988. *Managing Financial Institutions: An Asset/Liability Approach,* The Dryden Press, Chicago.

Grantier, B. J. 1988. "Convexity and bond performance: The benter the better," *Financial Analysts Journal:* 79–81.

Kahn, R. N., and R. Lochoff. 1990. "Convexity and exceptional return," *Journal of Portfolio Management:* 43–47.

Kaufman, G. G. 1984. "Measuring and managing interest rate risk: A primer," *Economics Perspectives*, Federal Reserve Bank of Chicago: 16–29.

Khang, C. 1979. "Bond immunization when short-term rates fluctuate more than long-term rates," *Journal of Financial and Quantitative Analysis:* 1035–40.

Little, P. K. 1986. "Financial futures and immunization," *Journal of Financial Research:* 1–12.

Litterman, R., and J. Scheinkman. 1988. "Common factors affecting bond returns," *Goldman Sachs Financial Strategies.*

McEnally, R. W. 1980. "How to neutralize reinvestment rate risk," *Journal of Portfolio Management:* 59–63.

Nawalkha, S. K., and N. J. Lacey. 1988. "Closed-form solutions of higher-order duration measures," *Financial Analysts Journal:* 82–4.

———, and T. Schneeweis. 1990. "Closed-form solutions of convexity and M-square," *Financial Analysts Journal:* 75–7.

Reilly, F. K., and R. S. Sidhu. 1980. "The many uses of bond duration," *Financial Analysts Journal:* 58–72.

Schnabel, J. A. 1990. "Is benter better? A cautionary note on maximizing convexity," *Financial Analysts Journal:* 78–79.

Toevs, A. 1983. "Gap management: Managing interest rate risk in banks and thrifts," *Economic Review*, Federal Reserve Bank of San Francisco: 20–35.

———, and W. C. Haney. 1986. "Measuring and managing interest rate risk: A guide to asset/liability models used in banks and thrifts," in *Controlling Interest Rate Risk*, ed. R. B. Platt, John Wiley & Sons, New York, 256–350.

Winkelmann, K. 1989. "Uses and abuses of duration," *Financial Analysts Journal:* 72–5.

Yawitz, J. B., and W. J. Marshall. 1981. "The shortcomings of duration as a risk measure for bonds," *Journal of Financial Research:* 91–101.

4

The Foreign Exchange Markets: Nature and Dynamics

The foreign exchange markets are global and continuous. They consist of the spot, forward, options, futures, and swap markets, each with its own contract characteristics, risk/return tradeoff, and suitability for the client's needs. What is commonly referred to as the *Forex markets* is by far the largest financial market in the world. Daily turnover was estimated to be about $900 billion in 1992, up from only $200 billion in 1986. This impressive increase is expected to continue, albeit at a slower rate, as financial markets continue to integrate, as world trade continues to rise, and as cross-border investments (both portfolio and direct) continue to mount.

Understanding investment opportunities in global financial markets cannot be achieved without a thorough understanding of the foreign exchange markets. These are simple and complex markets, promising and deceiving, vast and very narrow. The Forex markets present ample opportunities for risk bearing and risk shifting.

They represent a haven and a burial ground for speculators. An excellent information set and a superb sense of timing are indispensable tools for successful speculators. To control and take advantage of currency risk, it is essential to have a firm understanding of the international financial system. This chapter therefore provides an overview of the foreign exchange market and the economics of exchange rates. The first section reviews the recent history of the international financial system; an application to monetary convergence in Europe is covered next. The third section covers trading in the foreign exchange markets. The fourth section provides an overview of the major forces driving exchange rates, both in the long run and in the short run. The objective of this chapter is to provide a solid foundation for understanding the foreign exchange markets and using this knowledge as a basis for the more advanced analysis in the chapters to follow.

The International Financial System

A primary function of the international financial system is to provide a framework for the determination of the relative value of a currency. However, no international financial system ever devised had universal acceptance and steady success. In fact, one can argue that the present system is the result of compromises that left both advocates and antagonists dissatisfied. The current system, technically referred to as the *floating exchange rate regime*, is neither really floating nor a regime with disciplined adherents. Under this checkered umbrella lie various systems of currency value determination. We now briefly review the precursors to the present system.

The Gold Standard

The oldest of currency systems is the *gold standard*. This system has gone through a metamorphosis. It evolved from the gold-coin standard, where the actual currency was minted gold, which was in use in the earliest periods in history.

The gold-bullion standard followed. Here paper money was issued against gold deposits. Currencies could be fully exchanged for gold bullion. Each currency value was fixed in terms of gold and consequently in terms of other currencies. Externally, the country's currency was freely convertible to gold at a fixed ratio, and internally it was (fully or partially) backed by gold. Because each currency had a "par value" in terms of gold, it also had a par value in terms of all other currencies. If, for example, the British pound was valued at 1/4 of an ounce of gold, and the U.S. dollar at 1/20 of an ounce of gold, the par value of the pound would, therefore, be $5.

Under this system, these relative values, the exchange rates, were expected to remain constant. Some fluctuation of the exchange rates was possible, but with narrow limits around the par value. These limits were set by the cost of transferring gold. We can illustrate the permissible fluctuation in terms of shipping costs, though, in practice, very little gold was actually transferred physically: most of the world's reserves were kept in vaults in London and Fort Knox, and bookkeeping transactions were sufficient to change ownership. Let us suppose that the shipping cost of gold is 20 cents per ounce and that the par values of the dollar and the pound are 1/20 ounce and 1/4 ounce of gold, respectively, giving a par exchange rate of £1 = $5. If for any reason the market exchange rate for the pound rose to $5.12 in London, a currency trader could

1. Buy 1 oz. of gold in the United States for $20;
2. Ship this to London;
3. Sell the gold to the British central bank for £4.00;
4. Convert £4 into dollars at $5.12 per £, and obtain $20.48;
5. Make a net profit of $0.28 after paying shipping costs.

This process, known as *arbitrage*, involves selling the pound. Selling the pound will tend to bring the market value of the pound down to $5.05 per pound, (the limits being known as the gold import point and the gold export point), without any active steps by the monetary authorities. When the price of gold tends to exceed the limits, central banks are supposed to step in and buy and sell any amount of gold at par value.

Adjustments under the Gold Standard

Departures from the "range" were supposed to be strictly temporary under the gold standard. This is because, as we now illustrate, the system provides automatic adjustment mechanisms to return to equilibrium.

The most important of these is the *price–species flow* mechanism. This approach relies on the quantity theory of money, which postulates a relationship between M, the nominal money supply; q, total output; P, the nominal price level; and v, the velocity of money:

$$Mv = Pq.$$

The economic content of this theory is that the velocity of money is stable and output is fixed in the short run, so that changes in the money supply are proportionally reflected in changes in the price level.

Imagine now a world made up of two countries: the United States and Germany. Imagine also a fixed supply of gold divided (not necessarily equally) between the two countries. Each of the two countries has a comparative advantage in a basket of goods that it exports to the other country. Both countries agree to adhere to the gold standard.

Exhibit 4.1 presents the demand and supply for the foreign currency, which jointly determine the exchange rate. Here, the spot exchange rate is defined as the dollar price of the foreign currency and is measured in dollars per units of the foreign currency ($/FC$). The private demand curve for foreign currency is downward sloping because a higher quantity of foreign currency is demanded at a lower price. The supply curve is upward sloping.

Initially, the parity value of the spot rate is set at S_0, which is such that the private demand for the foreign currency exactly matches the private supply. For both countries, total exports equal total imports and the balance of trade (BOT) is in equilibrium.

Suppose now that the parity value is set at S_1, which is below the previous equilibrium level. At this price, the demand for the foreign currency, represented by the horizontal amount OA', exceeds the supply OA. The excess demand can arise, for instance, from the fact that a lower price for the foreign currency decreases the dollar price of foreign goods, which increases the demand for foreign goods.

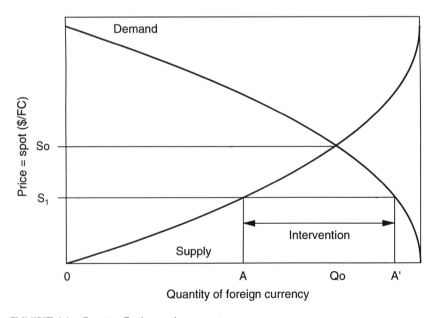

EXHIBIT 4.1   Foreign Exchange Intervention

Because the value of German imports exceeds that of U.S. exports, the U.S. balance of trade turns into a deficit.

To artificially maintain the spot rate at this level, the U.S. central bank must sell the foreign currency in exchange for dollars, in the amount of AA'. Under the gold standard, intervention was achieved by transfers of gold between central banks. Thus there is an outflow of gold from the United States to Germany. Because gold is a reserve asset, this leads to a fall in the U.S. money supply and an increase in the German money supply.

In effect, the BOT deficit means that Germany will have a net receipt of gold as U.S. nationals must pay with gold for their excess consumption; that is, they must use their national savings as they elect to live beyond their current means. This is analogous to consumers who wish to consume beyond their current income level and are therefore required to tap their savings.

Through the quantity theory of money, the decrease in M^{US}, and increase in M^{G}, leads to an decrease in the price of U.S. goods relative to the prices of German goods. U.S. goods become more competitive on world markets, and as a result, U.S. consumers buy fewer German goods, while German consumers buy more of the cheaper U.S. goods. This reduces the U.S. BOT deficit. The resulting leftward shift in the demand for foreign currency, along with the rightward shift in the supply of foreign currency, continues until the equilibrium spot rate becomes the parity rate set by the central banks. Alternatively, the adjustment mechanism can occur through changes in income, whereby, for instance, the decrease in the U.S. money supply reduces U.S. income, which decreases the demand for German imports. Changes in income have stabilizing effects on the trade balance and provide an alternative adjustment mechanism to the price–species flow approach. This obviously assumes that free trade continues and neither of the two governments cheats on the gold standard.

The gold standard was successful in automatic stabilization of exchange rates, but it suffered from two shortcomings. First, it made the world's money supply entirely dependent on the availability of gold, without any means to adjust it in accordance with economic conditions. Second, if wages and prices could not be reduced, a country reducing its money supply in response to an outflow of gold would run into a recession: instead of prices falling, employment and output would fall. Although this would bring about a reduction in the external deficit (because reduced income leads to reduced consumption of all goods, including imports), the cost of such an adjustment may not be considered acceptable. The gold standard was suspended in 1914, when, with the outbreak of World War I, controls were imposed on international transactions.

The Interwar Period, 1918–1939

For a period of five years after the end of World War I, international currency rates were allowed to fluctuate, as a temporary measure, until the world economy stabilized. After that, the major countries returned to fixed exchange rates, in the hope that the gold standard could be restored. However, the British attempt to restore the prewar parity between the pound and the dollar led to disastrous consequences. Given the changes in the fundamental economic position of Britain and the United States, the prewar rate of $4.8665 per pound was unrealistically high. Although Winston Churchill, the then chancellor of the Exchequer, regarded restoration of the prewar parity rate as a matter of national prestige, the overvaluation of the pound led to a loss of export markets and economic stagnation, because institutional factors did not permit sufficient reduction in domestic prices. In fact, the overvalued pound led to massive unemployment in Britain in the 1920s, before the worldwide depression of the 1930s.

The great depression of the 1930s led to the end of the gold standard, as the world went through a wave of devaluations. Countries attempted to export their unemployment through "beggar thy neighbor" policies, including exchange controls and competitive devaluation, and foreign exchange markets were extremely disorderly. With the onset of World War II in 1939, of course, most foreign transactions were subjected to strict controls and ordinary commercial activities were displaced by intergovernmental arrangements.

The Bretton Woods System

At the end of World War II, a new international monetary system was set up. The gold standard was recognized as too rigid, particularly in the provisions requiring monetary contraction by deficit countries, which led to unemployment. At the same time, new rules of the game were considered necessary to avoid the chaos of the 1930s. An international meeting in 1944 at Bretton Woods, New Hampshire, led to the adoption of a new international order. There were three cornerstones of the Bretton Woods agreement:

1. The foreign exchange markets were considered too important to be left to the forces of supply and demand. Government must be in control.
2. The U.S. dollar was to be pegged to gold, and all the other currencies pegged to the dollar. Only the U.S. dollar was convertible to gold at $35 per ounce. This was adopted in view of the fact that, after the war, few countries had enough gold to sustain a gold-exchange standard. Intervention in the foreign exchange markets was mandatory if the U.S. dollar value of a currency fluctuated by more than the permitted 1 percent around the par value – the pegged value in terms of the U.S. dollar.
3. The International Monetary Fund (IMF) was set up as an agency to monitor the foreign exchange markets and the extent of the adherence of member countries to the agreement.

The IMF also had the responsibility to help finance the intervention by member countries in the Forex markets and supervise necessary structural adjustments. Each member country provided a quota of capital to the IMF as a condition for membership. The size of the quota was initially computed from a complex formula involving the country's GNP and trade. Initially, the quota was paid 25 percent in gold and 75 percent in domestic currency. Later payments were to be made in major currencies instead of gold. The vast resources of the IMF were to be used "to promote exchange stability, to maintain orderly exchange arrangements among members, and to avoid competitive exchange depreciation." As of December 1992, 175 countries were members of the IMF.

A country with a short-term deficit in its balance of payments could borrow from the IMF to finance this deficit; the charges for such drawings were lower than market interest rates but rose with the duration of the borrowing. It should be noted that a country's international reserves, which are meant to meet short-term deficits, may not be adequate. To avoid resorting to deflationary policies – or devaluation or exchange controls – the IMF in effect created a line of credit for member countries. To some extent, the borrowing privilege was automatic – up to the "gold tranche," or 25 percent of a country's quota. Further borrowing usually involved some conditions, generally policy measures designed to eliminate the cause of the deficit. The *conditionality* principle reflected the idea that financing and adjustment must go together, since the IMF, with its objective of providing temporary balance of payments support, could not indefinitely finance deficits.

Adjustment, often involving contractionary fiscal and monetary policies, was necessary to correct the causes of the deficits. The conditions attached to loans have been criticized as penalizing countries for past shortcomings, but the IMF viewed them as essential to ensuring that its resources were used in ways that would strengthen the borrower's balance of payments. If the deficit was felt to be of a long-term nature, caused by "fundamental disequilibrium," the IMF would suggest devaluation. Similarly, countries with long-term surpluses were encouraged to revalue their currencies, but there were fewer cases of this kind.

Problems of the 1960s

The dollar-exchange standard just described performed very well during the 1940s and 1950s. Strains began to appear in the later 1960s, in large part because the dollar reigned supreme as the currency of choice for international transactions and holding reserves. The growth of world trade was thus largely dependent on U.S. balance of payments deficits, which were the only way in which the rest of the world could accumulate dollars. These deficits, however, were certainly not intended for that purpose, and their size was not even predictable.

The coverage of outstanding U.S. dollars in terms of gold was also declining over time, and as a result, many countries came to question the ability of the United States to convert dollars to gold on demand. Countries began to convert their dollars to gold, further reducing the ratio of gold to dollars, which led to a further erosion of confidence. The run on the dollar became so severe in 1968 that the United States suspended convertibility for private parties. A two-tier market for gold was established, with the official market – used for transactions between governments – valuing gold at $35 per ounce and a completely separate private market setting the price of gold by forces of supply and demand. For a while, this appeared to solve the confidence problem.

In spite of these measures, it became increasingly evident that the exchange rates between the major currencies were out of alignment, and no agreement emerged to ease the burden of adjustment. The United States wanted Japan and a number of Western European countries to revalue, while these countries wanted the United States to devalue relative to gold. Finally, on August 15, 1971, as part of the "New Economic Policy," which imposed peacetime price and wage controls for the first time in America, President Nixon cut off the link between the dollar and gold, abrogating the American commitment to convert dollars to gold at $35 an ounce. This cut the linkage of the dollar to any real commodity and placed price stability entirely in the hand of governments.

The Dirty Float

After being closed for a short period to digest this shock, currency markets opened to a new world of floating exchange rates. The dollar (and other currencies) in effect abandoned the old parities and floated freely for four months. In December 1971, the Smithsonian Agreement attempted to restore fixed rates, with new par values. The Japanese yen was revalued 8.5 percent and the German mark was revalued 5 percent with respect to gold. The dollar was devalued by 8.5 percent with respect to gold, the official valuation now being $38 per ounce of gold. However, the dollar remained inconvertible to gold. The parties to the Smithsonian Agreement agreed to try to support the new rates, but with bands wider than the 1 percent allowed under the Bretton Woods system. Fluctuations of up to 2.25 percent on either side of a currency's "central rate" against the dollar were now allowed. The United States continued to be passive in foreign exchange markets, leaving it to other countries to stabilize their currencies against the dollar.

The Smithsonian Agreement – an attempt to prop up the Bretton Woods system – lasted less than a year and a half. In early 1973, as the U.S. balance of payments deteriorated, there was a massive flight into deutsche marks and Swiss francs. In February 1973, the dollar was devalued another 10 percent; that is, the official price of gold was now $42 per ounce instead of $38. In March 1973, the major countries gave up the idea of trying to stay within the Smithsonian tunnel, and currencies were allowed to fluctuate in response to forces of supply and demand. After a considerable delay, this was "legitimized" by the IMF in 1978, when all original par values were abrogated. The system of floating exchange rates was thus borne, albeit with a major deformity: immediately after the floating rate system was announced, the United States was intervening in the spot market to "stabilize" the dollar.

The current situation is one of exchange rates of the major currencies fluctuating on a day-to-day basis, yet not floating with complete freedom. Governments do intervene from time to time. As we will discuss later, most of the major European currencies are in a managed, rather than a free, float. The U.S. government has also periodically engaged in attempts to stabilize currencies by intervening in the foreign exchange market. For instance, the unprecedented rise in the dollar over 1983–5 forced industrialized nations to sign the Plaza Agreement on September 20, 1985, which led to a coordinated attack on the dollar. Because of such intervention, the current situation is often characterized as a "managed" or "dirty" float.

Nowadays, many currencies are pegged to other currencies, mainly the U.S. dollar, or to currency baskets (a collection of currencies). Exhibit 4.2 breaks down the existing exchange rate systems into different types of arrangements.

Monetary Convergence in Europe

The European Monetary System (EMS) was seen from its inception as a foundation for the eventual economic and political unification of Europe. It was proposed by Helmut Schmidt during the 1978 meeting of the European Economic Community in Copenhagen. The EMS was established on March 13, 1979, to create a zone of "monetary stability" among member countries. It was a natural continuation of the 1958 Treaty of Rome, which formally established a customs union among EEC countries and led the European Community toward economic and political integration in Western Europe.

The EMS was created as a system of fixed but adjustable exchange rates, initially among the Belgian/Luxembourg franc, the Danish krone, the French franc, the German mark, the Irish punt, the Italian lira, and the Netherlands guilder. Together, these currencies are allowed to "float" against the dollar.

The EMS was also envisioned to be a mechanism for the imposition of monetary discipline on member countries. Any divergence from "average behavior" required intervention by the monetary authorities. That is, if the European Community average is moderate inflation, countries with too high (or too low) inflation would have to change their monetary policy to conform to the norm.

EXHIBIT 4.2   Exchange Rate Arrangements (December 1992)

	Currency Pegged to						Flexibility Limited in Terms of a Single Currency or Group of Currencies		More Flexible		
U.S. dollar	French franc	Russian ruble	Other currency	SDR	Other composite		Single currency	Cooperative arrangements	Adjusted according to a set of indicators	Other managed floating	Independence floating
Angola	Benin	Armenia	Bhutan (Indian rupee)	Iran, I.R. of	Algeria		Bahrain	Belgium	Chile	China, P.R.	Afghanistan
Antigua & Barbuda	Burkina Faso	Azerbaijan	Estonia (deutsche mark)	Libya	Austria		Qatar	Denmark	Colombia	Ecuador	Albania
Argentina	Cameroon	Belarus	Kiribati (Australian dollar)	Myanmar	Bangladesh		Saudi Arabia	France	Madagascar	Egypt	Australia
Bahamas, The	C. African Rep.	Georgia	Lesotho (South African rand)	Rwanda	Botswana		United Arab Emirates	Germany		Greece	Bolivia
Barbados	Chad	Kyrgyzstan	Namibia (South African rand)	Seychelles	Burundi			Ireland		Guinea	Brazil
Belize	Comoros	Moldova			Cape Verde			Luxembourg		Guinea-Bissau	Bulgaria
Djibouti	Congo				Cyprus			Netherlands		India	Canada
Dominica	Cote d'Ivoire				Czechoslovakia			Portugal		Indonesia	Costa Rica
Ethiopia	Equatorial Guinea				Fiji			Spain		Israel	Dominican Rep.
Grenada	Gabon				Hungary					Korea	El Salvador
Iraq	Mali				Iceland					Lao P.D. Rep.	Finland
Liberia	Niger				Jordan					Maldives	Gambia, The
Marshall Islands	Senegal				Kenya					Mexico	Ghana
Mongolia	Togo				Kuwait					Pakistan	Guatemala
Nicaragua					Malawi					Poland	Guyana
Oman					Malaysia					Sao Tome & Principe	Haiti
					Malta					Singapore	Honduras
										Somalia	Italy
										Sri Lanka	Jamaica
										Tunisia	Japan
											Latvia
											Lebanon

EXHIBIT 4.2 Exchange Rate Arrangements (December 1992) Continued

| Currency Pegged to | | | | | | Flexibility Limited in Terms of a Single Currency or Group of Currencies | | More Flexible | | |
U.S. dollar	French franc	Russian ruble	Other currency	SDR	Other composite	Single currency	Cooperative arrangements	Adjusted according to a set of indicators	Other managed floating	Independence floating
Panama			Swaziland (South African rand)	Mauritania	Papua New Guinea				Turkey	Lithuania
St. Kitts & Nevis				Mauritius	Guinea				Uruguay	Mozambique
St. Lucia				Morocco	Solomon Islands				Viet Nam	New Zealand
St. Vincent and the				Nepal	Islands					Nigeria
Grenadines					Tanzania					Norway
Suriname					Thailand					Paraguay
Syrian Arab Rep.					Tonga					Peru
Trinidad and					Vanuatu					Philippines
Tobago					Western					Romania
Yemen, Republic of					Samoa					Russia
					Zimbabwe					Sierra Leone
										South Africa
										Sudan
										Sweden
										Switzerland
										Uganda
										Ukraine
										United Kingdom
										United States
										Venezuela
										Zaire
										Zambia

Source: International Monetary Fund, 1992.

A critical component of the EMS is the *exchange rate mechanism* (ERM), which is reflected in a parity grid. This grid sets upper and lower limits for each pair of currencies. The range is 2.25 percent (6 percent for some currencies) above and 2.25 percent below the par value of the currency – the par value is fundamentally set against the ECU, which is a basket of currencies. All par values defined in terms of ECU are referred to as *central rates*. Given the central rates, one can calculate bilateral par values, the value of one currency against all other member currencies.

Countries whose currency value is at or close to the permissible limits must intervene. Intervention occurs directly in the foreign exchange market or in the money markets by altering interest rates. Intervention funds in the Forex markets are provided by the European Monetary Fund, the European equivalent of the IMF. The interesting feature of the Forex intervention, especially when compared with that under the Bretton Woods agreement, is that it is a no-fault intervention. Both countries, the one with the appreciating currency and the other with the depreciating currency, must intervene to bring the currency in line with the parity grid. If the DM appreciates against the French franc beyond the allowable limit, the French would have to buy the FF and the Bundesbank would have to sell DM. This rigid system allows the EMS members to avoid the problems experienced under the Bretton Woods mandated system, where a high-inflation country with sufficient political clout was allowed to systematically abuse the system.

The ECU

The *European currency unit* (ECU) serves as a benchmark for the ERM. The ECU operates as a basket of EEC currencies. Currency amounts in the ECU are set by the EC commission. The formal position of the European Community is that the composition of the ECU must be reconsidered every five years or in the unlikely event that the weight of a currency changes by more than 25 percent. In practice, redefinitions have been kept as infrequent as possible.

The ECU basket is constructed as the sum of a specific number of units of European currencies. The spot rate between the ECU and the dollar can be derived as follows: define x_i as the number of units of currency i in the ECU (FC_i), S_{it} as the base currency price of currency i at time t ($\$/FC_i$), and S_t^* as the base currency price of the ECU.

Because the ECU can be purchased either directly or through its individual components, the ECU spot rate should be

$$S_t^* = \sum_{i=1}^{N} x_i S_{it}. \qquad (4.1)$$

The weight of currency i in the ECU is derived as $w_{it} = x_i S_{it}/(\Sigma_i x_i S_{it})$ and can fluctuate over time with exchange rates. Exhibit 4.3 presents the composition of the ECU and percentage weights for different points in time. During the period 1979–89, there were two changes in the definition of the ECU. Each time, the number of currency units x_i was changed for all currencies so as to leave the external value of the ECU S_t^* unaffected.

The ECU replaced the European unit of account in 1979 and functions as the numeraire for the exchange rate mechanism, as the integral tool in the intervention and transfer of resources between the EMS monetary authorities, and as the basis for the divergence indicator. The divergence indicator indicates the extent to which a currency is out of step with other EMS currencies and is regularly published, for instance, in the *Financial Times* of London. If the Belgian franc is weak against the French franc and both Belgium and France are intervening in the Forex markets to shore up its value and keep it

EXHIBIT 4.3   Composition of the ECU

	National Currency Units			Percentage Weights				
	Mar 13 1979	Sep 14 1984	Sep 21 1989	Mar 13 1979	Sep 14 1984	Sep 17 1984	Sep 20 1989	Sep 21 1989
Deutsche mark	.828	.719	.6242	33.0	36.9	32.0	34.7	30.1
French franc	1.15	1.31	1.332	19.8	16.7	19.0	18.7	19.0
Pound sterling	.0885	.0878	.08784	13.3	15.1	15.0	13.0	13.0
Netherlands guilder	.286	.256	.2198	10.5	11.3	10.1	11.0	9.4
Italian lira	109.000	140.0	151.8	9.5	7.9	10.2	9.4	10.2
Belgian-Lux. franc	3.800	3.85	3.431	9.7	8.4	8.5	8.9	7.9
Danish krone	.217	.219	.1976	3.1	2.7	2.7	2.7	2.5
Irish pound	.00759	.00871	.008552	1.1	1.0	1.2	1.1	1.1
Greek drachma	—	1.15	1.440	—	—	1.3	0.6	0.8
Spanish peseta	—	—	6.885	—	—	—	—	5.3
Portuguese escudo	—	—	1.393	—	—	—	—	0.8

within the parity grid, the divergence indicator would point out the basic reason for the weakness of the Belgian franc. That is, it pinpoints that country which has diverged from the norm and compels it to take the appropriate fiscal and monetary adjustments to bring itself in line with the norm.

The ECU has an official side and a private side. Before venturing into the latter, let us say a few words about how ECUs are acquired by members of the EMS. Member countries put up 20 percent of their reserves (dollars, gold, etc.) and are issued ECUs. The ECUs, once again, are bookkeeping entries. Once acquired, ECUs may be used for official settlements between central banks and could be "converted" into reserve currencies. A member could also borrow foreign exchange from the fund in order to intervene in the Forex markets.

The ECU is also used to denominate transactions or assets in the private sector. In the Eurobond market, ECU-denominated bonds are fifth in rank in terms of volume, after the dollar-, pound-, yen-, and mark-denominated bonds. The ECU is viewed as an excellent diversification tool as it incorporates 12 European currencies and excludes the U.S. dollar.

Some companies nowadays are using ECUs for intracompany settlement. Other uses were reported in the January 13, 1990, issue of *The Economist*:

> The international airline cartel, IATA, now lets airlines settle with each other in ECU's, as well as in dollars and sterling. Iberia, Air France, Lufthansa and KLM are all likely to switch from the dollar to the ECU when the accounting procedures are in place. Many joint ventures between West and East European firms are denominated in ECU's. Italy's Fiat has just invested 1.2 billion ECU's ($1.4 billion) in a car factory in the Soviet Union, which will operate in an ECU enclave – all purchases and exports will be denominated in ECU's. The Australian wheat board denominates wheat contracts in the ECU. Even South American countries are accepting trade in ECU's, to reduce their exposure to the dollar.

European Monetary Union

Proponents of the ECU hope that it will eventually become the basis for a common European currency, with the same status as the dollar. A common ECU currency would become a dramatic step forward toward European economic integration. Parity values are now changed frequently. Twelve realignments have taken place between

1979 and 1990, and three more have occurred in the turmoil of Fall 1992, when the British pound and Italian lira went off the system. Full monetary integration would mean that these exchange rates would become permanently fixed and therefore central banks would have to relinquish their authority to one supranational central bank, which some central bankers are loath to accept. On the other hand, full monetary union would completely eliminate exchange rate risk and probably bring substantial benefits to Europe.

The story is sometimes told of an intrepid traveler who goes from one EEC country to another and exchanges an initial dollar from one currency to each next successive currency. After paying bank fees and commissions, he ends up with only 50 cents. Because a common currency would eliminate these transaction costs, the estimated savings are on the order of 16 billion ECU annually, or $20 billion. In addition, by enhancing price transparency, a common currency would also increase competition and substantially benefit consumers.

On the other hand, skeptics point to the well-known arguments in favor of flexible exchange rates, advanced as early as 1953 by Friedman.[1] In addition to the one-time costs of converting to a common currency, a fixed exchange rate system does not allow countries to adjust easily to external shocks, such as sudden change in oil or export prices. With flexible exchange rates, an economy such as Norway, for instance, that relies heavily on oil exports could easily depreciate its currency to compensate for the lost revenues from a sudden fall in oil prices. This is why a fixed exchange rate system, such as the one between U.S. states, works best when the economies of member countries are either diversified or are similar in terms of production. In addition, U.S. fiscal policies provide an automatic adjustment within the United States: states in recession provide less federal income taxes and receive more in federal funds, which smooths out the effect of transitory shocks. Finally, labor is relatively mobile among U.S. states, which again offsets the higher unemployment rate in some regions. Because of the lack of common fiscal policy as well as low labor mobility within Europe, some argue that a system of permanently fixed exchange rates in Europe is inappropriate and too costly.

Advocates of the European Monetary Union (EMU), EMU retort that these problems are outweighed by the reduction in business

---

[1]See, for instance, the case against EMU made by Feldstein in the June 13, 1992, issue of *The Economist*, and the reply from pro-EMU economists on July 4.

uncertainty and the benefits of bringing low inflation throughout Europe. The European Central Bank will have price stability as its sole objective and, therefore, should be as successful as the Bundesbank in maintaining low inflation. In addition, economic union should bring about more mobility in capital and labor, as well as the type of smoothing fiscal policies occurring in the United States. But the clinching argument, political and therefore more difficult to objectively assess, is that close cooperation between European countries on economic and monetary terms is likely to foster good relations and could be a small price to pay to avoid a repetition of the wars that have plagued Europe this century.

Europe is now slowly moving on the path toward EMU. Several years after the establishment of the EMS, a new impetus toward monetary union was created with the 1985 Delors report. The Delors report lays out three phases toward monetary union. Stage one, starting in July 1990, enlarged the ERM to current absentees and abolished remaining exchange rate controls. Stage two, scheduled for 1994, would create a European system of reserve banks, called the *European Monetary Institute* ("EuroFed"), similar to the U.S. Federal Reserve System. Exchange rate bands would be narrowed and realignment allowed only under exceptional circumstances. With the recent turmoil in the European foreign exchange market, the narrowing of bands has been put on hold. Finally, the last stage would involve a single currency, with binding monetary and budgetary controls, starting in 1999.

Because of the far-reaching consequences of EMU, amendments to the original Treaty of Rome must be approved by all member nations. These conditions for EMU were laid down by the Maastricht treaty, signed in December 1991 and ratified by 1994. The treaty put forth a series of conditions by which countries must abide to qualify for membership in a common European currency:

- The average CPI inflation rate must not exceed that of the best three countries by more than 1.5 percent;
- The budget deficit must not be excessive, where *excessive* is defined as more than 3 percent of GDP or a debt-to-GDP ratio of more than 60 percent;
- The country's currency must have been in the normal EMS bands for the prior two years;
- The average bond yield must not exceed that of the best three countries by more than 2 percent.

Clearly, these are extremely stringent conditions and are unlikely to be met by all candidate countries. Although escape clauses exist, these conditions are still viewed as necessary ingredients toward EMU, because they reflect healthy monetary and fiscal policies.

To some extent, EMU has already succeeded in forcing countries to address unsound economic policies. The path toward EMU is still fraught with danger, however. The EMS was rocked in September 1992 by unprecedented turbulence in the foreign exchange markets. Speculation against the pound reached such extent that the Bank of England, despite repeated promises to the contrary, was forced to leave the ERM. Further attacks also forced the Italian lira off the system as well as the realignment of other currencies.

The extent of speculative attacks against the Bank of England raises serious questions about the stability of the foreign exchange markets. If speculators really believe a currency is overvalued, then by selling this currency they could indeed force a devaluation, as in a self-fulfilling prophecy. In retrospect, however, speculation against the pound reflected valid doubts about the commitment of the British government to maintaining parity against the mark and therefore importing high German interest rates while the whole British economy was suffering from its worst postwar recession. In addition, some argued that the pound had entered the ERM at too high a rate, which was further aggravated by the high domestic inflation. As always, when faced with difficult choices between internal and external balances, governments have more often than not abandoned targeting external objectives for short-term political reasons.

Many obstacles, therefore, remain in the path to EMU. Only if governments demonstrate a long-term commitment to sound economic policies, converging all across Europe, will EMU become a reality. These will be fascinating developments to observe.

The Foreign Exchange Markets

The foreign exchange market is where currencies are traded. It is not a centralized market in the sense of a trading floor where all buyers and sellers meet to transact business. Transactions are effected over the Telex wire or by telephone. Face-to-face contact is hardly ever necessary. London, New York, and Tokyo are by far the most active financial centers. These centers are connected by sophisticated communications networks (SWIFT and CHIPS).[2] The market is a continuous one with no opening or closing hours and is the only major 24-hour financial market. It opens in Tokyo, then moves to Hong Kong, on to London, and then to the United States. Exhibit 4.4 describes how market activity passes from one center to the next. All markets open with a flurry of activity, cool down around lunch time, and pick up toward the end.

Exhibit 4.5 displays the activity in major financial centers, as reported by the Bank for International Settlements (BIS). Between 1986 and 1989, the market doubled, from $196 to $618 billion. It has grown by a further $260 billion from 1989 to 1992. The British market is dominated by brokers, and the others find room for banks and brokers to facilitate the flow of transactions. About 44 percent of gross volume in the New York market is conducted by the 13 recognized brokers. In comparison, daily trading volume on the NYSE, the largest organized stock exchange, amounts to $2–5 billion daily. Daily volume in the U.S. Treasury market, the largest bond market in the world, is $30 billion. The foreign exchange market is therefore by far the largest financial market in the world.

The Forex market is notable for its lack of regulation. Only exchange-traded derivative instruments are subject to formal regula-

EXHIBIT 4.4   Activity in the Forex Markets

Center	Daily Turnover ($bn)		
	April 1986	April 1989	April 1992
London	90	187	300
New York	58	129	192
Tokyo	48	115	126
Singapore	–	55	76
Zurich	–	57	68
Hong Kong	–	49	61
Paris	–	26	36
Others	–	–	21
Total	196	618	880

[2]SWIFT stands for Society for Worldwide Interbank Financial Telecommunication. CHIPS is the Clearing House Interbank Payments System.

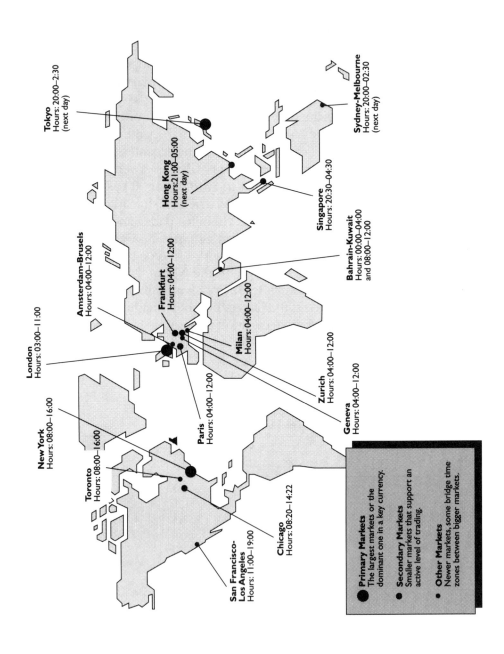

EXHIBIT 4.5   The Market That Never Stops

tion by the SEC and the CFTC in the United States.[3] The bank participants in the spot market are supervised by the Federal Reserve system and must report their foreign exchange position on a periodic basis. The Foreign Exchange Committee of the Federal Reserve Bank of New York, which consists of bank representatives (domestic and foreign), brokers and Forex dealers, and two ex-officio members of the Federal Reserve Bank, "develop suggested guidelines for the conduct of business by market makers, other dealers and brokers, and addresses a variety of technical operational and accounting issues."

Participants

The participants in the Forex markets include commercial banks, brokers, corporations, speculators, and central banks. *Commercial banks* account for a large proportion of total trading volume. Banks make two-way quotes, indicating that they are ready to buy or sell at posted prices. They make a profit from the bid–ask spreads. Intermarket spreads are about 3/100 of 1 percent, which is much lower than spreads in any other financial market except Treasury bills. Banks profit from the volume but can also speculate on currencies, adjusting positions and arbitraging across markets and time.

Brokers simply match buyers and sellers, in exchange for a fixed commission, and do not take positions, as banks do. Given the volume of trading and the size of the spreads, the foreign exchange market is by far the deepest and most liquid financial market.

Corporations use the foreign exchange market primarily to hedge their exposure to currency risk; increasingly, however, their foreign exchange desk also serves as an aggressive trading center. *Speculators* thus include corporations as well as investment managers for mutual funds and pension funds.

The role of *central banks* is not always a passive one (a transfer agent) in foreign exchange transactions. Central banks continue to intervene to maintain an "orderly market." They do so by trading with commercial banks or with each other. The greater is the role of the

---

[3] The Securities and Exchange Commission regulates primarily the stock, bond, and options on cash markets; the Commodities and Futures Trading Commission regulates primarily trading in futures and options on futures. As such, the SEC supervises options on currencies traded, while the CFTC supervises currency futures and options on futures.

central bank, the less freedom commercial banks enjoy and the less the foreign exchange rate is market determined.

Trading Mechanics

Trading in the foreign exchange markets generally involves the U.S. dollar. This is because of the depth of the dollar-currency market and the associated lower transaction costs. A British importer, for instance, wishing to buy Japanese yen to pay a Japanese exporter would sell pounds for dollars and then buy yen with the proceeds. Increasingly, however, "cross-transactions" in Europe use the mark as a reference currency.

The mechanics of a foreign exchange transaction are described in Exhibit 4.6. Intricate as this figure may appear, transactions are executed effectively and quickly. We must note, however, that no currency of whatever nationality has changed hands here. The foreign exchange contract is simply a bookkeeping entry. The correspondent banks in the United States that are called upon to execute foreign exchange transactions are usually New York banks. The 12 largest U.S. banks, anchored in New York, constitute the totality of the U.S. market. These banks, by arbitraging their own foreign exchange position and that of their clients, in a currency or across currencies, provide a continuous marketplace for currencies. Banks trading in New York can deal through brokers to preserve anonymity and centralize the communication network.

Transactions in the Forex Markets

Foreign exchange contracts can take the form of spot, forward, futures, options, and swap contracts. The latter four contracts are known as *derivative* contracts, since they can all be priced by arbitrage conditions relative to the current spot rate. Futures and options will be covered in more detail in the next chapter.

Spot Contract. A spot exchange contract is an agreement to buy or sell a foreign currency for delivery in two business days. For most currencies, standard quotes are for settlement two business days after the trade date. This gives enough time for the verification of transactions, given the large differences in time zones involved in international transactions.

Forward Contract. A forward exchange contract is an agreement to buy (sell) a certain amount of foreign currency at a specified price

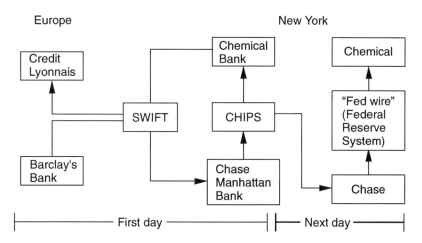

Steps in the transfer of funds:
1. Barclays Bank buys German marks from Crédit Lyonnais; to consummate this, it must transfer funds in the United States to Crédit Lyonnais's account at Chemical Bank in New York.
2. Barclays uses SWIFT to instruct the Chase Manhattan Bank to transfer funds out of Barclays's account.
3. The Chase debits Barclays's account and transfers the funds through CHIPS; those "clearing house funds" get credited to Chemical on the same day.
4. The next day, the net amount is settled between Federal Reserve member banks by transfer in "Fed Funds" – deposits held at the various Federal Reserve banks. This is done through the domestic interbank clearing system, the "Fed Wire."
5. Chemical credits Crédit Lyonnais's account and notifies Crédit Lyonnais through the SWIFT network.

Source: Ian Giddy, "Measuring the World Foreign Exchange Market," *Columbia Journal of World Business,* Winter 1979.

EXHIBIT 4.6   The International Dollar Payment System

for delivery at a specified date in the future (1, 2, 3, 6, or 12 months, usually). Commercial banks are the market makers for forward contracts, which are traded over the counter. A spot exchange contract, therefore, can be viewed as a special case of a forward contract.

Futures Contract.   A futures contract is an agreement to buy or sell a standardized size of a currency at a price set today for delivery at a designated time in the future. Futures contracts are traded on centralized exchanges, which set the size of the contracts, their time to maturity, and the required margin.

Option Contract.   An American call (put) option gives the holder of the long (short) position the right to buy (sell), if he or she chooses, a specified quantity of a foreign currency at a set price, called the *strike price*, any time during the life of the option. European options give the right of exercise only at expiration, but American options can be exercised at any time during the life of the option. For this right the holder pays a price called the *option premium*. Options are traded both OTC and on centralized exchanges.

Swap Contract.   A swap is the simultaneous purchase and sale of spot and forward exchange or two forward transactions of different maturities. A "swap-in," for instance, involves buying a foreign currency spot and selling the future amount forward back into the initial currency.

Spot Contracts

Let us consider first quotations for spot contracts. The *Financial Times of London* reports detailed daily bid and ask quotations for spot and forward contracts (Exhibit 4.7). Spot rates are quoted in either of two ways: direct or indirect. The direct quote gives the price of a unit of the foreign currency in terms of the domestic currency, that is, how many dollars it takes to buy, say, a British pound; it takes 1.5060 according to the second column of numbers in Exhibit 4.7; here the spot price S is represented as $S(\$/\pounds)$.

The indirect quote gives the price of a unit of domestic currency in terms of foreign currencies; that is, how many pounds it takes to purchase a dollar; the answer, according to Exhibit 4.7 $S(\pounds/\$)$, is .6645. The direct quote is referred to as the *U.S. basis* and the indirect quote as the *European basis*; each is the inverse of the other.

Each quote must reflect both sides of the market: the sell (ask) side and the buy (bid) side. Calling up your banker for a quotation on the $\$/\pounds$, he or she will quote, for example, 50 over 60. These, referred to as *points*, indicate that the dealer is quoting a *bid* at 1.5050 and an *ask* at 1.5060. In other words, the bank stands ready to buy the foreign currency from you at 1.5050 and to sell you the pound at 1.5060. The difference between the two rates is the *spread*, which is 10 points here. The arithmetic average of the two rates is known as the *mid rate*.

The bank acts as a dealer, realizing its profits from the spread. More often than not, the bank will turn around and pass the exposure created with one client to another. For instance, a bank that buys pounds from a U.S. client will try to cover its exposure by selling

EXHIBIT 4.7 Quotations from the *Financial Times*

POUND SPOT – FORWARD AGAINST THE POUND

Mar 31	Day's spread	Close	One month	% p.a.	Three months	% p.a.
US.............	1.4905 – 1.5075	1.5050 – 1.5060	0.37–0.35cpm	2.87	1.01–0.98pm	2.64
Canada......	1.8650 – 1.8950	1.8915 – 1.8925	0.18–0.15cpm	1.05	0.32–0.27pm	0.62
Netherlands.	2.7100 – 2.7375	2.7250 – 2.7350	$\frac{3}{8}$–$\frac{1}{2}$cdis	-1.92	1–$1\frac{1}{4}$dis	-1.65
Belgium......	49.60 – 50.10	49.95 – 50.05	10–12cdis	-2.64	25–30dis	-2.20
Denmark......	9.2625 – 9.3375	9.3225 – 9.3325	$4\frac{1}{4}$–$5\frac{1}{8}$cdis	-6.03	$11\frac{1}{4}$–$12\frac{1}{4}$dis	-5.04
Ireland........	0.9900 – 0.9980	0.9970 – 0.9980	0.29–0.34cdis	-3.79	0.80–0.89dis	-3.39
Germany......	2.4100 – 2.4300	2.4250 – 2.4300	$\frac{3}{8}$–$\frac{5}{8}$pfdis	-2.47	$1\frac{1}{8}$–$1\frac{3}{8}$dis	-2.06
Portugal......	222.75 – 225.00	223.25 – 224.25	258–286cdis	-14.59	576–632dis	-10.80
Spain...........	172.20 – 173.40	172.95 – 173.25	119–143cdis	-9.08	336–369dis	-8.15
Italy............	2379.50 – 2410.00	2401.50 – 2402.50	11–15liredis	-6.49	34–38dis	-6.00
Norway........	10.2675 – 10.3400	10.3300 – 10.3400	$2\frac{1}{2}$–$2\frac{7}{8}$oredis	-3.12	$7\frac{1}{4}$–$7\frac{7}{8}$dis	-2.88
France........	8.1725 – 8.2475	8.2375 – 8.2475	$3\frac{3}{8}$–4cdis	-5.37	$8\frac{3}{8}$–$9\frac{1}{2}$dis	-4.40
Sweden.....	11.4700 – 11.6875	11.6475 – 11.6575	$4\frac{1}{8}$–$4\frac{1}{4}$oredis	-4.57	$11\frac{1}{4}$–$12\frac{1}{2}$dis	-4.08
Japan........	171.50 – 173.50	172.50 – 173.50	$\frac{1}{2}$–$\frac{1}{8}$ypm	3.03	$1\frac{1}{4}$–1pm	2.60
Austria......	16.96 – 17.10	17.06 – 17.09	$2\frac{3}{8}$–$3\frac{1}{4}$grodis	-2.24	$6\frac{1}{4}$–$8\frac{5}{8}$dis	-1.74
Switzerland.	2.2300 – 2.2550	2.2450 – 2.2550	$\frac{1}{4}$–$\frac{1}{8}$cpm	1.00	$\frac{1}{2}$–$\frac{1}{4}$pm	0.67
Ecu............	1.2460 – 1.2550	1.2510 – 1.2520	0.34–0.39cdis	-3.50	0.83–1.01dis	-3.10

Commercial rates taken towards the end of London trading. Six-month forward dollar 1.87–1.82pm. 12 Month 3.25–3.15pm.

DOLLAR SPOT – FORWARD AGAINST THE DOLLAR

Mar 31	Day's spread	Close	One month	% p.a.	Three months	% p.a.
UK†.............	1.4905 – 1.5075	1.5050 – 1.5060	0.37–0.35cpm	2.87	1.01–0.98pm	2.64
Ireland†........	1.5000 – 1.5135	1.5105 – 1.5115	0.84–0.79cpm	6.47	2.28–2.18pm	5.90
Canada........	1.2500 – 1.2595	1.2575 – 1.2585	0.17–0.20cdis	-1.76	0.56–0.62dis	-1.88
Netherlands..	1.8080 – 1.8220	1.8125 – 1.8135	0.71–0.74cdis	-4.80	1.95–2.01dis	-4.37
Belgium......	33.15 – 33.35	33.15 – 33.25	15.00–17.00cdis	-5.78	39.00–43.00dis	-4.94
Denmark.......	6.1900 – 6.2175	6.1925 – 6.1975	4.00–5.00credis	-8.72	12.50–14.50dis	-8.72
Germany.......	1.6075 – 1.6210	1.6120 – 1.6130	0.71–0.72pfdis	-5.32	1.92–1.95dis	-4.80
Portugal.......	148.30 – 150.00	148.55 – 148.65	200–240cdis	-17.77	450–550dis	-13.46
Spain..........	114.90 – 115.65	115.15 – 118.25	103–106cdis	-10.99	303–308cdis	-10.61
Italy............	1591.75 – 1604.00	1595.25 – 1595.75	11.40–12.00liredis	-8.80	32.80–34.00dis	-8.37
Norway........	6.8400 – 6.8975	6.8625 – 6.8675	3.20–3.80oredis	-6.12	9.30–10.10dis	-6.81
France.........	5.4625 – 5.5000	5.4725 – 5.4775	3.30–3.45cdis	-7.40	9.20–9.45dis	-6.85
Sweden........	7.6875 – 7.7775	7.7375 – 7.7425	4.20–4.80oredis	-6.96	12.10–13.30dis	-6.56
Japan..........	114.55 – 115.75	114.85 – 114.95	0.01–0.02pdis	-0.16	0.01–0.03dis	-0.07
Austria........	11.3450 – 11.4000	11.3575 – 11.3625	4.45–4.80grodis	-4.89	11.85–12.95dis	-4.37
Switzerland.	1.4895 – 1.4980	1.4935 – 1.4945	0.29–0.31cdis	-2.41	0.71–0.75dis	-1.95
Ecu†............	1.1955 – 1.2040	1.2025 – 1.2035	0.65–0.63cpm	6.38	1.73–1.70pm	5.70

Commercial rates taken towards the end of London trading. † UK, Ireland and Ecu are quoted in US currency. Forward premiums and discounts apply to the US dollar and not to the individual currency.

Source: *Financial Times*, April 1, 1993.

pounds to another client or bank. But a bank that expects the pound to go up over the next few minutes may decide to wait before selling. Over the course of the day, the dealer will manage the bank's exposure in a way that is consistent with his or her short-term view on the currency. Toward the end of the day, the dealer will generally try to "square" the bank's position. A dealer who accumulates too large an inventory of pounds could induce clients to buy them by slightly

EXHIBIT 4.7 Quotations from the *Financial Times* Continued

EURO-CURRENCY INTEREST RATES

Mar 31	Short term	7 Days notice	One Month	Three Months	Six Months	One Year
Sterling.........	$6 - 5\frac{7}{8}$	$6 - 5\frac{7}{8}$	$6 - 5\frac{7}{8}$	$6 - 5\frac{7}{8}$	$5\frac{15}{16} - 5\frac{13}{16}$	$5\frac{15}{16} - 5\frac{13}{16}$
US Dollar........	$3\frac{9}{16} - 3\frac{7}{16}$	$3\frac{3}{16} - 3\frac{1}{16}$	$3\frac{3}{16} - 3\frac{1}{16}$	$3\frac{1}{4} - 3\frac{1}{8}$	$3\frac{3}{8} - 3\frac{1}{4}$	$3\frac{5}{8} - 3\frac{1}{2}$
Can. Dollar...	$4\frac{3}{4} - 4\frac{1}{2}$	$4\frac{7}{8} - 4\frac{5}{8}$	$5 - 4\frac{3}{4}$	$5\frac{1}{4} - 5$	$5\frac{9}{16} - 5\frac{5}{16}$	$6 - 5\frac{3}{4}$
Dutch Guilder...	$8\frac{1}{16} - 7\frac{15}{16}$	$7\frac{15}{16} - 7\frac{13}{16}$	$7\frac{13}{16} - 7\frac{11}{16}$	$7\frac{5}{8} - 7\frac{1}{2}$	$7\frac{3}{16} - 7\frac{1}{16}$	$6\frac{3}{4} - 6\frac{5}{8}$
Swiss Franc..	$5\frac{3}{4} - 5\frac{1}{2}$	$6\frac{1}{8} - 5\frac{7}{8}$	$5\frac{7}{16} - 5\frac{5}{16}$	$5\frac{3}{16} - 5\frac{1}{16}$	$4\frac{15}{16} - 4\frac{13}{16}$	$4\frac{5}{8} - 4\frac{1}{2}$
D-Mark........	$8\frac{5}{16} - 8\frac{3}{16}$	$8\frac{5}{16} - 8\frac{3}{16}$	$8\frac{5}{16} - 8\frac{3}{16}$	$8 - 7\frac{7}{8}$	$7\frac{9}{16} - 7\frac{7}{16}$	$6\frac{15}{16} - 6\frac{13}{16}$
French Franc...	$11 - 10\frac{3}{4}$	$10\frac{5}{8} - 10\frac{3}{8}$	$10\frac{1}{2} - 10\frac{1}{4}$	$10\frac{1}{2} - 10\frac{1}{4}$	$10\frac{1}{16} - 9\frac{15}{16}$	$9\frac{1}{4} - 9\frac{1}{8}$
Italian Lira......	$12\frac{1}{2} - 10\frac{1}{2}$	$11\frac{3}{4} - 11\frac{1}{4}$	$11\frac{3}{4} - 11\frac{1}{4}$	$11\frac{3}{4} - 11\frac{1}{4}$	$11\frac{3}{4} - 11\frac{3}{8}$	$11\frac{7}{8} - 11\frac{1}{2}$
Belgian Franc..	$9 - 8\frac{7}{8}$	$8\frac{7}{8} - 8\frac{5}{8}$	$8\frac{5}{8} - 8\frac{1}{2}$	$8\frac{7}{16} - 8\frac{9}{16}$	$7\frac{7}{8} - 7\frac{3}{4}$	$7\frac{7}{16} - 7\frac{9}{16}$
Yen........	$3\frac{3}{4} - 3\frac{11}{16}$	$3\frac{13}{32} - 3\frac{11}{32}$	$3\frac{5}{16} - 3\frac{1}{4}$	$3\frac{5}{16} - 3\frac{1}{4}$	$3\frac{11}{32} - 3\frac{9}{32}$	$3\frac{3}{8} - 3\frac{5}{16}$
Danish Krona..	$10 - 9$	$11\frac{1}{2} - 10$	$12\frac{1}{2} - 11$	$12\frac{1}{4} - 11\frac{1}{4}$	$12 - 11$	$11 - 10\frac{1}{4}$
Asian $Sing....	$4 - 3$	$4 - 3$	$3\frac{1}{2} - 2\frac{1}{2}$	$3\frac{1}{4} - 2\frac{1}{4}$	$3\frac{1}{4} - 2\frac{1}{4}$	$4 - 3$
Spanish Peseta	$14 - 13\frac{1}{2}$	$14 - 13\frac{1}{2}$	$13\frac{7}{8} - 13\frac{5}{8}$	$13\frac{3}{4} - 13\frac{1}{2}$	$13\frac{3}{8} - 13\frac{1}{8}$	$12\frac{7}{8} - 12\frac{5}{8}$
Portuguese Esc	$23\frac{1}{4} - 22$	$23\frac{1}{4} - 22$	$20\frac{5}{8} - 19\frac{7}{8}$	$17\frac{1}{4} - 16\frac{1}{2}$	$16\frac{1}{16} - 15\frac{7}{16}$	$16\frac{1}{16} - 15\frac{7}{16}$

Long term Eurodollars: two years $4\frac{1}{4}-4\frac{1}{8}$ per cent: three years $4\frac{3}{4}-4\frac{5}{8}$ per cent; four years $5\frac{1}{4}-5\frac{1}{8}$ per cent; five years $5\frac{5}{8}-5\frac{1}{2}$ per cent nominal. Short term rates are call for US Dollar and Japanese Yen; others, two days' notice.

EXCHANGE CROSS RATES

Mar. 31	£	$	DM	Yen	F Fr.	$ Fr.	H FL	Lira	C$	B Fr.	Pta.	Ecu
£	1	1.505	2.427	173.0	8.242	2.250	2.730	2402	1.892	50.00	173.1	1.251
$	0.664	1	1.613	115.0	5.476	1.495	1.814	1596	1.257	33.22	115.0	0.831
DM	0.412	0.620	1	71.28	3.396	0.927	1.125	969.7	0.780	20.60	71.32	0.515
YEN	5.780	8.699	14.03	1000.	47.64	13.01	15.78	13884	10.94	289.0	1001	7.231
F Fr.	1.213	1.826	2.945	209.9	10.	2.730	3.312	2914	2.296	60.66	210.0	1.518
$ Fr.	0.444	0.669	1.079	76.89	3.663	1	1.213	1068	0.841	22.22	76.93	0.558
H FL	0.366	0.551	0.889	63.37	3.019	0.824	1	879.9	0.693	18.32	63.41	0.458
Lira	0.416	0.627	1.010	72.02	3.431	0.937	1.137	1000.	0.788	20.82	72.06	0.521
C $	0.529	0.795	1.283	91.44	4.356	1.189	1.443	1270	1	26.43	91.49	0.661
B Fr.	2.000	3.010	4.854	346.0	16.48	4.500	5.480	4804	3.784	100.	346.2	2.502
Pta	0.578	0.869	1.402		4.761	1.300	1.577	1388	1.093	28.89	100.	0.723
Ecu	0.799	1.203	1.940	138.3	6.588	1.799	2.182	1920	1.512	39.97	138.4	1.

Yen per 1,000: French Fr. per 10: Lira per 1,000: Belgian Fr. per 100: Peseta per 100.

lowering the price, for instance, to 1.5048–1.5058. Therefore, because posted prices reflect inventory positions, it is advisable to check with several banks before deciding to enter into a transaction. Small differences can occur, worth the cost of a telephone call, but we do not expect large differences in pricing.

Consistency across markets requires that the price of the dollar in New York be the same as that in, say, London. If not, an arbitrage opportunity would present itself, leading to a flow of funds across borders. If the value of the pound were $2.10 in New York and $2.00 in London, arbitrageurs, starting with $2.0 million, would buy £1 million in London, where the price is low, and resell these pounds in New York, for a total of $2.1 million, thereby making a riskless profit of $100,000. The gain will be slightly less if transactions costs are accounted for. With minimal transactions costs and no impediments to the flow of funds, the price of one currency in terms of another should be the same.

Consistency across currencies is also called *triangular arbitrage*. If the equilibrium rate between the U.S. dollar and the British pound were $2 to £1 and that between the dollar and the franc FF4 to $1, the equilibrium rate between the franc and the pound would then have to be £1 = FF8. Restated, the equilibrium rates are

$$S(\$/\pounds) = 2, \ S(FF/\$) = 4, \ S(FF/\pounds) = 8.$$

And indeed we have $S(FF/\pounds) = S(\$/\pounds) \times S(FF/\$)$. Otherwise, arbitrage opportunities would present themselves. Had the pound sold for FF10, an arbitrageur, observing that the pound is overvalued, would buy dollars for francs, resell these dollar for pounds, which would then be resold at the high 10FF/£ rate. Starting, say, with FF400 we buy $100, sell the dollars for pounds, and get £50. We then cash the dollars for FF500 for a net profit of FF100. As this process continues, the price of the pound will fall until consistency across exchange rates is established.

Forward Contracts

Forward rates are also quoted in the direct and indirect ways with an interesting and sometimes confusing twist. A trader in New York may quote the German mark (deutsche mark or DM) spot – one-month and three-month – as follows: 1.5050–1.5060, 37–35 (or 37/35, or 37 to 35), 101–98. These quotes correspond to the following rates:

Maturity	Buy	Sell	Wire Quote
Spot	1.5050	1.5060	
1-month	1.5013	1.5025	37–35
3-month	1.4949	1.4962	101–98

Because the forward rate is lower than the spot rate, we say that the mark is selling at a (forward) discount. The size of the discount for one month is, using mid rates, 0.0036 or, divided by the spot rate, 0.0036/1.5055 = 0.00239, or 0.239 percent or an annual rate of 2.87 percent (0.232 × 12), which is the number reported by the *Financial*

Times. A possible reason for this premium is that the market expects the spot rate one month from now to be lower than the current spot rate. This point will be discussed later.

Whenever the currency is selling at a discount the quote from the trader will have a larger number (37, bid) followed by a smaller number (35, ask). These numbers must be subtracted from the spot rate quotation to arrive at the outright forward rate.

When a currency is selling at a premium, the trader's quote will be flashed in reverse order, with the smaller number (the bid) preceding the larger number (the ask). These numbers will have to be added to the spot quotation to arrive at the outright forward rate.

The preceding is based on the direct quotation system (the U.S. point of view). Using the European indirect quotation, we arrive at an opposite and important conclusion: the U.S. dollar is selling at a premium. The size of the premium (in percentage terms) is not exactly equal to the discount on the opposing currency simply because of the nature of the arithmetic. The reader can verify that, taking the inverse of direct quotes, the premium on the dollar relative to the pound is 2.88 percent per annum (pa), which differs slightly from the 2.87 percent pa number.

The forward exchange market is used for several purposes.

- *Covering Commercial Transactions or Hedging:* U.S. exporters expecting to receive foreign currency sell the currency forward to lock in a certain exchange rate. Alternatively, they may insist that they be paid in dollars, thereby shifting the risk to the buyer. The forwards market is also used to hedge against fluctuations in the value of assets or earnings subject to foreign exchange risk.

- *Arbitrage:* Arbitrageurs, using the foreign exchange market, attempt to capitalize on differences in interest rates across national boundaries by simultaneously buying and selling currency in two different markets to lock in a profit. An extensive discussion of this topic follows later.

- *Speculation:* Speculators try to outguess the market. They are actually betting that the expected spot rate implied by the forward rate will be different from the spot rate that will prevail at the end of the period covered in the forward contract.

  Speculators have a preference for the forwards market because little or no capital is required (the transaction is consummated in a margin account with a very low margin requirement). Speculation in the spot market could require commitment of 100 percent of the value of the contract. Speculators can buy foreign currency in the hope of selling it later at a profit. If they expect the spot rate to drop, they borrow the depreciating currency, sell it immediately, and buy back the currency in the market to repay their loans when these loans mature or when they deem the time is right. The speculators, in this case, profit if the currency depreciates and lose if it appreciates. Speculators may also speculate in the futures market, as we shall show later on.

Interest Rate Parity

Forward and spot rates are linked through a relationship known as *interest rate parity* (IRP). The equilibrium among the current exchange rate, the forward exchange rate, and the domestic and foreign rates of interest occurs through a process of arbitrage.

Consider a world made up of the United States and Great Britain and assume no government intervention in the flow of funds across national borders and no taxes. An investor ponders whether a profit could be made from higher foreign interest rates. Going back to the data from the *Financial Times*, the investor observes that the U.S. three-month interest rate is only 3.125 percent pa, while the British rate is 5.875 percent pa. The spot and forward rates are 1.5055 and 1.4955, respectively. Initially, assume that there are no transaction costs, so that we use mid rates.

For an initial investment of $1, investing for three months at the U.S. Eurodollar rate yields $(1 + iT) = [1 + (3.125/100)(3/12)] = (1 + 3.125/400) = 1.00781$. Alternatively, the investor can buy pounds and invest at the Eurosterling rate. To eliminate exchange risk, the investor will also sell forward the future amount of pounds into dollars. The proceeds will then be £1/1.5055 = 0.66423, which grows to £(1/1.5055)(1 + 5.875/400) = 0.67399, which can be converted into dollars at the forward rate F, yielding 0.67399 × 1.4955 = 1.00795. It is no coincidence that the two final amounts are very similar.[4] This reflects the fact that the investor can lock in a sure rate of interest in dollars or by a covered pound investment. Because all exchange and interest

---

[4] The small differences between the two numbers reflect bid–ask spreads. Readers can verify that slightly different numbers are obtained when using the appropriate bid and ask quotes.

rates are predetermined, the two alternative investments are risk free
and should provide the same payoffs.

From this, the payoff on a covered foreign currency investment is
$(1/S)(1 + i^*T)F$, using American quoting conventions. IRP can be
written as

$$(1 + iT) = (1 + i^*T)\,\frac{F[\$/FC]}{S[\$/FC]}, \qquad (4.2)$$

where S denotes the spot rate, expressed in dollars per units of the
foreign currency (FC), F is the forward rate, i and i^* are the U.S. and
foreign rates of interest, and T is the number of years to expiration.
Note that all contracts must be such that they expire on the same day.

A simplified version of IRP can be written as follows. Dividing both
sides of the equation by $(1 + i^*T)$, and subtracting 1, we get

$$\frac{F - S}{S} = \frac{1 + iT - 1 - i^*T}{1 + i^*T} \qquad (4.3)$$

$$\frac{F - S}{S} = \frac{iT - i^*T}{1 + i^*T} \approx (i - i^*)T.$$

Hence the forward premium or discount should be approximately
equal to the differential between the U.S. and foreign interest rates.

Stated differently, a forward contract can be duplicated by a long
position in the domestic currency generating a positive cash flow (iT)
and a short position in the foreign currency requiring a cash outflow
($-i^*T$).

The left-hand side of the equation is referred to as the *implicit rate*,
the right-hand side as the *interest rate differential*. Equation (4.3)
represents an important economic concept. It demonstrates that a
forward contract may be reproduced in the money market through a
long position in a U.S. bond paying an interest (an inflow) of i and
a short position in a foreign bond (an issuance of a foreign bond –
borrowing overseas) requiring the payment – (an outflow) of i^*.

Because this relationship is only an approximation, it can be written
more precisely as

$$\frac{F - S}{S} - \frac{iT - i^*T}{1 + i^*T} = AM, \qquad (4.4)$$

where AM is defined as the *arbitrage margin*. From Equation (4.2)
one can see that, if $i < i^*$, the forward pound must be at a discount

for *AM* to equal zero. That is, whenever a currency is at a discount, its country's interest rate must be higher than that of the other country for a no-arbitrage condition to exist.

Going back to the example of a three-month pound investment, we have

$$\frac{F - S}{S} = (1.5045 - 1.5055)/1.5055 = -0.00664,$$

$$\frac{iT - i^*T}{1 + i^*T} = (3.125/400 - 5.875/400)/(1 + 5.875/400) = -0.00677,$$

and therefore the arbitrage margin is 0.00013, or 0.05 percent annually. The interest rate differential slightly favors Britain. A U.S. investor observing this would decide to (1) buy pounds spot, (2) invest pounds at the posted rate, and simultaneously (3) sell the pound forward. He would invest in the U.S. had the arbitrage margin been possible.

One may observe deviations from IRP for the following reasons.

1. Investors face bid–ask spreads for spot and forward rates. Borrowers and lenders also face different rates. Direct measures of these transactions costs are not always possible. A worthwhile attempt was made by Hilley, Beidleman, and Greenleaf (1979). They divided transactions costs into two categories: those related to the spread in foreign exchange transactions (bid–ask) spread and other costs. The U.S. investor attempting to benefit from higher payoffs on the pound would face bid–ask spreads and other costs. The nonspread costs are summarized in the following equation:

$$K = (1 - t)(1 - t^*)(1 - t_s)(1 - t_f),$$

where

t = percent of transaction cost arising from brokerage fees and information costs involved in selling a home currency-denominated asset,

t^* = percent of transaction cost of buying a £-denominated asset,

t_s = percent of transaction cost of purchasing spot £,

t_f = percent of transaction cost of selling forward £.

Accounting for both K costs and the spread costs, the IRP equilibrium condition would look as follows:

$$\frac{F_b - S_a}{S_a} = \frac{(1 + iT) - K(1 + i^*T)}{K(1 + i^*T)} , \qquad (4.5)$$

where F_b is the bid forward exchange rate and S_a is the ask spot exchange rate. Empirical tests show that the K factor is significant and that, once costs are accounted for, covered interest arbitrage dominates in the foreign exchange markets.

2. Comparisons involving Eurocurrency deposits generally lead to very small deviations in IRP. This is because the deposits, denominated in different currencies but located in the same financial center, are very similar in terms of default and political risk, and taxation. Using Treasury bills in different countries introduces differences in these characteristics, even if currency and maturity are controlled for.

3. Existing or possible future restrictions on capital flows can also cause the condition to fail because it would prevent arbitrageurs enforcing IRP.

Explaining Exchange Rates

Is forecasting exchange rates an art or a science? No matter! Many services are selling foreign exchange forecasts to banks, corporations, investors, and speculators and appear to be making a profit.

The presence of these services and their profitability have interesting implications for the efficiency of the foreign exchange markets. A strongly efficient market requires that all information, publicly available or not, be reflected in the price of the security. A weakly efficient market, on the other hand, implies that technical analysis has no usefulness to portfolio managers. It asserts that historical records of foreign exchange rates cannot be relied on in forecasting future spot rates, implying that no one can devise a strategy that can consistently outperform a naive buy-and-hold strategy. Regardless of the technique employed – sophisticated econometric models, simple forecasting tools, or chart reading – efficient markets imply that the market cannot be beaten and that forecasting services have no reason to exist.

Because of the immense profits that can be generated from correctly timing exchange rate movements, however, speculators and forecasting services constantly hunt for new methods to forecast exchange rates. The methods used in forecasting exchange rates fall into two major categories: fundamental analysis and technical analysis. To attain a better understanding of methods used to forecast exchange rates, and also of the factors that drive exchange rates, we briefly review the exchange rate models that usually are at the basis of fundamental analysis. We present two classes of models. The first one focuses on transactions that produce a flow; that is, a quantity per unit time, demand for or flow supply of foreign exchange. This is the flow theory of exchange rate determination, which should be contrasted with the stock theory (asset market) or monetary theory of foreign exchange rate determination, which was detailed in the early part of this chapter and will also be discussed in some detail.

The Flow Demand and Supply of Foreign Exchange

This class of models views the demand for foreign exchange as a *derived* demand. Economic agents demand foreign currencies, not for the sake of having them but rather to purchase goods and services or to make portfolio investments abroad. Exhibit 4.8 summarizes the supply and demand factors for a currency, such as the dollar.

The demand and supply of goods and services are functions of price differentials between the United States and the rest of the world, income levels, and consumer taste. The demand for and supply of financial assets are functions of interest rate differentials between the

EXHIBIT 4.8   Supply and Demand for Dollars

Supply Factors (−)	Demand Factors (+)
1. Demand for foreign goods and services, which, in turn, is determined by a. Foreign prices relative to U.S. prices b. U.S. income levels c. Preferences for things foreign, e.g., foreign cars 2. Demand for foreign financial assets, which, in turn, is determined by a. Foreign interest rates relative to U.S. rates b. Perceived risk of foreign investment	1. Demand for U.S. goods and services, which, in turn, is determined by a. U.S. prices relative to foreign prices b. Foreign income levels c. Preferences for things American, e.g., Levi's jeans 2. Demand for U.S. financial assets which, in turn, is determined by a. U.S. interest rates relative to foreign rates b. Perceived risk of U.S. investment

United States and the rest of the world and the perceived risk of the investment. Much will be said in this chapter about the supply and demand for financial assets and the relationship between interest rates and exchange rates.

The linkages between the product and the financial markets and between both of these markets and the foreign exchange market are summarized in Exhibit 4.9. The first linkage (1) is internal to the economy (U.S. or foreign). It represents the relationship between the product market and the money and capital markets resulting from firms financing their inventories, capital equipment, physical facilities, and so forth. The second linkage (2) represents international trade between the United States and other countries and is affected by the factors listed in Exhibit 4.8. The third linkage (3) represents the role played by the foreign exchange markets in bridging the financial markets of the world as investors seek to maximize returns and minimize risk on their portfolios in an international setting.

The second and third linkages result in international transactions that are summarized and periodically reported as statistics in the *balance of payments*. The balance of payments is a record of the flow of transactions between residents of a country and of the rest of the world. As Exhibit 4.10 makes clear, there is a multitude of ways to measure whether the international transactions of the United States are in balance or not. Each "balance" has a different meaning and different implications.

1. The merchandise trade balance is the difference between exports and imports of goods. A negative balance indicates an excess in the value of U.S. imports over U.S. exports. The trade balance figures, published on a monthly basis, are useful indicators of the international competitiveness of U.S. products.
2. The balance on goods and services is the export of goods and services minus the import of goods and services. Services, usually referred to as *invisibles*, include performed services and debt service payments. Thus past portfolio or direct investment leads to interest or dividend payments that appear in the debt service account.
3. The current account balance is the preceding plus unilateral transfers, such as government grants and transfers or private transfers. The function of these transfer accounts is to have

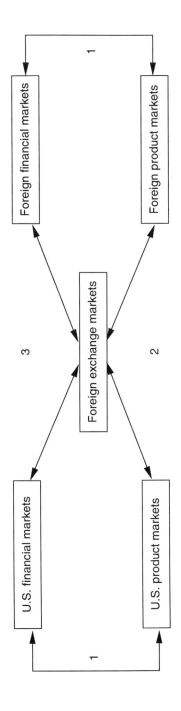

EXHIBIT 4.9   The Market Linkages

EXHIBIT 4.10   U.S. Balance of Payments: 1992 (billions of dollars)

Account	Receipts (+) (credits)	Payments (−) (debits)
Merchandise exports	439	
Merchandise imports		536
Merchandise Trade Balance		97
Services	179	123
Income on investments	109	99
Balance on Goods and Services		31
Unilateral transfers		31
Balance on Current Account		62
Private capital payments		
U.S. direct investments overseas		35
Other U.S. private investments overseas		13
Private capital receipt		
Foreign direct investments in the U.S.		4
Other foreign investments in the U.S.	84	
Change in U.S. government assets abroad		1
Balance on Capital Account	31	
Change in U.S. official reserve assets	4	
Change in foreign official assets in the U.S.	40	
Allocation of SDRs	0	
Statistical discrepancy		13

Source: *Survey of Current Business*, March 1993.

another accounting entry balance a capital flow for which there is no exchange of goods or services.

4. The capital account balance consists of private capital flows, including direct investments and portfolio investments into bank accounts, bonds, and stocks. Direct investment is defined as the purchase of shares in a company that involves some degree of control, usually defined as ownership exceeding 10 percent of the company. A positive balance indicates that there are more capital inflows into the United States than capital outflows.

5. The official reserve balance represents the net of U.S. and foreign official intervention in the Forex markets. As before, a positive balance indicates the buying of dollars or selling of foreign currencies or other reserve assets. A positive balance indicates that the central bank decreased its holdings of reserve assets to purchase dollars.

This account is sometimes viewed as the residual of all other accounts, in which case it is generally reported at the bottom of the balance of payments table and becomes *the* "balance of payments account" (BOP). When it is reported below the line, the BOP has the opposite sign to the changes in the official reserve account. In the previous case, a positive official reserve balance translates into a negative BOP. Therefore, a BOP in deficit indicates that central banks have been buying the domestic currency, probably because they wanted to prop up its value. Conversely, a surplus in the BOP indicates central bank selling of the domestic currency to offset increased private demand.

6. The "allocation of SDRs" account is affected whenever the IMF prints special drawing rights (SDRs), a basket of major currencies. In the early 1970s, this was viewed as a way to increase the world supply of reserve assets; the last allocation, however, dates back to 1981. The market for public and private SDRs has faded away.

7. The so-called statistical discrepancy account really represents errors and omissions. These arise because data on credits do not necessarily come from the same source as debits. Trade or real flows may be recorded on a different date from financial flows. Trade flows are ordinarily recorded at the time the merchandise crosses the border, while financial flows are recorded on the payment date. The two dates are usually not the same. Furthermore, the figures used in the accounting entries are frequently estimated, such as the amount of money spent by tourists; and some transactions (illegal ones, usually) are just not reported. For what follows, we assume that this account is zero.

The balance of payments is an accounting identity that states that the current account plus the capital account are equal to the balance of payment account. Hence, when there is no intervention in the Forex markets, the balance of payments is identically zero. Any current account deficit, that is, excess of imports over exports, must be financed by a capital account surplus, that is, inflows of funds from the rest of the world. This means that U.S. residents are consuming in excess of what they produce and that they must borrow funds from foreigners to finance their appetite for foreign goods.

Over the long run, fundamental equilibrium requires that the balance on current account be equal to zero, because foreign capital inflows that may have been offsetting a current account deficit generally begin to generate outflows in the form of profits and interest payments, which can worsen the external position of the country.

This approach is useful only if one assumes that flow buying and selling drives movements in exchange rates. For instance, a country with systematic current account deficits must either finance this excess consumption by foreign borrowing or by running down its foreign currency reserves. In either case, if automatic adjustment mechanisms are not allowed to take place, capital inflows cannot continue indefinitely and will at some point push down the value of the domestic currency.

The Asset Market Approach to Exchange Rates

Proponents of the asset market – or stock – approach, however, argue that exchange rates are not determined by the flow buying or selling during a particular period but rather by the market's assessment of value measured in terms of the outstanding stock or amount of two currencies. Thus the previous approach relies on volume of trading to drive exchange rates, whereas the latter relies on changes in the total supply or demand for a currency. The stock approach is also sometimes called the *asset market approach* to exchange rates, because it states that exchange rates are the prices of durable assets, currencies.

Over the years, the stock approach has become the dominant model because of the random-walk behavior of exchange rates, which conforms to the fact that movements in exchange rates are driven by changes in expectations due to "news" and that relative currency demands are driven by expectations.

Purchasing Power Parity.   Purchasing power parity (PPP) is a reduced form of the stock model and relates the exchange rate to relative prices. It is the oldest and simplest technique used in forecasting foreign exchange rates.

PPP extends the *law of one price* (LOP) to a basket of goods. The law of one price states that if the price of gold in the United States is $380 and the exchange rate is $S(SF/\$) = .77$, then the price in Zurich should be $380 \times .77 = 493.50\,SF$. Generally,

$$P = S(\$/FC)P^*, \tag{4.6}$$

where P and P^* represent the domestic (U.S.) and foreign currency prices, respectively.

The price of any tradable commodity in the United States should equal the price of that same commodity in Switzerland converted at the current spot rate. Otherwise, it will provide an opportunity for profit as arbitrageurs buy in the market where the commodity is cheap and sell in the market where it is dear. This assumes that transactions costs are negligible.

PPP, in its *absolute version*, states that the equilibrium exchange rate between any two currencies should be equal to the ratio of the price levels in their respective countries:

$$S_t(\$/FC) = P_t/P_t^*, \tag{4.7}$$

where P_t and P_t^* are now the price levels in the two countries at time t. The theory states that the long-run equilibrium value of the foreign currency relative to the dollar is given by the ratio P/P^*. For instance, if the cost of a typical consumption basket is DM200 in Germany and $100 in the United States, the spot rate should converge to DM 2/$. The *real* exchange rate, as opposed to the nominal rate, is defined as

$$s_t = S_t(\$/FC) \times P_t^*/P_t. \tag{4.8}$$

However, barriers to trade or structural differences between the U.S. and German product markets may invalidate this relationship. A weaker version of PPP, called the *relative version*, asserts that, relative to a period when equilibrium rates prevailed, changes in relative prices indicate the size of the adjustment in the exchange rate. The relative version of PPP is weaker in that it assumes that only *changes* in price levels – inflation rates – drive movements in exchange rates. We repeat Equation (4.7) at times t and $t + 1$, taking the ratio

$$S_{t+1}/S_t = (P_{t+1}/P_{t+1}^*)/(P_t/P_t^*) = (P_{t+1}/P_t)/(P_{t+1}^*/P_t^*). \tag{4.9}$$

In what follows, we assume that the measurement interval is unity, for example, one year, one quarter, or one month, and that all rates are adjusted for this horizon.

Alternatively, defining $\pi_{t+1} = (P_{t+1} - P_t)/P_t$ as the dollar inflation rate, from t to $t + 1$, or relative change in the price level P, and π^* as the foreign inflation rate, this is also

$$\Delta S = (S_{t+1} - S_t)/S_t = (1 + \pi_{t+1})/(1 + \pi^*_{t+1}) - 1,$$

which can be simplified to

$$\Delta S \approx \pi_{t+1} - \pi^*_{t+1}.$$

In fact, this relationship is not expected to hold perfectly at every time period, so that it is usually rewritten using expectations:

$$E_t[\Delta S] \approx E_t[\pi_{t+1}] - E_t[\pi^*_{t+1}]. \qquad (4.10)$$

Thus expected inflation rates drive movements in exchange rates.

Exhibit 4.11 displays the behavior of the real and nominal exchange rates for the $/pound and $/French franc since the beginning of this century. The nominal exchange rates appear to wander off without any tendency to revert to a common value: both the pound and the franc have substantially dropped in value against the U.S. dollar since the beginning of the century. In contrast, the real exchange rates appear to be strongly mean reverting. This suggests that PPP is a reasonable approximation of the behavior of exchange rates over the long run. Recent tests of PPP, using newly developed cointegration techniques, show that PPP generally appears to hold as a long-run relationship. Over five or more years, relative price levels do appear to influence the level of exchange rates.

As explained in Officer (1976), both versions of PPP have several drawbacks:

1. PPP involves an exclusive emphasis on monetary theory – a higher money supply (stock of money) leads to a higher rate of inflation and a lower value for the currency. This is an adequate description of currency movements in highly inflationary countries or times. Since monetary factors accumulate over the long run, PPP might be an adequate description of exchange rates over decades.

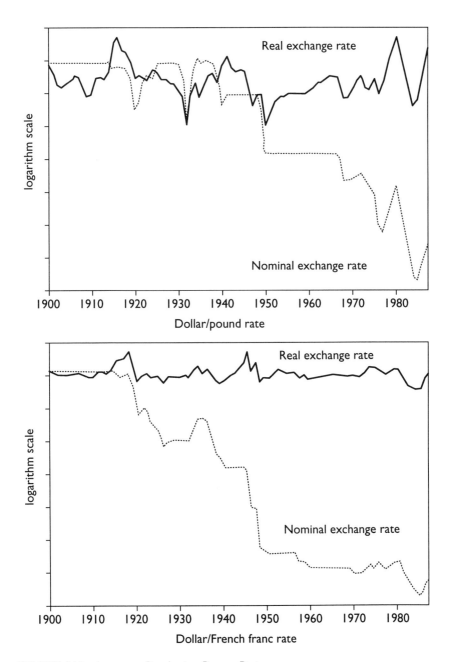

EXHIBIT 4.11   Long-run Purchasing Power Parity

In the short-run, however, PPP fails to explain the wide variations observed in flexible exchange rates. Additionally, structural considerations are also ignored. The sudden discovery of oil in the North Sea increased the demand for the British pound, despite a higher rate of inflation in Britain relative to its trading partners. The pound appreciated as a result. Japan experienced dramatic shifts in the relative prices of traded to nontraded goods, driven by innovations in the manufacturing, primarily export-oriented, sector. These shifts led to an appreciation of the yen in real terms over the last two decades.

2. There are some questions as to what indices should be used to measure PPP. The wholesale price index (WPI) and the consumer price index (CPI) are not free of deficiencies. The WPI measures goods that are and could be traded. It is not very adequate if heavily weighted with traded goods, the prices of which may reflect changes in the world markets rather than domestic inflationary pressures. The CPI suffers from being a mix between goods and services consumed by the citizens of a given country, and that mix may not be comparable across countries. Consumption in developed countries is skewed in favor of services, while that in developing countries is skewed in favor of goods. Thus differences in CPI would simply reflect difference in weights rather than in inflationary pressures. Some researchers have experimented with the export price index (XPI). The weakness of the XPI stems from the fact that it includes only traded goods and not potentially tradable goods. Despite its weaknesses, the WPI appears to be the best measure to use in testing the PPP theory.

Uncovered Interest Rate Parity.   Another component of the asset market approach to the determination of exchange rates is uncovered interest parity (UIP), also known as *forward parity*, or the *unbiasedness of forward rates*, or the *speculative efficiency hypothesis*.

Forward parity assumes that the forward rate, $F_{t,1}$, set at time t for delivery in 1 period is the best forecast available of the future spot rate S_{t+1}:

$$F_{t,1} = E_t[S_{t+1}]. \tag{4.11}$$

The meaning of an unbiased predictor is that the average difference between the forward rate and the future spot rate will be a small number, close to zero, over long periods of time. Also, there should be no systematic positive or negative error – that is, predictable patterns of positive or negative differences between the forward and the future spot rates.

Combined with IRP and assuming that $T = 1$, this implies that

$$\frac{F_{t,1} - S_t}{S_t} = E\left[\frac{S_{t+1} - S_t}{S_t}\right] \approx i - i^*. \tag{4.12}$$

One can see, therefore, that UIP suggests that the difference in interest rates between two countries is a good predictor of the change in the spot rate.

This hypothesis can be explained by a speculation argument. If the market as a whole expects the future spot rate to be much lower than the forward rate, then speculators will sell the foreign currency forward in the expectation of being able to buy it in the future at a lower price. In the process, this will push down the forward rate until equilibrium occurs.

Obviously, this argument ignores risk, which can create a wedge between the forward rate and the expected future spot rate. The chapter on international diversification presents a model of pricing of risk that is consistent with equilibrium in international capital markets. Whether UIP holds is ultimately an empirical issue. The chapter on anomalies will review the empirical evidence on this topic. Suffice it to say at this point, early tests of UIP were unable to detect systematic biases in the forward rate but more recent research has uncovered interesting puzzles.

UIP also has important implications for the decision of where to invest or borrow. If UIP holds, Equation (4.12) can also be written as

$$i \approx i^* + E\left[\frac{S_{t+1} - S_t}{S_t}\right]. \tag{4.13}$$

This shows that returns in dollars should *on average* equal uncovered returns from investing in a foreign currency. The latter include the nominal interest payment plus the appreciation of the foreign currency. UIP implies that, on average but not in every single period, the payoff from investing or cost of borrowing in different currencies is the same. Therefore, there is no reason to seek higher returns or lower capital costs in other currencies because, ultimately, all will be equalized.

An acceptance of this hypothesis has serious implications in terms of the market for foreign exchange forecasting services. If true, the forward rate, a costless forecast, should be better than the expensive forecasts sold by Forex advisory services. Finally, the relationship implies that the cost of hedging is the same as the expected cost of not hedging. In the former case, the rate is F; in the latter, the expected rate is $E[S]$.

The International Fisher Effect.   From the monetarist point of view, PPP and UIP are two relationships that drive exchange rate movements. A natural question, then, is whether these relationships are compatible with each other.

The link between PPP and UIP lies in real interest rates. Irving Fisher decomposed the nominal interest rate into two components: the expected inflation and the expected real interest rate,

$$i_t = E_t[\pi_{t+1}] + E_t[r_{t+1}], \qquad (4.14)$$

where $E_t[r_{t+1}]$ is the expectation of the future real rate, observed "ex post" at time $t + 1$. This definition can also be written for foreign currency.

The *Fisher open effect*, or *real interest parity*, assumes that expected real interest rates are equal across currencies:

$$E_t[r_{t+1}] = E_t[r^*_{t+1}]. \qquad (4.15)$$

The three conditions are closely linked, because they all emphasize the importance of inflationary expectations. It can be shown that any two of the conditions in Equations (4.7), (4.12), and (4.15) imply the third. For instance, take UIP and decompose the nominal interest rate,

$$E\left[\frac{S_{t+1} - S_t}{S_t}\right] = i - i^* = (E_t[\pi_{t+1}] + E_t[r_{t+1}]) - (E_t[\pi^*_{t+1}] + E_t[r^*_{t+1}]),$$

which, because of "Fisher open," becomes

$$E\left[\frac{S_{t+1} - S_t}{S_t}\right] = E_t[\pi_{t+1}] - E_t[\pi_{t+1}].$$

This is exactly purchasing power parity. So, forward parity plus Fisher open together imply purchasing power parity, and these three conditions are consistent with each other. Exhibit 4.12 presents an example of the consistency between these conditions. The forward discount

EXHIBIT 4.12   Parity Conditions: An Example

	U.S.	Britain
Interest rate (1 year)	5%	10%
Spot rate	–	$2.00 £
Forward rate (1 year)	–	$1.91 £
Forward discount	–	(1.91–2)/2 = –4.5%
Forward forecast	–	–4.5%
Real interest rates	2%	2%
Expected inflation	3%	8%
PPP forecast		(1.03/1.08) – 1 = –4.6%

on the pound, which is also the movement implied by UIP, is –4.5 percent. If real rates are identical, the change in exchange rate implied by PPP is –4.6 percent. Both forecasts are consistent with each other.[5]

Overshooting. The three propositions reflect the monetarist view of exchange rates, which emphasizes the importance of inflationary expectations to the detriment of real factors. In this approach, nominal interest rates are high because expected inflation is high and therefore should be associated with a depreciating currency. Goods prices are perfectly flexible, and therefore inflation immediately adjusts to changes in monetary conditions.

This approach, however, is an imperfect description of reality if goods prices are somewhat "sticky." Suppose, for instance, the Fed decides to expand the U.S. money supply by 10 percent. As shown in Exhibit 4.13, this expansion will ultimately lead to higher prices in the United States, by 10 percent, leading to a lower value of the dollar, also by 10 percent because of PPP. In the short run, goods prices cannot immediately adjust because of so-called menu costs: restaurants need to reprint their price lists, which is costly and will be done only when restaurant owners deem it necessary. Assume, for instance, that this price level adjustment takes one year.

In the meantime, the higher supply of dollars must be held by the public. With nominal prices fixed in the short run, the only way to induce the public to demand more dollars is to lower the nominal interest rate, which is the opportunity cost of holding cash (as opposed

[5]The two numbers are essentially identical. Small differences occur, however, because of errors in approximations due to discrete compounding. Continuous compounding would completely eliminate these differences.

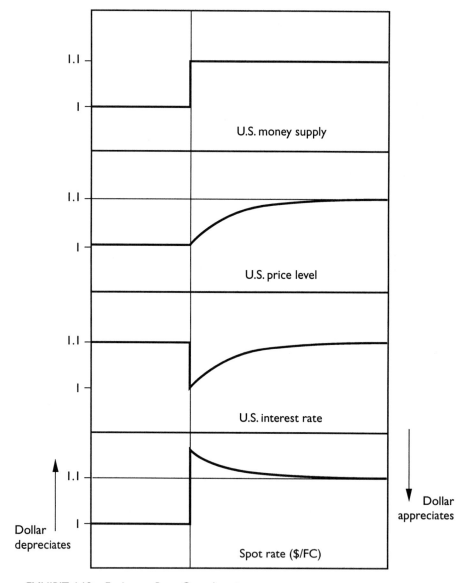

EXHIBIT 4.13   Exchange Rate Overshooting

to investing in deposits). Therefore U.S. nominal interest rates have to fall. Combined with the higher expected inflation, this leads to real interest rates being pushed down.

Consider now what happens to the dollar. After one year, it must have depreciated by 10 percent. In the meantime, dollar nominal interest rates are lower than foreign rates by 2 percent. By UIP, this means that global investors will be willing to hold dollars only if they expect an *appreciation* of the dollar over the next year. But this can occur only if the dollar immediately depreciates by 12 percent: 10 percent to account for the higher U.S. price level, and 2 percent that will be slowly eliminated by an appreciating dollar.

We observe, therefore, a phenomenon called *exchange rate overshooting*, initially described by Dornbusch (1976). The dollar immediately depreciates by more than its long-term value. With sticky goods prices, the money market and Forex markets must accommodate shocks in monetary policies and as a result are excessively volatile.

This model is particularly appealing because it explains why flexible exchange rates are so volatile. In addition, it is consistent with the evidence that real interest rates differ across countries. Mishkin (1984), for instance, focused on real rate parity over quarterly horizons and found systematic deviations in real interest rates across countries. These deviations suggest that real factors, in addition to nominal factors, have an important influence on exchange rates.

Government Intervention

The preceding models provide a framework to evaluate government intervention in the currency markets. Governments have rarely allowed foreign exchange markets to function free of intimidation or outright intervention. As discussed earlier, a government can intervene indirectly in the foreign exchange markets by influencing the real rate of interest or the rate of inflation using fiscal or monetary policy. Direct intervention by a government in the foreign exchange markets is achieved either by exchange controls or buy or sell transactions in these markets. Those transactions are typically entered into in the spot market. A speculator in the Forex markets or a tactical asset manager must be well acquainted with the nature and the effects of government intervention to avoid being fooled and bankrupted by the market.

Central banks intervene in the foreign exchange markets in various ways: by directly dealing with banks, by using commercial banks as agents operating within specified guidelines, and through various releases and actions, by attempting to dissuade speculators from a course of action.

Sources of Intervention Funds. Intervention by the U.S. government in the foreign exchange markets is undertaken by the Federal Reserve Bank of New York on behalf of the U.S. Treasury. The U.S. Treasury can directly intervene by selling securities denominated in foreign currencies.

The Fed's source of funds is the swap network. It works as follows. A swap contract is written at the end of each day that intervention takes place. To write a contract, the Federal Reserve calculates the dollar amount of the intervention and receives sufficient foreign exchange to cover its dollar purchases. The foreign bank's dollars are then invested in a nonnegotiable U.S. Treasury certificate of indebtedness until the swap is retired. Swaps are retired by purchasing the foreign bank's dollars at the original exchange rate.

Conditions for Intervention. The intervention of the Fed is officially justified on the basis that speculative activities in the market are either insufficient or "unwarranted." In either situation the activities of speculators, while essential to the efficiency of the foreign exchange market, can lead to temporary, unwarranted disequilibrium situations. Bureaucrats, usually very risk averse and much inclined to exert influence, are fearful that short-run phenomena could produce panic in the marketplace and generate problems whose solution requires a long period of adjustment. Bureaucrats, therefore, often opt for intervention.

Central banks are usually preoccupied by exchange patterns characterized as "disorderly." *Disorderly* is not well defined, but there seems to be a general understanding that a time path characterized by oscillations that are both frequent and of great amplitude is disorderly and unwarranted. Although price fluctuations certainly serve a purpose in a market economy, and one would not wish to forbid a price to go up just because there was a certain prospect that some day it would come down again, nevertheless most theorists would probably agree that "orderly" time paths are likely to be associated with higher social welfare. If the Fed had theoretical reason to believe that it could stabilize the time path of the exchange rate with little impact on other macroeconomic goals, it would probably have sufficient theoretical justification for its intervention. Exhibit 4.14 shows how the exchange rate can fluctuate around its intrinsic value.

Inefficiencies in the foreign exchange market, therefore, are a prime justification for intervention by the Fed. The issue of whether the

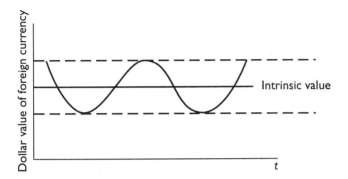

EXHIBIT 4.14   Fluctuations of Exchange Rates around Intrinsic Value

foreign exchange markets are efficient or not is unsettled. There is more agreement on the following:

1. An inefficient market implies that profitable opportunities have gone unexploited. As shown by Friedman (1953), stabilizing speculation creates profit for speculators, while the rest of society gains. This occurs because successful speculators buy when a currency is undervalued and sell when it is overvalued, thereby creating profits. Exhibit 4.14 shows that speculators who buy at the high points will put downward pressure on the exchange rate, thereby bringing it close to its intrinsic value and decreasing volatility. This process will force exchange rates to be closer to their true values.
2. If some actors have monopoly powers in the market, the lack of competition will prevent the foreign exchange markets from reaching equilibrium.

If either of these conditions occurs, then central banks have a rationale for intervention. Therefore, stabilizing currency intervention should lead to profits for the central bank.

Whether intervention actually results in profits for central banks is unclear, the reason being that central bankers are notoriously secretive about the extent of their intervention. Using the limited data available, present studies, however, seem to indicate that central banks systematically lose money from intervention. Taylor (1982), for instance, reported that, from 1973 to 1979, the central banks of major nations have collectively lost around $15 billion. During the more recent EMS turmoil of Fall 1992, European central banks are said to have lost more than $6 billion, most of which went to speculators and commercial banks. One can question the wisdom of a system that creates large transfers of wealth from taxpayers to speculators.

Effects of Intervention. To better understand the monetary implications of Forex intervention, consider the balance sheet of the Fed. Assets consist of claims on the private sector and the government, domestic credit, and reserves. Reserves are composed of claims on foreign central banks (foreign currencies), of gold, of the reserve position at the IMF, and of SDRs. Central bank liabilities consist of currency, coins and bills held by the public and commercial bank deposits, which constitute the monetary base. Exhibit 4.15 presents a simplified balance sheet as of December 1992.

Assume now that the Fed wants to sell the equivalent of $1 billion in DM reserves to support the dollar, at the spot rate of DM2/$. In the direct intervention method, the Fed consummates the operation with a commercial bank, which receives DM2 billion and pays $1 billion. The Fed's foreign currency reserves go down by $1 billion and so does the Fed's liabilities. Payment can be made in currency notes, in which case the currency held by the public decreases, or, more likely, takes the form of decreases in Fed's liabilities to commercial banks. As a result, the reserve base, a component of the money supply, decreases by $1 billion.

If intervention is allowed to have full impact on the money supply, it is called *unsterilized*. This, however, will have repercussions on the money market. Because interest rates represent the opportunity cost of holding cash, the public will reduce its demand for money

EXHIBIT 4.15 Balance Sheet of the U.S. Fed (billions of dollars, December 1992)

Assets			Liabilities		
Domestic Credit	=	289	Currency	=	297
Reserves	=	72	Deposits	=	74
For. Cur.	=	40			
Gold	=	11			
SDRs	=	9			
IMF Pos.	=	12			
Total	=	361	Total	=	361

only if U.S. nominal interest rates increase. Thus, in equilibrium, a lower money supply will put upward pressure on U.S. interest rates. Higher interest rates will make the dollar more attractive and induce investors to buy the dollar, which reinforces the effect of the initial purchase of dollars by the Fed.

On the other hand, if the Fed is unwilling to let the intervention affect the money supply, it will simultaneously buy government securities, Treasury bills, for instance, from commercial banks. Assuming that this purchase is made with currency notes, the amount of currency held by the public will increase by $1 billion, as will the Fed's claims on the government. This leaves the money supply unchanged. However, buying Treasury bills tends to push up their price or, equivalently, to bring down interest rates. This defeats the upward pressure on interest rates brought about by intervention in the foreign currency market. This type of intervention, which is offset by open market operations, is called *sterilized*. It is essentially equivalent to changing the composition of assets of the central bank, by selling foreign currencies and replacing them with government debt.

Intervention can now be evaluated using these two approaches. By most central banks' admission, sterilized intervention is not very effective. This suggests that what affects exchange rates is not the flow buying or selling by a market participant but rather the impact of these flows on the relative attractiveness of two currencies, which is determined mainly by interest rates. Therefore, the stock approach appears to be much more appropriate than the flow approach in describing the primary factors driving exchange rates.

The stock, or asset market, approach also explains why intervention is effective in some cases and not in others. When intervention signals an actual change in monetary policy, it is likely to have an impact on the exchange rate. In contrast, when intervention is not credibly accompanied by changes in economic policy, it is unlikely to affect exchange rates. This is especially true since the trading volume in the foreign exchange market, about $900 billion daily, is much greater than whatever amount the world's central banks can field. The total stock of reserves held by central banks is about $1 trillion and would be exhausted in a single day. In terms of relative volumes, intervention can be only a drop in the sea of foreign exchange trading. When governments cannot credibly signal their commitment to an exchange rate value, as happened in Fall 1992 with Britain and Italy, central banks cannot help but be swept by waves of speculative activity.

Forecasting Exchange Rates

Forecasting services usually rely on one of two methods: econometric or technical. Each has its drawbacks, which will be detailed. To these drawbacks must be added one major additional reservation about the wisdom of the whole process. To the extent that foreign exchange markets are efficient, the whole exercise is fruitless; that is, no additional price information useful for profitable trading can be gained by the most sophisticated of econometric models. These reservations, however, did not stop academicians and practitioners from trying. One reason is that the market, although efficient on the average, may not be permanently efficient, thus possibly creating substantial profit opportunities.

Econometric Models.   Purchasing power parity can be taken to be a simple econometric model of exchange rates, based on national price levels. It has been extended to a more complete monetary model, which directly focuses on the supply and demand for money in each country. The rationale for this is that money market conditions better anticipate inflationary pressures than the price level, especially when prices are controlled. By assuming that the demand for money is a stable function of parameters such as interest rates and real income, the monetary approach leads to the following regression:

$$s_t = b_0 + b_1 m_t - b_2 m_t^* - b_3 y_t + b_4 y_t^* + b_5(i - i^*) + s_{t-1} + \epsilon_t , \quad (4.16)$$

where

s_t = logarithm of the spot rate at time t (US\$/foreign currency),
m, m^* = logarithm of the U.S. and foreign money supplies,
y, y^* = logarithm of the U.S. and foreign real incomes,
i, i^* = U.S. and foreign nominal interest rates.

The model predicts that an expansion in the U.S. money supply, ceteris paribus, will lead to a depreciation of the dollar, or an increase in s. An increase in U.S. real income will increase the demand for U.S. dollar balances and lead to an appreciation of the dollar. According to the monetary model, higher U.S. nominal rates are associated with higher U.S. expected inflation and therefore lead to a depreciating dollar. This, however, can be modified to obtain a different relationship between exchange rates and interest rates. The model can be augmented by splitting $i - i^*$ into an expected inflation component $E[\pi] - E[\pi^*]$ and an expected real rate component $E[r] - E[r^*]$. With this extension, higher U.S. nominal interest rates, if associated with higher U.S. real rates, would lead to an appreciation of the dollar. This decomposition clearly shows that the link between interest rates and exchange rates fundamentally depends on the nature of the shocks affecting the economy.

Other variables have proven, especially with fixed exchange rates, to be valuable indicators of direction in a currency. For instance, with balance of payments data, a positive current balance is an indication of a stable if not appreciating currency. Also, larger reserves indicate greater liquidity, greater ability to meet unfavorable balances in the international account, and greater ability to support a currency level. These variables can be added to Equation (4.16).

The main drawbacks of econometric models are

1. The assumption that structural relationships do not change over time;
2. The estimated parameters are measured with imprecision, which may affect the quality and stability of forecast estimates;
3. The forcing, right-hand side, variables must be forecast first (it may be as difficult to forecast future interest rates as to forecast future exchange rates).

Meese and Rogoff (1983), for instance, have evaluated the predictive accuracy of such exchange rate models and found that, even with full knowledge of the (future) forcing variables, these models perform more poorly than a simple random-walk model. Drawbacks 1 and 2 therefore create serious difficulties in forecasting exchange rates.

Some forecasting services now use vector autoregression (VAR) models, in which both exchange rates and interest rates are simultaneously forecast from prior values of all variables of interest. To address the issues of stability and precision, Bayesian statistical techniques are used to measure and frequently update the estimated parameters.

Technical Analysis.   All the preceding analyses are of no value, technical analysts argue. It is better to spend time identifying past price patterns, because they are likely to be repeated. Exchange rates are determined by the interaction of supply and demand, which are influenced by both rational and irrational factors. Understanding those factors requires understanding the "psychology" of the market participants.

The techniques employed by technicians are varied – simplistic in some cases and very complex in others. A comprehensive review of forecasting techniques was undertaken by Stephen Goodman (1979), with a dual purpose: the examination of the merits of a given technique and simultaneously the testing of the hypothesis on market efficiency. Goodman evaluated six economics-oriented and four technically oriented services on the basis of their predictive accuracy with regard to six currencies against the dollar. The quality of services was evaluated using three criteria: accuracy in predicting trends, accuracy of their point estimates, and speculative return on capital at risk.

The results were startling in light of the accumulating literature indicating market efficiency:

> Blindly following the economics-oriented services' forecasts is profitable, but only marginally so. It is generally less profitable than a buy and hold strategy.
>
> All the technically oriented services do remarkably well. The speculative return on capital at risk for each of the services averages between 7.28% and 10.46% annually before transactions costs, compared with a 2.86% return on a buy and hold strategy. The average performance of the poorest technically oriented services is far better than the average performance of the best economics-oriented service.

Whereas the previous results focus on actual predictions, it is also useful to see how common technical methods fare over time. An objective review of the efficacy of filter rules was conducted by Sweeney (1991). The study concludes that

> On a practitioner level, the evidence seems to be that well-crafted technical approaches can generate persistent measured profits. These profits are subject to randomness, however, suggesting using a portfolio of currencies in any technical approach. It is possible that some of the randomness remaining to portfolios of currencies managed with technical approaches can be diversified away. For example, most estimates of foreign exchange betas are small, suggesting that a technical foreign exchange portfolio that is a small part of a well-diversified portfolio might add essentially no risk.

These studies can be interpreted as evidence of inefficiencies in foreign exchange markets. If justified, these results indicate that forecasting services have justified their existence and their charges. To some extent, this is not unexpected, because no forecasting service can permanently survive the onslaught of a market offering evidence contrary to the values forecast. On the other hand, it can be argued that many of the "new" technical models discovered using technical analysis are simply the result of data mining and are not stable enough to consistently produce profits. In particular, these rules have not been recognized by many forecasting services. Levich (1980), for instance, objectively evaluated the forecasting accuracy of foreign exchange advisory services and found that their forecasts are more often than not dominated by the forward rate, a freely available forecast. These issues will be explored further in the chapter on anomalies.

Conclusions

This chapter attempts to provide a condensed version of the relevant literature on the Forex markets, in the hope of building a solid ground for the management of foreign exchange risk.

We first covered the evolution of the international financial system from fixed to flexible exchange rates and illustrated the debate on exchange rate systems by studying problems of monetary convergence in Europe. The chapter then turned to the description of the foreign exchange markets, focusing on spot and forwards contracts.

Explaining flexible exchange rates is no easy matter. We contrasted two views, one based on flow demand and supply, the other taking an asset market approach, and showed that the latter is more satisfactory. In the context of the asset market approach, we showed that purchasing power parity can be used for long-term forecasting of exchange rates and that forward rates provide short-term forecasts. This led to the theory of "exchange rate overshooting," which integrates classical parity conditions with the important empirical observations that flexible exchange rates appear quite volatile and essentially unpredictable.

References

Dornbusch, R. 1976. "Expectations and exchange rate dynamics," *Journal of Political Economy* 84: 1161–76.
Friedman, M. 1953. "The case for flexible exchange rates," in *Essays in Positive Economics*, University of Chicago Press, Chicago.

Goodman, S. 1979."Foreign exchange forecasting techniques: Implications for business and policy," *Journal of Finance* 34: 415–27.

Hilley, J., C. Beidleman, and J. Greenleaf. 1979. "Does covered interest arbitrage dominate in foreign exchange markets?" *Columbia Journal of World Business* 14: 99–107.

Levich, R. 1980. "Analyzing the accuracy of foreign exchange advisory services: Theory and evidence," in *Exchange Risk and Exposure*, ed. R. Levich and C. Wihlborg, D. C. Heath, Lexington, Mass.

Meese, R., and K. Rogoff. 1983. "Empirical exchange rate models of the seventies: Do they fit out of sample?" *Journal of International Economics* 14: 3–24.

Mishkin, F. 1984. "Are real interest rates equal across countries? An empirical investigation of international parity conditions," *Journal of Finance* 39: 1345–57.

Mussa, M. 1979. "Empirical regularities in the behavior of exchange rates and theories of the foreign exchange market," in *Carnegie-Rochester Conference on Public Policy* 11: 9–57.

Officer, L. 1976. "The purchasing power parity theory of exchange rates: A review article," *International Monetary Fund Staff Papers* 23: 1–61.

Sweeney, R. 1991. "Technical strategies in foreign exchange markets: An interim report," in *Recent Developments in International Banking and Finance*, ed. S. J. Khoury, North-Holland, Elsevier.

Taylor, D. 1982. "Official intervention in the foreign exchange market, or bet against the central bank," *Journal of Political Economy* 355–368.

5

Currency Risk Management: Hedging and Speculating with Options and Futures

This chapter deals with derivative securities in the foreign exchange market. Derivative securities can be generally defined as securities valued in reference to underlying assets. In this context, the value underlying is the spot exchange rate. Although we focus on currency options and futures, the concepts developed here are fully transferable to any options and futures contracts.

The options and futures markets are fertile grounds for imaginative, quick-thinking individuals with any type of risk profile. The possibility set is limited only by the creativity of the participants.

Derivative instruments are essential risk management tools because they allow tight control over exposure to financial risk. As a result, there has been an explosion in the volume of trading in derivatives in the last decade. Futures and options exchanges are now sprouting all over the world, and U.S. exchanges are slowly losing their dominance to foreign markets.

Exhibit 5.1 displays the growth of derivatives markets from 1988 to 1992. In five years, the annual number of contracts traded on exchanges mushroomed from about 250 million contracts to 450 million contracts. On the Philadelphia Stock Exchange (PHLX) alone, the daily volume of currency options, reported in Exhibit 5.2, has grown from zero in 1982 to more than 50,000; given that the face value of PHLX contracts is about $50,000, this implies a notional daily trading

Derivatives contracts traded:

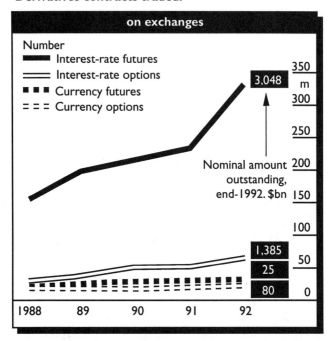

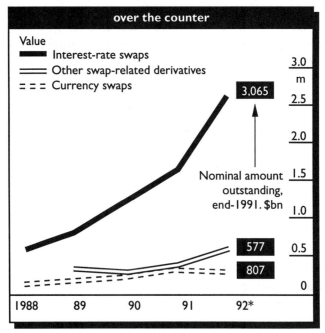

Source: Bank for International Settlements, 1993.

EXHIBIT 5.1   Growth in Derivatives Markets

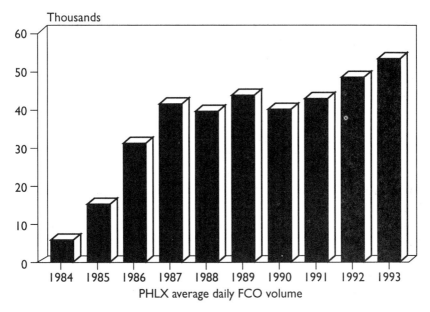

EXHIBIT 5.2   Growth in PHLX Currency Option Trading

volume of $2.5 billion. These are respectable numbers, even by the standards of the Forex markets.

Over-the-counter trading has also sharply increased over the last few years and is similar in size to exchange trading. Total amounts outstanding are $4.3 trillion and $4.5 trillion for OTC and exchange-traded contracts, respectively. The total value of OTC trading is now about $3.6 trillion annually, or about $15 billion daily. Although the bulk of trading is in interest rate swaps, there is also substantial activity in long-term currency swaps.

In this chapter, we develop strategies for options and futures both on the hedging and the speculative sides. After reviewing recent developments in derivatives markets, we present foreign currency futures. Futures are traded on exchanges and are standardized contracts, as opposed to forwards, which are traded over the counter and are tailored to clients' needs. The next section presents the market and uses of currency options. Because options contracts are valuable instruments and therefore carry a price, it is important to understand the factors driving this price, called the *option premium*. The third section explains the factors affecting the premium and discusses the Black-Scholes and binomial option pricing models. We also show

how to measure the sensitivity of the option value to different factors and the usefulness of these measures for the risk management of an option portfolio. Finally, we develop advanced hedging and speculation strategies using options. Although the mathematics is kept to a minimum, the topic is rather technical by nature.

Foreign Exchange Futures

The forward market lost its monopoly on foreign exchange contracts for future delivery on May 16, 1972, when the International Monetary Market (IMM), a subsidiary of the Chicago Mercantile Exchange, began trading futures contracts on foreign currencies. Today, futures contracts in the United States cover the Japanese yen, the deutsche mark, the Canadian dollar, the Swiss franc, and the Australian dollar.

The raison d'être of the futures market is to provide low-cost access to payoffs similar to forwards contracts. Up to 1972, speculators and hedgers could take forward positions only through the wholesale over-the-counter market. Participants first needed to establish lines of credit with commercial banks and also had to deal in large transaction sizes to benefit from low bid–ask spreads. This severely restricted access to the market.

Futures Contracts

In response, the IMM created standardized futures contracts on foreign currencies. A futures contract is a tradable obligation to the buyer (the seller) to buy (sell) a set amount of foreign exchange at a specified price at some future date. The buyer is said to have a "long" position, while the seller is said to be "short."

To ensure active trading, liquidity, and low transaction costs, the contracts are highly standardized: they have the same size, a limited number of expiration dates, typically four, and the same default risk. Contracts are available to investors who can put up the margin; the low amount of initial capital allows highly leveraged positions.

Exhibit 5.3 displays quotations as reported by the *Wall Street Journal*. One contract on the DM, for instance, bears on DM125,000 and is available for expiration in the next March, June, September, and December. The IMM uses the direct quotation system: the price of a unit of foreign currency in terms of domestic currency, such as the

EXHIBIT 5.3 Foreign Currency Futures Quotations

FUTURES PRICES

Wednesday, March 31, 1993

Open Interest Reflects Previous Trading Day

CURRENCY

	Open	High	Low	Settle	Change	Lifetime High	Lifetime Low	Open Interest
JAPAN YEN (CME) – 12.5 million yen; $ per yen (.00)								
June	.8583	.8726	.8574	.8704	+.0134	.8726	.7745	65,876
Sept	.8590	.8728	.8590	.8706	+.0134	.8728	.7945	2,406
Dec	.8700	.8712	.8700	.8714	+.0134	.8712	.7970	663
Est vol 25.402; vol Tues 10.556; open int 68.945. –31								
DEUTSCHEMARK (CME) – 125,000 marks; $ per mark								
June	.6121	.6158	.6105	.6156	+.0035	.6920	.5890	98,049
Sept	.6080	.6102	.6075	.6098	+.0034	.6720	.5863	4,731
Dec	.6008	.6050	.6038	.6057	+.0033	.6650	.5830	173
Est vol 45,378; vol Tues 45,656; open int 102,961, +3,869.								
CANADIAN DOLLAR (CME) – 100,000 dlrs.; $ per Can $								
June	.7950	.7950	.7904	.7913	–.0044	.8360	.7532	18,762
Sept	.7886	.7886	.7865	.7866	–.0047	.8335	.7515	616
Dec	.7848	.7848	.7838	.7818	–.0049	.8310	.7470	841
Mr94	....	....	....	.7772	–.0051	.7860	.7550	578
Est vol 5,970; vol Tues 9,370; open int 20,804. –2,013.								
BRITISH POUND (CME) – 62,500 pds.; $ per pound								
June	1.4846	1.5061	1.4846	1.5044	+.0206	1.9100	1.4020	29,737
Sept	1.4860	1.4970	1.4856	1.4954	+.0202	1.5580	1.3980	689
Est vol 15,627; vol Tues 8,489; open int 30,665. +389.								
SWISS FRANC (CME) – 125,000 francs; $ per franc								
June	.6665	.6689	.6653	.6683	+.0016	.8070	.6405	41,369
Sept	.6655	.6665	.6640	.6662	+.0014	.7100	.6380	1,244
Est vol 20,175; vol Tues 22,247; open int 42,624. + 362.								
AUSTRALIAN DOLLAR (CME) – 100,000 dlrs.; $ per A.$								
June	.7024	.7035	.7010	.7021	–.0068	.7158	.6590	3,452
Est vol 443; vol Tues 134; open int 3,480. –50.								
U.S. DOLLAR INDEX (FINEX) – 1,000 times USDX								
June	93.59	93.65	92.87	92.94	–.63	97.20	82.55	5,088
Sept	94.33	94.33	94.07	94.08	–.59	97.10	94.00	167
Est vol 2,430; vol Tues 2,081; open int 18,916. +42.								
The index: High 92.52; Low 91.87; Close 91.90 –.62								

Source: *Wall Street Journal*, April 1, 1993.

U.S. dollar. All foreign exchange rates are quoted with four digits to the right of the decimal except for the Japanese yen, which is quoted in cents per yen. Currency futures contracts expire on the Monday before the third Wednesday of the contract month.

After confirmation of the trade for both sides, the clearing corporation (CC) interposes itself as the legal counterpart to the trades. It becomes the seller to each buyer and the buyer to each seller. As such, the CC guarantees payments (delivery) on foreign exchange futures contracts traded on its exchange. The CC is, in turn, guaranteed by the capital of the member firms, who encompass most major securities and commodities firms. This very high level of safety, the standard size of the contracts, the centralized nature of the market, and large volume of trading account for the high level of liquidity the contracts enjoy. Because the clearing corporation has the highest credit rating, futures contracts have little or no default risk, which is not the case with forward contracts.

Initiating a position in futures contracts, whether short or long, requires the payment of a margin at the time of purchase. The typical initial margin requirement, $2,000 per contract, is set by the exchange. This margin, equivalent to a performance bond, is deposited in an equity account with the broker. It is intended to provide some protection in the event the market moves in a direction opposite to that expected by the buyer or the seller of the futures contract. This, incidentally, is not required for forward contracts.

An essential difference between futures and forward contracts is that futures positions are *marked to market* on a daily basis. Every day, the value of the equity is computed as the initial margin plus accumulated changes in the value of the futures contract. Profits are measured as $n(f_t - f_{t-1})$, where n is the contract position (positive if long, negative if short), and f_t is the daily futures price at settlement. This is set by the exchange and is generally, but not necessarily, the price at closing time. Any loss will necessitate additional margin deposited prior to the opening of the next day in the event the balance falls below the required maintenance level (typically $1,500). Clients unable to meet margin calls will see their positions liquidated. The margin can be met using interest-bearing instruments such as T-bills and does not represent an equity position in the underlying asset nor a cost to the position, because any interest fully accrues to the holder. The margin is simply a performance bond against which losses are offset. This is why a replenishment is necessary for losing positions, whether long or short.

Futures vs. Forwards

Futures and forwards are compared in Exhibit 5.4. Both contracts involve the obligation to buy at a specified price. Given the similarity between the contracts, prices must be very similar for identical maturities, otherwise arbitrageurs would step in and bring the prices into equality.

The main difference between the two types of contracts is the daily marking to market. Futures contracts require cash flows, possibly on a daily basis. This makes them sensitive to interest rate changes, as outflows have an explicit cost (borrowing rates) or implicit cost

EXHIBIT 5.4   Comparison of Futures and Forwards

	Forwards	Futures
Size of contract	Tailored to individual needs.	Standardized.
Delivery date	Tailored to individual needs.	Standardized.
Method of transaction	Established by the bank or broker via telephone contact with limited number of buyers and sellers.	Determined by open auction among many buyers and sellers on the exchange floor.
Participants	Banks, brokers, and multinational companies. Public speculation not encouraged.	Banks, brokers, and multinational companies. Qualified public speculation encouraged.
Commissions	Set by "spread" between bank's buy and sell price. Not easily determined by the customer.	Published small brokerage fee and negotiated rates on block trades.
Security deposit	None as such, but compensating bank balances required.	Published small security deposit required.
Clearing operation (financial)	Handling contingent on individual banks and brokers. No separate clearinghouse function.	Handled by exchange clearinghouse. Daily settlements to the market.
Marketplace	Over the telephone worldwide.	Central exchange floor with worldwide communications.
Economic justification	Facilitate world trade by providing hedge mechanism.	Same as forward market. In addition, it provides a broader market and an alternative hedging mechanism.
Accessibility	Limited to very large customers who deal in foreign trade.	Open to anyone who needs hedge facilities or has risk capital with which to speculate.
Regulating	Self-regulating.	April 1975 – regulated under the Commodity Futures Trading Commission.
Frequency of delivery	More than 90% settled by actual delivery.	Theoretically, no deliveries in a perfect market. In reality, less than 1%.
Market liquidity	Offsetting with other banks.	Public offset. Arbitrage offset.

Source: *Understanding Futures in Foreign Exchange.* International Monetary Market, Chicago, August 1979.

(opportunity cost) and inflows have to be reinvested at unpredictable rates. This is not the case with forward contracts, as they require no cash flows, initially or during the life of the contract.

As a result, the price on futures contracts might be slightly different from that on forward contracts. For example, a futures contract might be preferable to a forward contract if futures payoffs are positively correlated with interest rates. In that situation, when the long position creates profits, these can be reinvested at a higher interest rate. In theory, this should lead to futures prices slightly higher than forward prices. In practice, however, there is little discernible difference between the two prices.

In terms of transaction costs, both contracts involve similar spreads, even with different market structures. The forward market is a dealers' market, where dealers quote a bid and ask price, on the order of 0.05 percent for large transactions, above $1 million. The futures market, in contrast, is an auction market, where orders to buy and sell are transmitted to the floor; one broker may be selling, another may be buying. All transactions are consummated on the floor of the exchange. Although costs are less directly observable than in the forward market, spreads are also on the order of 0.05 percent. Note that the futures market brings the low transaction costs of the wholesale market down to small trades. This is the very reason futures markets have become so popular.

Forward contracts, however, are more flexible, because they can be tailored to the specific needs of a client. They remain fundamentally a wholesale market. Also, hedging results are guaranteed, because forward contracts are not subject to basis risk, as we will show.

Hedging Using Futures

Hedgers and speculators can use the futures market in a manner similar to that in the forward market. The hedger enters the futures market to offset a cash position (actual or prospective), expecting that the profits on the futures contract will offset those in the cash market. The success of the hedger is determined by movements in the *basis*, defined as the difference between the spot rate and the futures rate $S_t - f_t$. The basis is set primarily by interest rate differentials among countries, as demonstrated by interest rate parity $(S_t - f_t)/S_t = (i_{US} - i^*)/(1 + i^*)$. We now offer an example of a short hedge.

Hedging with Futures.   A short hedge involves a long position in the spot market and simultaneously a short position in the futures market. In contrast, a long hedge consists of a short position in the cash market and a long position in the futures market.

A naive hedge strategy matches the face value of the long position with that of the short (futures) position; as we show later, however, this is not always optimal. The hope is that whatever is lost in the long (spot) position due to a price decline will be gained in the short position. If all uncertainty in the total payoff is eliminated, the hedge is said to be perfect.

Consider, for instance, the case of an American tool maker with a German subsidiary in need of cash to meet operating expenses. The cash infusion into the subsidiary requires the purchase of DM against dollars and simultaneously the sale of a DM futures contract with a maturity closest to the debt repayment date. Assume that the spot rate on March 31 is $S_1 = 0.6170$, and the December futures rate is $f_1 = 0.5990$. The basis is initially $S_1 - f_1 = 0.0180$. Exhibit 5.5 presents three possible realizations for the future spot rate.

Before we comment on the preceding transactions and their consequences, let us review the alternative strategy of hedging in the forward market.[1] In that case, the hedge involves selling DM1 million at the forward rate $F_1(\$/DM) = 0.6020$. Defining $S_1 = 0.6170$ as the beginning spot rate and S_2 as the ending spot rate, the profit on the spot transaction is $DM1m(S_2 - S_1)$. The profit on the forward transaction is $-DM1m(S_2 - F_1)$. Therefore the total profit is $DM1m[(S_2 - S_1) - (S_2 - F_1)] = DM1m[(F_1 - S_1)] = -\$15,000$, which is a negative payout because the DM is cheaper in the forward market than in the spot market. With the forward contract, this payout occurs whatever the future spot rate is: this is a true hedge.

There are no such guarantees in the futures case, because of movements in the basis. The basis was initially 0.0180, for a total of 257 days to expiration. In case 1, interest rate differentials have not changed, and the basis shrinks linearly with time to expiration to $0.0180*43/257 = 0.0030$. In that case, the sum of the loss on the spot and futures contract is equal to $15,000; the hedge perfectly reproduces the payoff

---

[1]On March 31 the hedger can calculate the implied futures rate for a contract maturing on September 31, instead of December 13. This rate $= 0.6170 + (0.5990 - 0.6170) \, 214/257 = 0.6020$, where 214 days is the time period between March 31 and September 31, and 257 days is the time period between March 31 and December 13.

EXHIBIT 5.5   Short Futures Hedge

	Cash (Spot) Market	Futures Market
Mar 31:		
	Buy 1 million DM at 0.6170	Sold 8 Dec DM contracts at 0.5990
	Cost $617,500	Proceeds $599,000
Sep 31:		
Case 1	S($/DM) = 0.6100	f($/DM)= 0.6070
	Sell 1 million DM	Buy 8 Dec contracts back
	Proceeds $610,000	Cost $607,000
	Loss = (610,000 − 617,000) =	Loss = (599,000 − 607,000) =
	−$7,000	−$8,000
		Net loss = −7,000 − 8,000 =
		−$15,000
Case 2	S($/DM)= 0.5700	f($/DM)= 0.5680
	Sell 1 million DM	Buy 8 Dec contracts
	Proceeds $570,000	Cost $568,000
	Loss = (570,000 − 617,000) =	Profit = (599,000 − 568,000) =
	−$47,000	$31,000
		Net loss = −47,000 + 31,000 =
		−$16,000
Case 3	S($/DM) = 0.6300	f($/DM) = 0.6260
	Sell 1 million DM	Buy 8 Dec contracts
	Proceeds $630,000	Cost $626,000
	Profit = (630,000 − 617,000) =	Loss = (599,000 − 626,000) =
	$13,000	−$27,000
		Net loss = 13,000 − 27,000 =
		−$14,000

on the forward contract. In case 2, the DM has depreciated, possibly due to a decrease in DM interest rates; the basis shrinks to 0.0020, and the total loss is $16,000. Thus the futures hedge produces an additional loss of $1,000. In case 3, the DM has appreciated, possibly due to an increase in DM interest rates; the basis increases to 0.0040, and the total loss is $14,000. Thus the futures hedge produces a profit of $1,000.

In summary, the long cash–short futures position is exposed to basis risk. The hedger is said to be "long the basis," because increases in the basis create additional profits. In effect, the hedger substitutes basis risk for price risk. The bet is consequently on the relationship between rates instead of the rate level.

It should be emphasized, however, that this residual risk is very small compared to the risk of the unhedged position. Spot position profits range from −$47,000 to $13,000. The futures hedge has transformed these payoffs into a narrow range of −$14,000 to −$16,000. Hence the hedger can worry less about exchange rate volatility.

Given the hedger's expectations about the basis, it may not be necessary, however, to offset the cash position on a one-to-one basis by a futures position. This is referred to as a naive hedge. For instance, in this case, given the correlation between the spot rate and interest differentials, it may have been advantageous to purchase slightly more than eight contracts, so that the futures payoffs in cases 2 and 3 are $32,000 and −$28,000, respectively. This would lead to a total payoff of −$15,000 in both cases, which is a perfect hedge. One way to arrive at the "optimal" hedge ratio will follow.

Advanced Hedging with Futures.   From the preceding presentation, one concludes that the results of a hedge depend on the accurate measurement of the *hedge ratio*: the number of futures contracts necessary to provide the best hedge against a spot foreign exchange exposure. Profits or losses result from unexpected changes in the value of an asset arising from unexpected changes in the exchange rate.

Let

$$P = \text{profit} = V_t(S_0 + \Delta S_0^U + \Delta S_0^e) - V_0 S_0 , \qquad (5.1)$$

where

V_0, V_t = value of asset in foreign currency at time zero
and t, respectively,

$S_0 + \Delta S_0^U + \Delta S_0^e = S_t$,

ΔS_0^U = unexpected change in the spot rate,

ΔS_0^e = expected change in the spot rate,

$V_t = V_0(1 + r)$, with a possibly stochastic return r.

The hedger faces two sources of uncertainty: *quantity uncertainty*, because the foreign currency amount is uncertain at expiration, and *exchange rate uncertainty*. Hedging the currency exposure of an investment in foreign stocks, for instance, is difficult, because the investor does not know exactly how much of the foreign currency to sell forward since the future value of foreign investment is random.

Here, we shall address only exchange rate uncertainty. To simplify our presentation further we assume that our investment overseas consists of one unit of foreign currency and that the change in the spot rate is entirely unanticipated.

Assuming that N_f represents the number of long positions in futures contracts, our profit under these assumptions is

$$P = \Delta S + \Delta f\, N_f. \tag{5.2}$$

Since the profit in Equation (5.2) is risky, one should try to find that hedge that reduces risk to the minimum level.

The variance of profits is equal to

$$\sigma_P^2 = \sigma_{\Delta S}^2 + \sigma_{\Delta f}^2 N_f^2 + 2\sigma_{\Delta S,\Delta f} N_f.$$

Therefore,

$$\frac{\partial \sigma_P^2}{\partial N_f} = 2\sigma_{\Delta f}^2 N_f + 2\sigma_{\Delta S,\Delta f}. \tag{5.3}$$

Setting Equation (5.3) equal to zero and solving for N_f, we get

$$N_f^* = \frac{-\sigma_{\Delta S,\Delta f}}{\sigma_{\Delta f}^2}, \tag{5.4}$$

where $\sigma_{\Delta S,\Delta f}$ is the covariance between futures and spot price changes. N_f^* is the hedge ratio that minimizes the risk of the hedge, known as the *minimum variance hedge ratio.*

Further, we can measure the quality of the optimal hedge ratio in terms of the effectiveness of the hedge:

$$E = \frac{\sigma_{\Delta S}^2 - \sigma_P^2}{\sigma_{\Delta S}^2}. \tag{5.5}$$

Substituting the optimal hedge ratio into the value of σ_P^2, we get

$$\sigma_P^2 = \sigma_{\Delta S}^2 - \sigma_{\Delta S,\Delta f}^2/\sigma_{\Delta f}^2 = \sigma_{\Delta S}^2 - N_f^{*2}\sigma_{\Delta f}^2,$$

and as a result E simplifies to

$$E = \frac{N_f^{*2}\sigma_{\Delta f}^2}{\sigma_{\Delta S}^2}.$$

This is also the coefficient of determination, or the percentage of variance in ΔS explained by the independent variable Δf.

In practice, the optimal hedge ratio can be derived from a regression based on historical data. If the horizon is one day, the hedge ratio can be found from a regression of the price change over one day against the change in the futures rate:

$$\Delta S_t = a + b\Delta f_t + \epsilon_t. \tag{5.6}$$

Ederington (1979) showed that this equation could be used to derive the optimal hedge ratio, b, assuming historical data are in fact representative of today's reality.

The optimum (minimum variance) hedge ratio we have discussed thus far is applicable to a direct hedge. It can be adopted to a cross hedge as well. The latter involves hedging a Dutch guilder (DG) exposure using, for example, a DM futures contract. Here the correlation between the DG price changes and the DM price changes would serve as an adjustment to the hedge ratio calculated using the DM.

We must note that a portfolio of currencies may be "naturally" hedged as movements in currencies offset each other through diversification effects. For instance, if the correlation between the dollar/yen and dollar/mark rates is low, movements in one currency may be sometimes offset by movements in the other, so that a portfolio invested in both currencies will have lower risk than either exchange rate. The remaining, residual, risk could then be hedged using optimization techniques or a futures contract on a basket of currencies such as the ECU or a dollar index.

Hedging Long-Term Exposure.   Should an expected asset exposure be spread out over time intervals such as March, June, September, and December one may wish to hedge the exposure using strip hedges or rolling hedges.

In a *strip* hedge, each exposure per time period is hedged using the minimum variance number of futures contracts for that period. This assumes that each hedging instrument (each contract month) has an acceptable level of liquidity.

In a *rolling hedge*, on the other hand, the total exposure across all time periods is hedged up front using the appropriate number of futures contracts for the nearest contract (the most liquid contract) to the first spot maturity.

At the end of each period, the hedger closes out all outstanding futures contracts, and the remaining total exposure is then rolled forward to the next nearest futures contract. For example, a total initial exposure of $90 million would necessitate a hedge for the $90 million using the March contract. If, in the second period, the total remaining exposure were $65 million, it would be hedged using the appropriate number of minimum variance June futures contracts, and so on. Clearly, a rolling hedge exposes the investor to basis risk. As before, this risk can be avoided through using long-dated forwards contracts; these, however, are thinly traded for maturities longer than a year and can involve wide bid–ask spreads.

Speculating Using Futures

Futures markets have many features that are attractive to speculators: low commissions, low margin requirements, and very high liquidity.

Speculators who expected the DM to fall in value in relation to the dollar would sell a futures DM contract and buy it back at a lower price once their expectations had been realized. If, on the other hand, speculators expected the DM to strengthen against the dollar, they would purchase a DM futures contract and sell it at a higher price once the currencies had moved in the expected direction. In either case, speculators can close out their position in the futures market if their expectations do not materialize.

While the rewards may be great, the risks are commensurate. Speculation in foreign currencies is not for amateurs. Even "professionals" get burned and bring down organizations with them. Witness what happened to the Franklin National Bank. Its failure as a banking institution was primarily the result of excessive speculation in the foreign exchange market.

The currency futures markets offer interesting opportunities for speculators. These markets are characterized by high leverage possibilities, very high liquidity, low transactions costs, and a large body of information on the price behavior (past, actual, and expected) of the underlying security. Market participants may speculate on the level of the rate or on the relationship among rates.

Rate-Level Speculation.   Speculators are hedgers without offsetting positions in the cash market. They simply bet on the direction of exchange rates: long positions if an appreciation is expected, and short positions if a depreciation is expected. The "theories" on when to go long or short are actually more diverse than the theorists themselves. Speculators in the futures market rely extensively on technical analysis with some attention to the fundamentals.

A study by Stephen Taylor (1990) considers the effectiveness of three of the most prominent technical trading rules: the filter trading rule, the channel system, and the double moving-average system.

In *the filter rule,* each day the position is reviewed:

- If we are long on day $t - 1$ and today's closing price is more than x percent lower than the previous peak price, then we (i) close the long position and initiate a short position and (ii) let the trough price be today's closing price. The filter size, x, is typically between 0.5 percent and 10 percent.
- If we are short, and today's price is more than x percent higher than the previous trough price, then we (i) close the short position and initiate a long position and (ii) let the peak price be today's closing price.

The channel system generates trading signals whenever the price is outside the range of prices in a specified time interval. A high price compared with a particular number of recent prices is presumed to signal an upward trend in prices, and conversely, a low price signals a downward trend. The system has one parameter L, which is the length of the channel.

Each day the position is reviewed:

- If long on day $t - 1$, we calculate the minimum of the L closing prices for days $t - L$ to $t - 1$ inclusive. Then if today's price, on day t, is less than the minimum in the channel, we close the long position and initiate a short position. The trade is executed at the closing price on day t.
- If short on day $t - 1$, we calculate the maximum of the L closing prices for days $t - L$ to $t - 1$. If today's price is more than the maximum in the channel, we close the short position and initiate a long position. The trade is executed at the closing price on day t.

In *the double moving-average system,* a moving average is simply an average of past prices. The average of the N closing prices from days $t - N + 1$ to t inclusive is defined as A. The system we consider uses two moving averages, A_S and A_L, of duration N_S (short term) and

N_L (longer term). Proponents of the system argue that when the two moving averages cross, then the price trend has changed. If the short-term average is above the longer-term average, recent prices must be higher than more distant prices so the recent "trend" in price is upward. Conversely, when the short-term average is below the longer-term average, the trend is bearish. It has been said that the managers of most futures funds use the dual moving-average crossover system.

Each day the position is reviewed:

- If long on day $t - 1$ and $A_S < A_L$, then we close the long position and initiate a short position.
- If short on day $t - 1$ and $A_S > A_L$, then we close the short position and initiate a long position.

Rate-Relationship Speculation. A spread involves the concurrent sale of one contract and the purchase of another. The most frequently used spreads are intermonth spreads. The intermonth spread involves the sale (a short position) of one delivery month contract and simultaneously the purchase (a long position) of another delivery month contract on the same currency.

The purpose of spreads is to capitalize on aberrations in relationships among futures contracts traded in the financial futures markets. The speculator is betting that the price of the contract bought will rise by more than (or fall by less than) the price on the contract sold.

The empirical evidence on the price behavior of financial futures contracts suggests that near contracts (contracts with shorter maturities) are generally affected to a larger degree by a set of events than are distant contracts (contracts with longer maturities). A given economic event will always affect the near and the distant contracts in the same direction, albeit to a different degree. The spreader attempts to profit from that differential effect by predicting rate relationships instead of rate levels. A bullish spreader would, therefore, buy the near contract and sell the distant contract. The bearish spreader would do precisely the opposite. Profits will accrue, depending on whether the market is inverted (price of near contract (P_N) > price of distant contract (P_D)) or is noninverted $(P_N < P_D)$ and on whether the spread strengthens or weakens.

If $P_D - P_N$ is expected to go up, we say that the spread will strengthen, and we should go long the spread, that is buy the distant contract and sell the near contract. If the spread is expected to weaken, we should take the opposite position. Note that this reasoning is valid whether the market is inverted or normal. The price differentials reported on spreads are not absolute values. Practitioners prefer absolute values, however. We believe that our method is easier and can be consistently used across futures contracts regardless of the underlying instrument.

To illustrate the various intermonth strategies and their consequences, we analyze a bull spread in the inverted market case:

Buy   Jun 93 (near) SF   0.6683
Sell   Sep 93 (distant) SF 0.6662 $P_D - P_N = -0.0021$

The near contract should appreciate by more (depreciate by less) than the distant contract for the bull spread position to be profitable. Assume that the position is reversed at the following price:

Sell   Jun 93 (near) SF   0.6733
Buy   Sep 93 (distant) SF 0.6710 $P_D - P_N = -0.0023$

The spread here has strengthened, thus illustrating the profitability of a bull spread in an inverted market. The gain on the long position, 0.0050, more than offsets the loss on the short position, 0.0048. Relative to rate-level speculation, spread speculation offers much lower risk but also lower returns.

Foreign Currency Options

December 10, 1982, marked the birth of a new hedging vehicle for exchange rate risk: currency options. These new instruments, introduced by the Philadelphia Stock Exchange, have enjoyed a spectacular success. Since 1985, the IMM has traded options on currency futures, which have also been growing rapidly.

Currency options are valuable hedging and speculative instruments because of their unique feature: they add flexibility. A currency option is a right to buy (a call option) or to sell (a put option) a designated quantity of a foreign currency at a specified price (exchange rate), called the *strike price,* at or before a designated expiration date.

"American" options can be exercised at any time during their lifetimes, while "European" options can be exercised only at expiration.

However, it should be noted that the added feature from the possibility of early exercise may not be worth very much, because the option holder can resell the option on the exchange.

Call options where the present spot price is already above the strike price are said to be *in the money*. If immediately exercised, in-the-money options would generate a profit. In this case, the "intrinsic" value is the difference between the spot and the strike prices. Options where the spot is close to the strike are *"at the money."* If the spot price is below the strike price, the option is said to be *"out of the money."* The opposite holds for put options, which are *in the money* if the spot rate is below the strike price.

At expiration, a call option will be exercised only if it ends up in the money – that is, if the spot rate S_T is higher than the strike price X. Its value is therefore $c_T = \text{Max}(S_T - X, 0)$. In contrast, a put option will be exercised at expiration only if the spot rate is below the strike price. Its value is therefore $p_T = \text{Max}(X - S_T, 0)$.

Options Contracts

Exhibit 5.6 presents quotations for currency options taken from the *Wall Street Journal*. Like futures, options trade in standardized contracts, quoted for different strike prices and maturities. Because options can generate only future gains, or no gains at worst, they are valuable instruments; their value is called the option *premium.*

As with futures, options premiums are quoted using the U.S. quotation method. The premiums are expressed in cents per unit of currency, except for the Japanese yens which are expressed in hundredths of a cent and the French franc, which are expressed in tenths of a cent. For example, the price of a May 62 DM American call is $62,500 × 1.08¢ = $675; the price of a May 85 Yen American put is $6,250,000 × 0.55¢/100 = $343.75.

Strike prices are set by the exchange around the prevailing spot price. Contract months are March, June, September, and December plus two additional near-term months. Contracts expire on the Saturday before the third Wednesday of the contract month.

Trading on the Philadelphia Stock Exchange is almost 24 hours a day. The exchange began on September 24, 1990, to trade from 12:30 A.M. to 2:30 P.M. and from 7:00 P.M. to 11:00 P.M. The PHLX expanded trading in the hope of capturing more transactions from Europe and

EXHIBIT 5.6 Foreign Currency Options Quotations

OPTIONS

PHILADELPHIA EXCHANGE

Option & Underlying	Strike Price	Calls – Last			Puts – Last		
		Apr	May	Jun	Apr	May	Jun
50,000 Australian Dollars-cents per unit.							
ADollr	69	r	r	r	r	0.36	0.64
70.51	71	0.37	0.71	0.84	r	r	r
70.51	72	r	0.50	r	r	r	r
70.51	73	r	0.21	r	r	r	r
31,250 British Pound-German Mark cross.							
BPd-GMk	240	r	r	r	1.00	r	r
243.39	250	r	r	1.96	r	r	r
31,250 British Pounds-European Style.							
BPound	155	r	1.28	r	r	r	r
151.23	147½	r	r	r	r	r	2.54
31,250 British Pounds-cents per unit.							
BPound	137½	r	r	r	r	r	0.37
151.23	140	r	r	r	r	r	0.60
151.23	142½	r	r	r	r	0.48	1.15
151.23	145	r	r	r	r	r	1.62
151.23	147½	r	r	r	0.65	1.68	r
151.23	150	1.50	3.30	r	1.25	r	r
151.23	152½	1.25	2.00	2.65	2.58	r	r
151.23	155	0.40	1.05	1.92	r	r	r
151.23	162½	r	r	0.54	r	r	r
50,000 Canadian Dollars-cents per unit.							
CDollr	77	r	r	r	r	r	0.19
79.51	78½	r	r	r	r	0.30	r
79.51	79½	0.39	0.54	r	0.40	0.70	r
79.51	80	0.18	r	r	r	1.00	r
79.51	80½	r	0.25	r	1.05	r	r
79.51	81	8.05	r	r	r	r	r
250,000 French Francs-10ths of a cent per unit.							
FFranc	17	r	r	r	r	r	0.84
183.02	17½	r	r	r	r	1.80	r
250,000 French Francs-European Style.							
FFranc	17½	r	r	r	r	1.20	r
183.02	18	r	r	4.20	1.26	2.82	r
183.02	18½	r	1.76	r	r	r	r
62,500 German Mark-Japanese Yen cross.							
GMk-JYn	72½	0.26	0.56	r	r	r	r
71.45	74	r	0.27	r	r	r	r
62,500 German Marks-European Style.							
DMark	60½	r	r	r	0.23	r	r
62.14	61	r	r	r	0.38	r	1.31
62.14	62	0.70	r	r	r	r	1.81
62.14	62½	0.44	0.81	r	r	r	r
62.14	63	r	r	r	r	r	2.50
62.14	63½	r	r	0.76	r	r	r
62.14	64½	0.08	r	r	r	r	r

Source: *Wall Street Journal*, April 1, 1993.

the Far East. Yet the PHLX continues to face stiff competition from other exchanges all over the world.

As was the case for futures, the default risk on an option contract is very small, because all contracts are guaranteed by Options Clearing Corporation (OCC), which interposes itself between every buyer and every seller.

Relative to futures, long positions in currency options do not require posting a margin. Considering that 100 percent of the option premium is paid in advance by the long position holder, no additional commit-

EXHIBIT 5.6 Foreign Currency Options Quotations (cont.)

Option & Underlying	Strike Price	Calls – Last			Puts – Last		
		Apr	May	Jun	Apr	May	Jun
62,500 German Marks-cents per unit.							
DMark	56½	r	r	r	r	0.05	r
62.14	57	r	r	r	r	r	0.19
62.14	58	r	r	r	r	r	0.32
62.14	58½	r	r	r	r	0.20	r
62.14	59	r	3.01	r	r	0.28	0.50
62.14	59½	r	r	r	0.08	0.40	0.65
62.14	60	2.03	r	2.45	0.13	0.49	0.81
62.14	60½	1.68	r	r	0.20	0.69	r
62.14	61	1.33	1.45	1.83	0.32	0.86	1.30
62.14	61½	0.99	1.30	r	0.53	1.12	r
62.14	62	0.75	1.08	1.30	0.73	r	1.74
62.14	62½	0.54	0.79	r	1.15	r	r
62.14	63	0.37	0.67	0.90	1.40	r	2.40
62.14	63½	0.26	0.57	r	1.78	r	r
62.14	64	0.31	0.40	0.53	r	r	r
62.14	64½	r	r	0.50	r	r	r
6,250,000 Japanese Yen-100ths of a cent per unit.							
JYen	80	r	r	r	r	0.04	r
87.00	82	r	r	r	r	0.12	r
87.00	83½	r	r	r	0.07	r	r
87.00	84½	r	r	r	0.15	r	0.72
87.00	85	2.21	r	2.93	0.21	0.55	0.90
87.00	85½	1.86	r	r	0.34	0.74	r
87.00	86	1.02	1.92	2.20	0.49	r	r
87.00	86½	1.11	r	1.91	0.66	r	r
87.00	87	0.95	1.37	1.63	0.94	r	r
87.00	87½	0.67	r	r	1.18	r	r
87.00	88	0.37	r	r	r	r	r
87.00	89	0.30	r	r	r	r	r
87.00	90	r	r	0.70	r	r	r
6,250,000 Japanese Yen-European Style.							
JYen	80	r	r	r	r	r	0.09
87.00	87½	r	1.20	r	r	r	r
87.00	89	r	0.74	r	r	r	r
62,500 Swiss Francs-European Style.							
SFranc	65½	r	r	r	0.29	r	r
67.04	69	0.20	r	r	r	r	r
67.04	70	r	0.37	r	r	r	r
62,500 Swiss Francs-cents per unit.							
SFranc	65½	0.96	r	r	0.27	r	r
67.04	66	r	r	2.06	0.47	1.04	1.42
67.04	66½	1.00	r	r	r	r	1.60
67.04	67	0.76	r	r	0.88	r	r
67.04	67½	r	1.06	r	r	r	r
67.04	68	0.45	r	r	r	r	r
67.04	69	r	0.59	0.86	r	r	r
31,250 British Pound EOM-cents per unit.							
BPound	147½	r	4.68	r	r	r	3.18
62,500 German Marks EOM-cents per unit.							
DMark	59	r	r	r	r	0.42	0.65
62.14	61	r	r	r	0.61	r	r
62.14	63	0.56	r	r	r	r	r
62.14	64	0.31	r	r	r	r	r
62.14	61½	r	r	1.57	r	r	1.70
6,250,000 Japanese Yen EOM-100ths of a cent per unit.							
JYen	86	1.70	r	r	0.70	r	r
62,500 Swiss Francs EOM-cents per unit.							
SFranc	67	r	r	r	1.24	r	r

Total Call Vol 27,456   Call Open Int 624,080
Total Put Vol 22,982   Put Open Int 474,963

Source: *Wall Street Journal*, April 1, 1993.

ment will be called for during the life of the option. The option premium represents the maximum commitment and consequently the maximum loss. Compared to futures, however, the entirety of the premium can be lost even if prices do not change from the purchase price if the option was initially out of or at the money. In contrast, no loss will be incurred in the futures market if prices remain constant. For short put positions, however, a margin has to be deposited with a broker, as for futures contracts.

The accounting rules for options are standardized by GAAP and depend on whether the option position is a hedge (option plus a cash position in the underlying) or a speculation (no cash counterpart to the option position). This distinction also affects the taxability of the option position.

Using Options

We present in this section some simple, yet the most prevalent, uses of currency options. The strategies we cover are described in Exhibit 5.7. More advanced strategies will be presented later.

Exhibit 5.8 shows a graphical representation of the payoff at expiration for a long (buy) (a) call and a short (sell) (b) call. Exhibit 5.9 shows the payoff function from long (a) and short (b) put positions.

A *long call* position is established when the investor purchases a call. The call premium is the maximum that can be lost, and the gain is theoretically unlimited.

An investor or speculator who is bullish on a currency could purchase the currency itself, a forward contract, a futures contract, or a

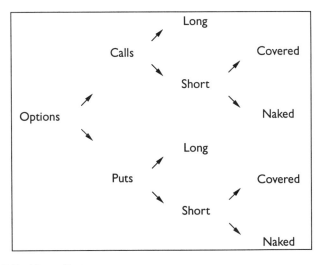

EXHIBIT 5.7   Using Options

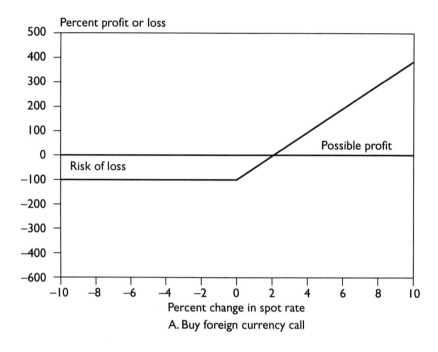

A. Buy foreign currency call

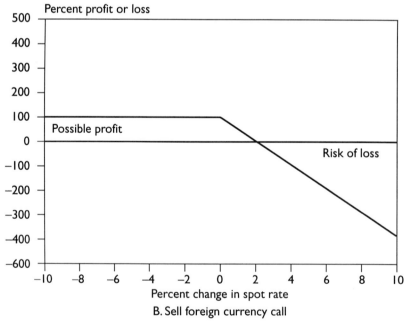

B. Sell foreign currency call

EXHIBIT 5.8   Payoff at Expiration of a Call

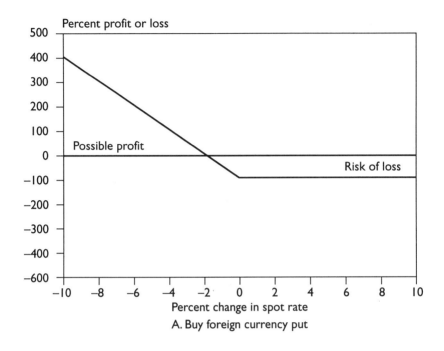

A. Buy foreign currency put

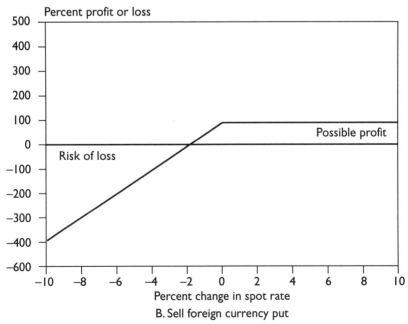

B. Sell foreign currency put

EXHIBIT 5.9   Payoff at Expiration of a Put

call option. The consequences of a long call option are best illustrated using an example.

From Exhibit 5.6, assume the June 1993 DM call option with the 63 strike price is purchased. The option is out of the money because the strike price exceeds the market price of the DM ($S = 0.6214$). No one wants to buy DM at the 0.63 strike price if it could be purchased for $0.6214 in the marketplace. The premium on the DM June 63 is equal to DM 62,500 × U.S. cent 90 = $562.50.

Assume three possible prices at the expiration of the DM June 63 call option: $0.65, $0.63, $0.61. If the DM trades at 0.63 or below, the option will expire worthless. If the DM increases in value to 0.65 the call will be in the money and it could be exercised or sold profitably, with a gain of 62,500 × (0.65 − 0.63) = $1,250.

A *short call* position represents an obligation to the seller (the writer) of the option. By selling an American call option, the seller is committed to sell shares at the strike price whenever the buyer chooses during the life of the options contract. For this commitment the seller is compensated by a premium. The short call position is said to be *covered* if the seller is also long the underlying asset.

It is important to note here the difference in the expectations of the buyers (the long) and the sellers (the short) of the call options. While the buyer hopes for a maximum upward movement in the value of the DM, the covered seller wishes no price movement to occur. A downward movement in the value of the DM, although not resulting in the exercise of the option, will produce a loss in the underlying cash position. A covered option writer, therefore, is one who expects little movement in the value of the underlying currency and wishes to earn additional income by collecting the premium.

Let us now examine the consequences of a short call position assuming the previous price movements. If the DM moves to $0.65, the option will be exercised. The option writer would earn the full premium, which means effectively succeeding in selling DMs for 0.63 + 0.0090 = 0.6390 while the DM market price at the time the short position was established was only 0.6214. However, had the short option seller not sold the call, it could have been sold at the new 0.65 market price. The opportunity loss is equal to 0.65 − 0.6390 = $0.0110.

If the value of the DM remains at $0.63, the full premium is realized by the short seller with no loss in the long cash position.

A drop in the value of the DM to $0.61 would lead to no option exercise but would produce a book loss of 0.6214 – 0.61, or $0.0114 per DM, assuming that the long cash position was established at the same time the option was written. This demonstrates the importance of price stability to the option writer.

A *naked or uncovered short call* is much riskier than a covered short call because the writer has no position in the underlying security to deliver in the event the option is exercised. The risk here is that, if the spot rate increases in value to, say, $.70, the naked writer would have to buy DMs at $.70 and deliver them to the exercising call holder at the $.63 strike price. However, the naked writer need not wait for the DM to reach $.70. The writer may, and in many cases should, buy a call to offset the short position.

Let us further explore the consequences of a naked short call assuming the earlier price movements. A DM movement to $.65 is not desirable for it requires, as indicated earlier, the purchase of DMs at $.65 and their sale at $.63. The loss is real and equal to $.02 minus the call premium. If the DM stays at about $.63 or better yet falls, the naked writer earns the full premium and avoids the book loss of the covered counterpart. Therefore, the naked writer expects currency values to remain constant or fall, while the covered writer is counting on their constancy.

A *long put* position is intended to capitalize on a downward movement in the value of a currency. It can also be used, among other things, to protect a long position in a currency as a call option is used to protect a short position in the currency. A put gives the holder an option to sell at a fixed price. If the value of the currency falls below the strike price, the put is in the money (a situation opposite that of a call) and if it rises above the strike price, the put is out of the money because no one would want to buy at the high market price and sell at the lower strike price.

A put holder would lose the full premium if currency values rise appreciably and would make money if currency values fall. Currency values would have to fall beyond the strike price minus the put premium if a profit were to be realized from the exercise of the option.

A pound June 145 put could have been purchased for U.S. cent 1.62 × 31,250 = $506.25. The put is out of the money because the strike price (1.45) is below the spot price (1.5123). If during the remaining life of the put the pound does not fall below $1.45, the full put premium would be lost. If the fall occurs, on the other hand, a profit could be made.

A *short put* position creates an obligation on the seller (the short) to buy whenever the underlying currency is "put" (sold) to him or her during the life of the option. For this commitment the option writer is paid a premium. The full premium is earned if the market value remains at or higher than the strike price, and a loss is realized (cushioned by the premium received, of course) if the market value of the currency falls below the strike price. A put option writer would, therefore, write an option only when expecting the value of the currency to remain the same or to rise.

Because the option writer can potentially realize a large loss, a margin deposit is required to establish the position. As for calls, short positions in put options can be either covered, that is, offsetting a short position in the asset or in a futures contract on the asset, or naked.

Hedging Contingent Claims

As seen in the previous sections, options are uniquely flexible instruments because they allow new patterns of exposure to market risk, such as the risk of exchange rates. Options, however, can also protect against other risks such as credit risk or the uncertainty of a bid outcome.

Consider the case of a company bidding for a contract denominated in a foreign currency. Rejection or acceptance of the bid will be known in three months, and payment, if any, will be received after another three months.

In this case, the forward market offers inadequate protection. The company that sells the bid amount six months forward faces the possibility that the bid will be rejected and the foreign currency will appreciate in the first three months, which could lead to a substantial loss. On the other hand, not hedging leaves the company exposed for three months; if the bid is accepted and the foreign currency depreciates, a loss will occur.

In the case of this contingent exposure, hedging can be effective by buying a three-month put option on the foreign currency. If the bid is accepted, the put option will offer protection if the foreign currency appreciates after three months; a short position can then be established in the forward market or through another put option for

the remaining three months. If the bid is rejected, the most the company can lose is the option premium; the position is then closed and
profits, if any, realized.

Futures and Options

As we now show, forwards or futures contracts can be reproduced
in the options market as follows:

$$\text{Long forward} = \begin{bmatrix} \text{long call} \\ + \\ \text{short put} \end{bmatrix} \quad \text{Short forward} = \begin{bmatrix} \text{short call} \\ + \\ \text{long put} \end{bmatrix}$$

The relationship between options and forwards contracts is best illustrated through graphical presentations. Exhibit 5.10 presents the payoff
on a forwards contract at expiration.

As the spot rate increases, the profits on a long position also increase
in a one-to-one fashion. This is the same as holding a long call and
a short put. In fact, Exhibit 5.10 results from a vertical addition of
Exhibits 5.8a and 5.9b. At expiration, as the price of the underlying

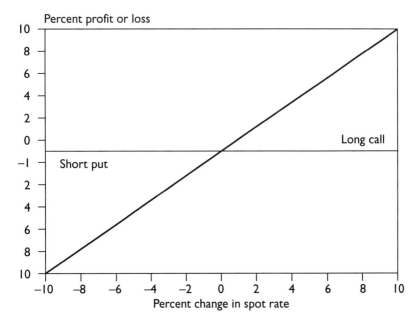

EXHIBIT 5.10   Buy Currency Forward

asset rises by one point, the in-the-money call option realizes a one-point profit. The short put is irrelevant as the holder has no incentive to exercise it. A drop of one point below the strike price causes a one-point loss in the short put position as the short holder must buy the underlying asset at the higher strike price while the market price is actually below that. This is equivalent to the loss on the forward position.

More formally, we can construct a portfolio long one European call (a cash outflow of $-c$), short one European put (a cash inflow of $+p$), with investment in cash, that will exactly replicate the payoff on a forward contract. The investment in cash is for the present value of $X - F$, or $(X - F)/(1 + i)$, where X is the strike price and F is the forward price. This investment is needed because the holder of the forward contract promises to pay F, whereas the holder of the call/put position effectively will pay X, so that an additional amount $X - F$ is needed at expiration to equalize the payoffs on the option portfolio and on the forward contract.

Exhibit 5.11 shows that for a final spot rate either above or below the strike price, the payoff is $S_T - F$, where S_T is the spot rate at expiration. This is the same as that on the forward contract. Therefore, the value of the initial portfolio must be exactly equal to that of a forward contract, which is zero: $-c + p - (X - F)/(1 + i) = 0$. This is known as *put–call parity* and formalizes the reasoning that a long futures contract is equal to a long call plus a short put:

$$c - p = (F - X)/(1 + i). \qquad (5.7)$$

Note that the equality is strictly valid only for European options, which cannot be exercised before expiration. For American options, the short

	Inflow (+), Outflow (−)		
	Now	Expiration	
		$S_T < X$	$S_T \geq X$
Buy call	$-c$	0	$S_T - X$
Sell put	$+p$	$-(X - S_T)$	0
Invest	$-(X - F)/(1 + i)$	$X - F$	$X - F$
Net	$-c + p - (X - F)/(1 + i)$	$S_T - F$	$S_T - F$
Buy forward	0	$S_T - F$	$S_T - F$

EXHIBIT 5.11   Put–Call Parity

put position can be exercised early, which invalidates the argument because the investor is not sure of being able to exactly replicate a forward contract. In general, we denote American-type call options as C. Obviously, the value of an American option must be no less than that of a European option:

$$C \geq c, \quad P \geq p. \tag{5.8}$$

Option Prices

The option price or premium is that amount one must pay in full upon the purchase of an option contract. We now examine the factors influencing the premium, then explain how currency options can be priced.

Factors Influencing Options Premiums

Exhibit 5.6 shows that the price of an April 61 DM contract listed on the Philadelphia Stock Exchange is 1.33 cents. The reader who looks horizontally at option prices would observe that the price gets larger with *maturity*. It increases from 1.33 to 1.83 for the June option. The difference is the time premium, that portion of the total premium attributable to that extra time in the life of the option that increases the probability that the option will become profitable. We have now isolated time as an explanatory variable. The price of an American option is a strictly increasing function of the time to expiration. However, the "time value premium" does *not* decay linearly as the option approaches maturity. As Exhibit 5.12 shows, the time decay accelerates close to expiration.

Looking vertically under the DM April call option, one sees a decreasing price as the *strike price* increases. The reason is that the option moves progressively from being in the money, that is, profitable to exercise, to being well out of the money, very unprofitable to exercise. A call option is said to be in the money if $S > X$. The exact opposite holds for put options.

As the *spot rate* increases, the value of the call also increases. The difference between S and X, $(S - X)$, is referred to as the *intrinsic value*. The difference between the option price and the intrinsic value is called the *time value*, because it would be zero if the option was at expiration. The value of an American option can never fall below

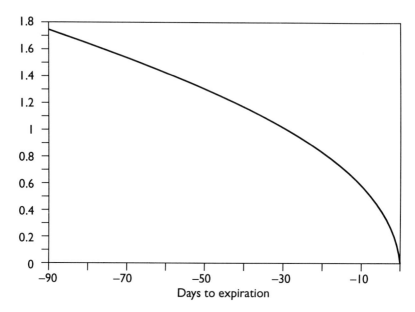

EXHIBIT 5.12   Time Decay of the Premium

the intrinsic value for, if it did, one would have the equivalent of a printing press: buy the option, exercise it, and make money. The minimum intrinsic value is zero; otherwise, assuming a zero time premium, a negative value implies that the seller of the option would have to pay the buyer to hold an option. Therefore, the value of the call, C, is such that

$$C \geq \text{Max}(0, S - X).$$

Also, the value of the call cannot exceed that of the underlying currency. That is $C < S$; otherwise, no one would want to purchase the option rather than the underlying currency.

These two relationships are shown graphically in Exhibit 5.13, which displays the current value of the option as a function of the current spot price S. The option value region is between S and $S - X$; these are represented by two lines with slopes equal to unity, the first emanating from zero, the other from X on the horizontal axis.

The option price curve represents the sum of the time value premium and intrinsic value, and it increases as S increases. To the right of point X, $S > X$, and the call is in the money; for higher values of S, the value of the call gets closer to $S - X$, since the option holder

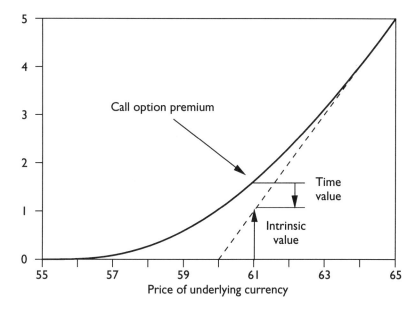

EXHIBIT 5.13   Components of the Option Premium

becomes more sure of exercising it. To the left of X, the call has no intrinsic value. The value of the option is simply its time value. As the call option moves into the money, the intrinsic value begins to dominate until it completely overshadows the time premium when the call is well in the money.

We have thus far identified three variables influencing option prices: S, X, and T. It is obvious from Exhibit 5.6 that the higher S is, ceteris paribus, the higher is the value of the call option. The higher X is, the lower is the value of the option. And the longer T is, the higher is the value of the option.

Options are especially valuable instruments because of the volatility of the underlying asset. The time value of the call option involves a *volatility* component. The volatility component is measured, typically, by evaluating a log-normal distribution of prices for the underlying asset. Such a distribution implies that prices could rise to infinity but not fall below zero. The call option price depends on the probability that the price of the asset will exceed the exercise price, that is, the probability that the option will be profitable to exercise.

The probability of being above one point at the end of a specified time horizon is measured by the area under the curve to the right of that point. This probability shrinks, at an increasing rate, as the time to maturity shrinks.

Exhibit 5.14 shows, ceteris paribus, that the variance of the underlying currency determines the probability. The more "spread out" the distribution is, the greater is the probability, hence the preference of a call option buyer for a high-variance currency. A high-variance currency is preferred because it has a greater probability of being in the money, as the call option holder realizes a profit only when the intrinsic value is positive $(S - X > 0)$ and does not lose when it is not. Thus, the focus is on the positive tail of the probability distribution.

As to the role of *interest rates* in determining option values, we should note that an option buyer does not pay until exercising the option, if ever. The higher the domestic interest rate, the lower is the present value of the payment. Thus higher domestic interest rates effectively reduce the exercise price, which increases the value of the call option.

Options on currencies are influenced, however, by two interest rates simultaneously. Foreign currencies are at a premium or discount relative to the domestic currency and that premium (discount) is determined by the differential in interest rates as demonstrated by the

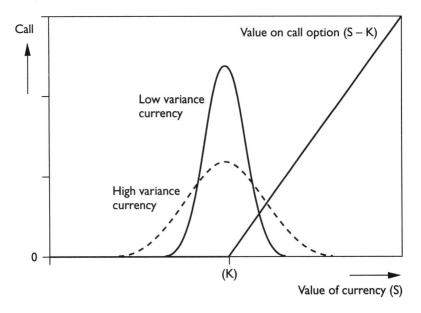

EXHIBIT 5.14   Payoffs on a Call Option

interest rate parity theory. Call option values rise, consequently, when the interest rate differential rises and fall when it shrinks.

We can now summarize those variables that influence the pricing of call options:

$$C = f(\overset{+}{S}, \overset{-}{X}, \overset{+}{\sigma^2}, \overset{+}{t}, \overset{+}{i - i^*}).$$

The signs (+, −) atop the independent variables describe the nature of the relationship between that variable and the call option price. All the variables are known with certainty when the option is being priced except for σ^2, which has to be estimated.

The challenge now is to find a way to integrate these variables to arrive at a closed form solution for valuing a call option.

Arbitrage Bounds

Before introducing the Black-Scholes model of pricing call options, let us illustrate the parallel between buying a call option in a foreign currency and taking an outright position in the foreign currency. But, first, we define the price of a zero coupon bond maturing at T with a face value equal to \$1 as $B(T)$. This is also $B(T) = \dfrac{1}{e^{rT}} = e^{-rT}$. Similarly, $B^*(T) = e^{-r^*T}$, where r and r^* are the instantaneous continuously compounded risk-free rates in the local and foreign currencies, respectively.

Based on this, the interest parity theory developed previously can be restated as

$$\frac{F}{S} = \frac{1 + iT}{1 + i^*T} = \frac{B^*(T)}{B(T)}. \tag{5.9}$$

Assume now that one is faced with two investment strategies:

1. Buy a European call option on the foreign currency, plus X domestic bonds.
2. Purchase one foreign zero coupon bond $B^*(T)$.

The total outlay of strategy 1 is $c + XB$; the total investment of strategy 2 is $SB^*(T)$. One must note that both investments would benefit from an appreciation in the value of the foreign currency. The first will realize a profit from the call, and the second will realize a profit from the face value of the bond, which is denominated in the now higher-valued foreign currency. Let us now look at the payoff under two states of the world: $S > X$ and $S < X$.

	Payoff	
	$S_T < X$	$S_T \geq X$
Strategy 1	X	S_T (Exercise)
Strategy 2	S_T	S_T

Since strategy 1 yields X when there is no exercise, precisely in those states where $S_T < X$, strategy 1 will always have a higher payoff than strategy 2. We conclude, therefore, that, initially, the cost of strategy 1 must be higher than that of strategy 2: $c + XB(T) \geq SB^*(T)$, or

$$c \geq SB^*(T) - XB(T). \tag{5.10}$$

Equivalently,

$$C \geq c \geq \text{Max}[0, SB^*(T) - XB(T)]. \tag{5.11}$$

Equation (5.11) will be used to show how a call option on a currency may be reproduced by the appropriate combination of a long position in a foreign bond (B^*) and a short position in the domestic bond (an issuance of a domestic bond requiring a negative cash flow).

The Black-Scholes Option Pricing Model

The Black-Scholes (B&S) option pricing model is possibly the most successful model in applied economics. It was first applied to stock options and then extended to options on other instruments, such as currencies. The model provides a closed-form solution for European options. The derivation of the solution is based the following assumptions:

1. The price of the underlying asset is continuous.
2. Interest rates are known and constant.
3. The variance of returns is constant.
4. There are perfect capital markets: short sales are allowed, with no transaction costs or taxes, and the markets operate continuously.

The most important assumption behind the model is that prices are continuous. This rules out discontinuities in the sample path, such as jumps, which invalidate the continuous hedging argument behind the B&S model. The statistical process generating the returns can be modeled by a geometric Brownian motion: over any arbitrary time interval, dt, the logarithmic return has a normal distribution with mean $= \mu dt$ and variance $= \sigma^2 dt$. The total return can be modeled as

$$dS/S = \mu dt + \sigma dz,$$

where the first term represents the drift component, and the second is the stochastic component, with dz distributed normally with mean zero and variance dt.

Based on these assumptions, Black and Scholes (1973) derived a closed-form formula for European options on a non-dividend-paying stock. Merton (1973) expanded their model to the case of a stock paying a continuous dividend yield. Since foreign currencies pay a continuous rate of interest, which can be interpreted as a "dividend" yield, the B&S model can be directly extended to currency options, as shown by Garman and Kohlhagen (1983).

Black and Scholes derived the appropriate weights that can force equality in Equation (5.10); that is, there is a combination of long and short bonds that produces the exact equivalent of a call option:

$$c = a[SB^*(T)] - b[XB(T)]. \qquad (5.12)$$

The Black-Scholes model gives us a mechanism for arriving at the values of a and b. It turns out that $a = N(d_1)$ and $b = N(d_2)$, where $N(d)$ is the cumulative distribution function for the standard normal distribution:

$$N(d) = \frac{1}{\sqrt{2\pi}} \int_{-\infty}^{d} e^{-1/2 U^2} dU.$$

This is also the area to the left of a standard normal $N(0, 1)$ variable with value equal to d. It is illustrated in Exhibit 5.15.

The values of d_1 and d_2 are arrived at using the following equation:

$$d_1 = \frac{\ln(SB^*/XB)}{\sigma\sqrt{T}} + .5\sigma\sqrt{T}, \; d_2 = d_1 - \sigma\sqrt{T}.$$

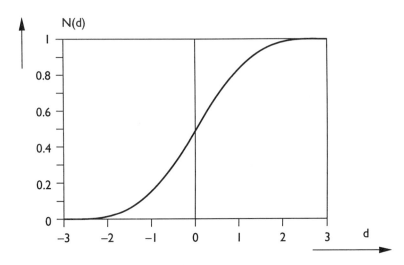

EXHIBIT 5.15   Cumulative Standard Normal Function

The expression $\sigma\sqrt{T}$ measures the volatility over the life of the option; if the volatility (σ) is measured on a per annum basis, then T must be expressed in number of years.

The call option value is therefore

$$c = SB^*N(d_1) - XBN(d_2). \qquad (5.13)$$

Alternatively, all occurrences of SB^* can be replaced by FB in the preceding formula, given interest rate parity. This yields

$$c = FBN(d_1) - XBN(d_2), \; d_1 = \frac{\ln(F/X)}{\sigma\sqrt{T}} + .5\sigma\sqrt{T}, \; d_2 = d_1 - \sigma\sqrt{T}.$$
$$(5.14)$$

It is interesting to note that the expected rate of return on the underlying asset does not appear in the pricing model. This reflects the fundamental observation by Black and Scholes that the option can be priced using an arbitrage argument by constructing a portfolio of the stock and call that is locally risk free. Alternatively, the B&S formula can be derived from direct evaluation of the integral

$$c = e^{-rT} E[\text{Max}(S - K, 0)] = e^{-rT} \left[\int_K^\infty (S - K)f(S)dS \right], \quad (5.15)$$

where the discounting is done using the risk-free rate and the stock is expected to grow at the risk-free rate, instead of μ. Thus, it is "as if" the option price could be derived in a risk-neutral world, where all assets yield the risk-free rate. This property is essential, because it allows researchers to short-circuit the derivation of option values, by setting all expected returns equal to the risk-free rate.

By put–call parity, the put option value is

$$p = SB^*[N(d_1) - 1] - XB[N(d_2) - 1]. \qquad (5.16)$$

For example, let

S = \$2.0000/pound
X = \$2.0000/pound
T = .25 of a year
$B(T)$ = .9876, or r = 5% pa
$B^*(T)$ = .9753, or r^* = 10% pa
σ = .13

$$d_1 = \frac{\ln\left(\dfrac{2.0000 \times .9753}{2.0000 \times .9876}\right)}{.13\sqrt{.25}} + (1/2).13\sqrt{.25},\ d_2 = d_1 - (.13)\sqrt{.25}$$

d_1 = −.1598, d_2 = −.2248
$N(d_1)$ = .4365, $N(d_2)$ = .4111
c = (2.0000)(.9753)(−.1598) − (2.0000)(.9876)(−.2248) = 0.0396

or 3.96 cents per each underlying pound for a total value (call premium) of $0.0396 \times 31{,}250$ = \$1237.5.

Lest we get overly enthusiastic about the simple and elegant Black-Scholes model, we must remind ourselves of its limitations.

1. Time is not consistent – time intervals are not uniform across time periods. Although the Forex markets are "continuous," they are interrupted by weekends and holidays (zero volatility intervals). These interruptions are not uniform across time periods. Therefore the debate is whether the call option price should be calculated using calendar time or trading days within a time period.
2. The constancy of both risk-free rates throughout the life of the option and the assumed equality of borrowing and lending rates could be inconsistent with the realities of the market. Further,

Black and Scholes assume that no relationship exists between interest rate changes and exchange rate changes. This is often not the case.

3. The risk may not be constant throughout the life of the option. One way to see that volatility changes over time is to derive an *implied volatility* measure. This is the value of the volatility parameter that equates the B&S model to the market price, and it can be viewed as the market's estimate of future volatility. This implied volatility can substantially change from one day to the next, thus indicating that risk changes and that one of the assumptions underlying the model is not strictly valid.

   Hull and White (1987) proposed a model where σ follows its own stochastic process. This requires the estimation of new parameters and considerably complicates the derivation of the option price. Another attempt to incorporate unstable volatility in the pricing of call options was undertaken by Melino and Turnbull (1990). These approaches require additional assumptions and are computationally difficult to implement. Further, they yield option values that do not fit the data much better than those found by using the B&S model with an implied volatility.

4. Currency returns may not be lognormally distributed. This is a serious problem, which may cause actual option prices to diverge substantially from the B&S prices. For instance, if there are jumps in exchange rates, out-of-the-money options may be worth more because of the higher probability that the spot rate will suddenly move above the strike price.

5. The option replication strategy may not be easy to implement because of costs. Leland (1985) addressed the issue of transaction costs and proposed an adjustment to the B&S pricing model. The option pricing model is changed to

$$c = SB^*N(\hat{d}_1) - XBN(\hat{d}_1 - \hat{\sigma}\sqrt{T}),$$

   and

$$\hat{d}_1 = \ln(SB^*/XB)/\hat{\sigma}\sqrt{T} + .5\hat{\sigma}\sqrt{T} \quad \hat{\sigma}^2 = \sigma^2[1 + k\sqrt{2\pi}/\sigma\sqrt{\Delta t}]^{1/2},$$

   where k is the round-trip transaction cost, measured as a fraction of value, and Δt is the revision interval, or time after which the hedge is reexamined for possible adjustment.

The Binomial Option Pricing Model

The B&S model provides an elegant closed-form solution to the pricing of options. Its main drawback is that it is strictly applicable only to

European options, which can be exercised only at expiration. Most traded options, however, are American style and can be exercised at any time during the life of the option.

This is less of a problem than might appear at first sight, because in many cases it does not pay to exercise the option early. As a result, the additional value due to the American feature is generally small. The main reason why early exercise may not be very valuable is that doing so effectively kills the remaining time value in the option. Options are traded assets, so it is generally more beneficial to *sell* the option than to exercise it, because selling preserves the time value of the option. In fact, when the underlying asset pays no dividend, there is never any reason to exercise a call early. This is because early exercise forces the option holder to pay the strike price now, when it could be paid later. Given the time value of money, the former alternative is preferable. When the underlying asset pays no dividend or interest, there is absolutely no reason to exercise early. Thus the value of an American call on an asset that pays no dividend is exactly the same as that of a European call.

For puts, however, it may be preferable to receive money now rather than later. Therefore put options are slightly more valuable with an American feature, even when the underlying asset pays no dividend.

The binomial model provides an easy method to numerically value American options and was originally derived by Cox, Ross, and Rubinstein (1979). It can also be used to value more complex options, where, for instance, the option disappears whenever the spot rate falls below a prespecified value (the "knock-out" option). Complex options are becoming more prevalent in the OTC market, where bankers continuously come up with new instruments to sell to clients.

The binomial model can be viewed as a discrete equivalent to the B&S model. First, the time to expiration T is subdivided into n intervals $\Delta t = T/n$. At each "node," the stock price is assumed to go either up or down from S to uS or dS, with probability p, or $1 - p$ for up and down moves, respectively. The parameters u, d, p are chosen so that, for a small time interval, the expected return and variance equal those of the continuous process. One could choose, for instance,[2]

---

[2]This can be demonstrated as follows. After one move, the expected stock price and its variance are, respectively,

$$E[S] = puS + (1 - p)dS = Se^{\mu\Delta t}$$
$$V[S] = p(uS - Se^{\mu\Delta t})^2 + (1 - p)(dS - Se^{\mu\Delta t})^2 = S\sigma^2\Delta t.$$

These equations impose two conditions on the three variables. Assuming $d = 1/u$,

$$u = e^{\sigma\sqrt{\Delta t}}, \quad d = (1/u), \quad p = \frac{e^{\mu\Delta t} - d}{u - d}. \quad\quad (5.17)$$

It can be shown that in the limit as $\Delta t \to 0$, the binomial model converges to the geometric Brownian motion model underlying the B&S model. Exhibit 5.16 shows how a binomial tree is constructed.

To evaluate options, we use the risk-neutral equivalence discussed in the previous section and set

$$a = e^{(r-r^*)\Delta t}, \quad p = \frac{a - d}{u - d},$$

where r is the risk-free rate instead of the expected stock return and r^* is the foreign risk-free rate. As r^* can be considered a yield on the underlying asset, the total expected return on the foreign currency is equal to the risk-free rate r.

Options are then evaluated by starting at the end of the tree and working backward to the initial time. At time T and node j, the call option is worth $\text{Max}(S_{T_j} - K, 0)$. At time $T - 1$ and node j, the call option is the present value of the call options at time T and nodes j and $j + 1$,

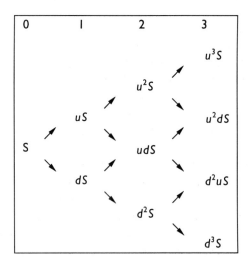

EXHIBIT 5.16   Binomial Tree

we can show that, after expanding e^x in series as $1 + x + x^2/2 + \ldots$, the final result obtains.

$$c_{T-1,j} = e^{-r\Delta t}[pc_{T,j+1} + (1 - p)c_{T,j}].\qquad(5.18)$$

Note that this is valid as long as there is no possibility of early exercise. For American options, the holder compares at any point the value of the option alive and dead (i.e., exercised). Thus the American call option value at this node is

$$C_{T-1,j} = \text{Max}\{S_{T-1,j} - K,\ e^{-r\Delta t}[pC_{T,j+1} + (1 - p)C_{T,j}]\}.\qquad(5.19)$$

By working backward through the tree, one can find the value of a European option, American option, or almost any other "exotic" option. In practice, the quality of the numerical approximation can be excellent if the interval Δt is chosen sufficiently small. With the ever-falling cost of computing power, it has become very easy to implement the binomial model with any required accuracy. For instance, setting the interval Δt equal to one day will produce binomial European option values virtually undistinguishable from closed-form exact solutions, especially when real-life bid–ask spreads are considered.

Going back to the example in the previous B&S model section, we wish to determine the value of an American call option. First, we divide the 0.25-year period into four intervals; for instance, so that $\Delta t = 0.0625$. The discounting factor over one interval is $e^{-r\Delta t} = 0.9969$. We then compute

$$u = e^{\sigma\sqrt{\Delta t}} = e^{0.13\sqrt{0.0625}} = 1.0330,$$
$$d = (1/u) = 0.9680,$$
$$a = e^{(r-r^*)\Delta t} = 0.9969,$$
$$p = \frac{a - d}{u - d} = (0.9969 - 0.9680)/(1.0330 - 0.9680) = 0.4439.$$

Exhibit 5.17 shows the steps involved. First, we lay out the tree for the spot price, starting with $S = 2.000$ at time $t = 0$, then $uS = 2.066$ and $dS = 1.936$ at time $t = 1$, and so on. We rank nodes so that the lowest spot rate corresponds to node $j = 1$.

Let us first show how the European call option value can be computed by the binomial method. We start from the end, at time $t = 4$, and set the call price to $c = S - K = 2.278 - 2.000 = 0.278$ for the highest spot rate, 0.134 for the next rate, and so on, down to $c = 0$ if the spot rate is below $K = 2.000$. The value of the call at time $t = 3$ and node $j = 4$ is the expected present value of two options valued at 0.278 and 0.134,

	0	1	2	3	4
Spot price	→	→	→	→	→
					2.278
				2.205	2.134
			2.134	2.066	2.000
		2.066	2.000	1.936	1.874
	2.000	1.936	1.874	1.814	1.756
European call	←	←	←	←	←
					0.278
				0.198	0.134
			0.121	0.060	0.000
		0.068	0.026	0.000	0.000
	0.0369	0.012	0.000	0.000	0.000
Exercised call					
					0.278
				0.205	0.134
			0.134	0.066	0.000
		0.066	0.000	0.000	0.000
	0.000	0.000	0.000	0.000	0.000
American call	←	←	←	←	←
					0.278
				0.205	0.134
			0.134	0.066	0.000
		0.076	0.029	0.000	0.000
	0.0409	0.013	0.000	0.000	0.000

EXHIBIT 5.17   Computation of American Option Value

$$c = 0.9969[0.4439 \times 0.278 + (1 - 0.4439) \times 0.134] = 0.198.$$

Continuing through the tree to time 0 yields a European call value of $0.0369. Note that we obtained a value very close to the B&S formula of $0.0396 simply by using four intervals. A finer partition would quickly lead to an option value very close to the exact number.

Next we examine the computation of the American call value. At time $t = 4$, the values are the same as previously because the call expires at this time. At time $t = 3$ and node $j = 4$, the option holder can either keep the call, in which case the value is as previously, $0.198, or exercise it. When exercised, the option yields $S - K = 2.205 - 2.000 = 0.205$; because this value is higher than $0.198, the option holder would rationally exercise the call. This means that the option value at this node is $0.205. Relative to the tree for the European call, we examine the value of early exercise at each node. Going through the tree in the same fashion, we find an initial value of $0.0409, which is (4/10)th of a cent higher than that of the European call. The value of the American premium is hence relatively small. In this example, the foreign rate of interest is 10 percent, against 5 percent for the domestic rate. The American premium would be even smaller if the foreign rate of interest were closer to the U.S. interest rate.

To conclude, this example has shown that the binomial approach provides a straightforward method to value American options. Other exotic options can be evaluated easily using the binomial method.

Comparative Statics

Considering that the variables influencing option prices have been identified, we can now examine how the option price reacts to each in isolation (assuming the others remain constant); that is, we look at the partial derivatives. These derivatives can be found in closed-form solution for the Black-Scholes model and by numerical derivation for the binomial model.

Let *delta*, Δ, be the change in the call price for a given change in the underlying spot price:

$$\Delta = \frac{\partial C}{\partial S}.$$

The absolute value of Δ is always between zero and unity. The Δ of a deep in-the-money call option ($S \gg X$) is about equal to 1. That of an at-the-money option is equal to about 0.5, and that of an out-of-the-money call option is low or zero. The same values hold for put options, for which the values of Δ are negative, however. By definition, a long spot position has a Δ of unity.

For example, assume a pound call option has a Δ of 0.5 and the position of the investor consists of one long pound position, worth £31,250, and one short call. A long position has a Δ of 1. A short call will have the Δ of a long call multiplied by (−1). The net Δ of the position is

$$1 + (-1)(0.5) = 1 - 0.5 = 0.5.$$

This "hedged" position (short call hedging the long position) is hedged only at expiration. In the meantime, there is residual exposure, equal to

$$31,250 \times 0.5 = £15,625.$$

A *delta-neutral* hedge is one with a net Δ equal to zero. A pound position of £31,250 hedged by two short call options each with $\Delta = 0.5$ produces a net Δ of

$$1 + (-1)(2)(0.5) = 0.$$

Thus the hedge is perfect over a very short horizon. The same results would have been obtained if the long spot position were hedged using two long puts, each with a delta = 0.5.

Therefore, Δ measures the sensitivity of the option value to movements in the price of the underlying asset. Measuring this exposure, Δ, is an essential part of the risk management of options. Traders, for instance, continuously take positions in options with different strike prices or maturities. It would be too complicated to have a zero net position in each traded option. Instead, traders use Δ to offset positions in different options and try to attain a delta-neutral position. Similar to duration hedging, delta hedging "immunizes" the portfolio to first-order movements in the price of the underlying asset.

The problem with a delta-neutral position is that it needs to be continually adjusted, as Δ is unstable over time. To capture these changes, we calculate γ as

$$\frac{\partial \Delta}{\partial S} \text{ or } \frac{\partial^2 C}{\partial S^2} = \gamma$$

The γ measures the change in Δ given a small change in the spot rate. For long option positions, the γ is positive. The γ has an interesting behavior. It rises with shorter maturity. For a given maturity, the at-the-money option has the highest γ. Also, γ tends to rise with volatility for short-term options (≤ 45 days) that are out of the money and fall with higher volatility for at-the-money options. A high γ indicates that the delta hedge needs to be actively managed.

For example, assume the investor's position consists of

$$A \text{ long pound call} \begin{cases} \Delta = 0.54 \\ \gamma = 0.10 \end{cases}$$

$$A \text{ short pound put} \begin{cases} \Delta = 0.49 \\ \gamma = 0.15 \end{cases}$$

The net position Δ = 0.54 + (−1)(−0.49) = 1.03. The net γ = 0.10 + (−1)(0.15) = −0.05. The net Δ in pound terms is equivalent to

$$1.03 \times 31{,}250 = 32{,}187.50 \text{ pounds.}$$

The negative net γ indicates that, as the spot price increases, Δ will fall.

Theta, θ, shows how an option changes value with the passage of time. The value of θ is always negative. A θ of −0.10 means that the call option loses

$$\theta = \frac{\partial C}{\partial T} = 10 \text{ cents per day.}$$

Vega, also written λ, is the partial derivative of the option price with respect to the volatility:

$$V = \lambda = \frac{\partial C}{\partial \sigma}.$$

We have already determined that all options respond positively (increase in price) as volatility increases and decrease in price as volatility decreases. Therefore a speculator expecting σ^2 to fall should construct a net short position (short volatility) in options, and one expecting σ^2 to rise should be long volatility.

Trading Strategies with Options

The comparative statics developed in the previous section allow traders to quantify the net exposure of a portfolio of options to underlying factors. A trading strategy can then be implemented that focuses on one particular factor, volatility, for instance, while avoiding exposure to underlying price risk.

Bankers involved in the over-the-counter options market felt for a long time that a "book," the collection of positions, provided a natural hedge (a pooled insurance) given the dispersion of exercise prices and maturities and balance between puts and calls. Any remaining exposure would be managed such as to reflect the bias of the trader. This turned out to be a suboptimal strategy, as many bankers have discovered; hence, the shift to a delta-neutral hedging strategy.

A delta-neutral (hedged) position produces no profit if the value of the currency changes. There is, however, a residual exposure through γ, which measures the speed at which Δ changes. Ideally, a portfolio should be delta and gamma hedged to provide the best protection against price risk. Also, a delta hedge is effective only if the estimate of volatility was correctly made at the point of implementation. The market crash of October 19, 1987, proved that, when volatility explodes, the portfolio may be in just as bad a position as if it were not hedged at all.

We now turn to the discussion of advanced option trading strategies. The development and the explanation of each of the advanced option trading strategies discussed will be based on Exhibits 5.18 and 5.19. The data were provided for our use by Rich Abrahams and John Tumolo, floor traders on the Philadephia Stock Exchange.

Combinations

A combination consists of a call and a put with the same or different strike prices and maturities. When the strike prices of the call and the put and their maturities are the same, the combination is referred to as a *straddle*. When the strike prices are different, the combination is referred to as a *strangle*.

Straddles.   Straddles are best used when the direction of the market is unpredictable; otherwise one should prefer a simple call or a put. Dramatic changes in economic variables such as oil prices or inflation cause dramatic price changes in exchange rates. A speculator unable to predict the direction of either variable would find the straddles very attractive even though the put is a "drag" on the profits from the call in an "up market," and the call is a "drag" on the profits from the put in a "down market." The "drag" is the cost of insuring one's position.

A long straddle consists of a long position in both a call and a put with the same maturity and strike price. Using the DM data in Exhibits 5.18 and 5.19, we can construct the following straddle:

EXHIBIT 5.18   DM Calls

STRIKE	DEC					JAN					MAR					JUN				
	P	Δ	V	G	T	P	Δ	V	G	T	P	Δ	V	G	T	P	Δ	V	G	T
63	4.516	98	1	3	-.1	4.565	94	3	5	-.2	4.732	86	8	6	-.3	4.947	80	13	6	-.2
64	3.560	94	2	6	-.4	3.665	88	5	7	-.5	3.923	79	11	7	-.4	4.207	73	15	7	-.3
65	2.662	86	4	9	-.8	2.841	79	8	10	-.7	3.193	71	13	8	-.5	3.540	66	18	7	-.4
66	1.863	75	6	14	-1.2	2.118	68	10	11	-.9	2.550	62	14	8	-.6	2.947	59	19	7	-.4
67	1.204	59	8	16	-1.4	1.511	57	11	11	-1.0	1.994	54	15	8	-.6	2.424	52	20	7	-.4
68	0.718	41	8	16	-1.4	1.035	45	11	11	-1.0	1.532	44	15	8	-.6	1.979	44	20	6	-.4
69	0.401	26	6	13	-1.2	0.683	31	10	11	-.9	1.157	36	14	8	-.6	1.600	38	19	6	-.4
70	0.211	15	5	9	-.9	0.435	22	8	9	-.8	0.858	29	13	7	-.6	1.280	32	18	6	-.4
71	0.108	8	3	5	-.6	0.269	14	6	6	-.6	0.625	22	11	6	-.5	1.014	27	17	5	-.4

where P = premium on option

Δ = Δ measured in percent

V = vega = the Street's equivalent of our $\lambda = \frac{\partial C}{\partial \sigma}$

G = γ

T = θ

EXHIBIT 5.19 DM Puts

STRIKE	DEC					JAN					MAR					JUN				
	P	Δ	V	G	T	P	Δ	V	G	T	P	Δ	V	G	T	P	Δ	V	G	T
63	0.044	-3	2	2	-.3	0.145	-8	4	4	-.5	0.449	-16	9	5	-.5	0.874	-22	15	5	-.5
64	0.096	-7	3	5	-.6	0.259	-13	6	6	-.7	0.655	-22	11	6	-.6	1.150	-27	17	5	-.5
65	0.202	-14	4	9	-.9	0.441	-21	8	9	-.9	0.929	-29	13	7	-.7	1.485	-33	18	6	-.6
66	0.402	-25	6	14	-1.3	0.717	-31	10	11	-1.0	1.280	-36	14	8	-.8	1.881	-39	19	6	-.6
67	0.740	-40	8	16	-1.5	1.104	-43	11	11	-1.1	1.712	-44	15	7	-.8	2.338	-45	20	6	-.6
68	1.250	-59	8	15	-1.5	1.619	-56	11	11	-1.1	2.233	-54	15	8	-.8	2.867	-52	19	6	-.6
69	1.926	-74	6	13	-1.3	2.257	-67	10	11	-1.0	2.839	-62	14	8	-.8	3.457	-58	19	6	-.6
70	2.730	-85	5	9	-1.0	2.998	-77	8	9	-.9	3.519	-69	13	7	-.7	1.280	64	18	6	-.6
71	3.620	-91	3	5	-.7	3.820	-84	6	6	-.7	4.265	-75	11	6	-.6	1.014	-69	17	5	-.5

	Price	Δ	γ	θ	Vega
1 March 67 Call	1.994	54	15	−0.6	8
1 March 67 Put	1.712	−44	15	−0.8	7
Net	3.706	10	30	−1.4	15

Because the components of the straddle move in opposite directions, the net Δ is small, at +10. However, because large price changes are expected, one should note that the net Δ is relevant only in a restricted range.

The graphical representation of a straddle is shown in Exhibit 5.20, which shows that the straddle is the vertical sum of the two options. The maximum loss (the sum of both premiums) is realized when the market value of the DM stays at 67 (the strike price). The profit is realized only when S rises above $X + P + C$ or falls below $X − P − C$.

A straddle is very attractive for it has a limited risk and unlimited profit potential. Thus the greater is the volatility (the combined vega), the more desirable the long straddle would be. Of course, such a strategy is worthwhile only if the trader's view on volatility is that the market underestimates future volatility or, in other words, that option premiums are cheap.

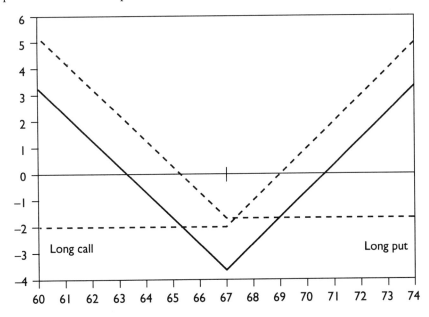

EXHIBIT 5.20   Straddle

Strangles.   Strangles are combinations of calls and puts with the same maturity but different strike prices. A strangle is represented in Exhibit 5.21.

As with a long straddle, a strangle needs large price movements to be profitable. A strangle ordinarily includes out-of-the-money options and therefore is cheaper than a straddle. When both options are in the money, the strangle is called *guts*.

Consider a strangle with 10 June 68 calls and 20 June 63 puts.

Price		Δ	γ	θ	Vega
10 June 68 Calls	19.79	10 × 44 = 440	10 × 20 = 200	10 × −.4 = −4	10 × 6 = 60
20 June 63 Puts	17.48	20 × −22 = −440	20 × 15 = 300	20 × −.5 = −10	20 × 5 = 100
Net	37.27	0	500	−14	160

The position is delta neutral. As the volatility increases, so would the value of the position. The positive γ indicates how the value of the position increases as the price of the underlying contract increases by a large amount. It measures the sensitivity of the strangle to large price moves. Finally, the position is "short" time. As time passes, the value of the position will decrease.

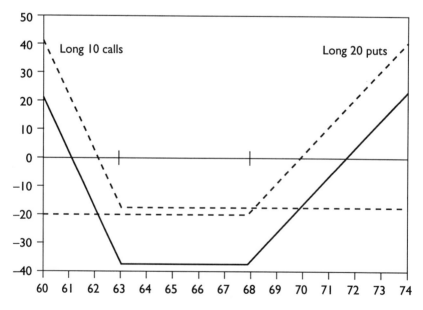

EXHIBIT 5.21   Strangle

Clearly, the strangle is much more flexible than the straddle, the latter being a special case of the former that allows for a much wider set of combinations for the available calls and puts on any currency.

Spreads

We have thus far concentrated on positions involving two classes of options. One can, however, establish positions with one class of option with different maturities (horizontal spreads) or strike prices (vertical spreads). The names of the spreads are derived from the manner in which they are listed in the *Wall Street Journal*; time is listed horizontally and strike prices are listed vertically.

Vertical Spread. The "simple" vertical spread is formed by buying one option with one exercise price (X_1) and selling another with a different exercise price (X_2). Both options will have the same maturity. Exhibit 5.22 shows the profile of a vertical spread where the spreader is long the call with an X_1 strike price (the more in-the-money call) and short that with an X_2 strike price. The maximum profit built into a vertical spread position is known in advance and equal to $X_2 - X_1 + C_2 - C_1$. The maximum loss is the difference in the call premiums.

From Exhibit 5.18, we can construct an example of a simple DM vertical spread:

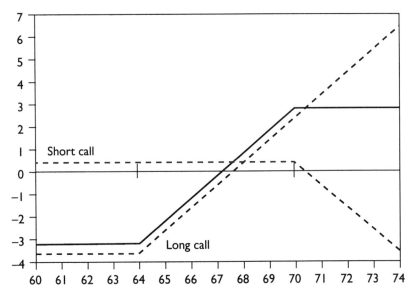

EXHIBIT 5.22   Bull Vertical Spread

Long January 64 call	$C_1 = 3.665$
Short January 70 call	$C_2 = 0.435$
Net commitment of funds	3.230

Here the spreader is buying the spread – that is, paying more premium for the call option bought than will be collected from the option sold. Because the position is based on bullish expectations, it is referred to as a *bull vertical call* spread.

The risk of this position is much lower than either the long or the short call position. Against this insurance one must settle for a limited upside potential. The net Δ of this position is .66, which is equivalent to owning DM62,500 × .66 = DM41,250 in the spot market, given that DM62,500 is the option contract size.

The reverse of this position produces a *bear vertical call* spread. This type of position would be established with bearish expectations, because it has a negative Δ.

Backspreads. A call backspread involves the sale of a number of call options with a low exercise price and the purchase of a higher number of call options with a higher exercise price. A call backspread, typically, results in a cash inflow. Thus, if the market falls drastically the call backspreader will keep the net premiums as the short options expire worthless. Should the market appreciate very dramatically, the call backspreader will also profit. As for straddles, backspreads involve small losses if the asset price does not move too much.

The typical characteristics of a call backspread are a small Δ, a positive γ, a positive vega, and a negative net θ. It is clear from this that the spreader is long the volatility, expecting a major price move upward.

Ratio Vertical Spread. A ratio vertical spread is the opposite of the backspread. It consists of more short contracts than long contracts. This spread may be done with calls or puts. With calls, the strategy involves selling the calls with a higher strike price and buying a larger number of the lower strike price call. The call version has an unlimited risk on the upside, and the put version has an unlimited risk on the downside. The ideal results are obtained when the price of the currency does not change much.

Calendar (Horizontal or Time) Spreads. Calendar or time spreads involve a short position in one contract month and a long position in another. When the distant option is bought and the near one is sold, the spreader is said to be long the time spread. When the opposite is true, the spreader is said to be short the time spread.

A horizontal bull call spread is one that results in a debt – a net commitment of funds by the spreader. This necessitates a long spread as the distant contract is priced at a higher price than the near one. A time spread resulting in a credit is a bear spread (short the time spread).

Butterfly Spreads.   Spreads involving more than two positions are referred to as *butterfly* or *sandwich spreads*. The latter is the opposite of the former.

A butterfly spread involves a long call at the strike price, two short calls at a higher strike price, and a long call position at an even higher strike price. All calls have the same maturity. An example of a butterfly spread is illustrated in Exhibit 5.23; it has two short March calls at 67 flanked by a long March call at 63 and another at 71.

The characteristics of this position are

Price		Δ	γ	θ	Vega
I long March 63	−4.732	I × 86 = 86	I × 6 = 6	I × −.3 = −.3	I × 8 = 8
2 short March 67	3.988	2 × −54 = −108	2 × −8 = −16	2 × .6 = 1.2	2 × −15 = −30
I long March 71	−0.625	I × 22 = 22	I × 6 = 6	I × −0.5 = −0.5	I × 11 = 11
Net	−1.369	0	−4	0.4	−11

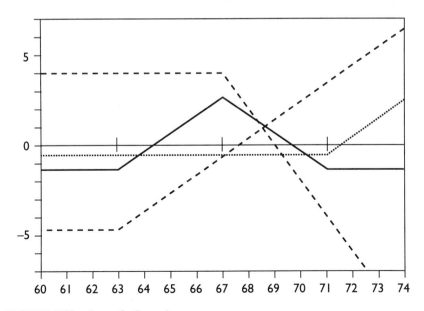

EXHIBIT 5.23   Butterfly Spread

The position is long time ($\theta > 0$); that is, as time passes the position earns money. It also has short volatility: as volatility increases by 1 percent, the value of the butterfly position falls by 0.11 percent. This butterfly should be set up only if one expects volatility to fall.

Diagonal Spreads. A diagonal spread involves the purchase of one option and the sale of another in the same class and on the same underlying currency, with the options having different strike prices *and* different maturities.

The position could be bullish or bearish. The diagonal nature of the spread translates into an expanded set of opportunities, relative to either time or vertical spreads.

Conclusions

This chapter covered futures and options, as well as advanced strategies for speculating and hedging using derivative markets. The most fundamental observation that can be made is that the options and futures markets are very fertile ground for the sober and imaginative investor, provided one learns the basics thoroughly and develops a "feel" for the markets!

The chapter has also shown that measuring the partial derivatives of option prices to underlying variables is an essential component of the risk management of a portfolio of options. In that sense, the Δ and γ of an option are as important as the duration and convexity of a bond and must be perfectly understood to control market risk. Although options and futures are presented in the context of the foreign exchange markets, the tools developed in this chapter are fully transferable to other securities markets.

References

Black, F., and M. Scholes. 1973. "The pricing of options and corporate liabilities," *Journal of Political Economy* 81: 637–59.

Cox, J., S. Ross, and M. Rubinstein. 1979. "Option pricing: A simplified approach," *Journal of Financial Economics* 7: 229–63.

Ederington, L. 1979. "The hedging performance of the new futures markets," *Journal of Finance* 34: 157–70.

Garman, M., and S. Kohlhagen. 1983. "Foreign currency option values," *Journal of International Money and Finance* 2: 231–38.

Hull, J., and A. White. 1987. "The pricing of options on assets with stochastic volatilities," *The Journal of Finance* 42: 281–300.

Leland, H. 1985. "Option pricing and replication with transactions costs," *Journal of Finance* 40: 1283–1301.

Melino, A., and S. Turnbull. 1990. "Pricing foreign currency options with stochastic volatility," *Journal of Econometrics* 45: 239–65.

Merton, R. 1973. "Theory of rational option pricing," *Bell Journal of Economics* 4: 141–83.

Taylor, S. 1990. "Profitable currency futures trading: A comparison of technical and time series trading rules," in *The Currency Hedging Debate*, ed. L. Thomas, IFR Publishing, London.

6

Portfolio Risk Management: Domestic Dimensions

"Fools and prophets don't diversify." Exceptions to this advice make for interesting case studies. Untold fortunes have been realized throughout the history of the United States from portfolios that were decidedly undiversified. The typical household portfolio remains dominated by the housing component, and pension funds remain underdiversified in terms of international securities.

Absent special skills to peer systematically and successfully into the future, one can construct a potent argument in favor of portfolio diversification, for it can eliminate idiosyncratic, or firm-specific, risk for which the market offers no compensation. Diversification is therefore akin to a free lunch, because it provides lower risk at no cost.

The purpose of this chapter is to treat comprehensively all aspects of portfolio diversification taking into consideration only domestic securities. In contrast with the previous chapters, where the principal source of risk was interest rates or exchange rates, we do not identify the sources of risk but instead focus on the diversification benefits obtained from including a large number of assets in a portfolio. This chapter thus takes a general view of risky assets and is applicable to portfolios of stocks, where returns are affected by a multitude of different factors. Later, in chapter 7, we will extend the menu of assets to stocks and currencies.

The first section reviews the measurement of risk and return for a portfolio of risky assets and presents the construction of efficiently diversified portfolios. Combining the investment portfolios with investor risk–return tradeoffs leads to the construction of mean–variance optimal portfolios. The normative theory of portfolio choice was developed by Markowitz and led to positive theories of how stocks should be priced if all investors efficiently diversify. Two theories are presented and discussed in the next sections, the CAPM and the more recent APT. The implications of these models for investment management and performance measurement are then discussed. Chapter 7 will further discuss portfolio risk management in an international context. Anomalies, or deviations from the usual asset pricing models, are left for Chapter 8.

Portfolio Choice

This section briefly reviews the concept of risk and expected return for investments in risky assets. We then show how the menu of possible investment assets can be summarized by the "Markowitz" efficient frontier.

Security Risk and Return

Returns on risky assets consist of income payments plus capital appreciation. If future prices are unknown, returns can be considered random variables. The range of possible payoffs on a security can be described by its probability distribution function. If the distribution is "normal," or Gaussian, the entire distribution can be characterized by its first two moments, the mean and variance.

In practice, the distribution of rates of return is usually estimated over a number of previous periods, assuming all observations are identically and independently distributed. If we consider a total number T of observations $x_1, \ldots, x_T$, the expected return $E(X)$ can be estimated by the sample mean,

$$\hat{\mu} = (1/T)\sum_{i=1}^{T} x_i \, , \tag{6.1}$$

and the variance $\sigma^2(X) = E[(X - \mu)^2]$ can be estimated by the sample variance

$$\hat{\sigma}^2 = [1/(T-1)]\sum_{i=1}^{T} (x_i - \hat{\mu})^2 . \tag{6.2}$$

The square root of σ^2 is the standard deviation of X, often referred to as the *volatility*. It measures the risk of a security as the dispersion of outcomes around its expected value. A flatter distribution indicates greater risk, and a tighter distribution, lower risk.

Portfolio Risk and Return

The return on a portfolio consists of a linear combination of the return on underlying securities. Assume for instance that we deal with the sum of two random variables X_1 and X_2. The variance of the sum is

$$
\begin{aligned}
\sigma^2(X_1 + X_2) &= E[(X_1 + X_2) - E(X_1 + X_2)]^2 \\
&= E[(X_1 - \mu_1)^2 + (X_2 - \mu_2)^2 + 2(X_1 - \mu_1)(X_2 - \mu_2)] (6.3) \\
&= \sigma^2(X_1) + \sigma^2(X_2) + 2\sigma(X_1, X_2),
\end{aligned}
$$

where $\sigma(X_1, X_2)$ is the covariance of X_1 and X_2, written more compactly as σ_{12}. It can be estimated from sample data as follows:

$$
\hat{\sigma}_{12} = [1/(T - 1)] \sum_{i=1}^{T} (x_{1i} - \hat{\mu}_1)(x_{2i} - \hat{\mu}_2). \tag{6.4}
$$

Note that if the random variable X is multiplied by a constant a, the variance of the new variable is $\sigma^2(aX) = a^2\sigma^2(X)$.

Covariance is a measure of the extent to which two variables move linearly together. If two variables are independent, their covariance is equal to zero. A positive covariance means that the two variables tend to move in the same direction; a negative covariance means that they tend to move in opposite directions. The *correlation coefficient* is a convenient, scale-free, measure of linear dependence:

$$
\rho_{12} = \sigma_{12}/(\sigma_1\sigma_2). \tag{6.5}
$$

The correlation coefficient ρ always lies between -1 and $+1$. When equal to one, the two variables are said to be perfectly correlated. When zero, the variables are uncorrelated. Equation (6.3) then reduces to

$$
\sigma^2(X_1 + X_2) = \sigma^2(X_1) + \sigma^2(X_2). \tag{6.6}
$$

Therefore, the variance of the sum of random variables is equal to the sum of variances only if the variables are uncorrelated.

By extension of the previous formulas, the variance of a sum of n random variables $(\sum_{i=1}^{n} X_i)$ is

$$
\sigma^2\left(\sum_{i=1}^{n} X_i\right) = \sum_{i=1}^{n} \sigma_i^2 + \sum_{i=1}^{n} \sum_{j=1, j\neq i}^{n} \sigma_{ij}. \tag{6.7}
$$

The first sum, over the variances, consists of n terms, whereas the second term, over the covariances, consists of $n(n - 1)$ terms.

We are now ready to compute the risk of a portfolio of securities. The return on a portfolio of assets is simply the weighted average of individual security returns ($Y = \sum_{i=1}^{n} w_i X_i$), where the w_i are the weights of individual securities in the portfolio. The variance of Y then becomes

$$\mathrm{Var}(Y) = \sum_{i=1}^{n} w_i^2 \sigma_i^2 + \sum_{i=1}^{n} \sum_{j=1, j \neq i}^{n} w_i w_j \sigma_{ij} . \tag{6.8}$$

This can be written more compactly in matrix notation:

$$\sigma_Y^2 = [w_1 \ \ldots \ w_n] \begin{bmatrix} \sigma_{11} & \sigma_{12} & \sigma_{13} & \cdots & \sigma_{1n} \\ \vdots & & & & \\ \sigma_{n1} & \sigma_{n2} & \sigma_{n3} & \cdots & \sigma_{nn} \end{bmatrix} \begin{bmatrix} w_1 \\ \vdots \\ w_n \end{bmatrix} .$$

Representing w as the column vector of values of w, w' as its (row) transpose, and Σ as the covariance matrix, the portfolio variance is also $\sigma_Y^2 = w' \Sigma w$. Note that if all X_i are uncorrelated, $\sigma_{ij, i \neq j} = 0$, the off-diagonal elements are all zero, and $\sigma_Y^2 = \sum_{i=1}^{n} w_i^2 \sigma_i^2$.

Suppose now that an existing portfolio is made up of $n - 1$ securities, numbered $j = 1, \ldots, n - 1$. Adding one security, numbered $i = 1$, creates a new portfolio. The risk of this new portfolio is changed not by the variance of security i, but rather by how security i covaries with the securities j. This marginal contribution to risk is at the heart of portfolio theory.

In fact, the contribution of a single asset i to the portfolio risk can be measured by differentiating Equation (6.8) with respect to w_i:

$$\frac{\partial \mathrm{Var}(Y)}{\partial w_i} = 2 w_i \sigma_i^2 + 2 \sum_{j=1, j \neq i}^{n} w_j \sigma_{ij} = 2\mathrm{Cov}(X_i, Y). \tag{6.9}$$

Rewriting this in terms of volatility and noting that $\partial \sigma^2 / \partial w_i = 2 \sigma \partial \sigma / \partial w_i$, the sensitivity of the relative change in portfolio volatility to a change in the weight is

$$\frac{\partial \sigma(Y)}{\sigma(Y) \partial w_i} = \mathrm{Cov}(X_i, Y) / \mathrm{Var}(Y) = \beta(X_i, Y). \tag{6.10}$$

Therefore, this sensitivity of portfolio risk to addition of securities is also the β of asset i relative to the total portfolio. This risk that cannot be diversified is referred to, as we amply explain later, as *systematic* or *nondiversifiable risk.*

Portfolio Risk – An Illustration. A portfolio represents a collection of securities. In this section, our discussion will concentrate on portfolios made up of only two securities, so that the mathematics as well as the graphic presentations are made easier.

Consider an investor with $\$A$ to invest. The percentage of A to be committed to each security is represented by w_i (where i = 1,2). If choosing to invest all of A in the first security, then w_1 = 1. If A is invested in the second security, then w_2 = 1. In any case, the budget constraint is that

$$w_1 + w_2 = 1. \tag{6.11}$$

We shall also assume that short sales are permitted. Therefore, w_1 or w_2 can assume negative values. If $w_1 = -3$, assuming short sellers have access to the proceeds from the short sale, then w_2 must equal 4 if the constraint $w_1 + w_2$ = 1 is binding.

Assume now that the expected rate of return from the first security is equal to $E(R_1)$ and that from the second security is $E(R_2)$. Let R_p be the rate of return on the entire portfolio. The expected rate of return on the portfolio is equal to

$$E(R_p) = \sum_i w_i E(R_i) = w_1 E(R_1) + w_2 E(R_2). \tag{6.12}$$

The variance of the portfolio is equal to

$$\sigma_p^2 = w_1^2 \sigma_1^2 + w_2^2 \sigma_2^2 + 2w_1 w_2 \sigma_{12} \tag{6.13}$$
$$= w_1^2 \sigma_1^2 + (1 - w_1)^2 \sigma_2^2 + 2w_1(1 - w_1)\rho\sigma_1\sigma_2$$

since $w_2 = 1 - w_1$ and $\sigma_{12} = \rho\sigma_1\sigma_2$. For values of $\rho = +1$ and $\rho = -1$, the relationship between $E(R_p)$ and σ_p is linear. This can be proven in the first case as follows:

$$\sigma_p^2 = w_1^2 \sigma_1^2 + (1 - w_1)^2 \sigma_2^2 + 2w_1(1 - w_1)\sigma_1\sigma_2 \tag{6.14}$$
$$\sigma_p = \sqrt{[w_1\sigma_1 + (1 - w_1)\sigma_2]^2} = w_1\sigma_1 + (1 - w_1)\sigma_2 ,$$

assuming that the last term is positive. (For some values of w_1, however, the term will be negative, in which case its sign must be switched. We classified the assets so that $\sigma_1 > \sigma_2$.) Then, $w_1 = (\sigma_p - \sigma_2)/(\sigma_1 - \sigma_2)$, and replacing w_1 in $E(R_p)$, we have

$$E(R_p) = E(R_1)(\sigma_p - \sigma_2)/(\sigma_1 - \sigma_2) + E(R_2)(\sigma_1 - \sigma_p)/(\sigma_1 - \sigma_2) \qquad (6.15)$$

$$E(R_p) = \left[E(R_2) - \frac{E(R_1) - E(R_2)}{\sigma_1 - \sigma_2}\sigma_2 \right] + \left[\frac{E(R_1) - E(R_2)}{\sigma_1 - \sigma_2} \right]\sigma_p,$$

which implies a linear relationship between $E(R_p)$ and σ_p when $\rho = 1$.

To illustrate, armed with Equations (6.12) and (6.13), we calculate $E(R_p)$ and σ_p assuming that $\sigma_1 = 4$, $\sigma_2 = 3$, $E(R_1) = 12$, $E(R_2) = 8$, under three assumptions for the value of $\rho:\rho = 0$, $\rho = -1$, and $\rho = +1$. The results are shown in Exhibit 6.1.

The linear relationship between $E(R_p)$ and σ_p is further confirmed by Exhibit 6.1. When $\rho = 1$, the portfolio standard deviation is simply the weighted average of the standard deviation of the individual securities. There are no diversification effects.

Plotting $E(R_p)$ against σ_p for $\rho = \pm1$ and $\rho = 0$, we get (assuming no short position) Exhibit 6.2. When $\rho = 0$, the relationship between $E(R_p)$ and σ_p is curvilinear. If short positions are not permitted, the maximum return is that on the highest yielding security. The minimum portfolio variance is achieved when $\rho = -1$, $\sigma_p = 0$.

Exhibit 6.3 now allows short sales, assuming $\rho = 0.5$. We observe the following:

EXHIBIT 6.1   Investment Portfolios

					No Short Position Permitted				Short Position Is Possible				
$\rho = 0$													
w_1	0	0.20	0.40	0.428	0.60	0.80	1.0	−.5	−1	−3	2	1.5
w_2	1	0.80	0.60	0.572	0.40	0.20	0.0	+1.5	+2	+4	−1	−.5
$E(R_p)$	8%	8.80	9.60	9.710	10.40	11.20	12.0	6	4	−4	16	14
σ_p	3	2.53	2.41	2.420	2.68	3.25	4.0	4.92	7.21	16.97	8.54	6.18
$\rho = -1$													
w_1	0	0.20	0.40	0.428	0.60	0.80	1.0	−.5	−1	−3	2	1.5
w_2	1	0.80	0.60	0.572	0.40	0.20	0.0	1.5	+2	+4	−1	−.5
$E(R_p)$	8%	8.80	9.60	9.710	10.40	11.20	12.0	6	4	−4	16	14
σ_p	3	1.60	0.20	0.000	1.20	2.60	4.0	6.5	10	24	11	7.5
$\rho = +1$													
w_1	0	0.20	0.40	0.428	0.60	0.80	1.0	−.5	−1	−3	2	1.5
w_2	1	0.80	0.60	0.572	0.40	0.20	0.0	1.5	+2	+4	−1	−.5
$E(R_p)$	8%	8.80	9.60	9.710	10.40	11.20	12.0	6	4	−4	16	14
σ_p	3	3.20	3.40	3.428	3.60	3.80	4.0	2.5	2	0	5	4.5

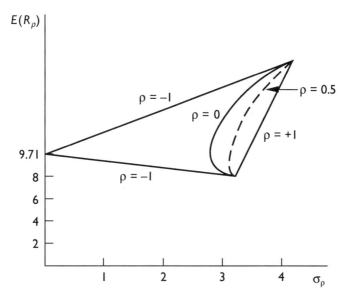

EXHIBIT 6.2   Representation of an Investment Strategy

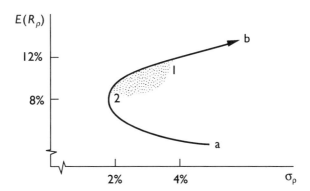

EXHIBIT 6.3   The Effect of a Short Position

1. Every short position in the first security ($w_1 < 0$) yields rates of
   return that are dominated by the expected rates of return where
   a short position is not permitted. Additionally, the standard deviations of the short position are higher than those of the no short
   position when $\rho = 0$ and $\rho = -1$. The lower standard deviations
   when $\rho = +1$ (short positions are permitted) produce very low
   expected rates of return – indeed, negative expected rates of
   return in some cases. The exceptions to this occur when the short
   position is established in the security with the lower expected rate

of return and when $w_1 \geq |w_2|$. This is illustrated by the w_1 = 1.5, w_2 = 0.5 case. Note, however, that while succeeding in improving the expected rate of return on the portfolio, the short position (w_2 = −0.5) produces higher risk than otherwise would be the case if both $w_1 \leq d$ and $w_2 \geq 0$. The impact of a short position is shown in Exhibit 6.2, assuming ρ = 0.5.

2. Point 1 represents the case where w_2 = 0 and w_1 = 1. Point 2 represents the case where w_2 = 1 and w_1 = 0, which also happens to be the global minimum risk portfolio. This portfolio clearly dominates segment 2–a, which produces higher risk and lower rates of return; along segment 2–b, portfolios have higher returns only at the expense of higher risk.
3. Segment 2–1–b in Exhibit 6.3 represents that combination offering the best risk–return tradeoff for a given value of ρ. Formally, an *efficiency frontier* is that locus of points where, for a given level of risk, the investor receives the highest rate of return. Alternatively, for a given level of return, the investor assumes the lowest possible risk.

The efficiency frontier we shall use henceforth is illustrated in Exhibit 6.4. Its shape here is concave. Can the frontier have convex portions, as illustrated in Exhibit 6.5? The answer is no. Point T is not efficient because a feasible combination of weights exists that would produce a higher return for that given level of risk (σ_{p1}). That combina-

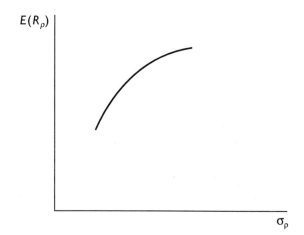

EXHIBIT 6.4   Efficiency Frontier

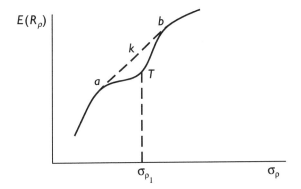

EXHIBIT 6.5   Variant of Efficiency Frontier

tion is represented by point k (a combination of efficient portfolios a and b). At worst, line akb would be straight if a and b were perfectly correlated. Otherwise, it would follow the curvature of the efficiency frontier.

The composition of the global minimum-variance portfolios can be determined as follows. Differentiating Equation (6.13) with respect to w_1, we get

$$\frac{d\sigma_p^2}{dw_1} = 2w_1\sigma_1^2 - 2(1 - w_1)\sigma_2^2 + 2\sigma_{12} - 4w_1\sigma_{12}. \qquad (6.16)$$

Setting Equation (6.16) equal to zero and solving for w_1, we get:

$$w_1 = \frac{\sigma_2^2 - \sigma_{12}}{\sigma_1^2 + \sigma_2^2 - 2\sigma_{12}}, \qquad (6.17)$$

$w_2 = 1 - w_1$, and it can be verified that this is indeed a minimum, because $d^2\sigma_p^2/dw_1^2 > 0$.

Referring back to the data in Exhibit 6.1, we can calculate w_1 and w_2. In the case where $\rho = 1$, we get $w_1 = (9 - 12)/[16 + 9 - 2(12)] = -3$, $w_2 = 4$. When $\rho = -1$, we get $w_1 = 0.428$, $w_2 = 0.572$, and $\sigma_p^2(w_1 = 0.428) = 0$. A correlation coefficient of -1 eliminates risk totally if the proper weights are assigned.

Having determined those combinations of w_1 and w_2 that produce minimum-variance portfolios (MVP), the exact point where the investor chooses to be is not yet settled. That combination of $E(R_p)$ and σ_p on the efficiency frontier preferred by the investor is determined by individual preferences.

Markowitz's Efficient Frontier

The efficient frontier represented in Exhibit 6.4 was derived using only two securities. For any number of securities, the efficient frontier may be derived in either of two ways: finding the locus of points yielding maximum return for a given level of risk or having a minimum risk for a given level of return. In addition, if short sales are allowed, the portfolios can be analytically derived; otherwise, a numerical method, based on quadratic programming, must be used.

The mathematical representation of the portfolio optimization is

$$\text{Minimize } \sigma_p^2 = \sum_{i=1}^{n} w_i^2 \sigma_i^2 + \sum_{i=1}^{n} \sum_{j \neq i}^{n} w_i w_j \sigma_{ij} \qquad (6.18)$$

Subject to

$\Sigma_i w_i = 1$
$\overline{R}_p = \Sigma_{i=1}^{n} w_i \overline{R}_i$
$w_i \geq 0$ for all $i = 1, 2, \ldots, n$,

where $\overline{R}_p$ is the target portfolio return and $\overline{R}_i$ is the expected return on security i. The first constraint indicates that the portfolio is fully invested. The second constraint forces the portfolio's expected return to be equal to that of the target. The third constraint is the nonnegativity constraint or the no short selling constraint; all weights must be positive or zero in this case.

When short sales are allowed, the portfolios on the minimum-variance frontier are a linear combination of two portfolios. In general, these are taken as the global minimum-variance (MV) portfolio and the tangency portfolio. Thus any portfolio can be written as a vector of weights

$$w = k w_{MV} + (1 - k) w_{TG}, \qquad (6.19)$$

where k represents the weight on the MV portfolio.

The MV portfolio solves an optimization problem with $\Sigma_i w_i = 1$ as the sole constraint. The solution, written in matrix notation, is

$$w_{MV} = \Sigma^{-1} 1 / (1' \Sigma^{-1} 1), \qquad (6.20)$$

where Σ is the covariance matrix of returns and 1 is a column vector of ones. Note that the solution does not depend on expected returns, since these do not enter the objective function or the constraints. The denominator ensures that premultiplying the weights by $1'$, which is equivalent to adding the weights, indeed yields unity.

The second portfolio maximizes the ratio of expected return to risk and is at the tangency point of a ray emanating from the origin. Its composition is

$$w_{TG} = \Sigma^{-1}\mu/(1'\Sigma^{-1}\mu), \qquad (6.21)$$

where μ represents the vector of expected returns $\bar{R}_i$, $i = 1, 2, \ldots,$ n. Here again the sum of the weights equals unity.

When short sales are not allowed, Markowitz (1959), a mathematician turned portfolio strategist, derived the details of the efficient frontier. The efficient frontier is fully characterized by a finite number of "corner portfolios," which are such that the weights for any portfolio between "corners" i and $i + 1$ are described by

$$w = kw_i + (1 - k)w_{i+1}.$$

The corner portfolios thus fully describe the constrained efficient set in the same sense that the MV and TG portfolios fully describe the unconstrained efficient set. The quadratic programming algorithm starts with the asset with the highest return as portfolio one (the first corner portfolio), then selects a second portfolio down the efficient set, and so on.

It should be emphasized that mean–variance optimization can uniquely integrate the portfolio objectives with policy constraints and efficient use of information. For instance, the optimization problem can be formulated with short-sales restrictions, transaction costs, liquidity constraints, and turnover constraints. Because of its ability to incorporate various investor constraints and preferences, mean–variance optimization is a remarkably flexible tool.

Portfolio Optimization in Practice

However, an enigma remains: if MV optimization is so powerful, why is it not used more extensively? MV optimization appears to be largely ignored by the majority of investment managers.

The main reason for this resistance to using optimizers is the lack of confidence in the quality of input parameters. The analysis so far has assumed that the investor had access to expected returns, measures of risk, and covariances on all considered assets and that all were measured without error.

In practice, historical averages are typically used to infer $\bar{R}_i$. Variances and covariance terms are also derived from historical returns. Risk and return estimates, however, are inevitably subject to estimation error. MV optimization then significantly overweights (underweights) those securities that have large (small) estimated returns. The size of estimation errors can be significant, as demonstrated by Jobson and Korkie (1981). As a result, the weights produced by an MV model can be unstable and very sensitive to small changes in input parameters. This is why Michaud (1989) calls MV optimizers *estimation-error maximizers*.

In addition, a number of other reasons have been advanced for this situation:

1. There still remains much resistance to the idea that asset allocation is a mechanical and impersonal process. Managers would like to see investment policy committees generate the thrust of a portfolio strategy. MV models, if used in this context, become nothing more than one tool or reference framework, but not ends in and of themselves, and are systematically overridden.
2. Many important factors are typically ignored in MV models. These include liquidity and relative size of the investment in a particular security or asset class.

Methods, however, are available to improve the application of the MV model. For instance, Jorion (1986) proposed a Bayesian adjustment, whereby widely different means are shrunk toward a common average, derived from historical data. This adjustment smooths the data and reduces the bias of the estimation resulting from the use of historical data. Ambachtsheer (1977) recommended the use of an IC (information coefficient) adjustment. The IC parameter, defined as the correlation coefficient between the realized and forecast measures of excess performance in a cross-section, is used to adjust forecasts of future excess performance.

These adjustments do produce a more stable, efficient frontier. The efficient frontier delineates the available efficient combinations of securities in a risky portfolio. The remaining problem, however, is to decide on the precise set of weights most appropriate for a given investor with a particular risk profile. We will show how specific risk profiles may be incorporated in the optimization process. We must begin, however, with a discussion of utility functions that, under conditions of risk, completely summarize the investor's attitude toward risk and return.

Utility and Risk

Investment opportunities present choices involving a desirable good (the expected rate of return) and an undesirable good (risk). The typical investor wishes to maximize the expected rate of return and minimize risk. In this context, utility or, more precisely, expected utility $E(U)$, is maximized by moving in a northwesterly direction, as shown in Exhibit 6.6.

The slope of the indifference curves indicates the extent to which the investor is concerned with avoiding risk. Stated differently, the slope indicates the extent to which the investor wishes to be compensated for assuming one additional unit of risk. The steeper is the slope of the utility curve, the greater is the risk aversion – that is, the greater is the compensation demanded per unit of risk.

With normally distributed returns and assuming a constant absolute risk aversion, the investor's objective is to maximize

$$U(w|\mu,\Sigma) = U(\mu_p, \sigma_p^2) = \mu_p - (1/2\lambda)\sigma_p^2 , \qquad (6.22)$$

where λ is the investor's risk tolerance ($\lambda > 0$), or inverse of risk aversion. This function provides a convenient way to express the tradeoff between risk and return.

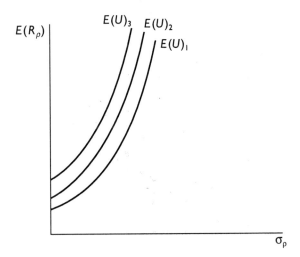

EXHIBIT 6.6   Indifference Curves

For instance, assume an investor is indifferent between investing in a risk-free asset or the stock market. Historically, U.S. stocks have had an excess return, in excess of the risk-free rate, of 8% per annum, with a volatility of 20%. Defining Rf as the risk-free return, the utility is

$$U(\mu_p, \sigma_p^2) = Rf - 0$$
$$= (Rf + 0.08) - (1/2\lambda)(0.20)^2.$$

Solving for λ, one finds $\lambda = 0.25$, which is the revealed risk tolerance of this investor.

Portfolio Selection

Since we have characterized the investor's preferences and investment opportunities, we can now describe the optimal portfolio choice.

Where along the efficiency frontier in Exhibit 6.4 would an investor then choose to be? Superimposing Exhibit 6.6 on Exhibit 6.4, we get Exhibit 6.7. Point S is the optimal point consistent with a minimum-variance portfolio theory and utility maximization. Precisely this point S necessitated all the preceding analysis, and it lays the foundation for further study of portfolio theory.

If investors can be characterized by a quadratic utility function, then they care about only the first and second moments of their portfolio. Alternatively, if asset returns are normally distributed, the full distribution is characterized by its mean and variance. In this case also, the

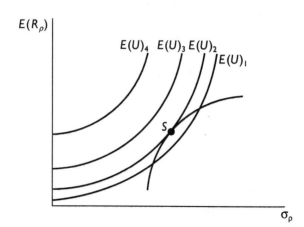

EXHIBIT 6.7 Optimal Portfolio Choice

expected utility maximization can be written in a mean–variance framework, whatever the investor's utility function.

In summary, the mean–variance portfolio choice model is based on the following assumptions:

1. Risk-averse investors who maximize expected utility,
2a. Over normally distributed asset returns or
2b. With a quadratic utility function.

The Capital Asset Pricing Model

The development of the capital asset pricing model (CAPM) began with the work of Sharpe (1964), followed by that of Lintner (1965). Sharpe extended Markowitz's pioneering work to show that, if all investors are rational mean–variance optimizers and have the same view of risk and return, market equilibrium requires that the "market" portfolio be mean–variance efficient.

The CAPM: Essentials

The capital asset pricing model assumptions are as follows:

1. Mean–variance portfolio choice assumptions plus
2. Securities markets are in equilibrium;
3. There is a risk-free asset, which can be used for borrowing or lending;
4. Capital markets are "perfect" – there are no transaction costs, securities are infinitely divisible, short sales are allowed, investors are price takers;
5. Investors have homogeneous expectations about the distribution of rates of return.

Several points need to be noted in connection with these assumptions. First, equilibrium implies that expected payoffs are such that optimal asset demands are precisely equal to the outstanding supply of assets. The latter is taken as fixed. In other words, this equilibrium is only partial, in the sense that the effects of securities markets on the production sector are ignored. Second, for a simple equilibrium to be worked out, we must assume that all investors have the same view of risk and expected returns for all assets. This is a reasonable assumption within a closed economy, but clearly not in an international environment, where investors use different currencies to measure value. U.S. investors, for instance, measure real prices in terms of the U.S. cost of living, whereas French investors measure value in terms of the French consumer price index. The implication of these differing views for equilibrium pricing will be further elaborated in a later chapter.

The introduction of a risk-free asset significantly expands the choice of portfolios available to an investor. Now he or she can either invest all in the risk-free asset, or borrow and invest in risky securities, or invest in the riskless and risky securities. We define M as the portfolio of risky assets in which the investor considers investing proportion w_2 and F as the riskless asset. The portfolio's expected return and variance are now

$$E(R_p) = w_1 R_F + w_2 E(R_M) \tag{6.23}$$
$$\sigma_p^2 = w_1^2 \sigma_F^2 + w_2^2 \sigma_M^2 + 2w_1 w_2 \sigma_{FM} , \tag{6.24}$$

where $w_1 = 1 - w_2$. But because F is riskless, all variance and covariance terms involving F are zero. Therefore, Equation (6.24) can be rewritten as

$$w_2 = \sigma_p / \sigma_M,$$

and Equation (6.23) is also

$$E(R_p) = (1 - \sigma_p / \sigma_M) R_F + \sigma_p / \sigma_M E(R_M) \tag{6.25}$$
$$E(R_p) = R_F + \frac{E(R_M) - R_F}{\sigma_M} \sigma_p .$$

Thus, from Equation (6.25), one can observe that the relationship between $E(R_p)$ and σ_p is linear. This is depicted in Exhibit 6.8 (segment $R_F M$).

If a short position in the risk-free security can be established, the line $R_F M$ extends as shown by the dashed line. If unlimited borrowing is possible, the extension is infinite in length.

Point M in Exhibit 6.8 represents $w_2 = 1$; that is, 100% of the investable funds are committed to risky securities. Point R_F represents 100% investment in the riskless asset. Any point between R_F and M represents a combination of risky and riskless securities: $1 > w_1 > 0$, $1 > w_2 > 0$, $w_1 + w_2 = 1$.

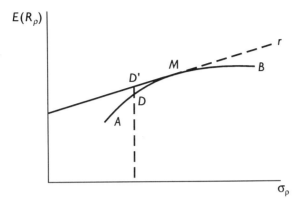

Key: M = Market portfolio; AB = efficiency frontier without the risk-free asset; $E(R_p)$ = expected portfolio rate of return; σ_p = standard deviation of portfolio rate of return; $R_F MT$ = efficiency frontier with borrowing and lending at the risk-free rate.

EXHIBIT 6.8   Capital Market Line

The efficiency frontier is no longer AMB, but rather $R_F MT$. The reason for this is that every point along AMB is dominated by a feasible point along $R_F MT$. Point D, for instance, is dominated by point D', for D' offers a higher return for the same level of risk. If there is no shorting of the riskless asset, the new efficiency frontier is $R_F MB$.

The slope of $R_F MT$ is equal to $[E(R_M) - R_F]/\sigma_M$, which represents the market price per unit of total risk. Line $R_F MT$ is referred to as the *capital market line*. The reader should observe that point M is unique across all investors if they have homogeneous expectations. That is, the choice of a portfolio of risky securities is limited strictly to portfolio M if the choice is to be consistent with the efficiency objective. Efficient portfolios plot along $R_F MT$ and consist of a combination of risk-free assets (long or short) and portfolio M. This is so regardless of the shape of the individual's utility curve.

This is referred to as the *separation theorem*, illustrated in Exhibit 6.9. The allocation of wealth between risky assets and risk-free assets is separated from the wealth allocation among risky assets.

Utility curve U_1 indicates that the investor wishes to combine risky securities with the riskless asset. The closer the tangency point is to the efficiency frontier R_F, the larger is the percentage of funds invested in riskless assets; the farther it is from R_F, the larger is the percentage of funds invested in risky assets. Thus utility curves help the investor decide where along the efficiency frontier he or she must be – that

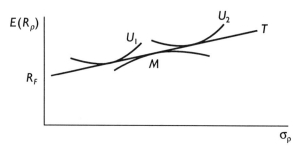

EXHIBIT 6.9   Separation Theorem

is, how much to borrow or lend at the risk-free rate and consequently how much to commit to portfolio M.

In equilibrium, the demand for all stocks equates the supply of all stocks. Because portfolio M is the only portfolio of risky assets any investor will hold and it is the same for all investors, this implies that, in equilibrium, the demand (portfolio composition) equates the supply and that the optimal portfolio must be the market.

The composition of market portfolio can be derived from the number of outstanding shares n_i and their market value P_i: $x_i = n_i P_i / \Sigma_j n_j P_j = n_i P_i / V_m$, where V_m is the total value of all publicly traded shares.

The CAPM: Technical Derivation

The preceding discussion centers on the relationship between return and risk for portfolios. The securities market, however, prices securities individually.

Consider a portfolio made up of a risky asset i and the market portfolio. The expected return on this portfolio and its variance are calculated as follows:

$$E(R_p) = w_i E(R_i) + (1 - w_i)E(R_M), \qquad (6.26)$$

$$\sigma_p = \sqrt{w_i^2 \sigma_i^2 + (1 - w_i)^2 \sigma_M^2 + 2w_i(1 - w_i)\sigma_{iM}}. \qquad (6.27)$$

Using the fact that $\dfrac{\partial E(R_p)}{\partial \sigma_p} = \dfrac{\partial E(R_p)/\partial w_i}{\partial \sigma_p / \partial w_i}$, we find that

$$\frac{\partial E(R_p)}{\partial \sigma_p} = \frac{E(R_i) - E(R_M)}{1/2[w_i^2 \sigma_i^2 + (1 - w_i)^2 \sigma_M^2 + 2w_i(1 - w_i)\sigma_{iM}]^{-1/2}}$$
$$\times \frac{1}{[2w_i\sigma_i^2 + 2w_i\sigma_M^2 - 2\sigma_M^2 + 2\sigma_{iM} - 4w_i\sigma_{iM}]}.$$

Security i, however, could not exist outside portfolio M because M is the market portfolio. Therefore w_i is zero in equilibrium and the preceding simplifies to

$$\frac{\partial E(R_p)}{\partial \sigma_p} = \frac{E(R_i) - E(R_M)}{1/2[\sigma_M^2]^{-1/2}[-2\sigma_M^2 + 2\sigma_{iM}]} = \frac{E(R_i) - E(R_M)}{(\sigma_{iM} - \sigma_M^2)/\sigma_M} \cdot \quad (6.28)$$

This represents a new price of risk that must be equivalent to that derived earlier $[E(R_M) - R_F]/\sigma_M$. Therefore,

$$\frac{E(R_M) - R_F}{\sigma_M} = \frac{E(R_i) - E(R_M)}{(\sigma_{iM} - \sigma_M^2)/\sigma_M} \cdot \quad (6.29)$$

Solving for $E(R_i)$, we get

$$E(R_i) = R_F + [E(R_M) - R_F]\frac{\sigma_{iM}}{\sigma_M^2}, \quad (6.30)$$

where

$E(R_M) - R_F$ is the marketwide risk premium,
$\sigma_{iM}/\sigma_M^2 = \beta_i$ is the measure of systematic risk.

The CAPM thus shows that the risk premium on any risky asset should be determined by the product of its β coefficient with the marketwide risk premium.

The linear relationship between the rate of return on a security and β shown in Equation (6.30) holds even if a risk-free asset does not exist. Black (1972) showed that the linear relationship also holds, with a zero β portfolio replacing the risk-free asset:

$$E(R_i) = E(R_0) + [E(R_M) - E(R_0)]\frac{\sigma_{iM}}{\sigma_M} \cdot \quad (6.31)$$

The CAPM: Implications

The CAPM has created a revolution in finance by transforming the way investors view capital markets. As stated by Stephen Ross (1978),

The CAPM theory . . . not only "explains" asset prices, but it does so by providing an analytic basis for a brilliant, if not entirely reliable, intuition. Asset risk premia depend not on the total risk of the asset, but rather on the relationship of the asset to the overall market m. Since

m aggregates all risk borne by the market portfolio, only the relationship between the asset and the market portfolio, its beta, can determine the premium for an individual asset.

The required return on a security is no longer wholly determined by its total risk σ_i but by the correlation of that security's rate of return with the market rate of return, as seen in the equation

$$\beta_{iM} = \frac{\rho_{iM}\sigma_i\sigma_M}{\sigma_M^2} = \frac{\rho_{iM}\sigma_i}{\sigma_M} ,$$

where β_{iM} measures the extra risk that security i adds to the portfolio.

Exhibit 6.10 depicts the security market line (SML), which relates expected return to β. Securities with rates of return lying above the SML are undervalued: they have too high a return given their level of risk. Those with rates of return plotting below the line are considered overvalued: they have too low a return given their level of risk. In equilibrium, every security should plot on the market line.

Beta and the Market Model

The CAPM provides equilibrium expected returns based on β. Systematic risk is generally measured from a statistical model called the *market model*. We can decompose the return on an asset into a component perfectly correlated with the market and another independent of, or orthogonal to, the market:

$$R_{i,t} = a_i + b_i R_{M,t} + \epsilon_{i,t} , \tag{6.32}$$

where the residual $\epsilon_{i,t}$ has zero mean $E[\epsilon_{i,t}] = 0$ and is not correlated with the market $\text{Cov}(\epsilon_{i,t}, R_{M,t}) = 0$. Note that there is no requirement that the intercept be equal to the risk-free rate. Therefore this model

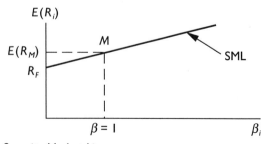

EXHIBIT 6.10 Security Market Line

is more general than the CAPM, because it does not impose cross-sectional restrictions on the pricing of assets.

This regression equation can be estimated in any spreadsheet or statistical package. Regressing the rate of return on the selected stock on the market return, one could obtain, for example,

$$Y = -0.049 + 0.993\ X, \quad R^2 = 30.1\% \quad (6.33)$$
$$(0.096)\ (0.218)$$

The values in parentheses are standard errors. Although the stock β is approximately one, there is substantial uncertainty as to what the true value is. We can for instance construct a confidence interval that will contain the true value with a 95 percent probability. With a normal distribution, this would be included within two standard deviations from the mean. The lower end of the interval is therefore 0.993 − 2(0.218) = 0.557, whereas the upper end is 0.993 + 2(0.218) = 1.429. The variance of the stock return as written in Equation (6.32) is

$$\sigma_i^2 = b_i^2 \sigma_M^2 + \sigma_\epsilon^2. \quad (6.34)$$

The total variance of the rate of return on a security is, therefore, separable into systematic risk $b_i^2 \sigma_M^2$ and unsystematic risk σ_ϵ^2. A sufficiently diversified portfolio should have a $\sigma_\epsilon^2 = 0$. Thus, the concern of investors should logically focus on systematic risk, for which they seek compensation in the form of higher rates of return. In the preceding equation, the R^2 measures the proportion of variance attributable to market movements: $R^2 = b_i^2 \sigma_M^2 / \sigma_i^2$.

Given that a portfolio return is the weighted average of individual stock returns, the systematic risk of a portfolio is measured by the weighted average of the values of β of each of the stocks in the portfolio:

$$b_p = \sum_i b_i w_i. \quad (6.35)$$

Thus, β is additive, in the same way that the Δ of a portfolio of options is equal to the weighted sum of the individual values of each Δ.

Empirical Tests of the CAPM

In terms of empirical verification, however, the CAPM is not directly testable because expectations are unobservable. In practice, empirical tests are based on the "rational expectations" assumption: we assume that the "ex-post" distribution from which returns are drawn is the same as the one perceived "ex ante" by investor.

The empirical testing of the CAPM ordinarily proceeds as follows:

1. Estimate β_i using time series data for several stocks over, say, five years. Define the months as $\{1, 60\}$. These measured values of β contain estimates of the true values of β plus an estimation error.

2. Form portfolios based on the magnitudes of their β. Dealing with portfolios instead of individual securities considerably lowers the number of assets to deal with and also increases the precision of the measured β.

3. Compute the average portfolio returns and β in a period outside the portfolio formation period. Define this for example as months $\{61, 120\}$. The reason for this is that the measured portfolio β contains estimates of true β plus estimation error. By choosing another period to measure β, we hope to keep useful information about the true β and to decrease the random estimation error.

4. Regress the average returns $\overline{R}_i$ on the values of $\hat{\beta}_i$ in a single cross-section:

$$\overline{R}_i = \gamma_0 + \gamma_1 \hat{\beta}_i + \epsilon_i. \qquad (6.36)$$

The estimated intercept γ_0 of the regression equation is then compared with the risk-free rate and the slope γ_1 with the excess rate of return $(R_M - R_F)$. This approach was implemented by Black, Jensen, and Scholes (1972), who found general support for the CAPM. Their approach, however, still suffers from measurement problems in the combined β: high measured β probably contains truly high values of β but also also positive estimation error and is therefore likely to be upward biased; similarly, low measured combined β is probably too low. This could explain why the intercept γ_0 was found to be higher than the risk-free rate.

In the two-step procedure pioneered by Fama and McBeth (1973), the regression is performed using returns in month 121 and prior values of β measured over $\{61, 120\}$ and then repeated for each subsequent month in the sample. Inference is made on γ_0 and γ_1 from the monthly time series. This approach completely avoids the problem of error in the measured values of β, which still affects the other procedure described previously.

The evidence in these papers indicates that the estimated intercept is significantly different from the T-bill rate, used as a proxy for R_F, and that the estimated slope is less than $R_M - R_F$. This indicates that low-β securities outperform the market (as predicted by the CAPM) and high-β securities underperform the market. These results are consistent with Black's zero β model presented in Equation (6.31).

The CAPM Controversy

Lest we leave the reader with the impression that the CAPM is the answer to the financial analyst's problems, we should note that the model has been the subject of intense controversy. Criticisms of the CAPM center on theoretical considerations and empirical findings; the latter will be described in the "anomalies" chapter.

On a theoretical level, the seeds of the controversy were planted by an article written by Richard Roll (1977), who questions the very foundation of the CAPM. His fundamental point is that, for a theory that acquired its reputation on the base of easy testability, the CAPM has never been correctly and unambiguously tested and there is practically no possibility that such a test can be accomplished in the future. The logic is the following:

1. The development of the CAPM implies that the market portfolio M is mean–variance efficient. The linearity between the expected rate of return and β summarized in the SML, however, holds for any portfolio on the efficient frontier.
2. The market portfolio M in the CAPM includes all invested assets. The use of proxies like the S&P 500 composite index is inadequate. Those proxies may be mean–variance efficient while the market is not and mean–variance inefficient while the market is. Unless the composition of the market portfolio is known and measurable, Roll argued, the testability of the theory is not possible. Roll (1978) supported his point by showing that different proxies against which portfolio performances are measured yield different rankings. The value of β is therefore open to question. Ross (1978) tempered this view somewhat:

> Roll's analysis does not say that we must observe M to test the theory. For example, we can all agree that M has only positive

components, and this means that the CAPM could be refuted by refuting the existence of a positive (ex ante) efficient portfolio. This is a testable proposition, but as Roll's second point shows, the construction of suitable powerful tests will be difficult. More generally, even though M is unobservable, a proxy P can be used for testing if we know something about $M - P$. By bounding the difference between M and P – for instance, by bounding the total wealth not included in our sample – it might be possible to construct tests of the efficiency of M by using P. This will not be easy, but it should be possible.

3. Although the preceding criticism concentrates on the empirical aspects of the CAPM, Ross found problems with the fundamental assumptions[1] of the theory, specifically with the normality of the distribution of rates of return or with the quadratic preferences of investors.

The limitations of the CAPM led Ross to develop an alternative model published in 1976 as the *arbitrage pricing theory* (APT).

The Arbitrage Pricing Theory

We must note at the outset that both the CAPM and the APT assert that every asset must be compensated only according to its systematic risk. The APT considers systematic risk as covariability with not only one factor (the market index in the case of CAPM), but also possibly with several economic factors. For both models, unsystematic risk, given that it can be diversified away, should not be compensated.

The models, however, differ in several respects:

1. The CAPM requires the economy to be in equilibrium while the APT requires only that the economy have no arbitrage opportuni-

---

[1]It must be noted that other assumptions have been relaxed without any significant impact on the validity of the CAPM. Fama (1965) investigated the normality assumption and found that returns were not normally distributed. The validity of the CAPM is preserved, however, if the distribution (not the variance) is used. Mayers (1972) showed that the validity of the CAPM is unaffected by the presence of nonmarketable assets. In a continuous (as opposed to a discrete) time framework, Merton (1973) showed that the CAPM is robust. The expected rate of return is replaced by an instantaneous rate of return. Lintner (1969) showed that heterogeneous expectations can be adjusted for mathematically, but that the testability of the CAPM is severely impaired.

ties. The latter is a necessary but not a sufficient condition for the economy to be in equilibrium. The APT therefore represents a more fundamental economic relationship. Its rejection implies the rejection of CAPM, but not vice versa.

2. The APT requires no assumptions about utility functions except the assumptions of monotonicity and concavity. It is also more general because it holds for n periods just as it does for a single period.

APT: Technical Derivation

To simplify the derivation of the APT model, assume initially that there is only one factor, called the *market*. Returns are generated by the following linear process:

$$\tilde{r}_i = E_i + \beta_i \tilde{\delta} + \tilde{\epsilon}_i ,   (6.37)$$

where E_i is the expected return, β_i is the β – or loading – on the factor, $\tilde{\delta}$ is a zero-mean common (to all securities) factor representing, for instance, the deviation of the market return from its trend. Here, tildes are used to signify random variables.

Of the n assets available for investment, we pick the arbitrage portfolio x, representing a vector of weights, that is, the proportions invested in each security. The arbitrage portfolio uses zero wealth, that is, the sum of the long positions must be offset by the sum of short positions; hence the components of the vector x can be positive or negative. Defining 1 as a vector of ones, we can represent the fact that all portfolio weights sum to zero as $x'1 = 0$.

The return on the arbitrage portfolio is equal to

$$x'\tilde{r} = x'E + (x'\beta)\tilde{\delta} + x'\tilde{\epsilon}.   (6.38)$$

If the portfolio is large enough, we have $x'\tilde{\epsilon} \approx 0$. Thus $x'\tilde{r} \approx x'E + (x'\beta)\tilde{\delta}$.

If the arbitrage portfolio is chosen to have no systematic risk, that is $x'\beta = 0$, then

$$x'\tilde{r} \approx x'E.   (6.39)$$

In the absence of arbitrage opportunities, the expected return on the portfolio must be zero, because the portfolio uses no wealth. Since $x'E = x'1 = x'\beta = 0$, the vectors E, 1, and β are in the same vector space and E is "spanned" by (is a linear combination of) 1 and β,

$$E_i = \mu + \lambda\beta_i , \qquad (6.40)$$

where μ and λ are constants. Put differently, there is an infinity of portfolios x_i, $i = 1, \ldots, n$ such that the two conditions $x'1 = 0$, $x'\beta = 0$ are satisfied. The E_i, however, must all be such that $x'E$ is always zero, for whatever values of x_i we have chosen. This can occur only if $E_i = \mu + \lambda\beta_i$, since then $x'E = x'\mu1 + x'\lambda\beta = \mu(x'1) + \lambda(x'\beta) = \mu0 + \lambda0$ is identically zero.

APT: Implications

The one-factor APT implies that expected returns on all assets must be proportional to their exposure to this factor. If this were not the case, one could construct a portfolio with no invested wealth but with a positive payoff. This situation would lead to "arbitrage" profits, because they occur with no risk. Equation (6.40) is depicted in Exhibit 6.11, which is similar to the SML.

For example, assume that expected returns and β for three securities are as follows:

Security	Expected rate of return	β
1	8%	0.5
2	11%	1.0
3	12%	1.5

If security 2 had an expected return of 10 percent, all expected returns would plot on a line with an intercept equal to 6 percent and a slope equal to 4 percent. Instead, security 2 has an expected return of 11 percent, higher than that implied by the APT. If this were the case, we could then form a portfolio that is long security 2 and short securities 1 and 3, with no net investment. For instance, choose the

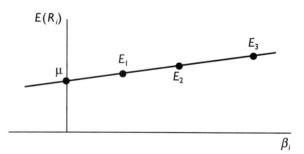

EXHIBIT 6.11 Graphic Depiction of the APT

weights −0.5, 1, −0.5, which indeed sum to zero and in addition are such that the net exposure is β = (−0.5) × 0.5 + (1.0) × 1.0 + (−0.5) × 1.5 = 0. This portfolio has no exposure to the common source of risk and, in addition, will have little residual idiosyncratic risk if it contains enough securities (three may not be enough). As a result, it is approximately riskless. But its expected return is $E(R)$ = (−0.5) × 8% + (1.0) × 11% + (−0.5) × 12% = 1%. Given the assumptions behind the APT, this situation cannot occur, because earning 1 percent on a portfolio that costs nothing and has no risk is an arbitrage opportunity. Note that this reasoning involved no aggregation across investors, just the absence of arbitrage opportunities.

Going back to Exhibit 6.11, we can see that μ represents the zero β portfolio or the risk-free rate if a riskless asset exists. For any portfolio m with a positive β, λ must represent the excess return on that portfolio over the zero β rate or the risk-free rate. Thus Equation (6.40) can be written (very similarly to the SML) as

$$E_i = \mu + (E_m - \mu)\beta_i \,, \qquad (6.41)$$

where E_m = rate of return on portfolio m. In this case, E_m represents the rate of return on the market portfolio.

A more general version of the preceding is the K factor model:

$$\tilde{r} = E + \beta_1\tilde{\delta}_1 + \beta_2\tilde{\delta}_2 + \ldots + \beta_K\tilde{\delta}_K + \tilde{\epsilon}, \qquad (6.42)$$

where $\tilde{\delta}_k$ is the unexpected component on factor k. The pricing equation directly extends Equation (6.41)

$$E_i = \lambda_0 + \sum_{k=1}^{K}\lambda_k b_{ik} \,, \qquad (6.43)$$

where λ_0 is the risk-free rate and λ_k represents the market price of factor k. Note that, in general, the APT does not require that the market portfolio (the single index in the CAPM) be mean–variance efficient.

APT: Empirical Tests

An obvious difficulty with the APT is that economic theory provides no guidance as to what the factors may be. As a result, the theory is further removed from practice than the CAPM. Two approaches have been taken by researchers in empirical tests.

The first method used to identify the significant factors is factor analysis. This is a statistical method that attempts to replicate the structure of comovements between assets by a small number of factors. This method comes with heavy baggage, however. It does not allow the researcher to precisely pinpoint the exact number of factors, and the method becomes difficult to implement when the number of securities under consideration is large, that is, above 100. Nonetheless, Roll and Ross (1980) showed that a factor-based APT provides a noticeable improvement in the cross-sectional explanation of expected returns than the CAPM.

Another method is to prespecify the factors as economic variables that are likely to consistently influence stock returns. Chen, Roll, and Ross (1986) posited as factors: (i) the "industrial production growth," (ii) the "change in expected inflation," where expected inflation is constructed as the difference between the one-month U.S. Treasury bill rate and the real interest rate, (iii) the "unexpected inflation," (iv) the "risk premium" series, defined as the difference between returns on low-grade bonds and government bonds, and (v) the "term structure" series, defined as the difference between the return on a portfolio of long-term government bonds and the risk-free rate. Although more research needs to be done, the APT has proven promising in explaining deviations from the CAPM. In addition, factor models have become widespread in the investment management industry as a tool to control different sources of risk.

Finance Theory in Investment Management

The development of finance theory in the latest decades has had an irreversible impact on the practice of investment management. The "efficient market" theory, in combination with the CAPM, for instance, has provided the intellectual impetus for a rapid growth in "index" funds, which simply try to mimic a particular stock index, such as the S&P 500. This search for "passive" funds, which dissipate much less transaction costs than active managers, has also been caused by dissatisfaction with the accumulating evidence that few active managers consistently outperform the market.

Portfolio theory, however, also provides essential tools to structure the portfolio allocation process. Whims and tips are no longer valid inputs for managing portfolios in the 1990s. Instead, return forecasts must be combined with risk measures to quantitatively assess portfolio risk. Because performance is now routinely measured relative to a benchmark, it is essential to know in advance how large deviations can occur relative to the index. This is why quantitative techniques, based on modern portfolio theory, have become indispensable tools in the management of investment portfolios. We now present two applications of "modern portfolio theory" (MPT) to investment management.

The Wells Fargo Model

Wells Fargo Investment Advisors, an investment subsidiary of the San Francisco bank, has developed a unique approach to investment management based on modern portfolio theory. The approach combines the β analysis with the discounted cash flow technique.

Wells Fargo analysts are required to forecast the following:

1. Dividends and earnings for the next five years;
2. Expected earnings per share, growth rate, and dividend payout ratio for the fifth year;
3. The length of period between the fifth year and the moment when "normal" earnings growth rate begins (*normal* here means a long-run steady-state growth rate, consistent with an economy in midcycle, between expansions and recessions);
4. The expected growth rate and payout ratio for the steady-state period and for the intervening period (after five years and before the steady-state period begins).

Armed with these values, which yield dividend flows over an infinite time horizon, and with the current market price of the stock, the analyst calculates the value of discount rate K_e that equates the present value of the dividend flows to the market price of the stock. This is done for every stock Wells Fargo follows.

In the next step, an estimate of β is computed using historical data and whatever pertinent information the analyst possesses about current and future operations of the firm. Note that the resulting β values are projected into the future, instead of reflecting past values. Stocks are then divided into risk classes in accordance with their β. For each β range a security market line is then estimated by fitting a straight line through the data points (K_{ei}, β_i). This line suggests the average rate of return the market expects for that level of risk.

The recommendation of the analyst is then based on where a given stock plots in relation to the expected SML. A stock plotting above the SML would be considered underpriced and one below the SML overpriced. The model allows portfolio managers to load the portfolio with securities deemed underpriced and to sell (or short) securities deemed overpriced, departing in the process from the distribution of weights in the market portfolio.

The BARRA Model

A unique feature of the Wells Fargo model is the use of fundamental information to forecast estimates of β. This was due to Barr Rosenberg, who initially worked as a consultant for Wells Fargo, then set up his own firm, BARRA. The firm was initially in the service of providing β forecasts.

Following the trend in finance toward multifactor models, BARRA has now extended the range of its services from a one-factor model to a more complete, multifactor view of risk management.

The BARRA E1 model, for instance, provides six risk indices that characterize movements in stock returns. The indices measure market variability, earnings variability, success, size, growth, and financial risk. The exposure to each risk index is built from a number of underlying fundamental factors. For instance, the exposure to the market variability factor is measured using a composite of historical β, historical volatility, share turnover, trading volume, and so on.

Although BARRA does not provide estimates of expected returns, the risk measures can be combined with analysts' return forecasts to tightly control portfolio risk. Tracking error can be minimized by constructing a portfolio where the loadings on risk factors are similar to those for the market. In addition, knowing the ex-ante loading on the risk factors as well as the ex-post payoffs on the risk factors leads to a performance decomposition of returns. Portfolio managers can then better understand the source of underperformance or outperformance. Multifactor models, therefore, have become essential tools in the construction of investment portfolios.

Measuring the Performance of Portfolio Managers

By emphasizing that risky securities should have higher returns than less risky securities, the CAPM demonstrates the need to adjust for risk when measuring performance. William Sharpe (1966) used total risk to devise an index of portfolio performance:

$$S_i = \frac{\overline{R}_i - R_F}{\sigma_i}, \qquad (6.44)$$

where

S_i = "Sharpe ratio"= portfolio i performance index,
$\overline{R}_i$ = average return on ith portfolio,
R_F = risk-free rate,
σ_i = standard deviation of returns for portfolio i (ex-post total risk).

The higher is the value of S_i, the better is the performance of the fund – that is, the higher is the risk premium per unit of total risk. An example of ranking based on Sharpe ratio is shown in Exhibit 6.12. The value of S_i represents the price per unit of total risk. The more risk-averse a person is, the higher is the S_i he or she will require.

The Sharpe ratio is appropriate when total risk matters; that is, when most of an investor's wealth is invested in this asset. When the asset, however, is considered only in relation to a large, diversified portfolio, measuring risk by total volatility is inappropriate. Treynor (1965) proposed an alternative performance measure emphasizing systematic rather than total risk. His index is

$$T_i = \frac{\overline{R}_i - R_F}{b_i}, \qquad (6.45)$$

where b_i is the measure of the fund's systematic risk, or slope of the characteristic line. The higher is the slope, the greater the sensitivity of the fund's return to the market portfolio's return.

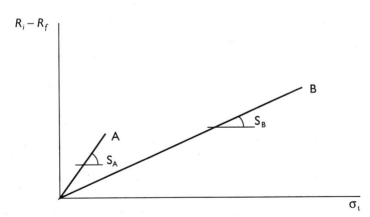

EXHIBIT 6.12   Ranking Based on Sharpe Ratios

The Sharpe and Treynor measures represent the risk premium per unit of total and systematic risk and assume that investors can borrow and lend at the risk-free rate. These performance measures can be compared to those of a benchmark index such as the S&P 500. In practice, studies of U.S. mutual funds show considerable consistency between the rankings observed for the two measures.

Another performance measure based on the market model was advanced by Jensen in 1968. The ranking of mutual fund i is determined by the intercept α_i in the regression

$$R_{i,t} - R_{F,t} = \alpha_i + \beta_i(R_{M,t} - R_{F,t}) + \epsilon_{i,t} .$$ (6.46)

A positive and significant α_i indicates that the fund manager had consistently outperformed the market, after adjusting for systematic risk. A negative and significant α_i indicates consistent underperformance.

Using this performance measure, Jensen (1968) was able to demonstrate, for 115 mutual funds during the 1945–1965 period,

> not only that these 115 mutual funds were on average not able to predict security prices well enough to outperform a buy-the-market-and-hold policy, but also that there is very little evidence that any individual fund was able to do significantly better than that which we expected from mere random chance. . . . Thus on average the funds apparently were not quite successful enough in their trading activities to recoup even their brokerage expenses.

Jensen's results were later questioned by Norman Mains (1977). The criticism centered on the method used to calculate return and risk. Focusing on possible biases in the risk estimates, Friend and Blume (1970) reestimated the relationships in the Jensen study and found that the risk-adjusted performance was significantly inversely correlated with risk. That is, low-risk portfolios achieved higher risk-adjusted performance than high-risk portfolios. Friend and Blume attributed the results primarily to the assumption of equality of the borrowing and lending rates with the risk-free rate in the capital asset pricing model. If the Black model holds, however, this problem can be corrected by empirically estimating the zero β portfolio, which then can be used instead of the risk-free rate. A related problem is the fact that performance measures appear to be very sensitive to the choice of the benchmark, as demonstrated by Lehmann and Modest

(1987). This goes back to Roll's criticism that it is difficult to distinguish between investment performance and benchmark inefficiency.

Robert Klemkosky (1973) also examined the bias issue using quarterly data on 40 actual portfolios between the years 1966 and 1971. His results showed a bias in a positive direction (opposite that of Friend and Blume); that is, higher-risk portfolios have higher risk-adjusted performance.

Another point raised by Fabozzi and Francis (1979) is the stability of β. The fund manager, by adjusting the portfolio's β upward in a bull market and downward in a bear market, can improve investment performance through market timing. But if β differs with market conditions, the use of β estimated over a long period can mask the market-timing skills of managers under different market conditions. Using monthly data on 85 mutual funds over 1966 to 1971, Fabozzi and Francis reported that mutual fund managers do not appear to adjust their portfolio's β as market conditions change. These results were later supported by Alexander and Stover (1980).

Tests of performance, however, can be seriously biased if managers attempt to time the market. In the SML in Exhibit 6.13, we assume that there are two states of the market return: high and low. If managers correctly anticipate the high state, they will move into high β stocks; with low return projected, they will move into low β stocks. The problem for performance measurement is that the measured long-run

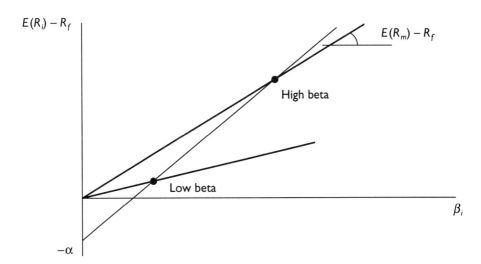

EXHIBIT 6.13   Apparent Underperformance Due to Market Timing

β will be too high, and the resulting α will appear to be too low. Thus, even if the SML holds, accurate market timing will result in an apparent underperformance!

Treynor and Mazuy (1966) added a quadratic term to Equation (6.46) to try to detect market-timing ability. They argued that a greater proportion of the assets should be invested in risky stocks if the market is expected to rise. However, they could detect market-timing ability for only 1 of the 57 surveyed funds.

It appears, therefore, that mutual fund managers have no special insight into the behavior of the market. Market timing can be separately analyzed using a method proposed by Henriksson and Merton (1981). Suppose that a manager has to decide whether to invest in bills or in stocks. He will invest in bills if returns $E(R_M) < R_F$. We observe, however, only R_M and R_F. Define n_1 as the number of outcomes where $R_F < R_M$ is predicted correctly, and n_2 as the number of unsuccessful predictions that $R_F < R_M$. Comparing the predicted with actual returns, we can construct a contigency table:

Predicted return	Actual return	
	$R_F < R_M$	$R_F \geq R_M$
$R_F < R_M$	n_1	n_2
$R_F > R_M$	$N_1 - n_1$	$N_2 - n_2$
Totals	N_1	N_2

Define also $n = n_1 + n_2$ and $N = N_1 + N_2$. Henriksson and Merton (1981) show that to test a forecaster's market-timing ability, we must determine whether $E(n_1/N_1) + E[(N_2 - n_2)/N_2] = 1$, or whether $E(n_1/N_1) = E(n_2/N_2)$. Let us think, for instance, of an eternal pessimist. The forecaster always predicts stocks will go down, and he or she will be right in many cases, every time the stock market falls: $n_1 = N_1$ and $n_2 = N_2$. But clearly, there is no forecasting ability. The normal approximation to the test statistic is

$$z = (n_1 - nN_1/N)/\sqrt{[nN_1N_2(N - n)]/[N^2(N - 1)]}. \qquad (6.47)$$

An answer to the puzzle of poor investment performance may be found in work by Grinblatt and Titman (1989). They collected the quarterly holdings of mutual funds, which were then applied to the returns on underlying stocks to create a hypothetical portfolio performance. For some fund categories, these hypothetical returns were found to be about 2 percent higher than actual returns, which were generally no better than the market. Because transaction costs and management fees are not factored in hypothetical returns, this indicates that some managers are able to outperform the market before costs, but not after costs. From an economic perspective, this is not unexpected: managers who have special talents may be able to charge fees or capture rents that will reflect this value added.

Conclusions

This chapter has discussed the measurement of risk for portfolios of risky securities, as well as implications for the pricing of risky assets in a domestic context. It lays the foundation for a chapter covering diversification in an international context, as well as for a chapter covering empirical tests of asset pricing models and recently discovered anomalies.

We have focused on the risk and return of individual securities as well as portfolios. In this context, β has several interpretations. Relative to a particular portfolio, it measures the marginal contribution of one asset to total portfolio risk. This has led to the theory of the capital asset pricing model: when β is measured relative to the market, there should be a linear relationship between expected returns on all assets and their market β. No other factor should be priced. The CAPM, however, is currently the subject of intense controversy.

Alternatively, β can be used as a measure of the sensitivity of a particular stock to general movements in the market. Like duration, which measures the exposure of a bond to movements in yields, β measures the exposure to general market movements. To obtain more explanatory power, more factors can be considered, which leads to a multiple β approach. As a result, β and the factor models have become essential tools for the management of risky assets.

References

Alexander, G., and R. Stover. 1980. "Consistency of mutual fund performance during varying market conditions," *Journal of Economics and Business* 225.

Ambachtsheer, K. 1977. "Where are the customer's alpha's?" *Journal of Portfolio Management*.

Black, F. 1972. "Capital market equilibrium with restricted borrowing," *Journal of Business* 45: 444–55.

——, M. Jensen and M. Scholes. 1972. "The capital asset pricing model: Some empirical tests," in *Studies in the Theory of Capital Markets*, ed. M. C. Jensen, Praeger, New York.

Chen, N. F., R. Roll, and S. Ross. 1986. "Economic forces and the stock market," *Journal of Business* 59: 383–403.

Fabozzi, F., and J. Francis. 1979. "Mutual fund systematic risk for bull and bear markets: An empirical examination," *Journal of Finance* 34: 1243–49.

Fama, F. 1965. "Portfolio analysis in a stable Paretian market," *Management Science*: 404–19.

—— and J. McBeth. 1973. "Tests of a multiperiod two parameter model," *Journal of Political Economy* 81: 607–36.

Friend, I., and M. Blume. 1970. "Measurement of portfolio performance under uncertainty," *American Economic Review* 60: 561–75.

——. 1975. "The demand for risky assets," *American Economic Review* 65: 900–22.

Grinblatt, M., and S. Titman. 1989. "Mutual fund performance: An analysis of quarterly portfolio holdings," *Journal of Business* 61: 393–417.

Jensen, M. 1968. "The performance of mutual funds in the period 1945–1965," *Journal of Finance* 23: 389–416.

Jobson, J. D., and B. Korkie. 1981. "Putting Markowitz's theory to work," *Journal of Portfolio Management* 19: 6–11.

Jorion, P. 1986. "Bayes-Stein estimation for portfolio analysis," *Journal of Financial and Quantitative Analysis* 21: 279–92.

Klemkosky, R. 1973. "The bias in composite performance measures," *Journal of Financial and Quantitative Analysis* 8: 505–14.

Lehmann, B., and D. Modest. 1987. "Mutual fund performance comparison: A comparison of benchmarks and benchmark comparison," *Journal of Finance* 42: 233–55.

Lintner, J. 1965. "Security prices, risk and maximal gains from diversification," *Journal of Finance* 20: 587–615.

——. 1969. "The aggregation of investors' diverse judgements and preferences in purely competitive security markets," *Journal of Financial and Quantitative Analysis* 4: 347–400.

Mains, N. 1977. "Risk, the pricing of capital assets, and the evaluation of investment portfolios: Comment," *Journal of Business* 50.

Markowitz, H. 1959. *Portfolio Selection: Efficient Diversification of Investments*, Wiley & Sons, New York.

Mayers, D. 1972. "Non-marketable assets and the capital market equilibrium under uncertainty," in *Studies in the Theory of Capital Markets*, ed. M. C. Jensen, Praeger, New York, pp. 223–48.

Merton, R. 1973. "An intertemporal capital asset pricing model," *Econometrica* 41: 867–88.

Michaud, R. 1989. "The Markowitz optimization enigma: Is 'optimized' optimal?" *Financial Analysts Journal* 45: 31–42.

Roll, R. 1977 "A critique of the asset pricing theory's tests," *Journal of Financial Economics* 4: 129–76.

———. 1978. "Ambiguity when performance is measured by the securites market line," *Journal of Finance* 33: 1051–69.

——— and S. Ross. 1980. "An empirical investigation of the arbitrage pricing theory," *Journal of Finance* 35: 1073–1103.

Ross, S. 1976. "The arbitrage theory of capital asset pricing," *Journal of Economic Theory* 13: 341–60.

———. 1978. "The current status of the capital asset pricing model (CAPM)," *Journal of Finance* 33: 886.

Sharpe, W. 1964. "Capital asset prices: A theory of market equilibrium under conditions of risk," *Journal of Finance* 19: 425–42.

———. 1966. "Mutual fund performance," *Journal of Business*.

Treynor, J. 1965. "How to rate management of investment funds," *Harvard Business Review*: 63–75.

——— and K. K. Mazuy. 1966. "Can mutual funds outguess the market?" *Harvard Business Review*.

7

Portfolio Risk Management: International Dimensions

The global environment is characterized by several factors that are distinct from the domestic environment. To isolate these factors, it is useful to reflect upon the unique characteristics of international markets that cannot be found in domestic environments.

There are similarities in links between countries and links between states within federal governments. Countries, however, are delineated by differing commercial and monetary policies. National commercial policies introduce barriers to the movement of goods, labor, and capital. Monetary policies introduce different currencies. Hence exchange rates and barriers to capital flows are unique aspects of international finance. These unique aspects can be reinterpreted in terms of differences in consumption and investment opportunity sets, which constitute the focus of this chapter.

This chapter extends the previous chapter on the domestic dimensions of portfolio diversification to the international environment. We integrate the management of currency risk, developed in Chapters 4 and 5, with the management of portfolio risk.

In the first section, we present the case for diversifying internationally. International diversification allows investors to costlessly lower risk, with benefits that more than offset potential problem areas. The next section summarizes the evidence on foreign portfolio investment, showing that national portfolios are heavily invested in home assets. Given the benefits of international diversification, this home bias has become known as the "puzzle" of foreign portfolio investment. Portfolio choice with exchange risk is analyzed in the third section. We show that the domestic CAPM can be extended to an international environment but that closed-form solutions do not generally obtain. The fourth section, in contrast, assesses the impact of capital controls on asset pricing. Finally, empirical tests are discussed.

Why International?

The most compelling argument why investors should consider foreign markets is again *diversification*. The arguments leading to the conclusion that domestic investors should be well diversified apply with greater force in a global environment. International diversification, by expanding the choice of markets to invest in, provides an improved risk/return tradeoff.

And indeed, foreign stock and bond markets account for a large proportion of total wealth. Exhibit 7.1 breaks down the total capitalization of major stock and bond markets into U.S. and foreign components. Clearly, even U.S. financial markets currently represent no more than 40 percent of global markets. It makes little sense to ignore foreign markets, or 94 percent of the world population, or 80 percent

EXHIBIT 7.1   Size of Major Stock and Bond Markets (percentage of total world market capitalization)

Country	Stocks			Bonds		
	1980	1985	1990	1980	1985	1990
Canada	4.7	3.6	2.6	3.2	2.1	2.3
France	2.2	1.9	3.5	4.0	2.9	4.2
Germany	2.9	4.4	4.0	10.3	6.4	7.0
Japan	14.7	22.5	33.2	20.1	17.5	18.1
Netherlands	1.0	1.3	1.4	1.4	1.0	1.3
U.K.	7.8	8.1	10.4	7.8	3.2	2.1
Other	9.9	9.7	11.5	23.7	20.1	22.5
U.S.	56.8	48.4	33.3	29.5	46.8	42.5
Total Size ($ billion)	2,430	4,039	8,444	2,706	5,933	10,368

Sources: Morgan Stanley Capital International for stock market data. Ibbotson and Associates for 1980 bond market data; Salomon Brothers for 1985, 1989 bond market data.

of the world GNP. Investors cannot afford to be ethnocentric in an age where geocentricity is so pervasive.

Diversification: A Free Lunch

A global approach is particularly beneficial because diversification is much more effective across national markets than within the domestic economy. Diversification benefits are driven by correlations. Exhibit 7.2 presents correlations across national stock and bond markets, using returns translated into U.S. dollars. Most of the numbers are rather low. For instance, correlations with U.S. equities vary from 0.33 to 0.75, which implies that U.S. risk can be reduced simply by investing across national markets. The essential result of the table is that correlations across national markets are lower than correlations across stocks in most domestic markets.

Lower Risk. The first study to make this point forcefully was an article by Solnik (1974a), who related portfolio volatility to portfolio size and foreign content. Solnik built portfolios from fixed numbers of randomly chosen stocks and computed their volatility. As shown in Exhibit 7.3, portfolio volatility decreases as the number of stocks increases, but asymptotically converges to a lower limit. This limit is 25 percent of the average stock volatility in the United States. A striking result in Exhibit 7.3 is that, for the same portfolio size, using both U.S. and foreign stocks substantially lowers portfolio risk, which is driven down to 12 percent of average stock risk.

This study has been reproduced many times, using different time periods and subsets of countries, with remarkably consistent results. The simple and intuitive exposition of this powerful result made a vast impression on the investment community in the 1970s. Also, in 1974 ERISA gave U.S. pension funds the freedom to invest overseas. These factors opened the gates to international diversification for U.S. investors.

Roll (1992) investigated why correlations across stock markets appeared to be so low. He found that low correlations were partly explained by the fact that countries tend to specialize in specific industries. Energy stocks, for instance, are a driving factor in Norway and the Netherlands and also have an impact on Canada, Great Britain, and the United States. Some countries, such as Austria, Belgium, Germany, Sweden, and Japan, are more sensitive to the finance sector, and so on. In general, foreign industry returns explain about 50 percent

EXHIBIT 7.2   Correlations of Total Annual Returns of National Stock Markets in U.S. Dollars, 1970–1989

	1	2	3	4	5	6	7	8	9	10
1. Australia	1.00									
2. Canada	0.69	1.00								
3. France	0.56	0.34	1.00							
4. Germany	0.22	0.10	0.72	1.00						
5. Italy	0.52	0.28	0.84	0.60	1.00					
6. Japan	0.39	0.30	0.46	0.28	0.43	1.00				
7. Netherlands	0.61	0.50	0.76	0.77	0.62	0.41	1.00			
8. Switzerland	0.39	0.31	0.77	0.91	0.62	0.43	0.84	1.00		
9. United Kingdom	0.56	0.36	0.37	0.35	0.26	0.25	0.62	0.56	1.00	
10. United States	0.54	0.63	0.38	0.40	0.41	0.33	0.76	0.50	0.60	1.00

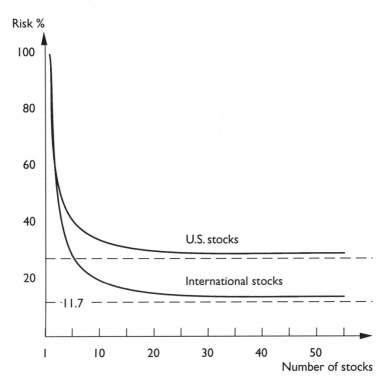

EXHIBIT 7.3   Effect of International Diversification on Portfolio Risk

of the variance of national returns. Interestingly, the lowest explanatory power, about 10 percent, is found for the United States, which suggests that going international is particularly advantageous from the viewpoint of U.S. investors.[1]

No Cost in Return.   The reduction in portfolio volatility, although encouraging, is only part of the picture. The other side of the coin is the impact of diversification on expected returns. We know, for instance, a very simple method to reduce risk: simply invest in short-term bills. In this case, lowering risk is exactly offset by lowering returns, which provides no risk-adjusted benefit. Therefore, there must be a presumption that going international reduces risk but does not adversely affect expected returns. In that sense, international diversification may pro-

---

[1]Other researchers have provided a detailed analysis of the transmission of innovations in daily returns and volatility across stock markets. See, for instance, Eun and Shim (1989) and Hamao, Masulis, and Ng (1990).

vide a "free lunch" because it permits lower risk at no opportunity cost.

The problem with the latter statement is that it is much more difficult to verify empirically. Whereas measures of risk and correlations can be estimated with reasonable precision, expected returns require very long periods, on the order of decades, to obtain the required statistical accuracy. This translates into measures of average returns that vary widely across periods and can veer far off the underlying true values. This problem becomes nearly insurmountable if, in addition, the unobserved expected returns change over time: using longer time series, when available, is then inappropriate.

To assess the benefits of going international in a risk/return framework, a number of studies have used "ex-post" estimates of average returns as proxy for expectations.[2] An efficient set, such as in Exhibit 7.4, purports to demonstrate the benefit from going international either in terms of increased returns for a given level of risk or decreased risk for a given level of return. The graph displays a series of efficient frontiers based on historical data from 1978 to 1993. Over this time period, returns on U.S. bonds and stocks were 10.6 percent and 15.4 percent per annum, respectively, against 12 percent and 16.6 percent for non-U.S. bonds and stocks, respectively.

The efficient combination of U.S. stocks and bonds is represented by the line along which point A lies. As we have seen previously, diversification in these two asset classes produces the curved line going from U.S. stocks to U.S. bonds. If the investor desires a level of risk equal to that of U.S. bonds, the highest attainable return is about 12.5 percent.

The introduction of foreign bonds into a portfolio with purely domestic bonds produces the efficiency frontier along which point B lies (between U.S. bonds and foreign bonds). Similarly, the combination of U.S. stocks and non-U.S. stocks produces the efficient frontier along which point C lies. In these two cases, it is notable to see that the minimum-risk portfolio, either along B or C, has much lower risk than simply investing in the U.S. asset. This confirms Solnik's findings that going international lowers the total portfolio risk and is actually *less* risky than investing solely in the United States.

Finally, the combination of all four asset classes, U.S. and foreign stocks and bonds, is represented by the line indexed by point D. This

---

[2]See, for instance, Grubel (1968), Levy and Sarnat (1970), Odier and Solnik (1993).

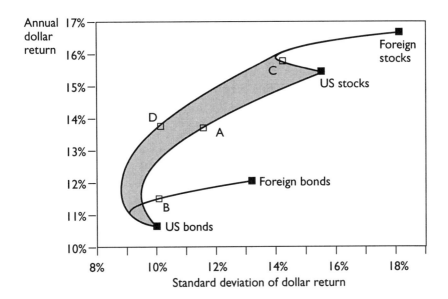

EXHIBIT 7.4   Ex-Post Mean–Variance Analysis of International Investments, Equity and Bond Markets, 1978–1993

Asset	Exp. Ret.	Std. Dev.	Correlations			
U.S. bonds	10.6	10.0	1.00			
Foreign bonds	12.0	13.1	0.41	1.00		
U.S. stocks	15.4	15.5	0.32	0.08	1.00	
Foreign stocks	17.0	18.0	0.22	0.63	0.42	1.00

efficient frontier clearly dominates any other investment choice. If the investor desires a level of risk equal to that of U.S. bonds, the highest attainable return from the choice of U.S. and foreign assets is about 13.5 percent. It appears, therefore, that allowing the investor access to foreign markets increases the portfolio performance from 12.5 percent to 13.5 percent, that is, a gain of 1 percent per annum. This is a substantial benefit, especially when obtained without undertaking additional risk.

It is not sufficiently appreciated, however, that this approach suffers because (i) expected returns are measured imprecisely and (ii) the performance measurement uses the same period as the portfolio optimization. Therefore the portfolios with apparent superior performance are likely to be tilted toward those assets with positive estimation error in expected returns. In other words, the value added can be only positive because, at worst, the optimizer could choose to remain in domestic assets. Hence, a substantial bias is imparted in the value added. Claims of higher returns based on "ex-post" data therefore should be viewed with some skepticism.[3]

Problem Areas

There are, however, many impediments to going international, which could explain the relatively low amount of foreign investment observed all over the world. High on the list are *information costs.* Processing financial information for foreign firms requires an enormous effort in understanding different cultures, languages, and accounting standards. One must also become familiar with foreign institutional arrangements, such as the conduct of monetary and fiscal policies. Information asymmetry is another problem. Acting on inside information is legal in certain countries, which puts the foreign investor at a disadvantage relative to locals.

Capital controls are also among the prime explanations for the lack of international investments. These can take the form of taxes or outright restrictions on amounts that can be invested overseas for domestic investors or, domestically, for foreign investors. Withholding taxes, for instance, apply mainly to dividend payments to foreign investors. When these taxes cannot be credited against domestic taxes, as is the case for tax-exempt investors, taxes create a symmetric wedge between national markets.

Exchange risk is also sometimes mentioned as an impediment to international investment. Exchange risk, however, is just another form of market risk, which can be tightly controlled and even eliminated, if so desired, through derivative instruments. Rather, as will be explained, exchange rate exposure should be considered in terms of risk and reward, along with exposure to foreign markets.

Political risk is another doubtful reason for avoiding foreign markets. Political risk is often associated with the threat of nationalization. But, in general, political risk arises from a wide range of government

---

[3]Jorion (1985) observes that the out-of-sample performance of optimal portfolios invariably falls short of what was expected. Michaud (1989) argues that optimizers are inherent "error maximizers," which explains why they are little used by practitioners. A simulation approach is presented in Jorion (1992a) to account for estimation error in optimized portfolio weights.

decisions. Although outright expropriation seldom occurs now in industrialized countries, corporations are constantly affected by changes in the conduct of monetary and fiscal policy, in barriers to trade, in price controls, in industrial regulations, and so forth. Thus political risk should be viewed more generally as the impact of changes in government actions on the value of the firm. Viewed in that context, political risk arises in all countries, and it would be irresponsible to consider one's own government as the most benign. Instead, prudence would actually dictate that investments be diversified across national sources of political risk.

Other reasons sometimes advanced, such as the high costs of transacting in non-U.S. markets or supposedly less efficient non-U.S. markets, may be valid to some extent but are asymmetrical in the sense that they do not explain why foreign investors have so little invested in countries outside their home markets. As we will show, this is best explained by information costs and capital controls.

The Puzzle of Foreign Portfolio Investment

Data on the extent of foreign portfolio investment (FPI) are notoriously hard to collect, in part because of the multiplicity of investors and countries, but also because no centralized agency is responsible for gathering such information. Across the world, however, pension funds are required to publish detailed information on their holdings. Information on foreign investments by pension funds is presented in Exhibit 7.5 for the years 1980, 1985, and 1990. The striking feature of this table is the low proportion generally invested in foreign assets. In the United States, for instance, pension funds have invested only 4 percent of their assets abroad. Another noteworthy feature is that FPI ratios are growing rapidly for all countries, except Canada, where pension funds were subject to a 10 percent foreign asset limit in 1990 that appeared to be binding.

The analysis in the rest of the chapter suggests that either capitalization ratios or import fractions may function as benchmarks in assessing the extent and composition of FPI. If the domestic CAPM also applies to the international environment, capitalization ratios should represent the optimal investment mix. The FPI ratios in Exhibit 7.5, however, appear to be much lower than the market capitalization ratios reported in Exhibit 7.1. For instance, nondollar stocks and bonds accounted

EXHIBIT 7.5   Foreign Investment by Pension Funds (percentage of assets invested abroad)

Country	1980	1985	1990
Canada	7	7	8
France	1	2	5
Germany	2	3	5
Japan	1	4	8
Netherlands	4	6	11
U.K.	9	15	26
U.S.	1	2	4
Total	2	4	8
($ billion)	19	95	347

Source: InterSec Research, Stamford, Connecticut. Pension fund data include public and private funds.

for 66.7 percent and 57.5 percent, respectively, of the world market in 1990. The portfolios of U.S. pension funds, for instance, are much closer to purely domestic portfolios than to capitalization-weighted world indices.

Alternative models, in contrast, state that foreign investment is used as a hedge against variations in domestic price levels due to exchange rates. We would then expect the optimal investment mix to represent the proportion of imports in total consumption. Data on the ratio of total imports over GNP are presented in Exhibit 7.6. The 1990 numbers range from 11 percent for the United States to 54 percent for the Netherlands. Again, FPI ratios appear much lower than expected. The

EXHIBIT 7.6   Import Penetration: Ratio of Imports to GNP (percent)

Country	1980	1985	1990
Canada	27	27	33
France	23	23	23
Germany	29	31	30
Japan	16	13	13
Netherlands	53	59	54
U.K.	25	28	27
U.S.	10	10	11

Source: International Monetary Fund, various issues.

only exception is the United Kingdom, which has recently attained a foreign investment ratio of 26 percent, close to the import fraction.

Therefore, foreign portfolio investment presents something of a puzzle: across countries, the actual proportions invested in foreign assets are much lower than the proportions implied by either market capitalization or import penetration. This has been termed the *home asset preference* (HAP) puzzle.

Portfolio Choice with Exchange Risk

In a multicountry environment, the portfolio decision problem for global investments involves a joint choice over the underlying assets and currencies. It is useful to detail the individual optimization problem not only because it marks the first step toward an equilibrium model but also because this process helps to understand the construction of international portfolios, as well as the more recent debate about currency hedging.

In general, with international investments, portfolio managers should make a decision both on the underlying assets, such as stocks or long-term bonds, *and* the currencies. This section forcefully shows that it is suboptimal to invest in foreign assets without paying attention to currencies. This is because a portfolio manager will rarely have similar views on a particular market and its associated currency. For instance, a U.S. manager with investments in German bonds may consider a most possible scenario as one of falling German interest rates. In this case the portfolio should be long German (long-term) bonds, but short the currency, because it is likely to depreciate if the fall in interest rates materializes. Therefore the positions in German bonds and German currency should have different signs and will be intrinsically different from just buying German bonds, which involve an equal position in German bonds and the German currency. In addition, the U.S. portfolio manager must consider the risk-reduction benefits from hedging currency risk. A uniform framework to address all of these considerations is presented in what follows.

Individual Portfolio Choice

For simplicity, we take the viewpoint of a U.S. investor who measures returns in U.S. dollars and in excess of the U.S. risk-free rate; inflation is nonstochastic. Investors are rational mean–variance optimizers who hold a combination of the domestic risk-free assets and a portfolio of all assets. The representative U.S. investor seeks to maximize a utility function that reflects the tradeoff between expected portfolio returns $\mu_p = w'\mu$ and risk $\sigma_p^2 = w'\Sigma w$, where w represents a vector of portfolio weights, μ represents a vector of expected returns on all assets, and Σ represents the covariance matrix of returns. With normally distributed returns and assuming a constant absolute risk aversion (necessary condition for a closed form solution), the investor's objective is to maximize

$$U(w|\mu, \Sigma) = U(\mu_p, \sigma_p^2) = \mu_p - (1/2\lambda)\sigma_p^2, \qquad (7.1)$$

where λ is the investor's risk tolerance ($\lambda > 0$), or inverse of risk aversion. These assumptions are summarized as follows:

1. Risk-averse investors who maximize expected utility;
2. Normally distributed asset returns;
3. Nonrandom inflation rates;
4. Perfect capital markets, with short sales allowed, no transaction costs, no barriers to capital flow.

Among these assumptions, normality ensures that the total distribution of returns is described by the first and second moments; returns can be measured in nominal dollars if inflation is nonrandom; with perfect capital markets, investors can solve the optimization problem without any constraint on positions.

The investment opportunity set consists of m risky assets, such as stocks or bonds, and n positions in short-term bills denominated in different currencies. The domestic bill is risk free. The other bills, however, are risky when measuring returns in the domestic currency. The optimal portfolio can be found by using only returns in excess of the risk-free rate; the position in the risk-free asset then simply follows from forcing the portfolio weights to sum to unity. In what follows, μ represents the expected return *in excess* of the domestic risk-free rate.

Note that if we allow unrestricted long and short positions in all securities, forward contracts are redundant assets because a long forward position can be replicated by a long position in the foreign bill financed by a short position in the domestic bill. In a previous chapter, we saw that interest rate parity (equation 4.2), on a continuously compounded basis, can be written as

$$i_t = \ln(F_{t,1}) - \ln(S_t) + i_t^*, \qquad (7.2)$$

where $F_{t,1}$ is the one-period forward rate observed at time t. The payoff from a long position in a foreign currency bill, in excess of the U.S. risk-free rate, is

$$[\ln(S_{t+1}) - \ln(S_t) + i_t^*] - i_t, \qquad (7.3)$$

where the bracketed term represents the currency appreciation plus the foreign interest rate. Using IRP, this is also equal to

$$[\ln(S_{t+1}) - \ln(S_t) + i_t^*] - i_t = \ln(S_{t+1}) - \ln(F_{t,1}). \qquad (7.4)$$

The latter term, the payoff on a long forward position, is thus exactly equivalent to the payoff on a position in foreign bills financed by domestic borrowing; both require no initial wealth. This demonstrates that, when unrestricted investment and borrowing are allowed for all currencies, forward contracts are redundant assets.

Returning to the optimization problem, we differentiate Equation (7.1) with respect to w,

$$\frac{\partial U}{\partial w} = \mu - 2(1/2\lambda)\Sigma w, \qquad (7.5)$$

and set the derivatives equal to zero. The optimal positions of N risky assets (the vector w_N) are given, in matrix notation, by

$$w_N = \lambda\Sigma^{-1}\mu. \qquad (7.6)$$

As explained before, this describes the portfolio weights for all risky assets, and the remainder of the portfolio is invested in the riskless asset. With an initial wealth of $1, the amount in the riskless asset is unity minus the sum of the weights in other assets, which can be written compactly as $w_{N+1} = 1 - \lambda(1'\Sigma^{-1}\mu)$,[4] where w_{N+1} is a . . . . the amount invested in cash. Thus the investment in risky assets is described by $w_N = \lambda\Sigma^{-1}\mu$, and the investment in the riskless asset is $w_{N+1} = 1 - \lambda(1'\Sigma^{-1}\mu)$, or $w_{N+1} = \lambda(1 - 1'\Sigma^{-1}\mu) + (1 - \lambda)$. In matrix notation, the composition of the optimal portfolio can be summarized as

---

[4]The term $\lambda 1'\Sigma^{-1}\mu$ denotes the multiplication of a row vector of ones ($1'$) with the vector of N weights, where $1'$ signifies the transpose of the column vector 1.

$$\begin{pmatrix} w_N \\ w_{N+1} \end{pmatrix} = \lambda \begin{pmatrix} \Sigma^{-1}\mu \\ 1 - 1'\Sigma^{-1}\mu \end{pmatrix} + (1 - \lambda)\begin{pmatrix} 0 \\ 1 \end{pmatrix}, \qquad (7.7)$$

where w_N describes positions in N assets, and w_{N+1} describes the position in the riskless asset.

Equation (7.7) is standard in the international finance literature; it also appears in Sercu (1980) and Stulz (1981a). As in the standard CAPM, it involves an investment in an optimally diversified portfolio, as well as in the risk-free asset that is the least risky or a minimum-variance portfolio. Adler and Dumas (1983) considered the more general case where domestic inflation is random. In this situation, the risk-free asset is replaced by the portfolio that minimizes the variance of real returns. Because the exposition of the more general model is quite burdensome, we prefer to continue with the simple version of the model that assumes that inflation is nonrandom.

It is essential to notice that the $\Sigma^{-1}\mu$ component is also the portfolio chosen by an investor with a logarithmic utility function, where $\lambda = 1$, (verifiable by calculating the value of relative risk aversion: $-(W) = \ln w \Rightarrow \lambda = 1$, hence its name, *log portfolio*. This is a fundamental result, since the log portfolio is independent of the currency of denomination and therefore universal across all investors. This can be proven, for instance, by noting that maximizing the expected logarithm of wealth, measured in dollars, W^{US}, can be written in terms of wealth measured in French francs (FF), $\log[W^{US}] = \log [W^{FF}/S(FF/US)] = \log[W^{FF}] - \log[S(FF/US)]$. Since the last term, the logarithm of the exchange rate, does not depend on portfolio allocations, maximizing utility when returns are measured in FF also maximizes utility when returns are measured in dollars. This portfolio also has the highest Sharpe ratio (μ_p/σ_p) among all possible portfolios and thus optimally balances returns against risk. This lays the foundation for describing the link between the stock decision and the currency decision.

Portfolio Allocation: Technical Derivations. One drawback of the preceding solution is that currency positions are contained in both foreign stocks and bills, while it might be useful to separately focus on currency positions.

Because positions in foreign bills combined with the domestic bill can be replicated by forward contracts, let us replace foreign bills by forward contracts. Next, we partition μ and Σ into components that correspond to underlying assets, such as stocks, represented by s, and currency forwards, represented by f:

$$\mu = \begin{pmatrix} \mu_s \\ \mu_f \end{pmatrix}, \ \Sigma = \begin{pmatrix} \Sigma_{ss} & \Sigma_{sf} \\ \Sigma_{fs} & \Sigma_{ff} \end{pmatrix}, \tag{7.8}$$

where Σ_{ss} represents the covariance matrix of stock returns only, measured in dollars, Σ_{ff} represents the covariance matrix of forward contract returns only, and Σ_{sf} measures the covariances between stocks and forward contracts.

We are now going to consider the impact of optimally hedging the positions in underlying stocks against currency risk using forward contracts. We define $\beta = \Sigma_{ff}^{-1}\Sigma_{fs}$ as the regression coefficients of the assets on the hedges, and $\Sigma_{s \bullet f} = \Sigma_{ss} - \beta'\Sigma_{ff}\beta$ as the covariance matrix of underlying asset returns conditional on the hedges. The β coefficients correspond to the positions in bills that provide a minimum-variance (MV) hedge against currency risk.[5]

The optimal portfolio can now be rewritten in terms of hedged stock returns y_s and positions in forward contracts y_f. The optimal portfolio is derived from the inverse of the partitioned matrix Σ, which is

$$\Sigma^{-1} = \begin{pmatrix} \Sigma_{s \bullet f}^{-1} & -\Sigma_{s \bullet f}^{-1}\beta' \\ -\beta\Sigma_{s \bullet f}^{-1} & \Sigma_{ff}^{-1} + \beta\Sigma_{s \bullet f}^{-1}\beta' \end{pmatrix}. \tag{7.9}$$

We can now rewrite the optimal positions as

$$\begin{pmatrix} y_s = \Sigma_{s \bullet f}^{-1}\mu_s - \Sigma_{s \bullet f}^{-1}\beta'\mu_f \\ y_f = \Sigma_{ff}^{-1}\mu_f - \beta y_s \end{pmatrix}. \tag{7.10}$$

Note that the optimal currency positions y_f depend on the optimal stock positions y_s, which themselves are affected by the presence of currencies in the portfolio. Also, the currency position has two purposes. The first term is a speculative component, $\Sigma_{ff}^{-1}\mu_f$, similar to the solution to Equation (7.6) and essentially driven by nonzero expected returns μ_f. The second term is the variance-reduction component βy_s and is directly related to the underlying stock position.

---

[5]With fixed positions in stocks, MV hedging aims at selecting a portfolio of bills to minimize the variance of the combined portfolio return, $w_s R_{s,t} - w_f R_{f,t}$. The variance is $w_s'\Sigma_{ss}w_s + w_f'\Sigma_{ff}w_f - 2w_f'\Sigma_{fs}w_s$, and therefore the minimum is attained at $2\Sigma_{ff}w_f - 2\Sigma_{fs}w_s = 0$, or when $w_f = \Sigma_{ff}^{-1}\Sigma_{fs}w_s = \beta w_s$. The β coefficients are also the slopes in the regression $R_{s,t} = \alpha + R_{f,t}\beta + \epsilon_t$, with $\Sigma_{s \bullet f}$ the covariance matrix of error terms ϵ.

This proves a very important point: in general, the stock selection decision cannot be made independent of the currency decision. As demonstrated in the preceding equations, both decisions are intimately related because the stock position y_s depends expected returns on currencies, μ_f, and on covariances between currencies and stocks. Also the position in currencies, y_f, depends on positions in stocks, y_s.

Portfolio Allocation: Main Results.   The previous section has shown that the portfolio allocation can be broken down into stocks and currencies. Currencies generally serve a dual purpose: achieving the highest possible Sharpe ratio with currency positions and providing the best, minimum-variance, hedge for the stock positions. Alternatively, the "log" portfolio can be decomposed into a portfolio of stocks optimally (MV) hedged against currency risk and additional positions in currencies for speculative motives.

This leads to the following separation theorem. For each investor, the optimal portfolio of stocks and bills can be decomposed into (a) a universal "log" portfolio and (b) a domestic risk-free bill. The relative amount invested in each component reflects the individual investor's risk aversion. The "log" portfolio can further be decomposed into (a.1) a portfolio of stocks optimally (minimum-variance) hedged against currency risk and (a.2) a portfolio of speculative positions in bills.

Portfolio Allocation: Example.   At this point, an illustration is in order. Exhibit 7.7 presents the expected returns and covariance matrix of returns for three stock markets, the United States, Japan, and the United Kingdom, and returns on foreign bills over 1974–1991. The estimates are *in percent per month*, based on continuously compounded returns including capital gains and dividends. Panel A presents returns in dollars, in excess of the U.S. dollar one-month Eurocurrency deposit rate, taken to be the risk-free bill rate. Panel B presents results in yen, in excess of the yen rate.

It should be noted that these numbers are used only for illustrative purposes. In practice, the estimated means measure the true, unobserved, means with error, which also imparts measurement errors into the optimal positions. In theory, measurement error should vanish for very large sample sizes, but practitioners are then exposed to structural changes in asset markets that may change expected returns over time. These optimal positions should be taken with a grain of salt. Instead, the purpose of Exhibit 7.7 is to compare the portfolio optimization process across currencies.

EXHIBIT 7.7   Portfolio Choice with Three Markets

| | (A) U.S. Viewpoint Excess Returns (per month) | | | | | Raw Return |
| | Stocks | | | Currencies | | |
	US	Japan	UK	JY	BP	US Risk Free
Exp. Returns (μ)	.229	.564	.534	.147	.147	.760*
Cov. matrix (Σ)						
US	23.34					
Japan	8.49	42.86				
UK	20.25	19.19	61.36			
JY	−.14	14.19	6.31	12.27		
BP	−.07	7.21	12.22	6.86	11.55	
Log Portfolio (ε'μ)	.18	1.27	.39	−.77	.53	−
Net Positions	.18	1.27	.39	−.77	.53	−1.60
"Hedges"				.60	−1.37	

| | (B) Japanese Viewpoint Excess Returns (per month) | | | | | Raw Return |
| | Stocks | | | Currencies | | |
	US	Japan	UK	US	₊BP	JY Risk Free
Exp. Returns	.089	.417	.387	−.147	.001	.533*
Cov. matrix						
US	35.88					
Japan	6.71	26.76				
UK	26.35	10.96	61.00			
US	12.41	−1.92	5.95	12.27		
BP	5.48	−1.57	11.31	5.41	10.10	
Log Portfolio	.18	1.27	.39	−1.60	.53	−
Net Positions	.18	1.27	.39	−1.60	.53	−.77
"Hedges"				8.89	−1.37	

Note: All returns are excess returns continuously compounded in percent per month, except for the risk-free rate, which is taken to be the nominal one-month Eurodeposit rate. Expected returns and covariance matrix are taken from "ex-post" data, measured over 1974–91. Expected returns are multiplied by 100 and variances and covariances by 10,000.

The bottom of each panel reports the optimal positions, measured as $\Sigma^{-1}\mu$. This log portfolio for the U.S. investor, is invested 18 percent in U.S. stocks, 127 percent in Japanese stocks, 39 percent in U.K. stocks is short 77 percent yen bills; and is long 53 percent pound bills. This amounts to a total of 260 percent of the portfolio; therefore, the portfolio must also have a short position of 160 percent in U.S. bills for the weights to add up to 100 percent. Note that the 53 percent long position in pound bills can be obtained either by borrowing in dollars and investing in pound bills or, more simply, by entering a forward purchase of pounds. Both choices involve no upfront investment.

The bottom panel, B, reports numbers in yen. Relative to the previous panel, the variance of the Japanese market decreases, from 42.86 to 26.76, while the variance of the U.S. market increases because currency risk is impounded asymmetrically on the two markets. Yet the optimal positions are remarkably similar: this reflects the universality of the logarithmic portfolio. The log portfolio with a yen perspective is invested 18 percent in U.S. stocks, 127 percent in Japanese stocks, 39 percent in U.K. stocks is short 160 percent U.S. bills; and is long 53 percent pound bills. This amounts to a total of 177 percent of the portfolio; therefore, the portfolio must also have a short position of 77 percent on yen bills. This is exactly equal to the optimal position of the U.S. investor in Japanese bills, or to any investor from any country who has a log utility function. The log portfolio is a universal portfolio.

Therefore, when bills are included with stocks and there are no restrictions on short sales, the optimal portfolio is the same for any reference currency. This substantially simplifies the portfolio decision across countries, because any investor should simply select from a combination of the domestic riskless asset and this universally optimal portfolio. The separation result takes the same importance as the two-fund separation theorem that underpins the CAPM.

International APM

As for the domestic CAPM, an international asset pricing model results from the aggregation of consumers across countries. The international APM (IAPM), as originally developed by Solnik (1974b) and expanded by Sercu (1980), allows consumption opportunity sets to differ across countries and is based on the following assumptions:

1. The portfolio choice assumptions plus
2. Investors within a country are identical,
3. Investors agree on the distribution of asset returns.

Within a country, all investors are identical, with wealth W^i and total positions in stocks are $W^i \lambda^i y_s$. Note that y_s is not indexed by i since it represents the "log" portfolio. In equilibrium, summing these optimal asset demands across countries must yield the total asset supplies. The following subsection details the derivation of equilibrium returns and again can be skipped to go directly to the main results in the following section.

IAPM: Technical Derivations. The total outstanding supply of each stock market can be measured as the market capitalization of all stocks times the weights in the stock market portfolio Mx_s. If we define a wealth-weighted risk tolerance as $\lambda = \Sigma_i W^i \lambda^i / (\Sigma_i W^i)$, the market-clearing condition for stocks is

$$\sum W^i \lambda^i y_s = Mx_s, \qquad (7.11)$$

or $\lambda W y_s = Mx_s$. Using Equation (7.10),

$$(\mu_s - \beta' \mu_f) = (M/W)(1/\lambda)\Sigma_{s \bullet f} x_s, \qquad (7.12)$$

which applies to the market as well, by premultiplying by x_s,

$$(\mu_m - x_s' \beta' \mu_f) = (M/W)(1/\lambda)\sigma^2_{s \bullet f}, \qquad (7.13)$$

where $\mu_m = x_s' \mu_s$ and $\sigma^2_{s \bullet f} = x_s' \Sigma_{s \bullet f} x_s$. Eliminating M, W, and λ from Equations (7.12) and (7.13) and defining $\beta_{s \bullet f} = \Sigma_{s \bullet f} x_s / \sigma^2_{s \bullet f}$, we arrive at a CAPM-like equation:

$$(\mu_s - \beta' \mu_f) = \beta_{s \bullet f}(\mu_m - x_s' \beta' \mu_f). \qquad (7.14)$$

Here, the expected excess returns on currency-hedged stocks are proportional to the β with the market, where all assets are currency hedged. Of course, since the derivation used only the supply conditions for stocks, this "partial pricing" approach does not allow us yet to price currencies.

To do so, we need to go back to the optimal portfolio positions for all investors. Currency j bills appear in two portfolios: the "log" portfolio of all investors and the minimum-variance portfolios of country j investors. Assuming that the bills are in zero net supply, the equilibrium condition is

$$\sum_i W^i \lambda^i y_f + (1 - \lambda^j) W^j = 0. \qquad (7.15)$$

Solving for μ_f in Equation (7.10),

$$\mu_f = \Sigma_{ff} y_f + \Sigma_{ff} \beta y_s,$$

and replacing y_f from Equation (7.15), we have

$$\mu_f = \Sigma_{ff} \beta y_s - \Sigma_{ff}(1 - \lambda^j) W^j/(\lambda W).$$

Recall that $\Sigma_{ff}\beta = \Sigma_{fs}$, and $\lambda W y_s = M x_s$. Also, multiplying and dividing the last term by $(1 - \lambda)$, we have

$$\mu_f = \Sigma_{fs}[x_s(M/\lambda W)] - [(1 - \lambda)/\lambda]\Sigma_{ff}[(1 - \lambda^j) W^j/(1 - \lambda)W].$$

Because bills are in zero net supply, total wealth is invested in stocks only and $M = W$. The last term between brackets represents a pseudo-portfolio, with positions summing to unity and related to each country's risk aversion weighted by wealth. Defining this to be a "hedge" portfolio, $x_h \equiv [(1 - \lambda^j) W^j/(1 - \lambda)W]$, the expected return on forwards can be written as

$$\mu_f = (1/\lambda)\text{Cov}(f, m) - [(1 - \lambda)/\lambda]\text{Cov}(f, h), \qquad (7.16)$$

where the pricing equation depends on the aggregate risk aversion. This is unfortunate, because, contrary to the domestic CAPM, this pricing equation involves unknown variables.

Going back to Equation (7.12) to replace μ_f, we obtain a pricing equation for stocks that does not depend on currencies:

$$\mu_s = \beta'\mu_f + (1/\lambda)\Sigma_{s\bullet f} x_s$$
$$\mu_s = (1/\lambda)\beta'\Sigma_{fs} x_s - [(1 - \lambda)/\lambda]\beta'\Sigma_{ff} x_h + (1/\lambda)\Sigma_{s\bullet f} x_s$$
$$\mu_s = (1/\lambda)[\Sigma_{sf}\Sigma_{ff}^{-1}\Sigma_{fs} + \Sigma_{s\bullet f}]x_s - [(1 - \lambda)/\lambda][\Sigma_{sf}\Sigma_{ff}^{-1}\Sigma_{ff}]x_h$$
$$\mu_s = (1/\lambda)\Sigma_{ss} x_s - [(1 - \lambda)/\lambda]\Sigma_{sf} x_h.$$

Therefore, the full pricing equation for stocks is

$$\mu_s = (1/\lambda)\text{Cov}(s, m) - [(1 - \lambda)/\lambda]\text{Cov}(s, h), \qquad (7.17)$$

which also depends on an unknown aggregate risk-aversion coefficient. Note that, in general, the pricing of stocks will differ from the

CAPM unless the λ coefficient, which is the wealth-weighted risk tolerance, is exactly equal to unity. In that case, expected returns are simply equal to the covariance between stocks and the market, which is a special case of the CAPM because this covariance is proportional to the market β.

IAPM: Main Results. Assuming that all investors have access to international capital markets and identical expectations about asset returns, the IAPM leads to equilibrium pricing equations for stocks and currencies. Unlike the domestic CAPM, however, the general pricing Equations (7.16) and (7.17) depend on the covariance with an unobserved "hedging" portfolio, whose composition depends on each country's risk aversion and wealth. Because these variables are not observed, this makes the IAPM less directly testable than the domestic CAPM. In addition, because of this second term, there is no simple linear relationship between expected returns and the covariance with the market. Therefore, the market is generally not mean–variance efficient, as in the CAPM.

If, however, every investor has a logarithmic utility function ($\lambda^j = 1$), then the pricing model simplifies to the international capital asset pricing model (ICAPM):

$$\mu_s = \text{Cov}(s,\ m), \quad \mu_f = \text{Cov}(f,\ m), \qquad (7.18)$$

where the market is again mean–variance efficient. In this world, however, nobody would need to hold any bills, because bills are not held as part of the hedge portfolio, because everybody holds the same proportion of bills in the log portfolio which is by construct equal to zero. The aggregate supply of bills is zero. Bills then become redundant assets, priced only at the margin. The ICAPM, therefore, must rely on additional strong assumptions to obtain tractable results.

IAPM: Example. The previous example may be further developed to demonstrate equilibrium positions and expected returns. Exhibit 7.8 presents positions for a U.S. investor. The stock market weights x_s are taken from the historical average capitalization ratios, 57 percent, 31 percent, and 12 percent, respectively, for the United States, Japan, and Great Britain. We do not know the risk aversion for these three countries, so we must arbitrarily assume values for national wealth ratios and risk tolerance; these are reported in the first panel of Exhibit 7.8. From these, we deduce that the world risk tolerance is 0.350 and that the hedge portfolio weights x_h are 23 percent for the United States, 62 percent for Japan, and 15 percent for the United Kingdom.

EXHIBIT 7.8   Portfolio Choice in Equilibrium

| | National Market Values, Wealth, Risk Tolerance | | | |
	Market Portfolio $x_{s,j}$	National Wealth w_j	Risk Tolerance λ^j	Hedge Portfolio $x_{h,j}$
US	0.5651	0.3	0.5	0.2308
Japan	0.3125	0.5	0.2	0.6154
UK	0.1224	0.2	0.5	0.1538
Total	1.0000	1.0		1.0000
World			0.350	

| | U.S. Viewpoint Computation of Equilibrium Returns | | | | | |
	Covariance with Market	Covariance with Hedge	Equilibrium Return μ	Log Portfolio $\Sigma^{-1}\mu$	Positions $\lambda^{US}\Sigma^{-1}\mu$	Equilibrium Hedges
Stocks:	Cov(s, m)	Cov(s, h)	μ_s			
US	18.32	−0.10	.525	1.615	0.807	
Japan	20.54	9.84	.404	0.893	0.446	
UK	24.96	5.76	.606	0.350	0.175	
Currencies:	Cov(f, m)	Cov(f, h)	μ_f			
JY	5.13	8.61	−.013	−1.143	−0.571	1.28
BP	3.71	6.00	−.005	−0.286	−0.143	0.82
$					0.714	
Total					1.000	

Note: Expected returns are multiplied by 100 and covariances by 10,000.

Based on these weights, and the pricing equations in the previous section, the second panel in Exhibit 7.8 presents the "equilibrium" expected returns that are consistent with the IAPM. Note that the expected returns on currency positions are different from zero, although small in this example.

As expected, the weights of the log portfolio, relative to each other, parallel the market weights. In that sense the IAPM is an equilibrium model. For all investors, expected returns are such that asset demands balance asset supplies.

Further, the Japanese stock position is 128 percent hedged, while the British stock position is 82 percent hedged. In addition, it can be shown that reconciliation of positions across U.S., Japanese, and British investors leads to a total zero supply of bills. With information about relative wealth and risk aversion, the IAPM thus provides a full description of the relationship between return and risk in global capital markets.

Implications for Currency Hedging

This section now explores the optimal hedging policy derived from equilibrium. The IAPM provides useful guidance for currency hedging, because it uses market-clearing conditions to derive equilibrium returns and positions for stocks and forward contracts. In the IAPM model, all portfolios contain some positions in currencies. These positions are sometimes, confusingly, termed *hedges*, even when they have both speculative and risk-minimization components.

IAPM Hedges. Because the universal "log" portfolio contains both stocks and bills, one can define a hedge ratio as minus the ratio of the weight of the currency i bill to that of stock i in the log portfolio: $h^i = -y_f^i/y_s^i$. This can accommodate a wide range of behavior toward risk. With low risk tolerance, the hedge ratio will be close to unity, which corresponds to pure risk minimization. The hedge ratio for a logarithmic investor is zero. For less-risk averse investors, the hedge ratio is even negative. For example, in Exhibit 7.7, the U.S. investor invests 127 percent of the portfolio in Japanese stocks and sells 77 percent of Japanese bills. The hedge ratio is thus $-(-77/127) = 60$ percent; for the United Kingdom, the hedge ratio is $-(53/39) = -137$ percent.

Note that, because the data are based on historical series, expected returns in Exhibit 7.7 do not conform to equilibrium relationships, that is, need not be consistent across countries. Imposing equilibrium, however, leads to additional insights. Because λ_i is the risk tolerance of investor i, and W_i the investor's wealth, this investor holds $(1 - \lambda_i)W_i$ in the domestic bill portfolio and $\lambda_i W_i$ in the log portfolio. Assuming the domestic bill is in zero net supply, it must then enter the log portfolio with a weight of $-(1 - \lambda_i)W_i$, for all investors. In equilibrium, the hedge ratio is therefore proportional to $h^i = (1 - \lambda^i)W^i/M^i$, where M^i is the market capitalization of country i's stocks.

Universal Hedges. Adding specific assumptions to the IAPM, Black (1990) suggested that there exists a *universal* equilibrium hedge ratio that is optimal for all investors. By assuming that (i) all investors have the same risk tolerance, $\lambda^i = \lambda$, and (ii) each national wealth is exactly equal to the value of each stock market, $W_i = M_i$, the optimal hedge ratio reduces to the "universal" value $b = (1 - \lambda)$.

Exhibit 7.9 presents the optimal allocation from the viewpoint of a U.S. investor with a risk tolerance of $\lambda = 0.5$, assuming the conditions behind universal hedging are satisfied. Note that the composition of the hedge portfolio b in the first column in this case is equal to the composition of the market portfolio m for Japan and the United Kingdom; these numbers were widely different in Exhibit 7.8. Solving for the equilibrium returns and associated optimal positions, the resulting positions in currencies are −15.6 percent in yen, −6.1 percent in pounds, and 21.7 percent in dollars. Because the stock positions are 56.5 percent in U.S. stocks, 31.3 percent in Japanese stocks, and 12.2 percent in U.K. stocks, the hedge ratio for Japan is 15.6 percent/ 31.3 percent = 0.50, and the hedge ratio for the United Kingdom is 6.1 percent/12.2 percent = 0.50. The ratios are the same (universal) and in addition equal to the risk tolerance coefficient.

Of course, these positions are valid only if they aggregate across all investors to the market. The lowest panel presents a reconciliation of positions across U.S., Japanese, and British investors. For all three investor classes, the stock portfolio is identical and equal to the market weights. Therefore it aggregates to the market portfolio. It is instructive to analyze next the currency positions. The yen position is −15.6 percent for U.S. and U.K. investors and 34.4 percent for Japanese investors; it is higher for the last because the yen is a risk-free asset for Japanese investors. Summing the three positions weighted by wealth yields a zero net supply of yen currency, which is consistent with the underlying model. The table therefore illustrates how investors' positions are consistent with equilibrium returns and add up to the outstanding supply of assets.

Black also showed that the aggregate risk aversion coefficient can be recovered from market data:

$$b = \frac{\mu_m - \sigma_m^2}{\mu_m - 0.5\sigma_e^2}, \qquad (7.19)$$

where μ_m and σ_m are the mean excess return on the market portfolio and its volatility and σ_e is the average exchange rate volatility. For instance, with values $\mu_m = 8$ percent, $\sigma_m = 15$ percent, and $\sigma_e = 10$ percent, the universal hedge ratio is 77 percent. This means that each

EXHIBIT 7.9   Universal Equilibrium Hedging

National Market Values, Wealth, Risk Tolerance			
	Market Portfolio $x_{s,j}$	National Wealth w_j	Risk Tolerance λ^j	Hedge Portfolio $x_{h,j}$
US	0.5651	0.5651	0.5	0.5651
Japan	0.3125	0.3125	0.5	0.3125
UK	0.1224	0.1224	0.5	0.1224
Total	1.0000	1.0000		1.0000
World			0.5	

U.S. Viewpoint Computation of Equilibrium Returns					
	Covariance with Market	Covariance with Hedge	Equilibrium Return μ	Log Portfolio $\Sigma^{-1}\mu$	Positions $\lambda^{US}\Sigma^{-1}\mu$	Equilibrium Hedges
Stocks:	Cov(s,m)	Cov(s,h)	μ_s			
US	18.32	−0.05	.367	1.130	0.565	
Japan	20.54	5.32	.358	0.625	0.313	
UK	24.96	3.47	.464	0.245	0.122	
Currencies:	Cov(f,m)	Cov(f,h)	μ_f			
JY	5.13	4.67	.056	−0.313	−0.156	0.50
BP	3.71	3.56	.039	−0.122	−0.061	0.50
$					0.217	
Total					1.000	

Reconciliation of Positions			
	Equilibrium Positions			Sum Weighted
	US Investor	Jap. Investor	UK Investor	by Wealth
US	0.565	0.565	0.565	0.565
Japan	0.313	0.313	0.313	0.313
UK	0.122	0.122	0.122	0.122
JY	−0.156	0.344	−0.156	0.000
BP	−0.061	−0.061	0.439	0.000
$	0.217	−0.283	−0.283	0.000
Total	1.000	1.000	1.000	1.000

dollar invested in a foreign stock should be hedged by a forward sale in the amount of $0.77.

This approach, however, has been criticized on various grounds. First, the hedging formula uses arbitrary nonmarket weights in the definition of μ_m and other quantities. Second, as discussed by Adler and Prasad (1992), the universality of the hedge ratio, far from being a general result, follows directly from the assumptions that impose homogeneity on world investors. These assumptions require foreign investment to be in balance for all countries at all times ($M_i = W_i$), which is questionable because this rules out trade deficits.

In summary, Black's "universal" hedge ratio actually involves speculative and variance-reduction components and relies on questionable assumptions. Instead, Adler and Prasad (1992) proposed focusing on the currency portfolio with a minimum-variance hedge function, represented by the second term in Equation (7.10), $y_f = \Sigma_{ff}^{-1} \mu_f - \beta y_s$. It turns out that this portfolio βy_s is invariant to the measurement currency. Adler and Jorion (1992) empirically estimated the regression hedge ratios for stock and bond portfolios and argued that this approach provides a component of a global portfolio that is common to all investors, whatever their nationality, thus simplifying the portfolio selection process for global managers.

Unitary Hedges.   Another view of currency hedging, *unitary* ("full") hedging has also attracted considerable attention since advocated as a "free lunch" by Pérold and Schulman (1988). Here, the full face value of the foreign investment is hedged in the forward market on a one to one basis. Proponents of unitary currency hedging argue that it reduces the volatility of returns without a commensurate reduction in returns and therefore that the benchmark against which to measure international portfolio performance should be always unit hedged against currency risks.[6]

Equation (7.10) can be used to discuss conditions under which unitary hedging is appropriate. The forward positions will be $y_f = -y_s$ if two assumptions are verified: the β matrix contains only zeros, except for ones when a foreign stock market is associated with its own currency, and $\mu_f = 0$. The first assumption is verified if *local*

---

[6]Indeed currency-hedged benchmarks have recently appeared in response to market demands. For instance, Morgan Stanley Capital International started to report currency-hedged international stock indices in June 1989; Salomon Brothers has constructed currency-hedged bond indices since March 1988.

market returns are uncorrelated with exchange rates. The matrix β then simplifies to unitary regression hedges.

The second assumption is verified if currency returns are expected to be zero. This, however, has no theoretical basis. It is often argued that there should be no long-term payoff from buying a forward contract on another currency, the reason being that any gains must be offset by losses to the counterpart: this is a zero-sum game. Because of this symmetry, due to the fact that forward contracts are in zero net supply, it has been claimed that no risk premium should exist for currencies. This is incorrect, however, as can be shown by an analogy with stock index futures. Stock index futures are also in zero net supply but are linked to the underlying stocks through a cost of carry relationship: when held to maturity, a long position in futures plus cash is equivalent to a long position in the underlying cash instruments. But it is generally accepted that stocks generate long-term excess returns of about 5–10 percent annually. Then this risk premium must also be imbedded in a long position in stock index futures. Therefore, the fact that a contract is in zero net supply does not necessarily imply a zero risk premium.

Instead, as seen earlier, international asset pricing models show that, in equilibrium, risk premiums depend on investors' risk aversion and whether countries are net investors or borrowers. To simplify, assume a world with two investors only, U.S. and Japanese. If Japanese investors as a whole are net investors in the United States, they will generally seek to reduce risk by hedging to some extent against exchange rate changes. Therefore, they will sell dollars even if it involves a slight loss – that is, if the forward price of the dollar is lower than the expected future spot price. In this world, U.S. investors must be net borrowers. Therefore, U.S. investors will seek to hedge by buying the yen forward, even if the forward price of the yen is above the expected future spot price. Thus, in equilibrium, there will be a nonzero expected return to forward contracts that is perfectly consistent with the fact that for every Japanese selling dollars, an American will be buying the currency. As an example, in Exhibit 7.8, Japan has a larger weight in the "hedge" portfolio than in the market (61 percent vs. 31 percent). This implies that Japanese have more wealth than the value of their stock market or are more averse to risk. As a result, there is an equilibrium negative return on the yen; Japanese investors must *lose* from selling dollars short to protect their investments in dollar markets.

Therefore, currencies could very well, in equilibrium, be character-ized by nonzero expected returns. If this is the case, unitary regression hedges are inappropriate.

Overlay Hedges. With the accelerating trend toward international investments, investors are now paying increasing attention to the impact of currency risk in their portfolios. It is widely believed, how-ever, that international equity managers have not developed sufficient expertise in exchange rates. In response, institutional investors are now turning to specialized "overlay" managers. In this setup, the "core" portfolio selection is delegated to a primary equity manager, either active or passive, while currency risk is managed separately. In 1992, out of a total of about $200 billion of U.S. pension funds invested abroad, about $15 billion in nominal value were actively managed as overlay portfolios.

The separation of functions typically occurs because the core man-ager lacks expertise in currencies, for many possible reasons. For instance, equity managers may neglect exchange rates because curren-cies are less risky than equities and thus may contribute less to the value added. Also, many equity managers may be regional specialists or tend to focus on micro rather than on macro factors during the course of the stock-picking process.

The overlay approach, however, is a second-best solution since the core portfolio is chosen without reference to currencies. In theory, core positions are communicated regularly to the currency manager, who then takes currency positions that should be optimal for the portfolio as a whole. Using the same notations as earlier, the optimal currency position given a predetermined stock position is

$$\begin{pmatrix} w_s = \Sigma_{ss}^{-1} \mu_s \\ w_f = \Sigma_{ff}^{-1} \mu_f - \beta w_s \end{pmatrix}. \tag{7.20}$$

As before, the optimal currency positions contain two components, a speculative position and an MV hedging position. The speculative position, represented by $\Sigma_{ff}^{-1} \mu_f$, aims at maximizing the Sharpe ratio of the portfolio of forward contracts; the MV hedging position, repre-sented by βw_s, provides the minimum-variance portfolio given the predetermined positions in the stocks, w_s.

The problem with this setup is that the underlying asset position completely ignores the impact of the currency overlay, which must suboptimal. Positions in Equation (7.10) and Equation (7.20) will be identical when $\Sigma_{sf} = 0$, which implies $\beta = 0$ and $\Sigma_{ss} = \Sigma_{s\bullet f}$. In other words, returns on underlying assets, measured in dollars, are uncorrelated with all exchange rates. In this situation, the globally optimal weights simplify to $w_s = \Sigma_{ss}^{-1} \mu_s$ and $w_f = \Sigma_{ff}^{-1} \mu_f$, which means that there is no loss of efficiency from separately optimizing on asset and currencies.

Going back to the example presented in Exhibit 7.7, we see that this condition is not satisfied for the sample of U.S., Japanese, and British stocks. For instance, the correlation between Japanese stock returns, measured in dollars, and the yen is $14.19/\sqrt{42.86 \times 12.27} = 0.619$, which is far from zero.

The overlay structure, therefore, is inherently suboptimal because it ignores interactions between the assets in the "core" portfolio and exchange rates. Overlays must be considered as a second-best solution to the global portfolio optimization problem. The efficiency loss, however, must be balanced against excess returns generated by specialized overlay managers. If anomalies in the foreign exchange market can be exploited by overlay managers, then the value added from active currency management may compensate the inherently suboptimal nature of currency overlays.

Hedges with Restrictions on Actual Portfolios. All of the previous developments rest on the assumption of unlimited short sales and positions in foreign markets. In reality, investors face restrictions on short selling foreign equity and bond markets. If this is the case, then forward contracts, instead of being perfectly redundant assets, may expand the menu of assets by allowing short positions in currencies that may otherwise not be implemented. The optimal portfolio allocation may therefore be substantially altered when short-selling restrictions are imposed. The empirical evidence on currency hedging, as well as the impact of short-selling restrictions, is analyzed in great detail in Glen and Jorion (1993).

Further, if the portfolio is heavily biased toward domestic assets, the optimal currency hedges may be very different from those in a completely unrestricted environment. When domestic investors have only a small percentage of their assets overseas, the risk reduction benefits of hedging should be measured in terms of the overall, mostly domestic, portfolio risk, using the systematic risk vis-à-vis the domestic portfolio. Studies that focus on the volatility of an asset and show how the risk of foreign stocks can be decreased simply by hedging are misleading in this context. Based on historical data, Jorion (1989) showed that unitary hedging involves a decrease in volatility of the foreign asset, offset by an *increase* in the correlation with the domestic asset, which leads to a mostly unchanged β. Therefore, full currency hedging is not so beneficial when viewed in the context of an overall portfolio with only 5–10 percent invested in foreign assets, as is the case for most U.S. pension funds. The debate on this point is far from settled.[7]

Summary and Implications. The following *theoretical* points have emerged from the preceding discussion:

- Currencies should be considered as a separate asset class. Managing currencies can improve the risk/return tradeoff of global portfolios.
- The IAPM provides equilibrium expected returns for stocks and currencies. These lead to optimal positions that are consistent across investors all over the world. In particular, there is a universal portfolio that contains optimally hedged stock. This demonstrates that currencies should be an integral part of any global investment portfolio. In the absence of strong views on returns or for long-term asset allocation, the expected returns generated by the IAPM can be most useful as benchmark returns. The IAPM in particular shows that currencies can be expected to generate nonzero returns, contrary to what many believe.
- Advocates of *unitary* or *universal* hedging should recognize that these are special cases of the general optimization decision, involving additional assumptions that may not be reasonable. As Odier and Solnik (1993) argued, simplistic assumptions lead to simplistic hedging rules.
- *Overlay* hedging is fundamentally a second-best solution because it ignores interactions between the core portfolio and currencies. In this setup, the onus is on overlay managers to prove their worth as active managers.

To summarize the different approaches to currency hedging, Exhibit 7.10 reviews the different approaches to hedging, along with a summary of assumptions and pros and cons.

---

[7]See also Filatov and Rappaport (1992). Thomas (1990) recently edited a book on this topic, *The Currency Hedging Debate.*

EXHIBIT 7.10 Currency Hedging: Overview of Approaches

	Mean–Variance Optimization	
Assumptions:	Risk aversion, normal distributions	
Positions:	$y_s = \Sigma_{ss}^{-1}\mu_s - \Sigma_{s\bullet f}^{-1}\beta'\mu_f$ $y_f = \Sigma_{ff}^{-1}\mu_f - \beta y_s$	
	IAPM Hedging	**MV Hedging**
Assumptions:	Market clears, homogeneous expectations no barriers to capital flows	Zero currency returns
Positions:	$y_s = x_s$ $y_f = -(1-\lambda)x_h$	$y_s = \lambda\Sigma_{s\bullet f}^{-1}\mu_s$ $y_f = -\beta y_s$
Advantages:	Consistent across investors	Few parameters to estimate
Problems:	Assumes rational investors and no capital controls	Inconsistent across investors

	Log Hedging	Universal Hedging	Unitary Hedging	No Hedging	Overlay Hedging
Assumptions:	Log utility	Same risk aversion, wealth is market cap.	Local returns uncorrelated with FX	Dollar returns uncorrelated with FX	MV optimization in two steps
Positions:	$y_s = x_s$ $y_f = 0$	$y_s = x_s$ $y_f = -(1-\lambda)x_s^-$	$y_s = \lambda\Sigma_{s\bullet f}^{-1}\mu_s$ $y_f = -y_s$	$y_s = \lambda\Sigma_{ss}^{-1}\mu_s$ $y_f = 0$	$y_s = \lambda\Sigma_{ss}^{-1}\mu_s$ $y_f = \Sigma_{ff}^{-1}\mu_f - \beta y_s$
Advantages:	Simplest	Simple	Simple, robust	Simplest	Use managers with specialized expertise
Problems:	Restrictive utility function	Restrictive assumptions	Approximate for stocks, less so for bonds	Assumptions blatantly false	Suboptimal relative to joint optimization

The table describes optimal positions in stocks y_s, and in currencies y_f, for each model. Expected returns for stocks and currencies are μ_s and μ_f. Covariance are Σ_{ss}, and Σ_{ff}, respectively; $\Sigma_{s\bullet f}$ is the variance of stocks conditional on currencies; β are the minimum-variance hedge ratios. Market weights for stocks are x_s, including dollar stocks; foreign stocks are defined as x_s^-.

This overview of currency hedging may be useful for plan sponsors who must decide on passive or active management, as well as on appropriate benchmarks for global or international portfolios. Most active portfolio managers, however, deeply believe that markets are inefficient and cannot be characterized by "equilibrium" relationships.

Instead, the investment process for active managers can be structured in two steps:

1. Identify anomalies that provide estimates of expected returns; these can be based on fundamental or technical models. Anomalies are discussed in the next chapter.
2. Structure the investment portfolio. This involves an optimization, as described in the "portfolio allocation" section, that accounts for the expected returns and volatilities of all assets, as well as correlations.

Equilibrium Models with Exchange Risk

The IAPM presented previously is the earliest, and perhaps most analytically tractable, model dealing with the general issue of differences in consumption opportunity sets. Other approaches and extensions have been proposed and are briefly summarized here.

An early competing model was that of Grauer, Litzenberger, and Stehle (1976). In their model, movements in national price levels are exactly offset by exchange rates, so that the price of the same consumption bundle is the same across countries. Exchange risk then disappears, and prices can be evaluated in real terms all over the world. This leads to a CAPM in real terms. Defining all returns to be in excess of the real risk-free asset, we have

$$\mu_s = [\text{Cov}(s,m)/\sigma^2(m)]\,\mu_m. \tag{7.21}$$

This approach has the merit of showing that exchange rate risk is related to purchasing power parity (PPP). Even though PPP might hold in terms of expectations, no empirical observer would claim that PPP holds instantaneously and perfectly. Therefore few researchers would view this approach as realistic.

Consumption and state-variable hedging enter the picture when, as in Stulz (1981a) and Adler and Dumas (1983), local inflation rates and opportunity sets are allowed to be stochastic. In addition to the universal logarithmic portfolio, investors will hold several hedge portfolios, some with weights that tend to replicate their consumption mixes and others that hedge state variables. The IAPM can be viewed as a special case where the hedge portfolio reduces to the domestic bond, which is riskless in real terms if inflation is nonstochastic.

Empirical tests have generally not been favorable to the more complex versions of the theory. In an illustration of the optimal composition of national hedge portfolios, Adler and Dumas (1983) regressed nine nations' inflation rates on a menu of stock indices and bond returns over the period 1971–9. As shown in Exhibit 7.11, they found each country's hedge portfolio to consist almost exclusively of that country's riskless bonds.

There may be sample-period bias in this result. The 1971–9 period was one of accommodating monetary policies which made domestic

EXHIBIT 7.11   Optimal Positions of U.S. and French Investors, Adler-Dumas Model (1971–9 data)

	Logarithmic Portfolio (weight sum to 1)	Hedge Portfolios U.S. Investor	Hedge Portfolios French Investor
Stocks			
Germany	−6.18	0.021	0.025
Belgium	6.15	0.000	−0.032
Canada	4.68	0.000	−0.028
France	−1.59	0.000	0.011
Japan	3.01	0.005	0.002
Netherlands	1.34	−0.011	0.014
United Kingdom	0.01	0.000	0.000
Switzerland	0.90	0.001	−0.022
United States	−6.75	−0.020	0.020
Bank Deposits			
Deutsche Mark	11.57	−0.029	−0.047
Belgian Franc	−9.22	−0.003	0.059
Canadian Dollar	−21.81	0.034	0.046
French Franc	3.02	0.004	0.988
Japanese Yen	−0.68	0.034	−0.007
Guilder	−2.79	0.016	−0.009
British Pound	−4.10	−0.024	−0.005
Swiss Franc	1.43	−0.017	0.017
U.S. Dollar	22.01	0.983	−0.032

interest rates superior predictors of home CPI inflation. The correlation between short-term interest rates and future inflation has fallen since.

This result can be explained by the fact that national CPI indices do not seem fully to reflect variations in import prices arising from exchange rate changes. This may be due to some importers' policies to absorb exchange rate changes into profits to keep their market share or to the fact that the measurement interval may be too short to account fully for the lagged impact of exchange rate movements on domestic prices. Until national price indices reflect more fully exchange rate variations, we cannot expect that empirically estimated consumption hedge portfolios will contain significant equity or foreign bond positions.

None of these models, therefore, can explain the "home asset preference" puzzle, particularly in relation to stocks. Actual portfolio compositions reveal more "home asset preference" than current theory would predict. For this reason economists have begun to seek explanations in other factors: transactions costs, as in Cooper and Kaplanis (1986), and, somewhat conveniently, asymmetric optimism, as in French and Poterba (1991). In addition, an emerging line of theory, exemplified by Eldor, Pines, and Schwartz (1988) and Stockman and Dellas (1989), seeks to base explanations of HAP on the presence of nontraded goods. At equilibrium in these models, home investors own all and foreigners none of the claims to the output of domestic nontraded goods. Hence with risk aversion, the presence of nontraded goods produces a bias toward domestic assets. These models, however, are partial equilibrium in nature and do not explain why some goods are not traded.

At present, however, the structure of these models does not permit one to judge how the HAP they produce affects investors' optimal financial asset demands for domestic bonds or for foreign versus domestic stocks. Nor can one tell whether ultimate optimal levels of foreign portfolio investment will converge to capitalization ratios, import ratios or some other market aggregate fraction.

Uppal (1993) explicitly modeled differences in consumption opportunities by introducing transaction costs for shipping goods across countries. He showed that, in such a setting, risk-averse investors will bias their portfolio *toward* foreign assets. This is because returns on foreign stocks hedge some of the uncertainty in the price of foreign goods. Thus current models are unable to explain the HAP puzzle.

International Arbitrage Pricing Theory

The previous utility-based models all assume markets in equilibrium, by equating optimal demand with supply. Because, in the presence of exchange risk, investors hold "hedge" portfolios, the main conclusion from the domestic CAPM that the market is mean–variance efficient does not translate to the international environment. The aggregation across heterogeneous investors makes the theory difficult to test.

An alternative to utility-based models is the arbitrage pricing theory (APT), which assumes perfect, or integrated, capital markets. The international APT (IAPT) has been developed by Solnik (1983), Ross and Walsh (1983), and Ikeda (1991). In an international setting, the APT requires investors to agree only on the factor model driving security returns:

$$\tilde{r}_i = E_i + \sum_{k=1}^{m} b_{ik}\tilde{\delta}_k + \tilde{\epsilon}_i, \; i = 1, \ldots, N \tag{7.22}$$

where $\tilde{r}_i$ is the actual return on the ith asset and E_i is its expected return. In this equation, $\tilde{\delta}_k$ is the random kth factor return and b_{ik} is called the factor loading of security i on factor k. This m-factor model assumes that there are m pervasive factors δ_k in the economy that drive asset returns and capture all systematic risks. As a result, the residual ϵ_i can be diversified away in a large portfolio. Both the residual and each of the factors are assumed to have zero mean.

As pointed out by Ross (1976), one could build an arbitrage portfolio with weights $x'1 = 0$, $x'b_k = 0$, so that it entails no net investment and has no exposure to any of the factors. This can be achieved with an infinite combination of weights of x', since the number of assets is much greater than the number of factors. Further, with a large number of assets, the portfolio will be well diversified so that $x'\epsilon = 0$. The return on this portfolio is $x'\tilde{r} = x'E + \sum_{k=1}^{m} x'b_k\tilde{\delta}_k + x'\epsilon = x'E$. The portfolio is therefore riskless and should have a zero expected return since it involves no net investment. But because $x'1 = 0$ and $x'b_k = 0$ for a wide range of x, $x'E = 0$ can be verified only if the N-vector E is a linear combination of the m-factor loadings:

$$E_i^j = \lambda_0^j + \sum_{k=1}^{m} \lambda_k^j b_{ik}^j , \tag{7.23}$$

where λ_0 is the risk-free rate and the j subscript is used to represent that returns are measured in currency j. The APT can be extended to the international environment if it is invariant to the reference currency.

In an international environment, Solnik (1983) showed that any arbitrage portfolio nominally riskless is riskless for all investors, irrespective of the currency of denomination. In addition, if exchange rates also follow the m-factor process, the factor structure is invariant to the currency of denomination. In the case where exchange rates do not follow the linear factor model, Ikeda (1991) proved that the pricing relation is

$$E_i^j - r_i - E[s_i^j] = \sum_{k=1}^{m} \lambda_k^j b_{ik}^j, \qquad (7.24)$$

where r_i is the riskless return in currency i and $E[s_i^j]$ is the expected currency movement. Therefore the IAPT (Equation 7.23) is a viable theory, internally consistent because it is independent of the numeraire currency j. The ex ante model can be aggregated to an ex post testable specification.

Although in theory the IAPT may provide a fruitful alternative to utility-based models, it should be recognized that it is subject to the same factor identification problems as the domestic APT. No theoretical guidance is offered as to which factors may be appropriate. In addition, the apparent testability of the IAPT, which does not rely on the troublesome aggregation of portfolios across national investors, is gained only at the expense of an additional assumption, which is that all investors agree on the same factor structure; this directly leads to the IAPT, because factors, unlike portfolios, need not be aggregated across countries. Nevertheless, the empirical evidence presented later shows that the IAPT is a useful approach to check if global or national factors are priced across countries, and it provides a benchmark model to test whether capital markets are integrated or segmented.

Capital Markets: Integrated or Segmented?

With the globalization of financial markets, it is widely believed that capital markets are becoming more integrated. The concept of integration, however, can be given many interpretations. In an efficient, integrated international capital market, the prices of all assets should fully reflect their relative investment values. Therefore, one interpretation of integration is that new information is efficiently transmitted across national stock markets. Given the increasing openness of national economies, the factors affecting stock values are becoming more international, which presumably implies that national markets should become more closely correlated with each other. The fact that returns on two assets are correlated, however, does not imply that these assets are efficiently priced. Instead of focusing on correlations, a more relevant definition of integration focuses on the *pricing* of assets: capital markets are said to be *integrated* when assets in different currencies or countries display the same risk-adjusted expected returns. Segmentation, in contrast, implies that the risk/return relationship in each national market is determined primarily by domestic factors. For example, assuming a world with only one currency, integration would imply that all assets are priced according to their β relative to the world index, while segmentation would describe a situation where the domestic β should be priced. The effect of integration vs. segmentation on the pricing of assets is described later in an example.

The question of whether capital markets are integrated has several important practical implications. For instance, if a multinational firm has a choice of raising capital in two countries, the cost of capital can be substantially different if these markets are not fully integrated. If the pricing of risk is different in a stock market and in the foreign exchange market, hedging currency risk may add value to the firm, and firms face optimal hedging decisions. More generally, many irrelevance propositions for corporate financial strategies break down in segmented capital markets. In addition, the issue of integration directly bears on the desirability of international diversification: if national stock markets are segmented, international portfolios should display superior risk-adjusted performance because some of the domestic systematic risk can be diversified away by investing internationally without paying a price in terms of lower returns.

One approach to measuring integration is to look for direct evidence of barriers to capital movements. Governments, keen on protecting their domestic economies, have often applied restrictions on capital movements. Among major economies, the United States imposed the Interest Equalization Tax from 1963 to 1974; Japanese financial markets were effectively closed to foreigners until the 1980s; and the United Kingdom, France, and Germany all experienced periods of capital controls in the last 20 years. Although many of these restrictions have been removed, some barriers to capital movements remain, including state restrictions on public pension funds in the United States. Legal restrictions on capital movements or on the ownership of foreign assets, for instance, can create wedges between expected returns or prices across markets. In equity markets, segmentations could also arise because of information effects, possibly due to differences in accounting rules, language barriers, and so on. Documenting such barriers, however, is not sufficient to prove segmentation, because prices are determined by marginal investors who may find innovative ways around capital controls.

When the same asset is traded in two different markets, integration can be directly tested, because efficient markets imply that prices should be identical across markets. More generally, comparing risky assets requires an asset pricing model, such as the capital asset pricing model or the arbitrage pricing theory to adjust for risk. Under integration, the same risk/return relationship should apply to domestic and foreign assets. In practice, however, it should be noted that the interpretation of empirical results reflects the joint nature of the assumption – integration and a pricing model; thus rejections could possibly occur because of misspecifications in the pricing model or, alternatively, because of auxiliary statistical assumptions.

Direct Evidence of Segmentation

The impact of capital controls can be observed most directly from comparing interest rates on short-term bank deposits denominated in the same currency but located in different financial centers. Because the currency of denomination, the investment horizon, and the credit risk are controlled for, any discrepancy in pricing reflects the effect of binding capital restrictions. During the early 1970s, for instance, Germany tried to stem capital inflows by taxing foreign residents' deposits in Germany. As a result, Eurocurrency interest rates were below those in the onshore market. A reverse phenomenon occurred in the early 1980s when France attempted to cut off capital outflows. Exhibit 7.12 displays such a comparison and shows that capital outflow restrictions induced at times a 15 percent differential between Eurocurrency and domestic interest rates. These comparisons are informative because there is no need to explicitly model risk and also because a specific opportunity cost can be attributed to capital controls.

The comparisons of "offshore" and "onshore" rates are probably the tests of integration least affected by the joint assumption problem. Unfortunately, they shed little light on issues of integration of long-term capital markets. Capital restrictions that are binding for short-

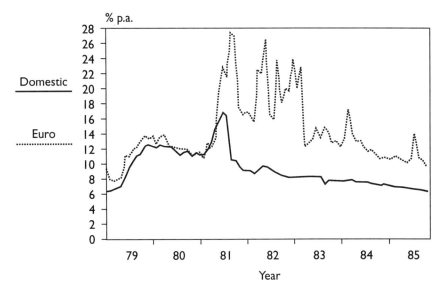

EXHIBIT 7.12   Effect of Capital Controls: Domestic and Euro French Franc Interest Rates

term capital movements may be less effective in long-term markets. For example, when trying to affect capital movements, governments often seem to focus on short-term rather than long-term capital, because of the perceived speculative nature of investments in assets with short maturities. In 1978–9, for instance, Japan prohibited foreigners from holding Japanese securities with maturities of less than five years. During the early 1970s, Germany also imposed heavier restrictions on short-term securities, which created higher implicit tax rates on short-term investments than on long-term investments.

Additional evidence of segmentations comes from the premiums observed in closed-end country mutual funds. If international capital markets were fully integrated, then the share price of a closed-end country fund should in principal equal its net asset value, computed from the price of underlying shares listed in the foreign market. Legal restrictions, however, could raise the fund's price relative to its net asset value by an amount that reflects what the marginal investor is willing to pay to circumvent capital controls. For a long time, for instance, the Korea Fund was selling at a price about twice the value of underlying Korean shares; this reflected the premium U.S. investors were willing to pay for access to a market in which foreigners were otherwise prohibited to invest. Admittedly, discrepancies also occur for domestic closed-end funds but on a lower scale. Bonser-Neal, Brauer, Neal, and Wheatley (1990) examined whether announcements of changes in investment restrictions created changes in the premiums. Over the period 1981–9, they found that a number of country funds experienced a significant decrease in premium either in anticipation or immediately following the announcement of liberalization of investment barriers. This is direct evidence that government restrictions have been effective in segmenting long-term capital markets.

Segmentation with the CAPM

As an illustration of the effect of segmentations on the pricing of assets, assume risk is priced according to the CAPM. If investors lack access or do not materially invest abroad, the pricing of domestic stocks should conform to

$$E[R_i] - R_f = \beta_i^{US}(E[R^{US}] - R_f), \qquad (7.25)$$

where β is defined as the systematic risk vis-à-vis the domestic (U.S.) market. If, however, investors hold portfolios that are diversified worldwide, then nondiversifiable risk will be measured by the systematic risk vis-à-vis the global market, measured as the value-weighted sum of world stock returns. Assuming away exchange rate risk, the pricing equation becomes

$$E[R_i] - R_f = \beta_i^{W}(E[R^{W}] - R_f). \qquad (7.26)$$

A numerical example is presented in Exhibit 7.13, which displays measures of risk and correlation for the U.S., world, and French markets. Assume that the fair risk premium for U.S. stocks is 5 percent. Then according to the segmented model, the fair risk premium on French stocks should be $\beta^{US}(E[R^{US}] - R_f) = 0.82 \times 5\% = 3.9\%$. With the integrated model, the 5 percent U.S. risk premium, maintained for consistency, implies a risk premium on world stocks of $5.0/1.06 = 4.7\%$, and for French stocks $1.09 \times 4.7\% = 5.1\%$. The two models, therefore, can lead to very different estimates of the risk premium, 3.9 percent for segmented markets and 5.1 percent for integrated markets.

These results can be interpreted as follows. Under the segmented model, the fair risk premium is what U.S. investors would require to invest in France. This is not necessarily related to the true expected

EXHIBIT 7.13   Pricing of Risk in Segmented and Integrated CAPM

| | | Segmented U.S. CAPM | | |
	Volatility	Correlation with US	β with US	Fair Risk Premium
US	18.4	1.0	1.0	5.0%
World	16.2	0.93	0.82	—
France	26.4	0.54	0.78	3.9%

| | | Integrated CAPM | | |
	Volatility	Correlation with World	β with World	Fair Risk Premium
World	16.2	1.0	1.0	4.7%
US	18.4	0.93	1.06	5.0%
France	26.4	0.67	1.09	5.1%

return for the French market, however. Any security analyst forecast above 3.9 percent implies that the French market is underpriced to U.S. investors. A major benefit from segmented markets is that international investors might be able to exploit mispricing opportunities. By going international, investors can in principle discover overpriced or underpriced securities, relative to the domestic market line.

Under the integrated model, even if the French market is fairly priced, there are still diversification benefits from going international for the same reason that apply in a domestic context. For instance, it makes no sense to invest solely in oil stocks when this industry risk can be diversified away in a larger portfolio and therefore is not compensated. The overall implication is that, whether capital markets are segmented or integrated, going international is beneficial. The models, however, have different implications for the pricing of assets.

In terms of welfare effects, Cohn and Pringle (1973) showed that, in general, the slope or the capital market line decreases as restrictions are lifted on international investments. Referring, for instance, to the logarithmic utility case in Equation (7.18), the risk premium is given by $E[R_i] - R_f = \sigma_i\sigma_m\rho_{i,m}$. As restrictions are lifted, the volatility of the market portfolio decreases because of diversification effects, and in addition the correlation term is also likely to decrease because of the addition of low-correlation securities in the market portfolio. Therefore the risk premium decreases as financial markets progressively become more integrated. Spreading risk across large markets should push down the market price of risk and increase stock values.

"Mild" Segmentation

The models already presented take extreme views: either complete segmentation or complete integration. The reality, however, is likely to fall somewhere between these extremes. This is why is it also useful to study models that account for specific forms of capital controls. Such models are also noteworthy because they provide a sharper alternative for empirical tests than either complete segmentation or integration.

The first satisfactory model of barriers to investments was proposed by Stulz (1981b). The approach considers a two-country world, where the domestic country investors face a tax on foreign investments but where foreign investors have free access to all markets. The model is rather involved because the tax occurs on both long and short positions, and hence the model loses its linearity.[8] For domestic stocks, a CAPM-like relationship holds, although the price of risk is different from the excess return on the market:

$$E[R_i] - R_f = \beta_i^m(E[R^m] - R_f - k), \qquad (7.27)$$

where the "market" represents the value-weighted average return on the domestic and foreign markets. Foreign stocks, however, do not plot on the security market line:

$$E[R_i] - R_f = \alpha_i + \beta_i^m(E[R^m] - R_f - k), \qquad (7.28)$$

where α depends on the amount of tax and wealth-weighted risk aversion of foreign and domestic investors; it is positive for foreign stocks held long and negative for foreign stocks held short.

Errunza and Losq (1985) proposed another model where domestic investors are restricted from buying any foreign securities. This can be viewed as a special case of the Stulz model with infinite tax rates on foreign investment. As before, domestic securities are priced according to the global market β:

$$E[R_i] - R_f = \beta_i^m\lambda. \qquad (7.29)$$

Foreign stocks, however, are also priced according to the β relative to the foreign market:

---

[8]Black (1974) assumed a positive tax on long positions and a negative tax on short positions. The latter, however, is hard to justify because it involves a subsidy on foreign short positions.

$$E[R_i] - R_f = \beta_i^f \lambda_3 + \beta_i^m \lambda_2, \qquad (7.30)$$

where β_i^f represents the covariance with the component of the foreign market orthogonal to the global market. This "super risk premium" in general will be positive, which suggests again that removing barriers to capital flows should reduce expected returns and hence increase prices. In both models, capital controls cause restricted assets to plot away from the SML and artificially create mispricings.

Empirical Tests

As noted before, comparing risky assets across national borders requires a method to adjust for risk – an asset pricing model. International asset pricing models can be classified into three classes: extensions of the domestic CAPM, APT, and consumption-based models. In addition, a new class of dynamic models has recently appeared. As the interpretation of empirical results should reflect the joint nature of the assumptions, integration plus a pricing model, it is useful to review the evidence for a number of different models.

At the outset, however, it should be emphasized that tests of international asset pricing models are beset by many difficulties. The usefulness of empirical tests critically depends on the ability of the researcher to model expected returns. Given that stock returns are so volatile, it proves difficult to precisely extract expected returns from ex post data. As a result, failure to reject can be interpreted in two ways: either the model truly fits the data quite well or, alternatively, there is too little information in the data. This latter interpretation is always a possibility, especially because international equity data have been available for a much shorter time period and are typically more volatile than U.S. equity data.

The first tests of integration extended the CAPM to an international environment, usually ignoring exchange risk. Stehle (1981), for instance, analyzed U.S. stocks and could not reject the hypothesis of integration or segmentation. His empirical tests are based on Equation (7.30) and attempt to distinguish whether expected returns are cross-sectionally related to a global or domestic β. Errunza and Losq (1985), on the other hand, explicitly modeled asymmetric investment restrictions and, using recent data from less developed countries, provided some evidence of mild segmentation, although their evidence is generally weak. Jorion and Schwartz (1986) and Mittoo (1992) addressed the question of integration of the Canadian equity market relative to the global North American market. They employed domestic and international versions of the CAPM and rejected the joint hypothesis of the CAPM and integration over the period 1968–82. In addition, they focused on a subset of Canadian stocks also interlisted in the United States and found that integration is rejected for both interlisted and domestic stocks alike. This points to legal barriers as the source of segmentations.

A difficulty with the international CAPM is that researchers must identify the world market portfolio. In theory, integration could be rejected merely because of an inappropriately chosen world market portfolio. While the Roll critique applies to all tests of the CAPM, the identification of the market portfolio is especially difficult in an international environment. The "global" index, for instance, should include all markets, even emerging markets, in proportion to available market capitalization. But conventional benchmarks, such as the Morgan Stanley Capital International index, assign large weights to Japanese stocks even though a substantial fraction of shares are cross-ownership agreements, which therefore are counted twice in the same supply of shares. In general, larger discrepancies occur between global indices than between domestic U.S. stock market indices.

On the other hand, the APT assigns no special role to the market portfolio and hence is free from this problem. Furthermore, the testability of the APT with a subset of assets makes studies easier to conduct, especially for the international markets, where data availability is always a constraint. Cho, Eun, and Senbet (1986) empirically examined the international APT and rejected the joint hypothesis of the integration and the APT. Korajczyk and Viallet (1989) compared CAPM- and APT-based models and also found evidence of segmentations. Comparing the performance of the single-factor CAPM and the multifactor APT models, the APT generally fares better in terms of pricing errors. They also noted that the models behave differently in later years, suggesting structural changes due to deregulation. Along the same lines, Gultekin, Gultekin, and Penati (1989) compared U.S. and Japanese stocks, splitting the sample in 1980, which corresponds to the relaxation of Japanese capital controls, and found that risk premiums appear to be closer across the two markets in the latter period.

Wheatley (1988) applied the Stulz (1981b) consumption-based model to international equity market integration. The advantage of this approach is that it does not require the identification of a market portfolio; instead, risk is measured relative to domestic consumption. He tested and could not reject that expected returns on foreign equities are in line with that country's asset pricing line. This approach, unfortunately, compounds the problem of identification of expected stock returns with imprecisely measured consumption data. So far, most tests of consumption-based models have been unable to reject anything of interest.

Most of the previous studies impose an auxiliary assumption of constant expected returns. There is, however, increasing evidence that the expected returns on a variety of financial assets are not constant, but rather can be predicted from ex ante information. Along these lines, Harvey (1991) investigated a version of the international CAPM with time-varying moments. If international financial markets were fully integrated, the conditional expected return on a country index should be determined by the country's exposure to the world risk. Using returns from 17 countries, the results suggest a single source of risk for most of the countries. One notable exception is Japan, where the model restrictions are consistently rejected.

More recent tests of integration have used the latent variable model, which is a less formal but explicitly dynamic model that allows for time variation in expected returns. When expected returns vary through time, the single latent variable model imposes meaningful cross-sectional restrictions on the pattern of time variation in expected returns. If integration prevails, then benchmark portfolio should be the common driving factor across different markets. Jorion (1992b) applied this methodology to the Eurocurrency fixed income market, which is free from capital controls, and found that the hypothesis of integration is supported by the data. The latent variable model has also been applied to the Japanese and the U.S. capital markets by Campbell and Hamao (1991), who reported weak evidence against integration.

Although corporate financial policy is not directly addressed here, it is informative to look at market reactions to policies aimed at circumventing the effect of market segmentations. In general, market segmentations can be avoided by listing on foreign stock markets or by international acquisitions. Alexander, Eun, and Janakiramanan (1988) reported that foreign securities that list on U.S. exchanges tend to experience slightly higher prices before the listing, then lower average returns in the three years following the listing, which is consistent with segmented capital markets. Fatemi (1984) found that firms that initiate international operations experience abnormal returns on the order of 15 percent in the year before going international. Although the sample size is limited, this suggests that direct investment in foreign markets leads to a lower degree of riskiness and possibly higher profits. International acquisitions were further investigated by Doukas and Travlos (1988), who reported that firms not operating in the target firm's country experience positive abnormal returns on the announcement date, whereas acquisitions made by firms already operating in the foreign country lead to negative valuation effects. Although much of this evidence is still preliminary, the burgeoning literature on market reactions to changes in financial policies suggests substantial segmentations in international capital markets.

Conclusions

International capital markets are characterized by two major factors: exchange risk and capital controls. When explicitly modeled, these factors cause deviations from the usual CAPM risk/return relationship. International asset pricing models offer many useful normative insights into international portfolio decisions. First, these models show how currency decisions can be made independent of underlying asset decisions; the models also provide the tools to formally evaluate the appropriateness of hedging policies such as unitary hedging, universal hedging, or overlay hedging. The different approaches to currency hedging are summarized in Exhibit 7.10. Another advantage of these models is that they provide benchmark expected returns that give rise to indexed portfolio allocations. International portfolios then can be managed by comparing security forecasts to those implied by these models and controlling risk.

Capital controls lead to apparent mispricing of assets across national borders, which can be interpreted as "segmentations." If there were no capital controls, efficient markets would lead to "integrated" pricing models. In terms of the empirical performance of these models, the body of evidence presented here seems to indicate that, over the last 20 years, segmented capital markets have prevailed more often than integrated capital markets. Global capital markets, however, are probably not totally integrated or segmented but can be more usefully described as a middle ground between these two extreme characterizations, especially in a changing environment of increasing financial deregulation. What matters to investors and corporations alike is the size of mispricings, which can translate into substantial opportunity costs or benefits for financial managers. Exploring these imperfections remains a major challenge to researchers in international finance.

References

Adler, M., and B. Dumas. 1983. "International portfolio choice and corporate finance: A synthesis," *Journal of Finance* 38: 925–84.
——, and P. Jorion. 1992. "Universal currency hedges for global portfolios," *Journal of Portfolio Management:* 18, 28–35.
——, and B. Prasad. 1992. "On universal currency hedges," *Journal of Financial and Quantitative Analysis* 27: 19–38.
Alexander, G., C. Eun, and S. Janakiramanan. 1988. "International listings and stock returns: Some empirical evidence," *Journal of Financial and Quantitative Analysis* 23: 135–51.
Black, F. 1974. "International capital market equilibrium with investment barriers," *Journal of Financial Economics* 1 (December): 337–52.
——. 1978. "The ins and outs of foreign investment," *Financial Analysts Journal* 34: 1–7.
——. 1990. "Equilibrium exchange rate hedging," *Journal of Finance*, Papers and Proceedings, 45: 899–907.
Bonser-Neal, C., G. Brauer, R. Neal, and S. Wheatley. 1990. "International investment restrictions and closed-end fund prices," *Journal of Finance* 45: 534–47.
Campbell, J., and Y. Hamao. 1991. "Predictable stock returns in the United States and Japan: A study of long-term capital market integration," *Journal of Finance* 47: 43–69.
Cho, D., C. Eun, and L. Senbet. 1986. "International arbitrage pricing theory: An empirical investigation," *Journal of Finance* 41: 313–29.
Cohn, R., and J. Pringle. 1973. "Imperfections in international financial markets: Implications for risk premia and the cost of capital to firms," *Journal of Finance* 28: 59–66.
Cooper, I., and E. Kaplanis. 1986. "Costs to cross-border investment and international equity market equilibrium," in *Recent Advances in Corporate Finance*, ed. J. Edwards et al., Cambridge University Press, Cambridge.

Doukas, J., and N. Travlos. 1988. "The effect of corporate multinationalism on shareholders' wealth: Evidence from international acquisitions," *Journal of Finance* 43: 1161–75.

Eldor, R., D. Pines, and A. Schwartz. 1988. "Home asset preference and production shocks," *Journal of International Economics* 25: 165–76.

Errunza, V., and E. Losq. 1985. "International asset pricing under mild segmentation: Theory and test," *Journal of Finance* 40: 105–24.

Eun, C., and B. Resnick. 1988. "Exchange rate uncertainty, forward contracts and international portfolio selection," *Journal of Finance* 43: 197–216.

Eun, C., and S. Shim. 1989. "International transmission of stock market movements," *Journal of Financial and Quantitative Analysis* 24: 241–56.

Fatemi, A. 1984. "Shareholder benefits from corporate international diversification," *Journal of Finance* 39: 1325–44.

Filatov, V., and P. Rappaport. 1992. "Is complete hedging optimal for international bond portfolios?" *Financial Analysts Journal* 48: 37–47.

French, K. R., and J. M. Poterba. 1991. "Investor diversification and international equity markets," *American Economic Review* 81: 222–26.

Glen, J., and P. Jorion. 1993. "Currency hedging for international portfolios," *Journal of Finance* 48: 1865–86.

Grauer, F., R. Litzenberger, and R. Stehle. 1976. "Sharing rules and equilibrium in an international capital market under uncertainty," *Journal of Financial Economics*.

Grubel, H. 1968. "Internationally diversified portfolios: Welfare gains and capital flows," *American Economic Review* 58: 1299–1314.

Gultekin, M., B. Gultekin, and A. Penati. 1989. "Capital controls and international capital market segmentation: The evidence from the Japanese and American stock markets," *Journal of Finance* 44: 849–69.

Hamao, Y. 1989. "An empirical investigation of the APT using Japanese data," *Japan and the World Economy* 1: 45–61.

———, R. Masulis, and V. Ng. 1990. "Correlations in price changes and volatility across international stock markets," *Review of Financial Studies* 3: 281–308.

Harvey, C. 1991. "The world price of covariance risk," *Journal of Finance* 46: 111–57.

Ikeda. 1991. "Arbitrage asset pricing under exchange risk," *Journal of Finance* 46: 447–55.

Jorion, P. 1985. "International portfolio diversification with estimation risk," *Journal of Business* 58: 259–78.

———. 1989. "Asset allocation with hedged and unhedged foreign assets," *Journal of Portfolio Management* 15: 49–54.

———. 1992a. "Portfolio optimization in practice," *Financial Analysts Journal* 48: 68–74.

———. 1992b. "Term premiums and the integration of the Eurocurrency markets," *Journal of International Money and Finance* 11: 17–39.

———. 1994. "A mean-variance analysis of currency overlays," *Financial Analysts Journal* 50: 48–56.

———, and E. Schwartz. 1986. "Integration vs. segmentation in the Canadian stock market," *Journal of Finance* 41: 603–16.

Korajczyk, R., and C. Viallet. 1989. "An empirical investigation of international asset pricing," *Review of Financial Studies* 2: 553–85.

Lee, A. 1987. "International asset and currency allocation," *Journal of Portfolio Management* 13: 68–73.

Levy, H., and M. Sarnat. 1970. "International diversification of investment portfolios," *American Economic Review* 60: 668–75.

Lucas, R. 1982. "Interest rates and the exchange rate in a two-country world," *Journal of Monetary Economics* 10: 335–60.

Michaud, R. 1989. "The Markowitz optimization enigma: Is optimized optimal?," *Financial Analysts Journal* 45: 31–42.

Mittoo, U. 1992. "Additional evidence on integration in the Canadian stock market," *Journal of Finance* 47: 2035–54.

Odier, P., and B. Solnik. 1993. "Lessons for international asset allocation," *Financial Analysts Journal* 49: 63–77.

Pérold, A., and E. Schulman. 1988. "The free lunch in currency hedging: Implications for investment policy and performance standards," *Financial Analysts Journal* 44: 45–50.

Roll, R. 1988. "The international crash of October 1987," *Financial Analysts Journal* 44: 19–35.

———. 1992. "Industrial market structure and the comparative behavior of international stock market indices," *Journal of Finance* 47, 3–41.

Ross, S. 1976. "The arbitrage theory of capital asset pricing," *Journal of Economic Theory.*

———, and Walsh. 1983. "A simple approach to the pricing of risky assets with uncertain exchange rates," in *Research in International Business and Finance,* ed. R. Hawkins, R. Levich, and C. Wihlborg, JAI Press, Greenwich, Conn.

Sercu, P. 1980. "A generalization of the international asset pricing model," *Finance.*

Shiller, R., F. Kon-Ya, and Y. Tsutsui. 1991. *Speculative Behavior in the Stock Markets: Evidence from the United States and Japan,* National Bureau of Economic Research, Working Paper no. 3613.

Solnik, B. 1974a. "Why not diversify internationally rather than domestically?" *Financial Analysts Journal* 30: 48–54.

———. 1974b. "An equilibrium model of the international capital market," *Journal of Economic Theory* 8: 500–24.

———. 1983. "International arbitrage pricing theory," *Journal of Finance* 38: 449–57.

Stehle, R. 1981. "A empirical test of the alternative hypotheses of national and international pricing of risky assets," *Journal of Finance* 32: 493–502.

Stockman, A., and H. Dellas. 1989. "International portfolio nondiversification and exchange rate variability," *Journal of International Economics* 26: 271–89.

Stulz, R. 1981a. "A model of international asset pricing," *Journal of Financial Economics* 9: 383–406.

———. 1981b. "On the effects of barriers to international investment," *Journal of Finance* 36: 923–34.

———. 1983. "The demand for foreign bonds," *Journal of International Economics* 15: 225–38.

Thomas, L. 1990. *The Currency Hedging Debate,* IFR Publishing, London.

Uppal, R. 1993. "A general equilibrium model of international portfolio choice," *Journal of Finance* 48: 529–53.

Wheatley, S. 1988. "Some tests of international equity integration," *Journal of Financial Economics* 21: 177–212.

8

The Search for Higher Returns: Anomalies

This chapter focuses on possible inefficiencies in the stock and foreign exchange markets. The intent is to identify profitable opportunities and their impact on resource allocation in financial markets. These opportunities can then be combined with the risk management models presented in previous chapters to construct portfolios that optimally balance risk and return.

Because inefficiencies can be defined only in relation to "normal" prices, we first review the efficient markets hypothesis (EMH). The EMH is possibly the most extensively analyzed proposition in economics. In its most generic form, the hypothesis implies that the market efficiently prices securities. In recent years, empirical research appeared to have dealt severe blows to the EMH-CAPM joint hypothesis. The evidence, termed *anomalies*, can either be construed as proof of inefficiency or, alternatively, one could argue that these results are consistent with more complicated models, such as implying rational time variation in expected returns or more general multifactor models.

In any event, these empirical tests are useful because they illustrate important aspects of the functioning of capital markets. Such studies improve our ability to describe the time-series and cross-sectional behavior of security returns and provide portfolio managers with tools for deviating from their benchmarks. In addition, provided performance is still measured using the CAPM, exploiting these anomalies should add value to their portfolios.

This chapter attempts to review the empirical evidence on efficient capital markets. Given the volume of literature on the topic, a comprehensive review appears hopeless. Instead, the emphasis will be on major trends, with a subjective evaluation of the most important work. The first section reviews the theory behind the EMH, and the implications for empirical testing. Anomalies in the equity markets are analyzed next; we show how stock returns are predictable based on past returns, seasonalities, and cross-sectional information. The third section reviews the main anomalies in the foreign exchange market, based on technical and fundamental data, and summarizes attempts to rationalize these results in terms of a risk premium.

EMH: Theory

Market efficiency implies a situation where information is rationally and quickly impounded in security prices. Market efficiency has severe implications for security analysis, investment management. If the market is efficient, then by definition there cannot exist mispriced securities, and the practice of security analysis cannot have any value. As a result, investors should simply "index" their portfolios, rather than try to choose active investment managers. From the viewpoint of corporate management, the EMH implies that the cost of capital accurately reflects firms' prospects. Therefore, capital will be efficiently allocated to firms according to their investment opportunities, which is beneficial to society as a whole.

Sufficient conditions for efficiency are the following:

1. Capital markets are "perfect," with no transaction costs, securities infinitely divisible, short sales allowed;
2. All relevant information is available at cost to all market participants;
3. All agree on the implications of current information for current prices and the distribution of future prices.

Depending on the information set, one can classify EMH into different definitions. We initially adopt the presentation by Fama (1970):

- *Weak form efficiency: there are no reliable time patterns to the random returns of any security.* In this definition, the information set consists of the history of price series. The reason why there can be no time patterns is that, if there were, reliable patterns would be noticed by traders who would try to sell at the high points and buy at the low points. This process would lead to price pressures that would lower the high points and raise the low points, thereby destroying the patterns. Hence weak form efficiency rules out technical analysis and seasonalities, such as turn of the year, day of the month, day of the week, in securities markets.

- *Semi-strong form efficiency: prices correctly reflect all available public information.* In this definition, the information set consists of all relevant publicly available information. The argument is that traders will quickly and rationally respond to public announcements of relevant information. Therefore, simple trading rules based on public information cannot earn abnormal profits.
- *Strong form efficiency: prices correctly reflect all available public and private information.* This is the strictest form of market efficiency and affirms that there is no such thing as capitalizing on insider information. It leads, however, to a paradox. If there is no benefit from acquiring information because of market efficiency and if information acquisition is costly, then there is no incentive to acquire information. But then, if nobody acquires information, the market cannot be efficient!

As shown by Grossman and Stiglitz (1980), a more economically sensible version of the EMH is that prices reflect information up to the point where the marginal benefits of acting on information do not exceed the marginal cost of acquiring information. Market efficiency appears to be a matter of degree. Instantaneous efficiency cannot exist, but rather must be muted by the impact of transaction costs. This implies, for instance, that mutual fund managers could add value through security analysis, but that returns to investors, net of transaction costs and investment management fees, cannot be abnormal.

Jensen (1978) has proposed an intermediate definition, which includes transaction costs: "A market is efficient with respect to a given information set if it is impossible to make economic profits by trading on the basis of this information set; by economic profits, we mean the risk adjusted returns net of all costs." In this definition, *costs* represents the costs of dealing in the market and also research and development costs, as well as the cost of processing the information required to manage the trading rule.

In a more recent survey of EMH, Fama (1991) expanded the weak form classification to *tests for return predictability,* which include forecasting returns based not only on previous price data, but also on other variables such as dividend yields and interest rates. The second and third categories are relabeled *event studies* and *tests for private information,* respectively. These new definitions are motivated by the growing body of empirical evidence that suggests that asset returns can be predicted. This changing tide is nowhere more apparent than in the work of Fama, who concluded his path-breaking research in 1965 with the sentence, "It seems safe to say that this paper has presented strong and voluminous evidence in favor of the random-walk hypothesis," and introduced a recent paper with the sentence, "There is much evidence that stock returns are predictable."

The EMH has been subject to extensive empirical tests in part because it is difficult to establish a clear-cut case of existence. In practice, the true value of the firm is never fully revealed and a model must be used as a benchmark of value. For instance, normal returns could be defined using an equilibrium model such as the capital asset pricing model. Of course, the model could be wrong, which would invalidate the test's results. This clearly shows that empirical tests are joint tests of EMH and the particular market structure chosen. The EMH hypothesis therefore leads to a rich source of empirical studies, because rejection can always be blamed on the model, in which case the search continues for another model, ad nauseam.

Equity Market

There is now mounting evidence that stock returns are predictable. To some extent, this evidence was made possible by the creation of the Center for Research in Security Prices (CRSP) database at the University of Chicago in the 1960s. CRSP for the first time made available to academics high-quality stock price information in computerized form.

Predictability of stock returns can be classified into time-series or cross-sectional evidence. On a time-series basis, returns can be forecast from past returns or from other variables such as dividend yields or interest rates. Across firms, returns can be explained by fundamentals and should be in some way related to risk. Each of these categories is now examined in turn.

Return Predictability: Past Returns

In the 1970s, research principally addressed the question of whether expected returns were constant over time by studying short-term auto-correlation. Fama (1965), for instance, regressed daily returns on lagged daily returns, as in

$$R_t = a + \rho_1 R_{t-1} + \ldots + \epsilon_t, \tag{8.1}$$

and found slightly positive, but insignificant, daily autocorrelation ρ_1 in stock returns.

In contrast, more recent research appears to find stronger effects, in part because of the availability of longer data series and more powerful statistical techniques. This has been confirmed more recently by Lo and McKinlay (1988), for instance, who found weekly autocorre-lations ranging from 0.09 to 0.30 and reported that the effect is more pronounced for small stocks. The fact that stronger effects appear for small stocks suggests, however, that autocorrelation may actually be induced by nonsynchronous trading.

This is because quoted prices can either represent actual trades or bid–ask prices posted by dealers. Because small stocks are traded less actively than large stocks, "stale" prices are more likely to appear; these do not represent actual trades but rather bid–ask prices at which it may be difficult to trade in any quantity. Consequently, these prices, which are not market clearing prices, do not fully reflect current information and will be correlated with old prices. As the flow of information is slowly impounded into quoted prices, spurious, or artificial, autocorrelation will result. After controlling for this effect, however, recent work such as that of Lo and McKinlay has shown that some detectable time variation in expected returns remains.

Although the evidence rejects the hypothesis of constant expected returns, the explanatory power of the regressions is very low, on the order of 1–5 percent. In other words, the R^2 of Equation (8.1) is such that only 1–5 percent of the variance of stock returns is explained by the previous day's return. This means that almost all of the short-horizon variation in stock returns is unexplained and this rule would be hard to put into practice. Thus statistical significance does not necessarily imply economic importance.

In trying to explain the large volatility in asset prices, economists have recently turned to "noise trading" as an explanation of excess volatility. Shiller (1981) started a vigorous debate by pointing out that the variability of stock prices appears to be too high relative to the variability of fundamentals, such as discounted dividends. Of course, this proposition can be tested only by imposing a model relating prices to fundamentals, which again reflects the joint nature of the tests. Early papers on volatility have assumed that interest rates and expected returns are constant and that all the variation in stock prices is entirely due to shocks in expected dividends. Given that dividend payouts are artificially smoothed by corporate managers and that some firms choose not to pay any dividend but instead reward investors with capital gains, it is not astonishing to find that dividends cannot explain movements in stock prices. Subsequent papers on excess volatility have shown that conclusions are particularly sensitive to the particular model chosen. The consensus on this line of research is that volatility tests, instead of testing market efficiency, can be interpreted as tests of time variation in expected returns.

Still, an intriguing observation emerges from the preceding. As long as rational investors are not completely dominated by noise traders, there should be some tendency for prices to gravitate back to fundamentals: prices should be mean reverting. Fama and French (1988) estimated over horizons of one to five years and indeed seemed to find some evidence of mean reversion over long horizons, but these results have been discredited on statistical grounds and anyway disappeared after the 1940s.

Another approach to mean reversion is to isolate extreme movements in stock prices. DeBondt and Thaler (1985) reported that a portfolio of firms identified as the most extreme losers over a three- to five-year period tended to have strong excess returns in subsequent years. Vice versa, past winners generally underperformed the market. Interestingly, most of the correction occurs in January, while other months provide little correction. Several other studies use a similar design and are reported in Exhibit 8.1. Here, most of the results are economically significant. For example, Bremer and Sweeney (1991) found excess returns of about 4 percent in the week following a large "down" move. By any measure, this is a large excess return.

DeBondt and Thaler argued that this is evidence of investor "overreaction" to news. They draw attention to the vast body of psychological and statistical research that shows that individuals exhibit inconsistency in their predictions. Individuals apparently are willing to make extremely strong inferences from small amounts of information and tend to underweight distributional information. The authors claim that

EXHIBIT 8.1   Short-Term Price Reversals: Literature Overview

	Sample	Methods	Summary of Selected Findings
Bremer and Sweeney (1991)	Daily returns 1962–1986 Fortune 500 companies	All 1-day (absolute) returns in excess of 7.5, 10, or 15%	Next 5 trading days winners: −0.004% losers: +3.95%
Brown, Harlow, and Tinic (1988)	Daily returns 1963–1985 200 largest companies in the S&P 500	All 1-day (market model) residual returns in excess of (absolute) 2.5%	Next 10 trading days winners: +0.003% losers: +0.37%
Howe (1986)	Weekly returns 1963–1981 NYSE and AMEX companies	All returns that rise or fall more than 50% within 1 week	Next 10 weeks winners: −13.0% losers: +13.8%
Lehmann (1990)	Weekly returns 1962–1986 NYSE and AMEX companies	Buy all stocks that lagged the market during the previous week ("losers") and sell short the equivalent "winners"	For $1 long on zero-investment arbitrage portfolio, earn 39 cents every 6 months; 2/3 of profits generated by prior "losers"
Rosenberg, Reid, and Lanstein (1985)	Monthly returns 1981–1984 NYSE companies	Buy stocks with negative residuals (relative to multi-factor model) and sell short stocks with positive residuals over the previous month	Arbitrage portfolio earns 1.36% per month; profits mostly generated by prior "losers"
Jegadeesh (1990)	Monthly returns 1945–1980 NYSE companies	Regressions relating Sharpe-Lintner residual returns to raw returns of previous month and returns in earlier years	Extreme decile portfolios: difference in residual returns is 2.5% per month
Brown and Harlow (1988)	1- to 6-month returns; 1946–1983 NYSE companies	Study stocks with residual returns that gain or lose (between absolute) 20 and 65% between 1 to 6 months	Large rebounds for losers; no decline for winners except in first month

only socio-psychological explanations can fully explain the observed short-term overreactions followed by long-term price reversals.

Aficionados of the EMH, however, maintain that these results are artificial. One explanation is the failure to adjust for risk. Chan (1988) indicated that the good performance of past losers is explained by increases in their β. Zarowin (1989) showed that the winner–loser results simply reflect a small stock effect, whereby losers are mainly small stocks that display higher than average, CAPM-adjusted, expected returns. As before, reversals could be explained by rationally changing risk premiums. Another explanation relates to methodological faults. Conrad and Kaul (1993), for instance, showed that the long-term reversals can be explained by the arithmetic cumulation of monthly returns, which does not represent a buy-and-hold strategy. When properly measured, long-term reversals disappear, and excess returns are solely due to the "January" effect described later. Although DeBondt and Thaler (1987), not unexpectedly, refuted these claims, at the very least this literature points to the existence of CAPM-adjusted excess returns.

Return Predictability: Seasonalities

An alternative to focusing on past returns is to search for seasonal patterns in stock returns. The availability of machine-readable CRSP data has started a thriving research profession of data dredging that has uncovered a number of seasonal anomalies. For instance, French (1980) and Gibbons and Hess (1981) reported that Monday returns are on average lower than the weekly average, by about 20 basis points. Returns are also higher the day before a holiday (Ariel 1990), by about 30–40 basis points, and toward the end of the month (Ariel 1987), by about 20–30 basis points.

The Monday seasonal is hard to explain, because one would expect a higher return given that Friday-to-Monday returns cover three calendar days. But it appears to be stable and occur in many markets. Jaffe and Westerfield (1985) also found weekly seasonals in foreign stock markets, although lowest returns are on Tuesdays for Japan and Australia. Flannery and Protopopadakis (1988) also found lower Monday returns in the U.S. government debt market. Among the many explanations that have been proposed, the most convincing is that negative information is typically held for release after the market is closed on Fridays. Indeed, Penman (1987) found that firms with unexpected good news tend to deliver the news on or before the date expected, whereas firms with bad news tend to delay disclosing their results. If the timing of information release is not systematically recognized by the market, low Monday returns could be explained by a bias toward negative information releases by corporations over the weekend.

The January effect is probably the most puzzling anomaly. It was revealed by Rozeff and Kinney (1976) and has been recently reviewed by Keim (1988). Stock returns, especially for small stocks, appear on average higher in January than in other months. This effect has received a tremendous degree of attention because of the magnitude of returns. Over 1926–86, small firms have on average outperformed the S&P 500 index by 5.5 percent in January. In addition, they have earned inferior returns in only 7 out of these 61 years. The January effect has also been documented in other markets, by Gultekin and Gultekin (1983) for foreign stocks and by Smirlock (1985) for low grade corporate bonds. In Japan, for instance, small stocks have returned 6.5 percent in January, versus only an average of 1.2 percent in other months.

Various explanations have been advanced for the January effect. The most popular is probably the tax-loss hypothesis. When capital gains are taxed, investors have an incentive to recognize losses early, by selling stocks that have decreased in value, and to delay realizing capital gains. December should thus be a month when losing securities should be sold to shield income from taxation. The evidence on tax-loss selling, however, is mixed. Schultz (1985) found no January effect from 1900 to 1917, when there was no significant income tax, but Jones, Pearce, and Wilson (1987) found opposite results in a longer sample period. Reinganum and Shapiro (1987) found positive gains in April, which corresponds to the new tax year for British investors, but also in January, which runs counter to the tax-loss argument. The January effect is also found in countries where there is no capital gain tax, for example, Japan and Canada before 1972. Hence there is only mixed support for the taxation hypothesis.

In addition, there is no reason for investors to keep the sale proceeds in cash and wait the turn of the year to buy new stocks. Instead, investors could very well reinvest the proceeds into other stocks, in which case there should be no monthly seasonal. Haugen and Lakonishok (1987) proposed another explanation, linked to incentive contracts of investment managers. If managers are compensated according to their performance during a calendar year, they have an incentive to establish superior performance by buying new stocks in January and, later in the year, to lock in their profits by slowly reverting to the benchmark. Because bargains are easier to establish among small, less well-known firms, this puts pressure on the prices of small firms in January. In addition, investment managers are believed to "window-dress" their portfolio toward the end of the year, especially by eliminating small, lesser known stocks that underperformed during the year. Overall, the January effect probably stems from a combination of tax-loss effects and investment manager behavior.

These anomalies, although not predicted by most asset pricing models, are in general not flagrant evidence of inefficiencies. A first caveat is that, with so many researchers spinning the same data tapes, some are bound to find "statistically significant" effects. For instance, we know that out of 20 regressions of returns on randomly selected explanatory variables, 1 is expected to be significant at the usual 5 percent level of confidence. It is important, therefore, to check for robustness outside the selected sample period or in other markets. Lakonishok and Smidt (1988) found that the January, Monday, holiday, and end-of-month effect also appear in other periods.

Exhibit 8.2, taken from Fama (1991), also shows how difficult it is to capture the January effect in practice. Monthly average returns are presented for the S&P 500, the CRSP Small Firm index, composed of the smallest quintile stocks, and the DFA Small fund, a mutual fund designed to mimic the CRSP Small Firm index. Over 1941–81, the CRSP Small Firm index outperformed the S&P by 8.1 − 1.3 = 6.8 percent in January, quite an impressive number. This outperformance persisted, although only by 2.1 percent, in the following eight years. The performance of the DFA fund, however, is only barely above the S&P 500 index in January. The reason for the deviation from the CRSP Small Firm index is that DFA, to minimize transaction costs, rationally

EXHIBIT 8.2   The January Effect: Average Monthly Returns

	1941–81			1982–90		
	Jan	Feb–Dec	All	Jan	Feb–Dec	All
S&P 500	1.3	0.9	1.0	3.2	1.2	1.4
CRSP Small	8.1	0.9	1.5	5.3	0.2	0.6
DFA Small				3.6	0.7	0.9

Source: Fama, E., "Efficient Capital Markets II," Journal of Finance 46 (1991): 1575–1617.

avoids the very smallest stocks and sells only when the stock values go up to the top of the third decile, instead of the first quintile. Apparently, small differences in portfolio composition, due to rational trading, can give rise to very significant mistracking. Fama's point is to advise caution when drawing inference based on the behavior of small stocks.

A final essential remark is that many of these seasonal effects are within the range of bid–ask spreads and therefore do not represent blatant profit opportunities. Some of theses seasonals can probably be explained by market microstructure effects, such as inventory adjustments by specialists or short sellers, which are too thin to be adequately represented by most asset pricing models.

Return Predictability: Other Variables

Financial analysts have long believed they could evaluate investment in common stocks by using, for instance, dividend yields or price–earnings ratios. If the stock price represents a claim to the future stream of dividends, the price can be exactly determined assuming constantly growing dividends and a known discount rate, as in the Gordon and Shapiro (1956) model:

$$P_t = \sum_{i=1}^{\infty} D_t(1 + g)^i/(1 + r)^i = \frac{D_{t+1}}{r - g}, \qquad (8.2)$$

where P is the stock price, D is the dividend, r is the discount rate, and g is the constant growth rate of dividends, where $r > g$. Although the model is not directly applicable to the case in which growth rates and discount rates vary through time, the model suggests that dividend yields should capture variations in expected stock returns. A more general valuation model recognizes that the stock price is a function of future expected cash flows and a discount rate.

Based on such models, researchers have tried to explain stock returns by variables such as dividend yields, price–earnings ratios, interest rates, and term-structure variables. The last are usually taken as the default spread (the difference between low-grade and high-grade bond yields) and the term spread (the difference between long-term and one-month bond yields). Most of these variables are usually found to be significant.[1] Generally, stock and corporate bond returns

---

[1] See, for instance, Shiller (1984), Keim and Stambaugh (1986), and Campbell (1987).

are positively related to dividend yields (high yields, or low prices, imply future price appreciation), positively related to the default and term spreads, with monthly R^2 going as high as 30 percent for small-stock portfolios.[2] Also, Fama and Schwert (1977) noted that monthly stock returns appear to be negatively correlated with the level of short-term interest rates.

This evidence has also been investigated for foreign stock markets. Harvey (1991) found that U.S. variables are also useful in forecasting returns on portfolios of foreign stocks. Thus the variation in expected returns using U.S. information is also international.

Whether this is evidence of inefficiency depends on one's stand on risk premiums. For instance, Fama and French (1989) and Chen (1991) argued that the systematic patterns in variation of expected returns are rationally linked to the business cycle. Dividend yields and default spreads tend to be high at low points in the business cycle, when low wealth puts a higher price on risk, thus leading to higher expected returns. The fact that variation in expected securities is common to different securities and markets provides support for the rational risk premium story. As always, the evidence on predictability of stocks and bonds can be given varying interpretations, but even if this represents time-varying rational premiums, these results can be exploited by portfolio managers whose performance is evaluated on the basis of constant β or σ – that is, without proper reference to these risk premiums.

Cross-Sectional Return Predictability

Return predictability on a cross-sectional basis is closely linked to tests of asset pricing models. The first cracks in the CAPM wall came from studies from Basu (1977), Banz (1981), and Reinganum (1981). These authors showed that, even after adjusting for β, earnings/price ratios and size are related to expected returns. High earnings/price ratios imply higher than average returns, while small stocks earn

---

[2] Fama and French (1988) presented long-horizon regressions, where one- to four-year overlapping index returns are regressed on yields and reported values of R^2 as high as 60 percent. These results, however, cannot be interpreted as usual because of statistical problems created by the data overlap. In addition, Nelson and Kim (1993) and Goetzmann and Jorion (1993) have shown that the coefficients obtained are much less unusual than one would expect under the null hypothesis of no predictability. Fuller and Kling (1990) argued that the out-of-sample predictive ability of dividend yields was erratic and unlikely to be useful to investors as a market-timing strategy.

higher than average returns. Fama and French (1991) further showed that high book-to-market equity ratios are also associated with high expected returns. Chan, Hamao, and Lakonishok (1991) got similar results for Japan.

First, let us examine the premier anomaly, the size effect. Banz (1981) sorted all NYSE firms into quintiles by size and reported that a dollar invested in the highest quintile (large stocks) would have grown to $109 from 1926 to 1980. In contrast, the same dollar invested in the lowest quintile (small stocks) would have grown to $524. This is a 5-to-1 ratio in favor of small firms! In other words, small stocks led to an annual return of 12.1 percent, versus only 8.9 percent for large stocks. It should be noted, however, that there have been periods where small firms underperformed large firms, but the small firm premium reappears over long horizons and different countries. In Britain, for instance, returns on small stocks have exceeded those on large stocks by 7 percent per annum over 1955–84. In Japan, Hamao has found that over 1971 to 1988, small stocks returned 23.7 percent versus 18.6 percent for large stocks. Thus there seems to be a consistent premium attached to investments in small stocks.

Next, we turn to the market-to-book effect, described in Exhibit 8.3. NYSE stocks are sorted into deciles according to their market-to-book ratios. As shown in the table, stocks with low market-to-book ratios had substantially higher returns than stocks with otherwise high

EXHIBIT 8.3   The Market-to-Book Value Effect (NYSE stocks, 1967–87)

Decile	Compound Annual Return (%)	Standard Deviation (%)	Ending Index Value ($)
1 (lowest)	16.0	17.1	22.6
2	17.1	21.5	27.6
3	15.7	21.1	17.8
4	12.8	20.3	12.6
5	11.1	19.7	9.1
6	9.8	17.7	7.1
7	10.9	19.1	8.8
8	9.3	20.6	6.5
9	7.9	17.4	5.0
10 (highest)	7.8	17.6	4.8

Source: Ibbotson Associates (1991).

ratios. For each dollar invested at the end of 1966, firms in the lowest deciles would have grown to $22.6 at the end of 1987, whereas firms in the highest decile would have grown to only $4.8.

Of course, these variables are not independent. For instance, small stocks are associated with high earnings/price ratios and high book-to-market ratios. The real anomaly, however, is the claim by Fama and French (1992) that, after controlling for book-to-market ratios, there remains no relationship between expected returns and βs. This claim, however, is still controversial because the results are sensitive to the grouping procedure used in the empirical tests.

One way to interpret these results is to recognize that market βs are measured with error and some of the additional priced variables may proxy for true differences in β. Chan and Chen (1988), for instance, found that size and β are nearly perfectly negatively correlated (with correlation of −0.988). Thus it may be difficult to tell whether size is truly priced or whether it is merely proxying for β.

Another interpretation is that these tests should be interpreted as evidence in favor of multifactor models, such as Ross's APT. Perhaps these reflect APT-type factors rationally priced or simply persistent mispricing of securities.

In any event, Haugen and Baker (1991) showed how cross-sectional deviations from the CAPM can be used to construct more efficient portfolios. They tracked the performance of the portfolio that minimizes volatility, without regard for expected return. The low-volatility portfolio was constructed from the population of the 1,000 largest U.S. stocks, subject to the constraints that (i) no more than 1.5 percent of the portfolio could be invested in one security, (ii) no more than 15 percent of the portfolio could be invested in one industry, and (iii) the minimum weight on any stock would be zero. This portfolio was constructed every quarter from 1972 to 1989, using the previous 24 months of data and assuming reasonable transaction costs. The performance was then recorded *out-of-sample*, i.e., outside the 24-month portfolio formation period, and compared to the benchmark, the Wilshire 5000 Index.

Exhibit 8.4 shows that this low-volatility portfolio has lower risk and higher returns than the index. It turns out that the stocks in the low-volatility portfolio tend to be generally "value" stocks, characterized by high book-to-market values, which is consistent with the results of Fama and French (1991). Haugen and Baker interpreted these results as evidence that few investors act as mean–variance optimizers, using

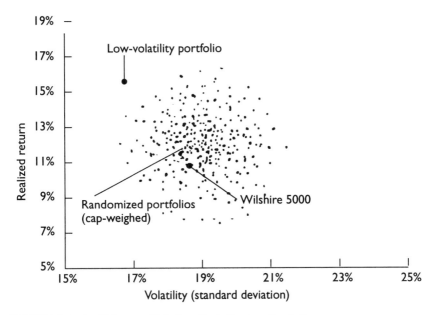

EXHIBIT 8.4   Inefficiency of Market-Capitalization Portfolios

the total portfolio volatility as a measure of risk; instead, they argued that most institutional investors focus on the tracking error relative to a benchmark portfolio. Minimizing the volatility of the tracking error, or relative returns, however, leads to very different portfolios from minimizing the volatility of absolute returns. This explains why capitalization-based portfolios are inefficient relative to low-volatility portfolios.

Event Studies

By now, the reader should feel frustration at the inability to distinguish between model failure and market inefficiency. In contrast, event studies come closest to allowing a break between market efficiency and equilibrium pricing issues. When the stock-price response to an event is large and concentrated over a few days, the estimation of expected returns has little effect on inferences. Brown and Warner (1985), for example, showed that excess returns on the order of a few percent over a short window are little affected by the measurement of expected returns, which are on the order of 10 percent annually. This translates into 0.04 percent daily, which is much smaller than price reactions to important events.

Event studies are now indispensible tools for corporate finance and have been used to study market reactions to security issues and redemptions, corporate-control transactions, dividend announcements, and so on. Generally, event studies have found that, on average, prices react within a day to announcements. This is consistent with efficiency.

Another approach to event studies is to measure returns over a longer period after the event. For instance, Ball and Brown (1968) reported abnormal returns after the announcement of quarterly earnings. Firms with unexpected high earnings tend to do better than the average in the ensuing three to six months. Watts (1978), for instance, found that a portfolio going long firms with a positive earnings surprise and short firms with a negative earnings numbers earned on average about 3 percent excess return in the following six months. This drift, however, is sensitive to assumptions about the measurement of expected returns, given that the risk characteristics of the firm may change over time. In addition, these excess returns are likely to be swamped by transaction costs.

Bernard and Thomas (1990) offered a more direct challenge to EMH. They showed that the market does not fully use the time-series properties of quarterly earnings, but instead takes the previous year earnings measure as an expectation of future earnings, as in the annual random walk model. As information contained in earnings one to four quarters back can be used to forecast the stock price response to the next earnings report, it appears that the market does not fully understand the autocorrelation structure of quarterly earnings.

For instance, assume an actual earnings process is characterized as follows:

$$e_t = e_{t-4} + 0.1 \times (e_{t-1} - e_{t-2}) + \epsilon_t, \qquad (8.3)$$

where e_t is the quarterly earnings per share, and ϵ_t is the unexpected component. Now assume that the market expectation is simply $E[e_t] = e_{t-4}$; that is, it ignores the most recent information and just takes last year's earnings as a forecast.

Exhibit 8.5 looks at the implications for the price reaction. After an increase from $10 to $20 in the fourth quarter, future quarterly numbers should drift up, as the increase is not totally transitory: earnings the following quarter should be $11 = 10 + 0.1 \times (20 - 10)$. The market, however, simply expects last year's earnings of $10 and is positively surprised when $11 appears. The following quarter, true expected

EXHIBIT 8.5   Price Reaction and Earnings Announcements

Quarter	Actual Earnings	Earnings Process: $e_t = e_{t-4} + 0.1*(e_{t-1}e_{t-2})$ Market Expectation	Price Reaction
I	10.0		
II	10.0		
III	10.0		
IV	20.0		
I	11.0	10.0	+
II	9.1	10.0	−
III	9.8	10.0	−
IV	20.1	20.0	+
I	12.0	11.0	+
II	8.3	9.1	−
III	9.4	9.8	−

earnings decrease to $9.1 = 10 + 0.1 \times (11 - 20)$, while the market still expects $10; it is negatively surprised.

The anomaly is that the price reaction can be forecast from past earnings data. This result is especially puzzling because so much time and effort are spent forecasting earnings. It is still not completely explained, although there is some evidence that this myopic earnings process occurs mainly for small stocks, which are followed by fewer analysts and are more expensive to trade. But clearly, because profits can be realized over a short announcement period, it would be hard to argue that they could be explained away by risk.

Foreign Exchange Market

The foreign exchange (Forex) market is the most active of all financial markets. A recent survey by the Bank of England estimates the amount of *daily* trading to be $1.0 trillion in 1992. Because the magnitude of this number is difficult to grasp, consider the following data: the *daily* U.S. GNP is $22 billion and worldwide daily exports amount to $13 billion. Alternatively, this number can be compared to the total stock of worldwide central bank reserves, which amounts to $1 trillion 35. Thus the daily volume of trading is equivalent to the sum total of all foreign currency reserves. Given this volume of trading, one might expect the foreign exchange market to be highly efficient.

In addition, whether exchange rates are correctly priced is particularly important since exchange rates simultaneously affect the relative prices of all foreign assets, goods, and factors of production. Misaligned exchange rates can lead to gross misallocation of resources across countries. As for the equity market, however, there is now an accumulation of recent evidence pointing to inefficiencies in the Forex market.

Return Predictability: Past Returns

Because exchange rates started to float in 1973, it is only in the 1980s that economists have had sufficient data to ascertain the profitability of technical trading rules in the foreign exchange market. In parallel, a whole new industry, dedicated to providing foreign exchange forecasts, has blossomed, driven mostly by technical models.

Financial economists have studied price patterns in the spot, forward, and futures currency markets.[3] Given interest rate parity, these three markets are closely linked together; any trend developing in one market should also appear in the others. For measuring profits, however, using only spot rates ignores interest rate differentials across currencies, which can bias the results if positions are left open for long periods of time. The researcher can instead use futures rates, or spot rates with some adjustment for the cost of carry, or forward rates after interpolation to reflect shorter horizons. The excess return on a foreign currency position is

$$R_t = \Delta s_t + i_t^* - i_t, \qquad (8.4)$$

where i and i^* are the overnight domestic and foreign interest rates, and Δs_t is the daily change in the exchange rate. The relationship is exact with continuous compounding, but ignores a cross-product term if discrete compounding is used to measure returns.

There is by now a burgeoning literature on technical analysis in the Forex markets, which, by and large, seems to find evidence of

---

[3]Closely related to technical analysis is the study of seasonalities in exchange rates. McFarland, Pettit, and Sung (1982) analyzed the statistical distribution of daily changes in exchange rates over 1976 to 1979 and found that Wednesday returns are typically higher than the average. The higher returns on Wednesday and lower returns on Thursday are consistent with settlement effects: transactions on Wednesday clear for "good" on Friday for foreign currencies but on the following Monday for the dollar. For dollar buyers, this results in the loss of two days' dollar interest, which lowers

profitability. Sweeney (1986) provided a good review and also showed how to control trading profits for a possible nonzero risk premium. Consider a technical rule that implies either going in a foreign currency or staying in dollars. We define N_{in}/N as the ratio of days "in" relative to the total number of days, and $R_{BH} = (1/N)\Sigma_t R_t$ and $R_{in} = (1/N)\Sigma_{t,in} R_t$ as the daily return on a buy and hold and on the filter rule, respectively. The appropriate test statistic is $X = R_{in} - (N_{in}/N)R_{BH}$. With a constant risk premium, the value of X should be zero under the hypothesis of no predictability. In addition, the standard deviation of this statistic is $\sigma_X = \sigma[(1 - N_{in}/N)(N_{in}/N)]^{.5}N^{.5}$, where σ is the volatility of currency returns. This permits formal statistical tests of whether risk-adjusted profits are significant.

Sweeney (1986) applied the filter rule to exchange rates over 1975–80. The filter is implemented as follows: a signal to buy is generated whenever the spot rate increases by more than f, a prespecified filter size, relative to a local trough; when long, a neutral position is initiated when the spot rate decreases by more than f relative to a local peak. Other implementations allow *short* positions, instead of no position, in the foreign currency whenever a "sell" signal is initiated. Of course, as with all technical rules, there is some subjectivity in the implementation because an essential degree of freedom, the size of the filter, is unknown. The filter size is usually derived from backtesting, but it should be recognized that, given a wide range of possible values, a particular filter can be found that will create apparent profits. In that sense, technical analysis is as much an art as a science.

As with most technical rules, a tradeoff must be found between low and high filter values. Low filters involve many transactions and thus large cumulative costs; large filters, in contrast, create fewer costs but may miss the beginning of trends and therefore be less profitable. Exhibit 8.6 reports Sweeney's main results.

The filter rules generate about 1–2 percent in excess returns. Even after transaction costs, the 1 percent rule appears to generate statistically significant profits. Further, Sweeney has divided the total sample of 1973–80 into two subperiods and shown that profitable filters in 1973–75 also appear profitable in 1976–80. This suggests that the

---

the demand for the dollar, or increases the price of foreign currencies on Wednesday. The effect is reversed on Thursday. The effect, however, is only about about five basis points. They also reported a Monday pattern, which disappeared in recent years.

EXHIBIT 8.6   Filter Rules Applied to the $/DM Rate (1975–1980)

Size (%)	R_{in} Return on Filter (%)	R_{BH} Return on Buy and Hold (%)	N_{in}/N Ratio of Days In	X Statistic Before Costs	X Statistic After Costs
0.5	2.4	1.6	0.55	1.6*	0.7
1.0	2.8	1.6	0.61	1.9*	1.5*
2.0	2.2	1.6	0.58	1.3	1.1
5.0	1.7	1.6	0.73	0.1	0.1

*Statistically significant at the 5% level.

optimal filter size could have been determined on the basis of prior information.

The notable feature of this test is that it is valid even if there is a constant risk premium on Forex returns, because it adjusts for buy-and-hold profits. Therefore, it encompasses CAPM- or APT-based models of asset pricing with constant risk premiums. One would have to believe that risk premiums increase precisely at times long positions are initiated to fully explain these results.

Sweeney and Surajaras (1988) extended this approach to rules based on single and double moving averages. A signal to buy now appears when the short-term average $MA_1 = \Sigma_{t=1}^{N_1} S_t$ (which specializes to the single MA when $N_1 = 1$) crosses the long-term average $MA_2 = \Sigma_{t=1}^{N_2} S_t$ from below. The evaluation period is mid-1980 to mid-1986, using prior data to determine the optimal parameters, filter size f, lag lengths N_1, N_2, for each method. After transaction costs, these rules generate profits of 2.0 percent (filter), 2.2 percent (double MA), and 2.6 percent (single MA), which are significant and appear to be stable over various subperiods.

Beyond these simple models, researchers are now exploring more sophisticated nonlinear models, where, for instance, the trend is related to the volatility of returns.[4] Although these approaches apparently enjoy good success, researchers should be aware of the fact that nonlinear models, as well as most technical rules, are particularly good at bending around the data; this is because they involve searching not only over parameter values, for which we have standard statistical

---

[4]See, for instance, Bilson (1990).

tests of significance, but also over different functional forms. There-fore, the evidence on nonlinear models should be tempered by the observation that these models are susceptible to serious biases due to data mining. In spite of these caveats, there appears to be some evidence of short-term forecastability in exchange rates.

The Forward Discount Bias

While technical models are still considered controversial, for reasons discussed previously, there is much more agreement among econo-mists on another type of anomaly, relating the forward premium to returns over monthly or longer horizons.

Whereas technical analysts have focused on daily, or intra-daily intervals, economists have analyzed returns over longer horizons, typically monthly because of data availability considerations.

To avoid exchange rate risk, investors can use hedging instruments such as forward contracts. The choice is then between hedging, or locking in a forward rate $F_{t,n}$ for delivery in n days, and not hedging, which involves an exchange at the future random exchange rate $\tilde{S}_{t+n}$. If investors are risk neutral and have rational expectations, the forward rate should reflect the market's expectation of the future spot rate as of time t:

$$F_{t,n} = E[\tilde{S}_{t+n}|t].\tag{8.5}$$

Alternatively, this implies that the forward *premium* should be an unbiased forecast of the future *appreciation* of the foreign currency. Because the forward premium is also the domestic minus the foreign nominal rate of interest, a low foreign interest rate, relative to the U.S. rate, should be associated with an appreciating currency. This is why this proposition is also known as *uncovered interest parity* (UIP), as opposed to the usual no-arbitrage (covered) interest parity.

Note that Equation (8.5) is sometimes interpreted as a test of the efficiency of the foreign exchange market. This, as we will note, is incorrect if there is a rational risk premium. Rather, tests of Equation (8.5) should be viewed as joint tests of the efficiency hypothesis plus a no-risk premium hypothesis.

Using monthly horizons, this can be tested by the following equa-tion:

$$(\tilde{S}_{t+n} - F_t)/S_t = a + b(i_t - i_t^*) + \tilde{\epsilon}_{t+n},\tag{8.6}$$

where $i_t(i^*_t)$ is the domestic (foreign) riskless interest rate, and $i^* - i$ is the forward discount. Under UIP, we would expect to find $a = b = 0$; that is, there should be no way to forecast the prediction error from the forward rate.

A voluminous literature, starting with Bilson (1981), reports on such tests, where researchers found that the slope coefficient is generally statistically negative and significant, although the explanatory power, expressed as the R^2, is always rather low. Thus, when a currency is selling at a discount in the forward market, $(i - i^*) < 0$, there is a positive expected return from buying that currency forward. The ensuing strategy is to sell a foreign currency forward when it is at a premium and, conversely, to purchase the foreign currency forward when it sells at a discount.

In fact, the average coefficient across some 75 published estimates is -1.88, even less than unity.[5] Adding $(F_t - S_t)/S_t = i - i^*$ to both sides, Equation (8.6) can be rewritten as

$$(\tilde{S}_{t+n} - S_t)/S_t = a + (b + 1)(i_t - i^*_t) + \tilde{\epsilon}_{t+n}. \tag{8.7}$$

This implies that when i^* exceeds i by one percentage point, the exchange rate not only refuses to go down by 1 percent, as predicted from the forward rate, but instead *appreciates* by $(b + 1) = -1.88 + 1 = -0.88$, which is slightly less than 1 percent. These puzzling results, as always, can either be explained by a rational time-varying risk premium or by expectational errors.

Time-Varying Risk Premiums

If investors are rational and risk averse, then the forward rate can be decomposed into an expected future spot rate plus a risk premium:

$$(F_{t,n} - S_t)/S_t = E[(\tilde{S}_{t+n} - S_t)/S_t] + RP_t, \tag{8.8}$$

where Equation (8.6) can also be written, more generally, as

$$(\tilde{S}_{t+n} - F_t)/S_t = RP_t + \tilde{\epsilon}_{t+n}.$$

Thus, maintaining the assumption of rationality, the risk premium must be correlated with interest differentials.

---

[5] See Froot and Thaler (1990).

In addition, the required behavior of the risk premium is most peculiar. As Fama (1984) pointed out, a slope coefficient that is greater than one in absolute value implies that the variance of RP_t must be greater than both the variance of $i - i^*$ and of the expected currency depreciation. The astonishing conclusion that the variance of RP exceeds that of expected currency movements has become known as the *puzzle of risk premium volatility*. For rationality to be maintained, academic researchers have tried to come up with models that could explain why risk premiums change so much over time.

One approach is to try to explain risk premiums in a simple mean–variance/CAPM framework. In the simplest situation with one representative agent and one risky asset, the risk premium can be written as

$$RP = \rho x \sigma^2, \tag{8.9}$$

where ρ is the risk aversion, x is the asset supply, and σ is the volatility. Frankel (1986) tried to explain movements in risk premiums by movements in asset supplies x, but found insufficient variability. But movements in risk premiums can also come from movements in risk. In fact, there is strong evidence of time variation in volatility, which can be captured by so-called generalized autoregressive conditional heteroscedasticity (GARCH) models, where the variance is described as

$$\sigma_t^2 = \alpha + \beta \sigma_{t-1}^2 + \gamma \epsilon_{t-1}^2. \tag{8.10}$$

In this process, the conditional variance is a linear function of the previous variance, as well as of the latest squared innovation.

In theory, changes in the volatility might explain the time pattern in risk premiums. Giovannini and Jorion (1989), however, found that the time variation in CAPM-β is completely inconsistent with the time variation of unrestricted risk premiums in Equation (8.8). Other attempts, such as Hodrick and Srivastava (1984), based on latent variable models, have also failed to rationally explain the risk premiums.

Since model after model is rejected, this clearly is a topic for endless academic research. In practice, however, profits are highly volatile. Bilson (1981), for example, uses these forecasts as inputs into a mean-variance optimizer and finds measured profits. The parameter estimates, however, are not updated and positions are very large, primarily involving a long position in the Belgian franc offset by a short position in the Dutch guilder. This position is explained by the fact that the franc offered higher interest rates and was closely tied to the guilder within the EMS. The strategy worked well until February 1982, when an 8 percent devaluation of the franc wiped out the profits of the previous two years.

Interpretation

At this juncture, many possible explanations can be offered. Even if expectational errors appear after the fact, they may not necessarily imply unexploited profit opportunities. If investors are in the process of *learning* about newly floating exchange rates, then there may exist apparent, but temporary, expectational errors. Lewis (1989), for instance, showed that investors' slow learning about the 1980–85 money supply process can explain part of the forward bias. The problem with this explanation is that deviations do not appear to diminish with time. Exhibit 8.7, for instance, provides estimates of the regression Equation (8.6) over 1976–80, 1981–85, and 1986–90. It shows that over these three subperiods, there is no tendency for the slope coefficient to revert to zero. In fact, no coefficient is ever positive and many coefficients, considering the small sample size, are significant.

An alternative interpretation is that these results reflect a *peso* problem, where investors take into account rare events, of a large magnitude, that may not be adequately represented in the sample. The *peso* term was initially coined to describe persistent forward discounts in the value of the Mexican peso over 1955–75, as investors were correctly anticipating a devaluation; over finite samples, however, these dis-

EXHIBIT 8.7   Tests of Unbiasedness of Forward Rates (1976–90)

Currency	1976–80			1981–85			1986–90		
	slope	t-stat	R^2	slope	t-stat	R^2	slope	t-stat	R^2
C$	−2.2*	−2.2	0.07	−3.7*	−2.6	0.11	−1.3	−0.8	0.01
Mark	−2.1	−1.4	0.03	−7.6*	−2.6	0.10	−6.4	−1.8	0.05
Pound	−2.1	−1.8	0.05	−3.9	−1.8	0.05	−6.1*	−2.0	0.06
Yen	−2.7*	−2.1	0.07	−4.9*	−3.3	0.15	−7.6	−1.9	0.06

*Statistically significant at the 5% level.

counts were not offset by a devaluation, thus creating biases in the estimated regressions.

The peso problem is probably most acute with fixed exchange rate systems, and is difficult to gauge from historical data. For instance, a growing number of portfolio managers have tried to take advantage of the forward bias by buying high-yielding currencies. To limit risk, positions have been implemented as cross-hedges within EMS currencies, where, for instance, the Italian lira is purchased against the dollar while the deutsche mark is sold against the dollar, thereby benefiting from high interest rates on the lira. This strategy worked particularly well until September 1992, at which time the EMS unraveled, and the lira dropped precipitously against the mark. As a result, many global managers reported sharp losses for 1992.

As a last resort explanation, these empirical regularities may be ascribed to inefficiencies. A simple story based on overshooting, described in a previous chapter, could be as follows. First, assume that investors need time to process information. They observe an increase in U.S. nominal interest rates. Over the long run, this increase will be accompanied by a depreciation of the dollar, which will offset the higher dollar interest rates. For this to occur, the dollar must rise now to depreciate later. If this initial appreciation takes time, however, then we might expect to find that high dollar interest rates are associated with an appreciating dollar. This is clearly an inefficiency because buying dollars as soon as dollar interest rates rise allows the wily speculator to profit from the subsequent appreciation, which in addition comes with a higher yield.

These profits, it should be mentioned, are risky. In Exhibit 8.7, the explanatory power, as measured by the R^2, is very low, on the order of 5–10 percent. This is to be expected, because most of the movements in flexible exchange rates are the result of "news," which by definition cannot be forecast. The low R^2, however, indicates that a strategy of speculating on this basis will be quite risky. For instance, with an initial investment of $1,000, estimates show that an increase of 1 percent per annum in nominal rates implies a return higher by about 2 percent per annum, or $20/12 per month. The volatility of exchange rates is about 14 percent annually, or 4 percent monthly. The expected profit, therefore, is about $2 per month, with a standard deviation of about $40 per month. Assuming a normal distribution, losses will occur about 48 percent of the time, which is quite high. This speculative strategy therefore entails a substantial amount of volatility. To some extent, risk can be mitigated by diversifying across currencies, across horizons, and perhaps across anomalies, but patience is certainly necessary.

Conclusions

By now, there appears to be a considerable body of academic evidence that returns in most financial markets can be forecast. This leads to many questions.

The first question is whether these results could be explained by chance. On an academic level, this evidence has been subject to classical statistical testing. However, additional biases are due, for instance, to testing many different models and reporting only "interesting" results. After a while, all researchers report variants of the same anomaly. This process, called *data mining,* could potentially explain many results.

The second question is whether some of these results could be explained away by data measurement problems or transaction costs. Autocorrelation in returns, for instance, can occur because of thin trading or because reported prices bounce between bid and ask quotes. Ultimately, the only way to address these issues is to try with real money in real time.

Finally, even if an actual track record generates profits, it is not clear that these results are proof of inefficiency. Hard-core proponents of EMH will always argue that risk premiums on different assets rationally change over time and that this pattern of time variation may be too complex to be captured by simplified models of asset pricing. Hence it is unlikely that there will ever be a clear-cut answer to whether markets are efficient.

References

Ariel, R. 1987. "A monthly effect in stock returns," *Journal of Financial Economics* 18: 161–74.
——. 1990. "High stock returns before holidays: Existence and evidence on possible causes," *Journal of Finance* 45: 1611–26.
Ball, R., and P. Brown. 1968. "An empirical evaluation of accounting income numbers," *Journal of Accounting Research* 6: 159–78.

Banz, R. 1981. "The relationship between return and market value of common stocks," *Journal of Financial Economics* 9: 3–18.

Basu, S. 1977. "Investment performance of common stocks in relation to their price-earnings ratios–A test of the efficient market hypothesis," *Journal of Finance* 32: 663–82.

Bernard, V., and J. Thomas. 1990. "Evidence that stock prices do not fully reflect the implications of current earnings for future earnings," *Journal of Accounting and Economics* 13: 305–40.

Bilson, J. 1981. "The speculative efficiency hypothesis," *Journal of Business* 54: 435–52.

——. 1990. "Technical currency trading," in *The Currency Hedging Debate*, ed. L. Thomas, IFR Publishing, London.

Bremer M., and R. Sweeney. 1991. "The reversal of large stock-price decreases," *Journal of Finance* 46: 747–54.

Brown, K., and W. V. Harlow. 1988. "Market overreaction: Magnitude and intensity," *Journal of Portfolio Management* 14: 6–13.

——, W. V. Harlow, and S. Tinic. 1988. "Risk aversion, uncertain information, and market efficiency," *Journal of Financial Economics* 22: 355–85.

Brown, S., and J. Warner. 1985. "Using daily stock returns: The case of event studies," *Journal of Financial Economics* 14: 3–31.

Chan, K. C. 1988. "On the contrarian investment strategy," *Journal of Business* 61: 147–65.

——, and N. F. Chen. 1988. "An unconditional asset-pricing test and the role of firm size as an instrumental variable for risk," *Journal of Finance* 43: 309–25.

Chan, L., Y. Hamao, and J. Lakonishok. 1991. "Fundamentals and stock returns in Japan," *Journal of Finance* 46: 1739–64.

Conrad, J., and G. Kaul. 1993. "Long-term market overreaction or biases in computed returns," *Journal of Finance* 48: 39–63.

DeBondt, W., and R. Thaler. 1985. "Does the stock market overreact?" *Journal of Finance* 40: 793–805.

——. 1987. "Further evidence on investor overreaction and stock market seasonality," *Journal of Finance* 42: 557–81.

——. 1989. "Anomalies: A mean-reverting walk down Wall Street," *Journal of Economic Perspectives* 3: 189–202.

Fama, E. 1965. "The behavior of stock market prices," *Journal of Business* 38: 35–105.

——. 1970. "Efficient capital markets," *Journal of Finance* 25: 383–417.

——. 1984. "Forward and spot exchange rates," *Journal of Monetary Economics* 36: 697–703.

——. 1991. "Efficient capital markets II," *Journal of Finance* 46: 1575–1617.

——, and K. French. 1988. "Dividend yields and expected stock returns," *Journal of Financial Economics* 22: 3–25.

——, and K. French. 1992. "The cross-section of expected stock returns," *Journal of Finance* 47: 427–65.

Flannery, M., and A. Protopopadakis. 1988. "From T-bills to common stocks: Investigating the generality of intra-week return seasonality," *Journal of Finance* 43: 431–50.

Frankel, J. 1986. "The implications of mean-variance optimization for four questions in international macroeconomics," *Journal of International Money and Finance* 5: 53–75.

——, and K. Froot. 1987. "Using survey data to test standard propositions on exchange rate expectations," *American Economic Review* 77: 133–53.

French, K. 1980. "Stock returns and the weekend effect," *Journal of Financial Economics* 8: 55–69.

Froot, K., and R. Thaler. 1990. "Anomalies: foreign exchange," *Journal of Economic Perspectives* 4, 179–92.

Gibbons, M., and P. Hess. 1981. "Day of the week effects and asset returns," *Journal of Business* 54: 579–96.

Giovannini, A., and P. Jorion. 1989. "The time variation of risk and return in the foreign exchange and stock markets," *Journal of Finance* 44: 307–25.

Gordon, M., and E. Shapiro. 1956. "Capital equilibrium analysis: The required rate of profit," *Management Science* 3: 102–10.

Grossman, S., and J. Stiglitz. 1980. "On the impossibility of informationally efficient capital markets," *American Economic Review* 70: 393–408.

Gultekin, M., and B. Gultekin. 1983. "Stock market seasonality: International evidence," *Journal of Financial Economics* 12: 469–81.

Haugen, R., and N. Baker. 1991. "The efficient market inefficiency of capitalization-weighted stock portfolios," *Journal of Portfolio Management* (Spring), 17: 35–40.

Haugen, R., and J. Lakonishok. 1987. *The Incredible January Effect: The Stock Market's Unsolved Mystery,* Dow Jones-Irwin, Homewood, Ill.

Hodrick, R. 1987. *The Empirical Evidence on the Efficiency of Forward and Futures Foreign Exchange Markets,* Harwood Academic Publishing, New York.

——, and S. Srivastava. 1984. "An investigation of risk and return in forward foreign exchange," *Journal of International Money and Finance* 3: 5–30.

Howe, J. 1986. "Evidence on stock market overreaction," *Financial Analysts Journal* 4: 74–77.

Ikenberry, D., and J. Lakonishok. 1988. "Seasonal anomalies in financial markets: A survey," in *A Reappraisal of the Efficiency of Financial Markets,* ed. R. Guimaraes, B. Kingsman, and S. Taylor, Springer-Verlag, Berlin.

Jaffe, J., and R. Westerfield. 1985. "The weekend effect in common stock returns: The international evidence," *Journal of Finance* 40: 433–54.

Jegadeesh, N. 1990. "Evidence of predictable behavior of security returns," *Journal of Finance* 45: 881–98.

Jensen, M. 1978. "Some anomalous evidence regarding market efficiency," *Journal of Financial Economics* 6: 95–101.

Jones, C., D. Pearce, and J. Wilson. 1987. "Can tax-loss selling explain the January effect? A note," *Journal of Finance* 42: 453–61.

Keim, D. 1989. "Trading patterns, bid–ask spreads, and estimated security returns: The case of common stocks at calendar turning points," *Journal of Financial Economics* 25: 75–97.

Lakonishok, J., and S. Smidt. 1988. "Are seasonal anomalies real? A 90 year perspective," *Review of Financial Studies* 1: 435–55.

Lehmann, B. 1990. "Fads, martingales and market efficiency," *Quarterly Journal of Economics* 105: 1–28.

Lewis, K. 1989. "Changing beliefs and systematic rational forecast errors with evidence from foreign exchange," *American Economic Review* 79: 621–36.

Lo, A., and C. McKinlay. 1988. "Stock prices do not follow random walks: Evidence from a simple specification test," *Review of Financial Studies* 3: 175–205.

McFarland, J., R. Pettit, and S. Sung. 1982. "The distribution of foreign exchange price changes: Trading day effects and risk measurement," *Journal of Finance* 37: 693–715.

Nelson, C., and M. Kim. 1993. "Predictable stock returns: Reality or statistical illusion?" *Journal of Finance* 48: 641–61.

Penman, S. 1987. "The distribution of earnings news over time and seasonalities in aggregate stock returns," *Journal of Financial Economics* 18: 199–228.

Reinganum, M. 1981. "Misspecification of capital asset pricing: Empirical anomalies based on earnings' yields and market values," *Journal of Financial Economics* 9: 19–46.

———, and A. Shapiro. 1987. "Taxes and stock return seasonality: Evidence from the London stock exchange," *Journal of Business* 60: 281–95.

Rosenberg, B., K. Reid, and R. Lanstein. 1985. "Persuasive evidence of market inefficiency," *Journal of Portfolio Management* 11: 9–16.

Rozeff, M., and W. Kinney. 1976. "Capital market seasonality: The case of stock returns," *Journal of Financial Economics* 3: 379–402.

Schultz, P. 1985. "Personal income taxes and the January effect: Small firm stock returns before the War Revenue Act of 1917: A note," *Journal of Finance* 40: 333–43.

Shiller, R. 1981. "Do stock prices move too much to be justified by subsequent changes in dividends?" *American Economic Review* 71: 421–36.

Smirlock, M. 1985. "Seasonality and bond market returns," *Journal of Portfolio Management* 11: 42–44.

Sweeney, R. 1986. "Beating the foreign exchange market," *Journal of Finance* 41: 163–82.

——, and P. Surajaras. 1988. "The stability of speculative profits in the foreign exchanges," in *A Reappraisal of the Efficiency of Financial Markets,* ed. R. Guimaraes, B. Kingsman, and S. Taylor, Springer-Verlag, Berlin.

Watts, R. 1978. "Systematic 'abnormal' returns after quarterly earnings announcements," *Journal of Financial Economics* 6: 127–50.

Zarowin, P. 1989. "Short-run market overreaction–Size and seasonality effects," *Journal of Portfolio Management* 15: 26–29.

Index

minimum variance portfolios (MVP),
    243, 248, 288, 300
Mishkin, F., 169
mispriced securities, 20
Mittoo, U., 316
modern portfolio theory (MPT), 263
Modest, D., 266
modified duration, 75
Modigliani, 59, 60
monetary integration, 138
monetary models, 174
monetary stability, 132
monetary theory, 162–4
money supply, 7
    and intervention, 172–3
monopolies, 171
Moody's ratings, 37
mortgage bonds, 36
mortgages, 28–9, 115
MPT. See modern portfolio theory
multiplicative stochastic process, 106–7
municipal bonds, 31–3
    See also general obligation bonds
municipal debt, 19
MV. See minimum variance
MV optimization. See mean-variance
    optimization
MVP. See minimum variance portfolios

naive hedges, 187
Natenberg, Sheldon, 224
national stock markets. See world stock
    markets
natural immunization (on balance
    sheet), 96
Nawalkha, S.K., 111, 113
Neal, R., 312
near contracts, 195
negative risk premium, 59
Nelson, C., 334n2
net interest income, 95–6
new security issues, 16
New York market, 141
New York Stock Exchange (NYSE), 15,
    28, 141
Ng, V., 277n1
Nixon, Richard M., 131

noise trading, 327, 328
nominal exchange rates, 162, 163
nondiversifiable risk, 239
nonlinear models, 342–3
nonlinear optimization, 50–1
normal distribution, 232, 252
NYSE. See New York Stock Exchange

OCC. See Options Clearing Corporation
Odier, P., 278n2, 302
off-balance sheet methods, 97
off-balance sheet products, 74
Officer, L., 162
official reserve balance, 159
oil price shocks, 4
oil prices, 7
on-balance sheet methods, 97
optimal asset demands, 250
optimal maturity, 20
option premium time decay, 207
option premiums, 141, 181, 195, 198,
    207–23
option prices. See option premiums
option pricing method, 43
option replication, 216
option values, 207–9
option volatility, 227
Options Clearing Corporation (OCC),
    197–8
options contracts, 196–99
options contracts, defined, 145–6
options markets, 123, 181
orderly time paths, 170
OTC. See over the counter
out-of-the-money options, 221, 222, 236
over the counter (OTC) market, 25, 32,
    146
over the counter trades, growth of, 181
overlay hedges, 300–1
overshooting
    and exchange rates, 167–9

par bonds, 79–80
par values, 134
    and abrogation, 131
    and arbitrage, 124
parallel shift, 105, 114